Psychological Perspectives on Deafness

Volume 2

Edited by

Marc Marschark
National Technical Institute for the Deaf—Rochester Institute of Technology

M. Diane Clark
Shippensburg University

LEA LAWRENCE ERLBAUM ASSOCIATES, PUBLISHERS
1998 Mahwah, New Jersey   London

Lawrence Erlbaum Associates, Inc., Publishers
10 Industrial Avenue
Mahwah, NJ 07430

Cover design by Kathryn Houghtaling Lacey

Library of Congress Cataloging-in-Publication Data

Psychological Perspectives on Deafness / Marc Marschark and
M. Diane Clark, editors.
p. cm.
Includes bibliographical references and indexes.
ISBN 0-8058-2709-9 (alk. paper)—0-8058-2710-2 (pbk: alk.
paper).
1. Deafness—Psychological aspects. I. Marschark, Marc. II.
Clark, M. Diane.
HV2380.P77   1998
362.4'2'019–dc20   92-4262
                                          CIP

Books published by Lawrence Erlbaum Associates are printed on
acid-free paper, and their bindings are chosen for strength and dura-
bility.

Printed in the United States of America
10 9 8 7 6 5 4 3 2 1

Contents

Preface

Five years ago, we edited a volume entitled *Psychological Perspectives on Deafness*. It was intended to be a one-time affair, but, obviously, that is not the way it turned out.

The present book, with *Volume 2* appended to its title, is in some sense a continuation of discussions begun in that 1993 book. With new topics and many new authors, however, it is more than that. In only 5 years, there has been considerable change in the field of deafness research. For example, it is hard enough to define this field without adding the problem of how to refer to it without using a term that some people now find discomfiting (*deafness*). So, we will not even try. Instead we focus on the substance of a field that is changing rapidly even while its progress sometimes seems painfully slow.

Most deaf children face significant educational and social challenges growing up, and, to put it bluntly, we have not done enough to eliminate those barriers. Even if research in the field is making great strides, and we believe it is, many deaf persons and service providers still feel frustrations in the "here and now." Part of that frustration concerns the fact that despite decades of investing time and resources in a better understanding of communication, social, and psychological issues associated with hearing loss, access to services and many of our educational methods remain woefully inadequate. Certainly, there has been considerable progress in these domains; it just is not coming as fast as we might like, and sometimes it does not seem to come in the right places.

Beyond the pace of change, part of the frustration stems from the fact that deaf people are rarely in the driver's seat of the research that involves them. This observation is not intended as a political statement, just a statement of fact. There are relatively few deaf researchers in the field—although the number is increasing—and there is a variety of differing perspectives on what research questions are most pressing. In our view, the field is in need of a collaborative model for inquiry that includes deaf children, deaf adults, teachers of deaf students, and researchers. The experiences and expertise of individuals within these groups can provide both the essential insider's view and an objective external perspective to ensure that key decisions are made in a culturally sensitive fashion and based on valid and reliable evidence rather than on political grounds or administrative or financial expediency. As Paolo Friere (1970) once noted, "a revolution for the people is a revolution against the people." A true revolution must be *with*, not *for* those seeking change.

An additional challenge and source of frustration falls on the boundary between the research community and those who might most benefit from our research programs: the stubborn gap between basic research and applied research (not to mention the chasm between research findings and their application). Somehow, we need to communicate to those involved in educating deaf children the implications of research on basic processes involved in areas such as early social processes, language development, and reading. At the same time, investigators interested in the basic processes of language and cognition among deaf individuals must understand the needs of those involved in educating deaf children and the ways in which their work might be disseminated and implemented.

When applied and basic research involve different methodologies and concerns with different levels of analysis, the situation is sometimes interpreted as reflecting different underlying goals. This is not necessarily so. Advances in educating deaf children have been led by scientific studies on the social–psychological impact of early intervention programs, the linguistics of American Sign Language, memory for linguistic and nonlinguistic information, and the problem-solving strategies employed (or not employed) by deaf students. Recent studies of teaching and learning processes among deaf students have moved these areas much closer together, and we hope that this volume can close the gap even more.

In both literal and metaphorical senses, our starting point here is where the previous volume ended, with Bill Stokoe, who wrote the final chapter in the 1993 volume and the first one in this volume. In his earlier chapter, Stokoe cautioned against both the oversimplification of the issues facing deaf individuals (e.g., those related to literacy and access) and overgeneralization of limited research findings. He pointed out the educational and psychological misconceptions inherent in viewing deafness as an engineering problem (i.e., an issue of hearing-aid technology), equating language with speech, and failing to consider scientific research in making informed decisions about teaching goals and methods. Stokoe then highlighted some of the recent progress made in the domains of linguistics, education, and psychology, helping to sharpen our psychological perspectives. Most centrally, he reminded us that "in order to *see* deaf people as individuals and as members of a social group, in order to *see* their language and their associations that language cements, their customs it preserves, and all the rest, it is necessary that our cognitive camera have a lens that passes, and film sensitive to, anthropological, cultural, sociological, linguistic, and semiotic, as well as psychological, phenomena" (p. 373). That seemed like a good starting point to us!

The present volume retains the title *Psychological Perspectives on Deafness*. Armed with the wisdom that comes from time and experience (theoretically at least), both for ourselves and the field at large, however, we promote here a broadening of that perspective. Some of the following chapters, for example, relate to topics that are generally part of the domain of developmental and cognitive psychology. Within these as well as the other chapters, the contributors to this book extend the camera angle to include sociological, pragmatic, anthropological, and clinical psychological issues. The contributors deal with the content of several other areas as well, with their methodologies, and with their theoretical underpinnings. Further, they help to provide the all-important bridges from applied research to basic research to application.

Above all else, this volume is intended to reflect, and hopefully encourage, the kinds of cross-community and cross-disciplinary collaboration that people like Bill Stokoe, Kay Meadow-Orlans, and Elissa Newport have advocated and have demonstrated in their own work. Such a *modus operandi* is not always easy to achieve, and we see that ourselves when potential collaborators are more or less willing (or able) to move "outside the box" and participate in activities like this one or in organized, collaborative research. For our part, we accept and applaud the progress that has been made; but we are not satisfied. We have a considerable distance to go, but at least we know we are moving in the right direction.

—*Marc Marschark*
—*M. Diane Clark*

1

A Very Long Perspective

William C. Stokoe
Gallaudet University

One perspective on deafness has changed a great deal even in the short time since the first volume of *Psychological Perspectives on Deafness* was published. As long as *speech* and *language* were taken to be alternate names for the same phenomenon, psychologists and educators could see deafness only as disease or a severely handicapping physical condition. A new perspective on the origin and evolution of language (Armstrong, Stokoe & Wilcox, 1995), however, revealed that sign languages have all the essential features of language—*syntax, semanticity, and creativity*—and that only visible gestures can connect a sign naturally to a great many things people talk about. An arbitrary social convention is necessary to link vocal sounds to meanings, and unless it was supernaturally established, such a convention could only have arisen after gestures and their meanings provided a set of paired forms and meanings for vocalizations (which may have accompanied the pairs) to represent.

This is a revolutionary change in perspective: Teachers, to be effective, instead of pretending they can make deaf children into hearing children must learn to see how ideas relate, how gesture directly expresses basic oppositions like up–down, in–out, close–far, and dozens of others on which cognition, the power of thought, depends. With sign language, deaf children are not handicapped. Teachers also need the perspective such change provides: (a) the arbitrary vocal expressions of spoken languages make understanding difficult; (b) hearing children have to acquire the

1

word–meaning pairs of their caretakers; and (c) deaf children have to be recognized as very effective at using their eyes, upper bodies, and brains to grow language again from its roots as they pair visible signs with meanings.

In the first volume of *Psychological Perspectives on Deafness*, Lillo-Martin (1993) presented the following account of how language acquisition is accomplished:

> A child is exposed to his or her native language daily, in the home, from birth on. As early as 6 months, the child begins babbling, using the sounds (or sign pieces) of the language to form meaningless syllables. ... After about a year of input and output, the child begins using words (whether spoken or signed) in a systematic, meaningful way. Later, the child combines words into phrases and short sentences, beginning at around 18 months. ... Although these early utterances are short and often devoid of grammatical morphemes, they display a consistent word order that represents various grammatical relations.
>
> By around the age of 3 years, the child uses sentences of many types to describe a vast array of experiences and feelings. (p. 312)

An entirely different perspective on language acquisition can be found in the work of Volterra (Volterra & Erting, 1990; Volterra & Iverson, 1995). Although it is true that an infant is exposed to language from birth, the hearing child does not begin babbling (nor the deaf child with deaf parents begin *finger babbling*) until about 6 months of age. This alone suggests that exposure to language (and/or an internal set of universal grammar rules) is exceedingly slow at making enough of an impression to elicit attempts at imitation. Volterra and Iverson reported that from a very early age all children, hearing and deaf alike, communicate with gestures. Even at 16 to 20 months, the many children they observed (in homes where different languages were in use) were still engaging in meaningful communication in the gestural–visual channel. This communication begins more than a year before the child begins to combine words (or sign language signs) into phrases and short sentences. Yet, the physiological ability to make the sounds of speech and the movements of sign has been apparent since the vocal or manual babbling began.

If language acquisition begins with passive exposure, if there is input from birth onward, but output begins to emerge only at 6 months or later and has reached virtual completion at about age 3,[1] it should be apparent that the language experience of a child in the first few months is crucial. This, of course, was the conclusion of Hart and Risley (1995), whose book

---

[1]Lillo-Martin (1993) wrote: "Although a child's linguistic performance is usually unsophisticated, many researchers claim that the linguistic competence available to the child at this age [3 years] approaches the adult level." (p. 312–313)

Meaningful Differences in the Everyday Experience of Young American Children, presented striking disparity in development measured at age 3 and at age 10 as the effect of just one variable: the amount and kind of language experiences the children had between birth and 3 years of age. The children scoring in the top third compared with those in the bottom third were exposed to several times as much language generally, and to language directed specifically at them in utterances of the kind that encourage and build a child's self-confidence and do not turn off the inquiring mind by commanding silence or discouraging questions.

When this new light on language acquisition is applied to the circumstance of childhood deafness, there can be no mistaking the implication. All children, hearing and deaf alike, communicate gesturally before they communicate linguistically. It is therefore imperative that they be communicated with in the gestures they naturally use and have the sensory equipment to perceive unimpeded. There is not the slightest advantage to be gained (quite the reverse) in withholding the perfectly natural use of gesture from deaf infants and children. Hart and Risley supplied copious unequivocal evidence that it is imperative to communicate with young deaf children gesturally, insofar as possible in a natural sign language.

OUR SPECIES ALSO HAD TO ACQUIRE LANGUAGE

This brief look at the acquisition of human communicative competence—which begins at birth, attains expressive power shortly thereafter, and shows effective employment in gestural form many months before recognizable linguistic forms emerge. Another perspective broader in scope and deeper in time is called for; that is, a view of acquisition by the human genus, first of effective gestural interaction, and from that, genuine language in gestural form.

Hard evidence is missing to show how gestural interaction began and became language. Nevertheless, human physiology and epistemology (the nature of cognition and knowing) make it impossible to disprove the hypothesis that language began with gesture and eventually changed from mainly addressing the eyes to mainly addressing the ears. Examination of circumstantial evidence well grounded in physiology began essentially with Kimura (1993), who pointed out that the brain centers controlling the sequential and parallel activities in the speech tract are the very centers, or lie adjacent to them, that control similar timing of upper limb movement. Although spoken language is addressed to hearing and signed language is addressed to vision, these activities are not separated in the human body and brain. Kimura, in the same work, reviewed much of the literature on aphasia and apraxia and showed how in the literature, brain damage in a specific location is said to cause certain kinds of language impairment, but the statement is made without any assessment of other motor activities. In a nutshell, Kimura's findings implied that language is movement. Whether the movement is mainly within the vocal tract or out where it can be seen, language is disrupted by any damage to the brain that impairs the ability to make complex simultaneous and sequential movements. Language is not not some wholly unique brain activity but the normal working of an evolved brain and body (Edelman, 1989).

The evidence, or argument, from epistemology is more fully explained later; it shows that signs of different nature are linked in the mind or behavior of some *interpretant* in different ways to what they signify.[2] This excursion into physiology, epistemology, and semiotics (the branch of philosophy that deals with signs and signification) may seem to take a reader some distance away from deafness, but distance between observer and observed is a requirement of perspective. Besides, if it once again became recognized that humans have always used both vision and hearing to get and exchange information, once it is seen that language is most likely to have evolved from gestures, the public and the professional view of deafness would change, improving the education and other treatment of those who cannot hear.

Although more than 99% of earth's people use spoken languages, there are also primary sign languages that deaf people use, and alternative sign languages used by tribal people whose contact with modern industrial cultures was relatively recent (Farnell, 1995; Kendon, 1988). Gesture, or gesticulation, is universally used with speech or alone in human interaction (McNeill, 1992). Moreover, gesture is useful and often necessary to make spoken language utterances understood. For example, the following order overheard at a delicatessen counter was immediately and correctly filled: "A half-pound of this and a quarter-pound of that, please." And yet, although gesturing, with or without speaking, is part of every known culture, it has been standard practice ever since writing was invented, to divide communication into what is redundantly called verbal language,[3] and its assumed categorical opposite, nonverbal communication. A better

---

[2]The word *interpretant*, unlike interpreter, was coined by C. S. Peirce to mean precisely and only that one (human or not) to which or to whom a sign has a significance (see Sebeok, 1994).

[3]Verbal implies words (Latin *verbi*) and words do not exist without language; thus, *verbal language* is awkwardly redundant. Most users of the phrase intend it to mean spoken language only, ignoring the now widely known fact that there are signed languages whose words are visible not audible.

perspective, aided by recent research, makes it possible to see both language and deafness in a different light.

A difference in perspective can often change the viewer's understanding substantially. For example, without previous knowledge, no one looking at caterpillars and butterflies would know that butterflies are transformed imagoes. Before their metamorphosis they were crawling caterpillars with nothing to suggest that they would become delicate airborne creatures. It is becoming more and more apparent that language before its metamorphosis was gesturally signed. What makes this likely is that only visible signs can relate naturally to what they denote.

A sign, as semiotian Peirce defined it, is anything that can be perceived to denote something besides itself, by some interpretant. Moreover, all of life works by virtue of signs (Sebeok, 1994). Pheromones are signs to insects that have the chemical senses to detect them, but the pheromone-triggered response is built into the organism. Organisms of greater neural complexity interpret various kinds of signs with well-differentiated sensory systems, and their brains provide them with a repertoire of responses that is lacking in simpler life forms. Among mammals, especially in the primate order, vision is highly developed, as it must have been for living in the treetops. Vision is also the main channel for social information transfer, which is more sophisticated in apes than in monkeys and is likely to have been even more so in hominids (King, 1994).

What this glimpse of semiotics and primatology reveals is that, for intelligent interpretants like anthropoids, seeing and interpreting each of their movements as signs is what makes their social existence possible. This fact is not disputed by those who think language is only vocal–auditory activity, but they consider it irrelevant to their theories of language and generally dismiss it as nonverbal communication.

This dualism is as untenable as the Cartesian myth that mind and body are separate. If mind and body were the complete strangers Descartes took them to be, psychology could have nothing to do with the mind, because as a science it must be based in the natural world. If verbal and nonverbal communication were essentially separate, verbal and nonverbal messages would have to be managed by totally different and separate parts of, or modules in, the brain. The best neuroscientists cannot find any such separation and do not look for it because that is not the way brain cells and circuits work (Edelman, 1988, 1989, 1991). Moreover, what is essential to language can be shown to derive from visible signs, as is demonstrated next.

The converse proposition, that language originated with vocal sounds, is a hypothesis easily disproved. Sounds by themselves are signs with very limited signifying power. Thunder is an exception; it signifies to sophisticated interpretants that lightning has flashed somewhere. (Long ago it was interpreted as a sign that a god had spoken.) Vocal sounds, if they signify directly, are a specific kind of sign—symptoms. We know that an infant's cries may be symptoms of hunger or some other discomfort. Yet, it is only by observing much more than the sound an infant makes that we can determine what caused it, what it means. Although we teach young children words like *meow*, *moo*, and *bow-wow*, while showing them pictures of animals, these sounds suggest but do not precisely reproduce the sounds domestic animals make. As signs to denote meanings on a more sophisticated level than nursery games, vocal sounds are almost completely useless. Even involuntary sounds that can be caused by sneezing, yawning, or flatulence are not allowed in most societies to stay in their natural state; they must either be suppressed or expressed in socially acceptable form.

How then could vocally produced sounds become bearers of the meanings we find in language? Ferdinand de Saussure (1967), the Swiss linguist, had a half-grasped answer to that question. He declared that words, as linguistic signs, had to be arbitrary, could not be motivated—could not be naturally related to what they mean. Then who are the arbiters? Who makes the arbitrary decisions linking the words of a language to their meanings? Why, it is we ourselves and all the users of a particular language who do that. We all have to use words to mean what others mean by them, or else we become like the character Humpty Dumpty that Alice met in Looking-Glass Land. There is a loophole here, however. Creative, innovative people, poets, teenagers, and others are continually changing word-to-meaning linkages in small and subtle ways. Nevertheless, both what makes sense and the acceptable way to phrase it are determined less by rigorous abstract rules than negotiated by social convention.

Saussure seemed not to have realized that the meanings, the relationships, the concepts into which we sort our world come to us only partly from our language. Much of our basic understanding of the world and ourselves comes directly from our senses and from our exploration and manipulation of things, not words. When we understand, however, that Saussure was talking only about spoken languages, not language as a whole as he thought, his observation is quite correct: In order for spoken words to have meanings there must be a convention; such as, a whole society or community agreeing to understand that certain words, patterns of sounds, denote certain meanings.

This is necessary because spoken words, like the sounds they are made of, have no natural connection to anything beyond what made them. Saussure failed to observe that signs of another kind (i.e., gestures) are not so completely dependent on convention, and that many languages are systems using just these kinds of signs. He, like others of his time and ours, did not think of language as anything except what people speak and hear. Visible gestures, however, show what they mean naturally, and they continue to do so until cultural, social pressure changes them to forms the community deems proper. With such change, they become conventional, more symbolic, and less natural.

This culturally imposed change of language signs (Frishberg, 1975) from natural to symbolic–conventional explains quite simply what has seemed to some a paradox: Gestures are iconic, but sign languages are by and large mutually unintelligible. Stated another way, many signs (i.e., words) of American Sign Language may be transparent or translucent, their meanings "guessable" more or less correctly by a naive observer, but there is no universal language of signs (See, e.g., Battison & Jordan, 1976; Jordan & Battison, 1976; Klima & Bellugi, 1979).

Gestures, unlike vocal sounds, denote naturally: Chimpanzees and even human observers know that when a chimp holds out an upraised palm toward another, with fingers curled and then pulls it inward, it is asking for a gift of food. Likewise, when one animal looks at another and makes picking movements with the fingers on the body, it is asking the one addressed by the head, face, and eye gesture to groom it in the place the fingers indicate. King (1994) presented strong arguments that hominids must have used more gestures than chimpanzees do for the transfer and donation of social information (just as chimpanzees use more than monkeys do), and thus our prehuman ancestors must have used many gestures that were immediately understood by each other.

These chimpanzee gestures and the similar (and probably more numerous early hominid gestures) would not yet have been language, nor even language-like. The problem, therefore, is to discover how such gestures could have become language. The search for the beginnings of language has been impeded since about 1957 by theorists such as Chomsky and those who accept his theory of langauge (see *The Linguistic Wars*, Harris, 1993). These adherents to a theory of abstract language deny flatly that gestures of this kind could have become language. They call gestures *proto-language* (Bickerton, 1990, 1995) or classify them as nonverbal communication. They deny that gesture could have evolved into language, because they insist that language must belong to a completely different category—a category as different from gesture as Descartes thought mind to be different from body.

HOW DO GESTURES MEAN?

For a mind ready to entertain the notion that language expression, like the butterfly, may not always have existed in its present form, the problem loses much of its difficulty. Certain gestures when carefully observed can be seen to contain an interesting structure in addition to their natural indication of what they signify. This structure is precisely the structure of a sentence. The argument can be made stronger when we analyze instead of a human gesture a gesture made by chimpanzees and observed among both captive and wild animals.

This gesture, already introduced, has been labeled the *gimme* gesture because it is directed toward another who is holding or eating food and it obviously indicates a desire that the food will be shared. Its formation can be described easily step-by-step:

(a) The maker of the gesture looks fixedly at the eater.
(b) Extends a forearm (usually the right) in the same direction.
(c) The forearm is held horizontally in supination (i.e., rotated to turn the ventral side of hand and forearm upward).
(d) The fingers are slightly curled as they would be if receiving a morsel of food.
(e) The upper arm flexes, pulling the forearm and hand toward the gesturer's body.

Of course, the description requires much more time than does performing the gesture itself, but this is usual when the forms of signs used in communicative systems are analyzed.

The parts of the gesture signify as follows: (a) and (b) unmistakably indicate *you*, the animal addressed, possessor of the food; (c) and (d) by their form suggest naturally that the upturned palm and fingers are ready to hold food; and (e) by its movement inward indicates that the suggested gift of food should *come to me,* the gesture-maker. It is easy for us, separated from the chimpanzee by geological ages (but different by only 1% at the molecular level; Kingdon, 1993) to see in these five parts of the gesture what we find also in a common syntactic structure, the three-argument predication:

(a) (b)	(e—movement)	(e—direction)	(c) (d)
Subject	Verb	Beneficiary	Object
YOU	GIVE	ME	FOOD

The analysis and labeling inevitably suggest a sequence, as of course does this glossing of the gesture with English words. However, the actual gesture is a single, coordinated muscle action. It is a gesture, not a sequence of gestures, and the order of its parts is an artifact of this analysis.[4] Its making, meaning, and result (the gift of food or not) are all part of chimpanzee life, which does not make or require any analysis. As Kendon (1991) remarked:

> Chimpanzees ... seem to be on the verge of developing a language, yet they have not done so. What is missing? What holds them back? ... Chimpanzees have not developed a system of language-like communication because they do not need to. (p. 212)

Early humans, it seems, must have had a pressing need to venture beyond the behavioral edge where the other primates stopped short. *Homo erectus*, at some point in a time span a million or more years long appears to have moved out of Africa, faced many different kinds of environments, and even changed them (Kingdon, 1993). Unlike chimpanzees then, creatures in our lineage did need to develop a system of language-like communication to be able to cope with migration, changing environment, and the new lifestyles that these imposed.

A much-debated question of our time, however, is whether a system of somewhat language-like communication could have evolved into a language. A growing number of scientists do believe that language did evolve. As a result of their broader view, perspectives on language and deafness—and attitudes toward people whose languages do not depend on speech—are changing.

Many common human gestures embody the kind of meaning found in what school grammars define as complete sentences. The nod and facial expression that together mean *I agree*, the shrug for *I don't know*, the arm movement that invites, *You, come closer*—all these translate into simple sentences, but there are other common gestures similarly translated that can show more clearly what have become separable parts in both signed and spoken languages. One of these is the gesture sometimes seen when a person speaks the italicized words at the end of this sentence:

He was leaving, but before he got in the car, *I caught him*.

The gesture is made when one hand catches and grasps the upright index finger of the other hand as it is moving outward. It would be perverse not to see that in this gesture the catching hand represents the speaker of the sentence, that the finger grasped represents the person caught, and that the hand's action reproduces directly the action the gesture reports redundantly.

David McNeill (1992), in *Hand and Mind*, examined several gestures of this kind made by speakers, and concluded that the spoken sentence

---

[4]It should be noted that in any manual gesture the nerve impulses that configure the hand reach the muscles involved immediately before those that cause the visible movement. (See Armstrong et al., 1995; pp. 178–182.)

and the gestural representation of the same elements in the same relation imply a single central language and/or cognitive process. This is very likely to be the case, but the concern here is with a time when, possibly, the gestural sentences could have been performed and understood, but the human vocal–auditory apparatus had not yet evolved to a stage that would permit a regular, reliable, and well-formed vocal representation.

This putative gestural stage could conceivably have been much earlier, because seeing the parts of such a gesture as denoting such meanings has been a simple matter ever since our species had something a little more sophisticated than a language-like system to use for thinking and communicating. Even before the meanings of the gesture's parts were discernible in the whole act, primates and perhaps other creatures were sending and getting messages visually that make most sense to us when translated into complete sentences.

It is difficult to make a reasonable guess at when early humans first saw that gestures, in addition to being single actions with meaning, also consist of parts that by themselves have meanings. Precisely when it happened, and whether it happened all at once or gradually, is not as important as the fact that it did happen. Once this discovery about gestures was made and shared, of course, its discoverers possessed—in a very real sense—both sentences and words.

The gesture itself is a sentence when it expresses a wish or effectively makes a command, declaration, or statement. The parts of the gesture, the appearance of the hand or hands and the position and movement of the arms, with or without facial and other visible signals, not only have meanings like the meanings words have, but they also have the grammatical values of words. Pointings and visible resemblances (as when the hand looks as if it was holding food, etc.) have the nature of vocally expressed nouns and pronouns; that is, they refer to substantive things. Arm–hand movements by their very nature represent verb meanings. In fact, they would have represented such meanings long before a vocal apparatus evolved that could produce spoken language verbs.

This step from language-like behavior to genuine language, then, could well have been made at the moment when some adventurous early humans began looking in a slightly different way at something that had been going on for a long time—using gestures to communicate. Surely the early humans who spread from Africa (or some other Eden) to the farthest reaches of Asia and Europe, and perhaps to the New World, must have been extremely innovative, adventurous creatures; otherwise, they would have stayed at home and avoided all change, as their near relatives the chimpanzees seem to have done.

THE NATURE OF A FIRST LANGUAGE

The nature of this new system, *language*, does not really match the usual linear descriptions we are given of language. In these descriptions, the constituents of a sentence are a noun phrase (NP) and a verb phrase (VP); the constituents of the NPs and VPs are a multitude of grammatical categories (nouns, verbs, determiners, auxiliaries, pronouns, suffixes, prefixes, etc.). The items found in these categories are composed of *morphemes*; morphemes are composed of *phonemes*; phonemes are composed of language sounds or *phones*; phones are groupings of distinctive features; and so on, like an ever-repeating fraction disappearing into the distance.

When a gesture is seen to be simultaneously a sign with a sentence kind of meaning and a sign composed of parts, each of which has a word kind of meaning, the system appears not linear but circular in the sense of being self-sustaining (like an electrical buzzer's circuit; Bateson, 1979). The parts (hand and motion) of the gesture appear word-like because they refer to specific things and actions, and also because within the gesture they have grammatical value as nouns or verbs; syntactic value as subjects, verbs, and objects; and semantic value as what acts, its action, and what is acted on. Defined thus, however, there cannot be words without sentences; equally, there cannot be sentences without words (whether made of gestural or vocal material). Furthermore, the gesture appears sentence-like because it expresses a unified meaning (or a complete thought), it shows how agent and action are related, and it has discernible parts.

Of course, this is seen from the perspective of the border, or *no man's land*, which has language on this side and something language-like but not quite language on the far side. We, as members of a species with language, take it for granted that there are words, and that with words we can construct sentences. If there were no sentences, how would we know what words are? Where could we find signs that are both specific in reference as words must be, and at the same time have the nature—that only being in a sentence can give them—of being nouns or verbs? It is little wonder that those who dismiss gesture as nonverbal deny that language could have evolved. Looking at language as something spoken, they have no possibility of seeing how sentences and words could have come into existence at the same time. To see that, it is necessary to look at gestures in this new way.

Although it is arguable that early in the existence of *Homo sapiens*, the most successful of them in the game of survival did look at gestures in just this way—as linking noun-like and verb-like concepts into special relationships; ever since *Homo sapiens* became a speaking animal, the knack of seeing gestures for what they are seems to have been lost. It nearly surfaced in that remarkable period of intellectual ferment in Europe and France especially. Mirzoeff (1996) summarized succinctly the way Condillac saw gesture:

> Epée's leap of comprehension took him beyond his philosophical mentor, Condillac, whose *Essay on Human Knowledge* investigated the origins of language. Condillac held that the first form of language was the gesture. Soon the gesture was accompanied by a sound which, in turn, came to replace the gesture altogether. Sounds were then combined to form phrases and sentences. It was thus impossible for a gestural langauge to have grammar, as it preceded the grammatical stage in the evolution of language. (p. 35)

But Epée did not find grammar, or syntax, in the sign language of Parisian deaf people he studied; instead, he supplemented the language of signs they were using with his own invented methodical signs. "These methodical signs as he called them stood for grammatical constructions which, in accompaniment with the natural French sign language vocabulary, were held to replicate the processes of speech" (p. 38). Seeing that the natural sign languages of deaf people (as well as the alternate sign languages of African, American, and Australian tribes) not only have grammar, but that something like them long ago may have begun grammar and language is difficult for language speakers in any period to see; and unless it is seen, any perspective on the origins of language is dim and confused indeed.

Once certain gestures were seen as both unitary signs that could naturally convey a coherent message and as constructions of parts that naturally signified specific things and actions (parts moreover that could be assembled differently), this system of communication with visible signs would certainly have possessed syntax, a critical, perhaps the most critical, feature of language. Syntax is built into this double-level signification. Indeed, seen thus, syntax is simply a name for this dual-level signification we know as words-in-sentences. Gestures that use hands and arms as agents to represent things and move them to depict actions obviously possess this double-level power of signifying.

Another characteristic of language, necessary as well as useful, is creativity; this comes as a product of syntax as it is considered here. Once the gesture has been seen as what moves plus its movement and has been simultaneously understood as predication, words-in-sentence, the gestural words could be used in other combinations. Even with no more than the basic and necessary categories of noun and verb, recombining members of these categories can be productive and creative. (One is reminded here of the evolving grammar of a 2-year-old, which has been characterized as having but two categories, pivot and open, or topic and comment; but this simple grammar allows the child to make many useful and appropriate sentences.) With a system for making gestural sentences composed of noun signs and verb signs, for designating creatures and things and actions, the users of this first genuine language system would have greatly increased their repertoire of objects and operations. Their new system for dealing with their culture would have enlarged and diversified its social and material sides, would have become creative, even as the growing culture enriched the language.

Language and Cognition

Discovering syntactic gestural communication and the power in it to multiply signs for concepts helps to explain how a system of communication that was language-like became language. It does not explain, however, something equally important—the difference in cognitive power between the human genus and that presumed to belong to *Australopithecus*. Once again, a clue can be found if gestural expression is pulled out of the nonverbal wastebasket and studied more closely. Language, though inescapably social, is not entirely a system of communication. It is also a system, as all biological sign systems are, with which the organisms of every species model their world (Sebeok, 1994). The human world, we believe with some justification, is more complex than the world modeled by any other species. What gives it this complexity is the capability, helped naturally by language, of consciously seeing and making distinctions. Language aside, no thought of consequence, no human model of the world is possible without a huge set of sharp, clear contrasts. The most fundamental of these is surely self–other.[5] Almost as fundamental are: this one–that one"; fight–flee; friendly–hostile; together–separate—the list could be extended beyond the space here to record it. There are also the oppositions of physical space.

Beginning with the statocyst, which uses gravity to tell very simple life forms that they are upright or tipped over, simple organisms have to know up from down. The statocyst evolved into our semicircular canals, which are indispensable for keeping our balance on two feet. And these organs, working with our other senses and motor mechanisms, help us know many other spatial contrasts; clockwise–counter-clockwise; in front of–behind;

---

[5]Laughlin and d'Aquili (1974) point to " ... the primitive, but universal, tendency to order reality into pairs that are usually subjectively experienced as opposites" and add: " ... the self–other dichotomy is a very important model of reality—probably one of the most fundamental *binary oppositions*. When this structure does not function properly, the boundaries of self are lost with resultant psychotic symptoms, such as auditory and visual hallucinations" (p. 115).

near–far; over–under; in–out; and so forth. Besides these static space relations, which teach us to know space by binary, polar opposition, there are dynamic oppositions: enter–emerge; arrive–depart; and stay–leave. This is only a beginning at cataloging the polarities on which our thinking, our modeling of the universe we know (or think we know) is based. However long the list when it is completed, one thing is quite clear. Every one of these oppositions is most clearly, directly, and efficiently expressed not by the words of any spoken language but by visible gestures. The conclusion is inescapable: Not only language but thought as well is firmly based in movement and vision, the master sense in humans (Donald, 1991; Gibson, 1966).

Vision does more than present us the images projected by light patterns on the retinas of our eyes. Because the neural connections between eyes and brain far outnumber the brain connections to all other sensory-end organs combined, vision itself is a kind of thinking. When we move our heads, the pattern of light reaching our eyes is not the same as it was the moment before, but the brain figures out what has really happened, and tells us that nothing has changed but our position. Although we see things from a different perspective, we see and know them to be unchanged. There is more than metaphor in the widespread use of *see* to mean *know*.

When human groups began to use upper limbs (which upright walking had freed from other uses) for representing such fundamental concepts as up there–down here and close by–far off, these visible representations greatly enhanced human ability to form concepts, an ability that even chimpanzees appear to possess (Edelman, 1989). This visual–motor representation as an aid to cognition (see also Donald, 1991), along with the gestural development of syntax, marked an important step from rudimentary concept formation to something akin to human thinking. Taking the view of things presented here makes it obvious that language and cognition coevolved, each contributing new power to the other. Ultimately, of course, *Homo sapiens*, or the later generations of *Homo erectus* would have had a sign system with every attribute languages have, except complete expressibility with vocal sounds. Spoken language would come in time—a long time—because it required the evolution of the vocal tract with its brain-centered control and the related evolution of the auditory system.

The Metamorphosis of Language

One question asked of us who maintain this perspective is: How do we then explain the change, if it ever occurred, from gesture-driven to speech-driven language? The first answer is that human communication never has been exclusively in a single mode or channel. As Gibson's classic study of the sensory systems showed, all organisms are genetically programmed to extract every bit of information important to their survival from the surroundings. Not only are there presently sign languages as well as speech languages, but there is also the constant use that speakers make of their eyes and bodies when they interact—films make it quite clear that even talkers on the telephone gesticulate when obviously they cannot be seen by the person on the other end.[6]

This question deserves a fuller answer. What seems most likely is that members of the human genus, whether erect or sapient, when they possessed a language and the coevolved cognitive abilities, would have so enlarged and enriched their material and social culture that they badly needed a system of communication that did not keep their upper limbs from doing other necessary things and did not demand unbroken visual contact. Besides, the persistence and constant use of gestural–visual communication in all cultures—the universality of vocal and silent information transfer—suggests that when language began as a gestural–visual system, it was in all likelihood accompanied by vocal noises.

It is likely also that just as manual gestures, facial expressions, and body English now carry affective information while a speaker's voice is making what are called linguistic signs; so, in the era before language metamorphosis, at the same time as a signer's upper-body movements were making the linguistic signs, the sounds made by the voice of the signer was most likely carrying much of the affective information.

These parallel channels for communication or information transfer probably never were isolated from one another. Never, that is, until the relatively recent invention of alphabetically writing the sounds of speech led to the study of language as recorded speech, the subsequent study of texts as records of speech, and the eventual misapprehension that speech is language. As we know, writing cannot capture what the speaker is showing by posture, movement, facial changes, and other visible forms of expression.

It is likely then, that there always has been, as there still is, a mix of sight and sound in human communication, but that in the course of evolution, the proportion of each of these devoted to producing sentences became interchanged. In the earliest uses of language, gestural expression would very likely have had an audible accompaniment. Habitual use of distinctive vocal sounds with certain gestural linguistic signs along with their meanings could then have led to the use of vocal output for more than just expressing affect. As regularly occurring phenomena, some of

---

[6]See Jonathan Miller's BBC documentary, *Born Talking, Episode 3*. Videotape. John McGreevy Productions, Toronto.

these vocal sounds would have begun to serve occasionally as surrogates for the gestural expression and what it meant—an interesting new perspective on the sociolinguistic and semiotic curiosities referred to as *speech surrogates*.

As the use of vocal sounds to stand for the sometimes omitted gestural expressions grew more acceptable, and perhaps at times more convenient than the full gestural delivery, so the refinement of the vocal sounds to make finer contrasts (and the coevolving ability to hear minute differences) would have proceeded—until at some period in the past the proportion shifted, and the linguistic signs humans used became more vocal and less gestural.[7]

IMPLICATIONS OF A NEW PERSPECTIVE

The preceding discussion may seem to present less a perspective on deafness than on the whole human species' acquisition of language. However, when the possibility is considered that gesture and vision allowed a new species on earth to represent what was learned of the world by using easily performed and naturally signifying signs, it can be said that this species invented language. Therefore, when this proposition is seriously considered, the implications of not being able to hear can be seen in a new light. Of course, to people who hear and speak and, against all evidence, believe that speech and language are the same thing, deafness is a calamity, a disease, or a condition to be altered at all costs—even by surgical invasion of infants' skulls. Thus, for Samuel Heinicke in the 18th century, Alexander Graham Bell in the 19th century, and oralists to the present day who confuse language with speech, the whole aim of education for the deaf was to inculcate artificial speech and implant the ability to decode speech, by watching speakers with or without sound amplification (see Lane, 1984; Lane, Hoffmeister, & Bahan, 1996).

However, when it becomes more widely recognized that arbitrary (i.e., spoken) signs could have become language only as surrogates for gestural signs with their meanings, deafness will have to be viewed in an entirely different light. Educators of deaf children will need to understand how fundamental distinctions, binary oppositions, have a dynamic and visual basis. They will seek out ways to translate effectively between signed and spoken language.

---

[7]No doubt at somewhere near the point at which articulate human speech is supposed to have emerged.

Many viewers now find it interesting to watch sign language interpreters appearing in televised programs (something unthinkable in the early days of television programming and bitter opposition from oralist organizations). In the coming century, such visual experiences and a growing recognition that cultures like those of Native Americans and Aboriginal Australians[8] as well as sign languages of the deaf have great value in a world of disappearing resources, not only because they make those who cannot hear able to cope with the modern world, but because they preserve more or less intact the roots of language and cognition. The preservation and use of alternate sign languages also adds something to human understanding, if only the demonstration that human information transfer is not limited to one mode or channel. The widening of the public perspective on sign languages can only bring benefit to those whose deafness makes a sign language their natural first language—a benefit, incidentally, to those whose professional attention is focused on deafness and deaf children and adults.

REFERENCES

Armstrong, D. F., Stokoe, W. C., & Wilcox, S. (1995). *Gesture and the nature of language*. New York: Cambridge University Press.
Bateson, G. (1979). *Mind and nature*. New York: Dutton.
Battison, R. M., & Jordan, I. K. (1976). Cross-cultural communication with foreign signers: Fact and fancy. *Sign Language Studies, 10*, 53–68.
Bickerton, D. (1990). *Language and species*. Chicago: University of Chicago Press.
Bickerton, D. (1995). *Language and human behavior*. Seattle: University of Washington Press.
De Sassure, F. (1967). Cours de Linguistique general. Wiesbeden: Harrassourtz.
Donald, M. (1991). *Origins of the modern mind*. Cambridge, MA: Harvard University Press.
Edelman, G. M. (1988). *Topobiology*. New York: Basic Books.
Edelman, G. M. (1989). *The remembered present: A biological theory of consciousness*. New York: Basic Books.
Edelman, G. M. (1991). *Bright air, brilliant fire: On the matter of mind*. New York: Basic Books.
Farnell, B. (1995). *Do you see what I mean? Plains Indian Sign Talk and the Embodiment of Action*. Austin, TX: University of Texas Press.
Frishberg, N. (1975). Arbitrariness and iconicity: Historical change in American Sign Language. *Language, 51*, 696–719.
Gibson, J. J. (1966). *The senses considered as perceptual systems*. Boston: Houghton Mifflin.
Harris, R. A. (1993). *The linguistic wars*. New York: Oxford University Press.
Hart, M., & Risley, T. R. (1995). *Meaningful differences in the everyday experience of young American children*. Baltimore, MD: Brookes.

---

[8]See Farnell (1995) and Kendon (1988).

Jordan, I. K., & Battison, R. M. (1976). A referential communication experiment with foreign sign langauges. *Sign Language Studies, 10,* 69–80.

Kendon, A. (1988). *The sign languages of Aboriginal Australia.* New York: Cambridge University Press.

Kimura, D. (1993). *Neuromotor mechanisms in human communication.* New York: Oxford University Press.

King, B. J. (1994). *The information continuum; Evolution of social information transfer in monkeys, apes, and hominids.* Santa Fe, NM: School of American Research Press.

Kingdon, J. (1993). *Self-made man: Human evolution from Eden to Extinction?* New York: Wiley.

Klima, E. S., & Bellugi, U. (1979). *The signs of language.* Cambridge, MA: Harvard University Press.

Lane, H. (1984). *When the mind hears.* New York: Random House.

Lane, H., Hoffmeister, R., & Bahan, B. (1996). *A journey into the deaf world.* San Diego, CA: Dawn Sign Press.

Laughlin, C., & d'Acquili, E. (1974). *Biogenetic structuralism.* New York: Columbia University Press.

Lillo-Martin, D. (1993). Deaf readers and universal grammar. In M. Marschark & M. Diane Clark (Eds.), *Psychological perspectives on deafness* (pp. 311–337). Hillsdale, NJ: Lawrence Erlbaum Associates.

McNeill, D. (1992). *Hand and mind: What gestures reveal about thought.* Chicago: University of Chicago Press.

Mirzoeff, N. (1996). *Silent poetry: Deafness, sign, and visual culture in modern France.* Princeton, NJ: Princeton University Press.

Sebeok, T. A. (1994). *Signs: An introduction to semiotics.* Toronto: University of Toronto Press.

Volterra, V. & Erting, C. J. (1990) From gesture to language in hearing and deaf children. New York: Springer-Verlag.

Volterra, V., & Iverson, J. M. (1995) When do modality factors affect the course of language acquisition? In K. Emmorey & J. Reilly (Eds.), *Language, gesture, and space.*

2

The Impact of Sign Language Use on Visuospatial Cognition

Karen Emmorey
The Salk Institute for Biological Studies

Online comprehension of sign language involves many visuospatial processes, such as handshape recognition, motion discrimination, identification of facial expressions, and recognition of linguistically relevant spatial contrasts. Production of sign language also involves visuospatial processes linked to motor processes, for example, production of distinct motion patterns, memory for spatial locations, and integration of mental images with signing space. In this chapter, studies are reviewed that have suggested the habitual use of a visuospatial language such as American Sign Language (ASL) may have an impact on nonlinguistic aspects of spatial cognition.

Many studies have investigated the visuospatial skills of deaf people; however, most of these studies are not applicable to the question addressed here because the language background of subjects was not examined. Attention to language background is critical because deaf people have varying degrees of exposure to ASL. Deaf people with deaf parents are generally exposed to ASL from birth and are native signers. Deaf people with hearing parents may first be exposed to ASL at differing ages (from early childhood to adulthood), and some deaf people never learn to sign. Thus, only those studies are reviewed that selected subjects for language background (studying fluent ASL signers) and those studies that addressed explicitly the question of how experience with sign language might affect non-linguistic visuospatial abilities.

Three domains of visuospatial cognition are discussed: motion processing, face processing, and imagery. Within each of these domains, there is strong evidence that experience with sign language enhances specific cognitive processes. These findings have important implications for the relationship between language and thought and for the modularity of mind hypothesis, which is discussed at the end of the chapter.

MOTION PROCESSING

Interpreting movement is critical to online processing of sign language. For example, Emmorey and Corina (1990) and Grosjean (1981) used a gating technique to track lexical recognition of ASL signs (isolated signs are presented repeatedly, increasing the length of each presentation by one videoframe, and subjects attempt to identify the sign at each presentation). Both studies found that movement identification coincided with lexical identification (when the movement of the sign was recognized, the sign itself was also identified). Such a direct correlation between lexical identification and a phonological element does not occur in English and may not occur in any spoken language. That is, there appears to be no phonological feature or segment, the identification of which leads directly to spoken word recognition.

Furthermore, several sign phonologists have identified movement as the most salient feature within a sign-based sonority hierarchy (Brentari, 1993; Corina, 1990). Differences in movement patterns also signal differences in aspect and agreement morphology (e.g., Klima & Bellugi, 1979). Given the significant role of movement in conveying phonological, morphological, and lexical contrasts in ASL, there is reason to expect that experience with processing motion within the linguistic domain might influence nonlinguistic motion processing. The studies reviewed here all find an influence of sign language use on different aspects of motion processing: motion detection, motion categorization, and the perception of apparent motion.

Detection of Motion in Peripheral Vision

Neville and Lawson (1987a, 1987b, 1987c) conducted a series of experiments that investigated the ability of deaf and hearing subjects to detect the direction of motion in the periphery of vision. Identification of movement in the periphery is important for sign perception because signers look at the face, rather than track the hands, when they are conversing or watching a sign narrative (Siple, 1978). Thus, lexical identification depends on peripheral vision when signs are produced away from the face. Neville and Lawson used an electrophysiological measure of brain activity (Event Related Potentials or ERPs) to study the neural activity associated with motion perception for deaf and hearing subjects. The subjects' task was to detect the direction of motion of a small, white square presented in either the left or right visual field (18° lateral of central fixation). The illusion of motion was created by presenting one square for 33 ms immediately followed by another square in an adjacent position for another 33 ms. The motion was thus very quick and could occur in eight possible directions (up, down, left, right, and 4 diagonal directions). The following subject groups were studied: native deaf signers (deaf subjects exposed to ASL from birth by their deaf parents), hearing native signers (hearing subjects with deaf parents exposed to ASL from birth), and hearing nonsigners (hearing subjects with no knowledge of a signed language).

Deaf signers were significantly faster than hearing nonsigners in detecting the direction of motion of the square. However, this enhanced detection ability appears to be an effect of auditory deprivation, rather than an effect of the use of sign language, because deaf native signers were also much faster than hearing native signers who performed similarly to hearing nonsigners. The effect of sign language use was not found in absolute performance level, but rather in the pattern of responses within the left and right visual fields. Both deaf and hearing ASL signers were more accurate in detecting motion in the right visual field (left hemisphere) compared to hearing nonsigners (see Fig. 2.1). In addition, the electrophysiological results showed that both groups of signers showed increased left hemisphere activation during the motion detection task compared to hearing nonsigners. Neville and Lawson hypothesized that the increased role of the left hemisphere may arise from the temporal coincidence of motion perception and the acquisition of ASL. That is, the acquisition of ASL requires the child to make linguistically significant distinctions based on movement. If the left hemisphere plays a greater role in acquiring ASL, then the left hemisphere may come to mediate the perception of temporal sequences of nonlanguage material as well as linguistically relevant motion. These results suggest that the acquisition of a signed language can alter the brain areas responsible for certain aspects of (nonlinguistic) motion perception.

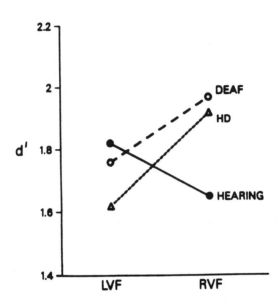

FIG. 2.1. Detection (d') of moving targets in the left and right visual fields (LVF and RVF) for hearing subjects, deaf subjects, and hearing subjects born to deaf parents (HD subjects). Reprinted from Neville and Lawson (1987c) with permission.

Perceptual Categorization of Motion

Just as the acquisition of a particular spoken language can alter the nature of perceptual categorization of speech sounds, the acquisition of a signed language may alter the perceptual categorization of motion. Many studies have shown that adult speakers of Japanese have difficulty distinguishing /l/ and /r/ (e.g., Eimas, 1975); whereas adult English speakers have difficulty distinguishing between dental and retroflex stops (/da/ vs. /Da/) found in languages like Hindi (Werker & Tees, 1983). Six-month-old hearing infants in Japan, India, and America can all distinguish these sound contrasts. By about 1 year of age, however, infants are performing like their adult counterparts, reliably distinguishing only those speech sounds relevant to their language. Thus, experience with a particular spoken language appears to cause a perceptual reorganization that fine-tunes the ability to perceive linguistically relevant distinctions (Kuhl, 1991; Werker; 1994). Similarly, Poizner and his colleagues discovered that experience with sign language can influence the perceptual categorization of linguistic movements (Poizner, 1981, 1983; Poizner, Fok, & Bellugi, 1989).

In Poizner's experiments, deaf native signers and hearing nonsigners were asked to make triadic comparisons of motion displays, deciding which two of three movements were most similar. Johansson's (1973) technique for presenting biological motion as patterns of moving lights was used to create the motion displays. A signer was filmed in a darkened room with lights attached to the head, shoulder, joints of the arm, and the index fingertip. Thus, subjects did not see the signer's face or hand configuration. Motion similarity judgments were based on the pattern of the movement alone. Poizner (1981, 1983) found that deaf and hearing subjects differed in their motion similarity judgments. Using multidimensional scaling techniques, Poizner found that certain linguistically relevant dimensions of movement were more salient for native ASL signers compared to hearing subjects with no knowledge of ASL. In particular, movement repetition and cyclicity were much more salient for the deaf signers, and repetition and cyclicity are both phonologically distinctive in ASL. For example, noun–verb pairs are distinguished by repetition (Supalla & Newport, 1978), and aspectual distinctions are conveyed by differences in cyclicity (Klima & Bellugi, 1979). These results suggest that the acquisition of American Sign Language can modify the perceptual categorization of linguistically relevant motion. ASL signers categorize such motion patterns differently than nonsigners for whom the patterns carry no linguistic information. However, the extent to which differences in motion categorization are due to differences in motion perception itself versus the cognitive process of categorization has yet to be determined.

Poizner, Fok, and Bellugi (1989) also found that the nature of motion categorization may depend on the particular sign language acquired, just as the categorization of speech sounds depend on the particular spoken language acquired. Using the same motion similarity judgment task, Poizner et al. (1989) found that deaf subjects from Hong Kong who acquired Chinese Sign Language as their first language exhibited a slightly different pattern of motion salience compared to native ASL signers. Both ASL and CSL signers found motion repetition to be particularly salient—in contrast to both the hearing English and hearing Chinese speakers. Repetition is phonologically significant for CSL, as it is for ASL (van Hoek, Bellugi, & Fok, 1986). However, the CSL signers weighted the "arcness" of motion as less salient than did the ASL signers. A straight versus arced movement is phonologically distinctive in ASL, but Poizner et al. (1989) speculated that arcness may not be distinctive in CSL. However, Yau (1987) and van Hoek et al. (1986) provided evidence that CSL distinguishes between several movement paths on the basis of arcness (e.g., distinguishing circular from straight paths). It is possible that arcness of motion is a more prevalent lexical contrast in ASL than in CSL, but until more comparative linguistic analysis is done, the interpretation of the differential sensitivity of ASL and CSL signers to this parameter of motion must remain open.

The previous studies indicate that acquisition of a signed language can alter the categorization of linguistically relevant movement. Note that these studies presented the movements of actual signs rather than nonlinguistic motion, and ASL signers were able to recognize these dynamic point light displays as signs (Poizner, Bellugi, & Lutes-Driscoll, 1981). Thus, the observed perceptual fine tuning might be limited to motion that is clearly linguistic.

However, results from Klima, Tzeng, Fok, Bellugi, and Corina (1996) and Bettger (1992) suggest that sign language acquisition can affect the categorization of movement that is not linguistic, i.e., that is not derived from signs. Klima et al. presented dynamic point light displays of Chinese pseudocharacters to deaf and hearing Americans (see Fig. 2.2). The subjects' tasks were to draw the Chinese characters that had been 'written in the air.' Because neither subject group was familiar with Chinese, no linguistic knowledge could be used to determine the underlying stroke pattern. Thus, the movement patterns were nonlinguistic for these subjects. Klima et al. found that the deaf ASL signers were significantly better at segmenting the continuous light image into discrete movement strokes. Deaf signers were better able to distinguish between transition and stroke components of the movement and were less likely to include transitional movements in their drawings compared to the hearing subjects. Klima et al. hypothesized that this enhanced ability to analyze movement may arise from the processing requirements of ASL. Signers must separate out phonologically significant and transitional movement online during sign perception. This linguistic processing skill may make signers more sensitive to the distinction between purposeful movement and transition. Bettger (1992) provided support for this hypothesis. Using the same experimental paradigm, Bettger found that hearing native ASL signers were also better able to segment the movement pattern into strokes and transitions compared to hearing nonsigners, suggesting that this skill is linked to language experience rather than to deafness.

In summary, the acquisition of a signed language can influence how motion is categorized perceptually. Signers not only categorize linguistic motion differently than nonsigners, but they may also have a heightened sensitivity to certain perceptual qualities of nonlinguistic motion.

Perception of Apparent Motion

Apparent motion is the perception of a single moving object when a static object occurs at one location, followed rapidly by a static object at another location. The object does not actually move, but it is perceived as moving from one location to another. For example, apparent motion accounts for

Point Light Motion	Target Structure
	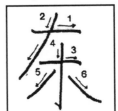

Hearing American Adults

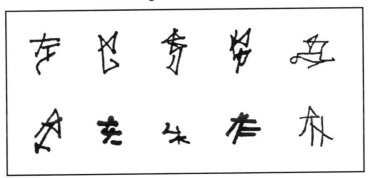

Deaf American Adults

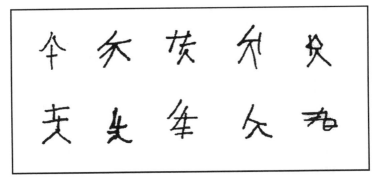

FIG. 2.2. Example of a point light motion stimulus, its target structure, and representative drawings from deaf ASL signers and hearing nonsigners. Adapted from Klima et al. (1996), with permission.

the perception of Christmas lights *moving* along a string. In reality, each light bulb simply blinks on and off—there is no real motion. It turns out that object identity usually does not alter how we perceive apparent motion. In general, we perceive objects taking the shortest path between two locations—even when such a path is not plausible in the real world (e.g., a solid object would have to pass through another solid object to get to the second location).

However, Shiffrar and colleagues have found object identity does affect how we perceive the path of motion when the object is a human figure (Chatterjee, Freyd, & Shiffrar, 1996; Shiffrar & Freyd, 1993). Shiffrar and Freyd (1990) found that apparent motion for the human body sometimes appears to take a longer, indirect path, when the shortest path would require it to pass through the body. For example, if the hand is shown first in front of the torso and then behind the torso, the shortest path would require it to go through the body. In fact, subjects report seeing this direct path at fast presentation rates (e.g., 150 ms between presentation of the two pictures). However, as presentation rate is slowed, subjects increasingly report seeing the longer, but physically possible path, in which the hand moves around the body.

When the two objects are not part of the human body, subjects continue to see one object moving through another at longer presentation rates, despite the physical impossibility of such motion. Thus, the visual system appears to utilize constraints on the perception of motion that are specific to biological motion. Furthermore, sensitivity to constraints on biological motion appears in young infants, suggesting that knowledge about the properties of biological motion may be innate (Bertenthal, 1993; Bertenthal, Proffitt, Kramer, & Spetner, 1987). However, it is possible that infants have sufficient visual exposure to the human body during the first few months of life to alter the sensitivity of the visual system for biological motion.

Recently, Wilson (1997) asked the following question: If the constraints on motion perception for the human body are acquired through experience, could experience with a rule-governed motion system (such as sign language) create additional constraints on the perception of biological motion? She presented deaf and hearing subjects with apparent motion stimuli derived from ASL signs. Subjects were presented with the beginning points and endpoints of a sign—they were not shown the actual motion of the sign. Two sets of signs were used: those that have an arc motion between two locations (e.g., BRIDGE, IMPROVE, MILLION)[1] and signs which have a straight path between two locations (e.g., BUSY, CREDIT CARD, FEVER). In the absence of other constraints, all subjects

---

[1]Words in capital letters represent English glosses for ASL signs.

should be biased to see a straight path motion between the endpoints of both sets of signs because this is the shortest path between locations. However, Wilson (1997) reasoned that if acquired knowledge of ASL can influence perceived biological motion, then deaf ASL signers (but not hearing nonsigners) should report seeing arced motion for those signs that lexically contain an arced movement.

Wilson (1997) found that for signs that used a straight path, both hearing and deaf subjects primarily reported seeing a direct path between locations. However, for signs which used an arc path, deaf subjects were significantly more likely to report an arced motion than hearing subjects. Furthermore, as presentation rate slowed, the tendency to report arced movement increased dramatically for the deaf subjects, but the increase was minimal for the hearing subjects. Wilson concluded that experience with ASL alters the probability of perceiving an indirect (arced) path of motion, when that motion path yields an ASL sign. She proposed a *lexicality constraint*, which is learned by the visual system through exposure to ASL. Wilson's results demonstrated that constraints on the perception of biological motion can be acquired. Furthermore, her results are the first to directly show that knowledge of ASL can alter motion *perception*. Deaf signers perceived the hand moving with an arc motion, whereas hearing non-signers perceived a straight path motion for the same stimuli.

FACE PROCESSING

Linguistic facial expression plays a significant role in the syntax and morphology of American Sign Language (Baker-Shenk, 1985). For example, the syntax of sentences is often determined by different eye and eyebrow movements, for example, raised eyebrows mark topic constructions; furrowed brows mark *wh*-questions. Unlike emotional facial expressions, linguistic facial expressions have a clear onset and offset and are coordinated with specific parts of the signed sentence (Reilly, McIntire, & Bellugi, 1991). In addition to their syntactic function, linguistic facial expressions constitute adverbials that co-occur with predicates and carry specific meanings (e.g., pursed lips indicates effortless action; tongue protrusion indicates careless action). Signers must be able to discriminate rapidly among many different expressions during language comprehension. In addition, as noted earlier, signers fixate on the face of their addressee rather than track the hands. The fact that signers focus on the face during sign perception and the fact that facial expressions convey grammatical and lexical distinctions may lead to the enhancement of certain aspects of face processing.

Face Discrimination: The Benton Faces Test

Several studies have shown that ASL signers exhibit superior performance on the Benton Test of Face Recognition (Benton, Hamsher, Varney, & Spreen, 1983). In the Benton Faces test, subjects match the canonical view of a target face with other views of the same person (see Fig. 2.3). The target faces and distractor faces are presented under different orientation and/or lighting conditions. Bellugi, O'Grady, Lillo-Martin, O'Grady, van Hoek, and Corina (1990) found that deaf signing children between the ages of 6 and 9 performed significantly better at every age level than hearing children on this test. Bettger (1992) replicated this result with adult signers, finding that both deaf and hearing ASL signers out-performed hearing nonsigners, suggesting this effect is language-linked. Furthermore, Parasnis, Samar, Bettger, and Sathe (1996) found that *oral* deaf (deaf people who do not know sign language) do not exhibit superior performance on the Benton Faces test compared to hearing subjects. Because these subjects were deaf, but had no experience with sign language, Parasnis et al.'s finding again suggested that the superior performance of the deaf subjects is due to their signing experience rather than to effects of deafness. Finally, results from Bettger (1992) indicated that exposure to ASL from birth is not required to improve performance. He tested deaf signers with hearing parents who had not been exposed to ASL at home or in grade school—they had only 4 years of signing experience. Bettger (1992) found that these non-native signers were more accurate on the Benton Faces test compared to hearing nonsigners, and the non-native deaf signers' performances did not differ significantly from the performance of the native deaf and hearing signers. Thus, it appears that life long experience with ASL is not required to enhance face processing skills.

Inverted Faces

Bettger, Emmorey, McCullough, and Bellugi (1997) found evidence suggesting this enhancement is linked to processes specifically involved in face perception, rather than a general enhancement of visual discrimination or object recognition. Deaf and hearing subjects (both children and adults) were presented with a version of the Benton Faces test in which the faces were turned upside down. It has been found that inversion impairs face recognition disproportionally compared to the recognition of other objects, such as houses (Yin, 1969). This inversion effect has been interpreted as indicating that there are unique mechanisms underlying face processing. Farah, Wilson, Drain, and Tanaka (1995) suggested that

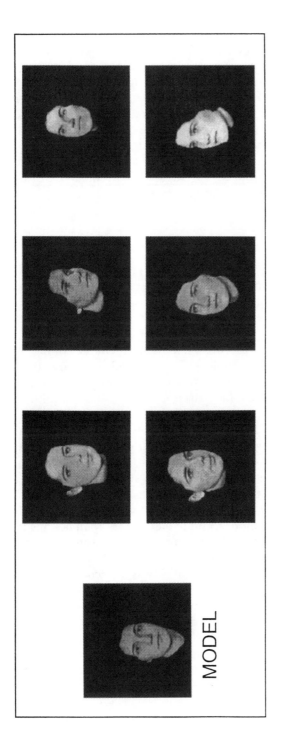

FIG. 2.3. Example stimulus from the Benton Faces test. The model face is the same face as the top middle, bottom middle, and bottom right face.

MODEL

these specialized mechanisms are not utilized when faces are turned upside down and that face perception systems are specific to upright faces. Bettger et al. (1997) found that deaf signers (both adults and children) were more accurate than hearing nonsigners when the Benton Faces were presented in their canonical upright orientation. However, deaf signers and hearing nonsigners (both adults and children) did not differ in performance when the faces were inverted. This result suggests that experience with sign language affects mechanisms specific to face processing and does not produce a general enhancement of discrimination abilities (even when the stimuli are faces).

Face Recognition

Recently, McCullough and Emmorey (1997) conducted a series of experiments that investigated whether enhanced performance extended to other aspects of face processing. Note that although the Benton Faces test is called a test of face recognition, it actually taps face *discrimination* by asking subjects to distinguish among faces that differ in lighting and profile. There is no memory component, as the target and the response choices are presented simultaneously. The first study conducted by McCullough and Emmorey, therefore, investigated whether the enhanced face discrimination abilities of ASL signers extended to face *recognition* as well.

Deaf signers and hearing nonsigners were presented with the Warrington (1984) Recognition Memory Test for Faces. In this test, subjects are first given a *foil* task in which they rate 50 individual faces as pleasant or unpleasant. Subjects are then given a surprise recognition test. They are presented with two faces and must decide which face they saw previously during the rating task. McCullough and Emmorey found that deaf signers were not more accurate on this task than hearing nonsigners. In another experiment, deaf and hearing subjects were given the same face recognition test but the stimuli were presented on the computer, and subjects were asked to respond as quickly as they could. Again, the subject groups did not differ in accuracy, and they had similar response times. These findings suggest that experience with ASL does not lead to an enhanced ability to recognize unfamiliar faces from memory. This result is actually not that surprising given that the face-processing skills required for ASL do not involve recognition of the faces of individual people—just the opposite, in fact. Signers must be able to generalize facial expressions across individuals, disregarding aspects of a face that are unique to an individual.

Gestalt Face Processing

McCullough and Emmorey (1997) explored other aspects of face processing using the Mooney Faces Closure Test (Mooney, 1957), which taps gestalt face processing ability. This test consists of high contrast pictures of human faces of various ages and different genders (see Fig. 2.4). Deaf and hearing subjects are asked to sort the pictures into different groups (boy, girl, adult man, adult woman, old man, old woman). Because few local facial features are shown in these high contrast images, subjects must rely on global information derived from the faces to identify and categorize the stimuli into different age and gender groups. Before individual features can be identified, recognition of the face must be achieved through the gestalt process of visual closure. McCullough and Emmorey found that deaf and hearing subjects did not differ on this task (in fact, deaf signers were slightly less accurate than hearing nonsigners). This result suggests that when a configurational analysis with a gestalt closure process is required for face identification, deaf signers perform on a par with hearing subjects. The fact that deaf signers were not superior to hearing subjects on the Mooney Faces Closure task suggests that the mechanism(s) responsible for their superior performance on the Benton Faces Test may involve processes related to local facial features rather than to global facial

FIG. 2.4. Example stimuli from Mooney Faces Test. The faces are those of an adult man and woman.

features. Such a hypothesis is reasonable given that signers must discriminate among facial expressions that involve individual facial features (e.g., eyebrows) rather than global features (e.g., the overall configuration of features within the face).

Discrimination of Facial Features

McCullough and Emmorey conducted a third experiment that investigated whether ASL signers exhibit a superior ability to discriminate subtle differences in local facial features. Deaf and hearing subjects' abilities to detect changes in facial features within the *same* face were compared. It was hypothesized that because ASL signers must attend to facial features in order to interpret signed sentences, they may perform better than nonsigners in detecting differences in facial features. In this experiment, subjects were first presented with a target face in the center of a computer screen. After several seconds, two response faces were presented side-by-side: One was exactly the same as the target face and the other was also the same face, but one facial feature had been replaced by a feature from a different face (either the eyes, nose, or mouth). Subjects had to indicate which face was the same as the target face (see Fig. 2.5).

McCullough and Emmorey found that deaf signers were significantly more accurate than hearing nonsigners in discriminating between faces that were identical except for a change in a single facial feature. When the performance of hearing signers was compared to both deaf signers and hearing nonsigners, the pattern that emerged suggested that both experience with ASL and experience with lip reading can lead to an enhanced ability to identify differences in facial features. Specifically, experience with ASL may lead to an enhanced ability to detect differences in eye configuration. Both deaf and hearing ASL signers were more accurate in detecting a difference in the eyes than hearing nonsigners. In ASL, changes in eye configuration (e.g., raised eyebrows, squinted eyes, furrowed brows) convey various syntactic distinctions that may lead to the observed enhancement. In contrast, deaf signers were more accurate than both hearing signers and non-signers in detecting differences in the mouth feature. This result suggests that experience with lip eading may lead to a superior ability to detect differences in mouth shape. Deaf signers receive extensive training in lip reading, unlike hearing signers. Finally, deaf and hearing subjects did not differ in their ability to detect alterations of the nose. This result was expected because ASL grammatical facial expressions do not involve the nose, and the nose is also not relevant for lip-reading skills. Thus, deaf signers were best able to remember and discriminate between just those facial features that are relevant for lip reading and ASL linguistic facial expressions.

Target Stimulus

Original

Altered

FIG. 2.5. Example stimuli set from McCullough and Emmorey (1997). The altered face has different eyes than the target face.

Recognition of Emotional Facial Expressions

Engberg-Pedersen (1993) pointed out the important role of affective facial expressions in sign language discourse. She proposed a concept termed *shifted attribution of expressive elements*, in which the emotions and attitude expressed by the signer's face or body posture are attributed to a referent within the discourse (rather than to the narrator). This use of affective facial expressions occurs during referential shift in which the narrator signals that the discourse reflects the point of view of a particular referent within the narrative, and affective facial expressions within the shift are attributed to that referent. Goldstein and Feldman (1996) explored the hypothesis that ASL signers might exhibit a heightened proficiency in the identification of emotional facial expressions. As in previous studies, they reasoned that because signers must attend to linguistic facial expressions, signers may also have heightened attention to emotional facial expressions. This hypothesis is even more plausible given the role of affective facial expressions in ASL narratives just described. Heightened attention to facial expressions (both linguistic and emotional) when comprehending ASL discourse might lead to a strengthened ability to identify emotional expressions.

Goldstein and Feldman (1996) presented a silent videotape of people expressing spontaneous emotions to hearing subjects who either had no knowledge of ASL or who had studied ASL for an average of 2 years (range: 10 months to 5 years). Subjects had to identify each facial expression as showing happiness, sadness, fear–surprise, anger, or disgust. Overall, ASL signers were significantly more accurate than nonsigners in identifying these emotional facial expressions. All subjects were equally good at identifying happy facial expressions. However, signers were more accurate in identifying disgusted and angry facial expressions. These are the emotions that are typically most difficult to distinguish (Coats & Feldman, 1995). Goldstein and Feldman (1996) suggested that the heightened saliency of facial expression for signers may lead to an increase in experience decoding facial expressions and thus improve their ability to identify facial expressions of affect.

In summary, the combined results of these studies suggest that ASL signers are not enhanced in all aspects of face processing. Specifically, deaf signers and hearing nonsigners do not differ in their ability to recognize faces from memory or in their gestalt face processing abilities. Enhancement of face processing skill appears to be most strongly tied to the ability to discriminate among faces that are very similar (as in the Benton Faces test) and to recognize subtle changes in specific facial features. These skills are most closely tied to recognizing and interpreting linguistic facial expression in ASL. To identify and categorize ASL facial expressions, signers need not recognize the person. Rather, signers must rely on featural processing of the face in order to identify specific facial expressions. The gestalt aspect of the face does not change with different facial expressions. Ability to generalize over individual faces and to focus on specific local features rather than on the global configuration of the face are characteristic of lipreading as well. Finally, experience with ASL appears to enhance the ability to identify emotional facial expressions. These expressions, like linguistic facial expressions, are generalized over individual faces and rely on changes in individual features. Thus, it appears that sign language use enhances face processing skills that are relevant to interpreting subtle differences in local feature configurations and that must be generalized over individual faces.

IMAGERY

Several studies have examined the relation between processing ASL and the use of visual mental imagery (Chamberlain & Mayberry, 1994; Emmorey, Kosslyn, & Bellugi, 1993; Emmorey & Kosslyn, 1996; Emmorey, Klima, & Hickok, 1997; Talbot & Haude, 1993). Specifically, these studies examined the ability of deaf and hearing subjects to transform images mentally (e.g., by rotation) and to generate mental images. Emmorey and colleagues hypothesized that these imagery abilities are integral to the production and comprehension of ASL and that their constant use may lead to an enhancement of imagery skills within the nonlinguistic domain for ASL signers. This hypothesis and other studies are reviewed, comparing the performance of signers and nonsigners on nonlinguistic tasks requiring mental rotation, image generation, and image maintenance.

Mental Rotation

McKee (1987) was one of the first to investigate mental rotation skills in deaf and hearing subjects. McKee used a task similar to the one devised by Shepard and Metzler (1971) in which subjects were shown three forms created by juxtaposing cubes to form angular shapes. The constructions were rotated in space around a vertical axis. One of the three shapes was a mirror image of the other two, and subjects were asked to indicate on an answer sheet which of the two constructions were exactly alike. Deaf signers were significantly more accurate on this task than hearing nonsigners.

Emmorey et al. (1993) used a similar task in which subjects were shown two separate two-dimensional shapes and were asked to decide as quickly as possible whether the two shapes were the same or mirror images, regardless of orientation (see Fig. 2.6). Both deaf and hearing signers had faster reaction times than nonsigners at all degrees of rotation. Emmorey et al. (1993) suggested originally that ASL signers may be faster in detecting mirror reversals rather than in rotation *per se* because they were faster even when no rotation was required (i.e., at 0°). However, research

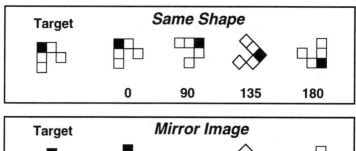

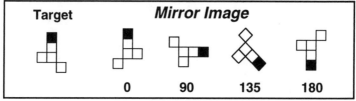

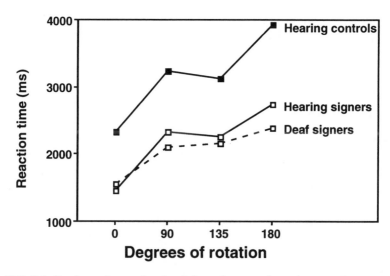

FIG. 2.6. Results and example stimuli from the mental rotation experiment conducted by Emmorey et al. (1993).

by Ilan and Miller (1994) indicated that different processes may be involved when mirror–same judgments were made at 0° within a mental rotation experiment, compared to when mental rotation was not required on any of the trials. In addition, results from Emmorey and Bettger (in preparation) indicated that when native ASL signers and hearing nonsigners were asked to make mirror–same judgments in a comparison task that did not involve mental rotation, these groups did not differ in accuracy or reaction time. This result suggested that signers' enhanced performances stemmed from processes critical to mental rotation tasks, rather than from processes that are specific to mirror-reversal detection.

The fact that deaf and hearing signers were both faster than hearing nonsigners suggests that the enhanced performance on mental rotation tasks is a result of experience with ASL. Further support for this hypothesis was found by Talbot and Haude (1993), who showed that mental rotation performance depended on ASL skill level. Using a variation of the mental rotation task developed by Vandenberg and Kuse (1978), Talbot and Haude (1993) found that hearing subjects who were student interpreters with 6 years of ASL experience performed significantly better than hearing subjects who had less than 1 year of experience or no experience with ASL. These results suggest that a lifetime of ASL experience or exposure to ASL at an early age are not required for an effect on nonlinguistic mental rotation tasks to be observed. Finally, Chamberlain and Mayberry (1994) found that deaf subjects who do not know sign language (*oral* deaf) do not exhibit enhanced performance on mental rotation tasks—their performance did not differ from hearing nonsigners. Together these results support the hypothesis that use of ASL can enhance mental rotation skills. Why? What is it about processing ASL that might lead to such an effect within a nonlinguistic domain of spatial cognition?

Emmorey et al. (1993) and Emmorey et al. (1997) hypothesized that mental rotation may play a crucial role in sign language processing because of the mental transformations that the sign perceiver (i.e., the addressee) must perform while comprehending certain types of discourse. In descriptions involving spatial locations, ASL signers manipulate signing space to isomorphically represent spatial relations in the real or an imagined world. For most locative expressions in ASL, there is a direct correspondence between the location of the hands in signing space and the position of physical objects in the world. When describing spatial scenes in ASL, the identity of each object is indicated by a lexical sign (e.g., TABLE, BED, CHAIR), and the location of the objects, their orientation, and their spatial relation vis-à-vis one another is indicated by where the appropriate classifier signs are articulated. Where English uses prepositions to express spatial relations, ASL uses the actual visual layout displayed by classifier signs positioned in signing space.

Crucially, these spatial scenes are most often described from the perspective of the narrator, such that the viewer, if facing the signer, must perform a 180° mental rotation to correctly comprehend the description. Often during sign comprehension, the perceiver (i.e., the addressee) must mentally reverse the spatial arrays created by the signer such that a spatial locus established on the right of the person signing (and thus on the left of the addressee) is understood as on the right in the scene being described by the signer. Such a situation arises when a particular point of view must be adopted (i.e., the scene must be understood from a particular vantage point, such as from the entrance to a room). As such scenes are most often described from the signer's perspective and not the addressee's, this transformation process may occur frequently.

The problem is not unlike that facing understanders of spoken languages who have to keep in mind the directions *left* and *right* with regard to the speaker. The crucial difference for ASL is that these directions are encoded spatially by the signer. The spatial loci used by the signer to depict a scene (e.g., describing the position of objects and people) must be understood as the reverse of what the addressee actually *observes* during discourse (assuming a face-to-face interaction). Emmorey and colleagues hypothesized that this habitual transformation during discourse comprehension may lead to enhanced mental rotation skills within the nonlinguistic domain.

However, one difficulty with this hypothesis is that the intuitions of native signers suggest that they do not actually mentally *rotate* locations within signing space when they are the addressee (the viewer). Signers report that they instantly know how to interpret the narrator's description (Emmorey et al., 1997). They do not experience a sensation of rotating a mental image of a scene or of objects within a scene. Signers may transform signing space not by mental rotation but by a transformation in which an image is reversed or instantly repositioned in an opposite position within a horizontal plane. If sign language processing involves mental reversal rather than mental rotation, then we must examine our explanation of enhanced mental rotation skills in ASL signers. One possibility is that signers may be more likely to apply a reversal transformation (rather than rotation) that may improve their accuracy on mental rotation tasks because these transformations are easier than rotation (Shepard & Cooper, 1982). Another possibility is that experience with ASL enhances other processes that are involved in mental rotation tasks. To perform mental rotation, subjects must generate an image, maintain that image, and then transform it (Kosslyn, 1980). Emmorey et al. (1993) and Emmorey and Kosslyn (1996) found that deaf and hearing ASL signers were faster at generating mental images than hearing nonsigners. Thus, signers may also be faster at mental rotation tasks because they are able to generate mental images quickly prior to manipulating them. We now turn to studies that investigated image generation skills in ASL signers.

Image Generation and Maintenance

Image generation is the process whereby an image (i.e., a short-term visual memory representation) is created on the basis of information stored in long-term memory (see Kosslyn, Brunn, Cave, & Wallach, 1985). In ASL, image generation and maintenance may be an important process underlying aspects of referential shift. Liddell (1990) argued that under referential shift, signers may imagine referents as present physically, and these visualized referents are relevant to the expression of verb agreement morphology. Liddell (1990) gave the following example involving the verb ASK, which is lexically specified to be directed at chin height:

> To direct the verb ASK toward an imagined referent, the signer must conceive of the location of the imaginary referent's head. For example, if the signer and addressee were to imagine that Wilt Chamberlain was standing beside them ready to give them advice on playing basketball, the sign ASK would be directed upward toward the imaged height of Wilt Chamberlain's head. ... It would be incorrect to sign the verb at the height of the signer's chin. ... This is exactly the way agreement works when a referent is present. Naturally, if the referent is imagined as laying down, standing on a chair, etc., the height and direction of the agreement verb reflects this. Since the signer must conceptualize the location of body parts of the referent imagined to be present, there is a sense in which an invisible body is present. The signer must conceptualize such a body in order to properly direct agreement verbs. (p. 184)

In addition, as we noted, ASL classifier verbs of location and motion often require precise representation of visual–spatial relations within a scene, and such explicit encoding may require one to generate detailed visual images. For example, when describing the layout of a room using the classifier system of ASL, it is impossible to sign "the bed is on the right and the chair on the left" without also specifying the orientation and location of the bed and chair, as well as their relation to each other. English does not require such explicit obligatory marking of spatial relations. Several adjunct phrases would be required to express the same layout; in fact, English speakers take longer than ASL signers to describe spatial scenes, despite the fact that ASL signs take longer than English words to articulate (Emmorey, 1996; Lane, Hoffmeister, & Bahan, 1996). Note, however, that other spoken languages, such as Navajo (Pinxten, van Dooren, & Harvey, 1983) or Tzeltal (Brown, 1991), require similar explicit linguistic marking of spatial relations on predicates of location and position. What is unique about ASL is that space itself is used to express spatial relationships. Thus, not only does ASL have a very rich linguistic system for expressing complex spatial relations, but these relations are also directly encoded in physical space. Emmorey et al. (1993)

and Emmorey and Kosslyn (1996) hypothesized that ASL signers generate images frequently because of the interaction between what must be
encoded from a referent object and how it is expressed in ASL.

If deaf subjects are in fact generating visual images prior to or during
sign production, then the speed of forming these images would be important, and signers might develop enhanced abilities to generate images. The
image generation task used by Emmorey et al. (1993) required subjects to
first memorize uppercase block letters. Subjects were then shown a series
of grids (or sets of brackets) that contained an X mark (see Fig. 2.7). A
lowercase letter preceded each grid, and subjects were asked to decide as
quickly as possible whether the corresponding uppercase block letter would
cover the X if it were in the grid. The crucial aspect of the experiment was
that the probe mark appeared in the grid only 500 ms after the lowercase
cue letter was presented. This was not enough time for the subjects to
complete forming the letter image. Thus, response times reflect in part the
time to generate the image. Kosslyn and colleagues used this task to show
that visual mental images are constructed serially from parts (e.g., Kosslyn,
Cave, Provost, & Von Gierke, 1988; Roth & Kosslyn, 1988). Subjects tend
to generate letter images segment by segment in the same order that the
letter is drawn. Therefore, when the probe X is covered by a segment that
is generated early (e.g., on the first stroke of the letter F), subjects have
faster reaction times, compared to when the probe is located under a
late-imaged segment. Crucially, this difference in response time based on
probe location is not found when image generation is not involved, such
as, when both the probe X and letter (shaded gray) are present physically.

Using this task, Emmorey et al. (1993) found that both deaf and
hearing signers formed images significantly faster than nonsigners. This
finding suggests that experience with ASL can affect the ability to generate
visual images mentally. Results from the perceptual baseline task indicated
that this enhancement was due to a difference in image-generation ability,
rather than to differences in scanning or inspection. The signing and
nonsigning subjects were equally accurate on the image-generation task,
which suggests that although signers create complex images faster than
nonsigners, they generate equally good images. Furthermore, deaf and
hearing subjects appeared to image letters in the same way: Both groups
of subjects required more time and made more errors for probes located
on late-imaged segments, and these effects were of comparable magnitude
in the two groups. This result indicates that neither group of subjects
generated images of letters as complete wholes, and both groups imaged
segments in the same order. Again, the fact that hearing signers performed
similarly to deaf signers suggests that the enhanced image generation
ability is due to experience with ASL, rather than to auditory deprivation.

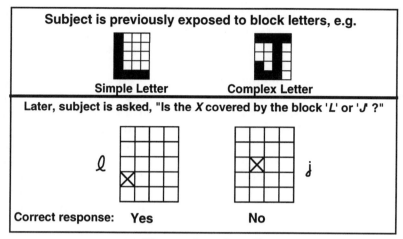

Example stimuli

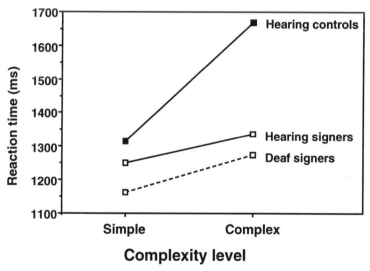

Complexity level

FIG. 2.7. Results and example stimuli from the image generation experiment conducted by Emmorey et al. (1993).

Emmorey and Kosslyn (1996) also investigated whether the processes underlying image generation were lateralized within the brain in the same way for deaf signers and hearing nonsigners. Kosslyn and colleagues argued that each cerebral hemisphere can generate mental images, but the images are constructed using two different types of spatial relations representations (Kosslyn, 1987, 1994; Kosslyn et al., 1988; Kosslyn, Maljkovic, Hamilton, Horwitz, & Thompson, 1995). This hypothesis is based in part on the finding that the hemispheres apparently encode different types of spatial relations, which subsequently may be differentially available for use in juxtaposing parts of an object in a visual mental image. Specifically, several research groups found that the left hemisphere encodes *categorical* spatial relations more efficiently than the right; such relations specify an equivalence class, such as *connected to* or *above*. In contrast, the right hemisphere processes *coordinate* spatial relations more efficiently than the left; these relations specify metric spatial properties, such as precise distance. Representations of categorical spatial relations are used when the precise arrangement among parts of an object can vary, but the general category of the relation remains constant. This type of spatial categorization has parallels to the categorical and symbolic nature of language. In contrast, coordinate spatial relations representations are used primarily to guide movements; for example, in navigation, one must be aware of precise distances in order to avoid collisions with objects.

Emmorey and Kosslyn (1996) used the same image generation task as Emmorey et al. (1993), but the stimuli were presented to either the right visual field (left hemisphere) or the left visual field (right hemisphere). Stimuli presented within grids were used to tap use of categorical spatial relations representations, and stimuli presented within brackets were used to tap use of coordinate spatial relations representations. Deaf signers were found to generate images more quickly when stimuli were presented to the right hemisphere, and generally were faster than hearing subjects. Furthermore, deaf signers exhibited a strong right hemisphere advantage for image generation using *either* categorical or coordinate spatial relations representations. In contrast, hearing subjects showed evidence of left hemisphere processing for categorical spatial relations representations, and no hemispheric asymmetry for coordinate spatial relations representations. These findings suggest that the enhanced image generation abilities in deaf ASL signers may be linked to right hemisphere processing.

However, it is clear that this enhanced image-generation ability of the right hemisphere is not a consequence of a right hemisphere dominance for processing sign language. There is abundant evidence that the left hemisphere of deaf signers is primarily responsible for processing sign language (e.g., Hickok, Bellugi, & Klima, 1996; Poizner, Klima, & Bellugi, 1987). Nevertheless, recent research suggested that the right hemisphere may play a more important role in processing certain aspects of sign language in ASL signers than it does in processing spoken language in

English speakers. For example, Emmorey and Corina (1993) found that deaf signers had a right hemisphere advantage for imageable ASL signs in a lateralized lexical decision task, whereas English speakers simply showed a weaker left hemisphere advantage for imageable words. Thus, it is possible that the right hemisphere of deaf signers is more proficient in using categorical spatial relations representations during image generation because it has a greater role in processing aspects of ASL that involve image-generation processes.

Emmorey et al. (1993) also investigated signers' abilities to maintain an image in short-term memory. In this experiment, subjects first studied a pattern within a grid or set of brackets. The patterns were created by blackening several contiguous cells within a 4 X 5 grid. After subjects memorized the pattern, it was removed and an X probe appeared in the empty grid or brackets after a delay of either 0.5 s or 2.5 s. Subjects indicated whether the X would have fallen on the pattern, were it still present. Thus, subjects did not need to retrieve information from long-term memory or generate the image; they simply needed to retain an image of the pattern in visual short-term memory. The results indicated experience with ASL did not enhance the ability to maintain a pattern in a visual image—at least not as tested by this task. It is possible that the memorized patterns were too simple and that more complex patterns might reveal a difference in image maintenance skill for signers and nonsigners. Also, image retention was measured over a relatively short delay, and it is possible that with a longer delay, differences in performance might emerge, particularly if images are maintained during a signed discourse for more than 2.5 s. Finally, although signers may not differ from nonsigners in their ability to maintain *visual* images, signers may have an enhanced ability to maintain *spatial* images. Farah, Hammond, Levine, and Calvanio (1988) argued that visual images are specifically *visual* and encode the appearance of objects, including perspective and color information, whereas spatial images are relatively abstract, amodal or multimodal representations of the layout of objects in space with respect to the viewer and each other. Wilson, Bettger, Niculae, and Klima (in press) provided data suggesting that signers may have a superior ability to maintain information spatially in short-term memory.

In sum, deaf signers exhibit an enhanced ability to generate mental images, and this ability appears to be linked to their use of ASL. Linguistic requirements may promote image generation during certain types of discourse, for example, referent visualization during referential shift and the generation of object images that may be necessary to encode object shape, orientation, and location when producing certain classifier constructions. Image-generation processes appear to be more strongly tied to the right hemisphere for deaf signers, which again suggests that experience with ASL can alter the neural organization for nonlinguistic visuospatial processes.

Spatial Imagery

Wilson et al. (in press) examined spatial working memory in children aged 8 to 10 who were either native deaf signers or hearing English speakers. Subjects were given the Corsi blocks task (Milner, 1971) in which they had to remember and reproduce a sequence of identically marked spatial locations. The deaf signers had a significantly longer spatial memory span than the hearing nonsigners. This result is complemented by the finding of Parasnis et al. (1996) who showed that deaf children who had no exposure to sign language performed as well as hearing children on the Corsi blocks task. Thus, the spatial memory advantage observed by Wilson et al. appears to be due to early exposure to ASL. One possible source of this advantage is an enhanced ability to maintain spatial images of locations. However, some other possible explanations are that there is a stronger relationship between motoric and spatial representations for signers or that signers coopt linguistic representations to encode nonlinguistic spatial information. More research is needed to tease apart these potential sources of explanation.

Recognition of Objects From Noncanonical Views

Kosslyn (1994) argued that imagery plays an important role in object recognition. This role is particularly crucial when recognizing objects that are distorted, partially occluded, or seen from an unusual view. During recognition, stored image representations of objects are activated and matched with the visual input. If the match fails, another mental image is generated based on a close competitor. There is imagery feedback that augments and adjusts the size, location, orientation of the image during the matching process. Emmorey and McCullough (1997) found evidence that the image generation process or the matching and feedback processes that occur during object recognition may be enhanced in deaf signers.

Deaf signers and hearing nonsigners were shown pictures of objects from a canonical point of view (generally from a point slightly above and to one side of the front of the object) and from a noncanonical point of view (e.g., from below, from above, or from a view that results in foreshortening). Figure 2.8 provides an example of an object shown from a canonical and a noncanonical viewpoint. Subjects were first shown objects from a noncanonical viewpoint and were asked to press the

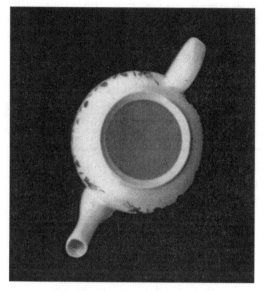

B

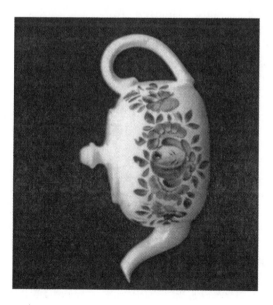

A

FIG. 2.8. Example stimuli from the experiment conducted by Emmorey and McCullough (1997). The teapot is shown from a canonical point of view (A) and a noncanonical point of view (B). The stimuli for this study were provided by Susan Carey and Rhea Diamond.

spacebar on the computer as soon as they had identified the object. Then the subject told the experimenter what they thought the object was. Subjects were then given the same objects to identify from a canonical perspective. Subjects were asked to respond as quickly and as accurately as possible.

Deaf signers were significantly more accurate than hearing nonsigners when identifying objects presented from a noncanonical point of view, and the subject groups did not differ in accuracy for identifying objects from the canonical viewpoint. The superior accuracy of the deaf subjects was not due to a speed–accuracy trade-off because the subject groups did not differ in their response times for identifying objects. Emmorey and McCullough (1997) hypothesized that deaf signers are more accurate in identifying objects from unusual views because they may generate images faster than nonsigners, and they may have more fine-tuned imagery feedback processes as well. Deaf signers may be better able mentally to transform their internal image of objects when attempting to identify an object seen from a vantage point that obscures important features or distorts the view of the object.

In summary, several studies showed that deaf and hearing ASL signers exhibit superior performance on mental imagery tasks compared to deaf and hearing nonsigners. The evidence suggests that signers do not actually *rotate* images faster (e.g., the slopes for mental rotation do not differ for signers and non-signers). Rather, ASL signers generate images faster, may be more likely to use reversal transformations rather than rotation, and may have more fine-tuned feedback between imagery and visual perception. Emmorey and colleagues argued that image-generation and transformation processes may occur much more frequently during the production and comprehension of ASL compared to spoken languages like English.

IMPLICATIONS

Before discussing some of the implications of the research reviewed here, it is important to point out that there are several visuospatial cognitive processes that do not appear to be influenced by sign language use. These include visuospatial constructive abilities (Bellugi et al., 1990), certain object localization skills (Bettger, 1992; McKee, 1987), unfamiliar face recognition (McCullough & Emmorey, 1997), and maintenance of visual images (Emmorey et al., 1993). Thus, sign language use does not create a general enhancement of visuospatial cognitive processes; rather, there appears to be a selective effect on certain processes argued to be involved in sign language production and comprehension. However, much more research is needed to determine the extent and nature of these enhancement effects. For example, are low-level perceptual processes, as well as higher cognitive functions, affected? Are there processes that might actually be impaired due to interference from sign language processing? How similar does a nonlinguistic visuospatial process have to be to the sign language process in order to be affected?

One result that emerges from the studies reviewed here is that life-long experience with ASL is not needed to enhance performance on certain cognitive tasks (e.g., face discrimination, facial expression identification, and mental rotation). Thus far, there is little evidence that early exposure to ASL is necessary to enhance performance. However, the requisite research in most domains has not been conducted. For example, Neville (1991) suggested that early exposure to ASL may result in a reorganization during development in which the left hemisphere comes to mediate aspects of motion perception. However, until subjects who acquire ASL later in life are studied, the extent of neural plasticity will not be clear, such as, can exposure to ASL shift motion detection processes from the right hemisphere to the left in late childhood or in adulthood? The fact that only a few years of experience with a signed language can influence at least some nonlinguistic cognitive processes suggests that there is a malleable and sensitive relation between linguistic and nonlinguistic visuospatial domains beyond childhood.

Is this influence of sign language use and knowledge on nonlinguistic cognition a *Whorfian effect*? That is, do these findings provide support for the linguistic relativity hypothesis? The answer depends on how one defines this hypothesis (for excellent discussions of linguistic relativity see Gumperz & Levinson, 1996; Lucy, 1992). Arguably, these studies do not provide evidence for the hypothesis that the language one uses can alter the *nature* of cognitive processes or representations. However, the evidence does suggest that the language one uses can enhance certain cognitive processes through practice. Through habitual use within the language domain, cognitive processes can be faster (as with image generation), more fine-tuned (as with face discrimination and aspects of motion processing), or more adept at coding certain types of information (as with memory for spatial sequences). Nonetheless, the effects of language use on cognitive behavior go beyond the thinking-for-speaking relativity hypothesis put forth by Slobin (1991, 1996). Slobin's hypothesis is that the nature of one's language (in particular the grammatical categories of one's language) affects cognitive processes *at the moment of speaking*. The results with users of American Sign Language (as well as recent work by Levinson [1996] and Pederson [1995] with users of different spoken languages) indicate that the language one uses can influence cognitive processes even when speaking–signing is not required.

The studies reviewed here are also interesting with respect to Fodor's (1985) modularity of mind hypothesis. Fodor argued that linguistic processes are encapsulated, insulated from other types of processes. The findings with ASL signers suggest that the processes that underlie human language are not entirely modular. Although the cognitive processes discussed here (motion detection–categorization, face discrimination, and imagery) are involved in the *processing* of ASL, they may or may not be related to the principles that underlie ASL grammar. The grammar of ASL has been shown to conform to principles of universal grammar (see, for example, Lillo-Martin, 1991), and we may find that the principles that underlie natural human language may be autonomous and not shared by other cognitive modules. We may also find that processing modularity applies only to linguistic systems that are auditorily based. The same modularity questions can be raised regarding the relationship between auditory language processing and nonlinguistic auditory processing. However, in the auditory domain, these questions are difficult to study because auditory processing cannot be observed in the absence of experience with speech. The visual domain, in contrast, provides an ideal means of studying these questions because visuospatial processes can be observed with and without the influence of a visuospatial language. By comparing visuospatial functions in deaf and hearing subjects, we gain a window into the nature of cognitive modularity. The results reviewed here suggest that central aspects of ASL processing are not domain specific and are not insulated from other types of visual processing. As Fodor himself has pointed out, the notion of modularity ought to admit of degrees (Fodor, 1983). Studies with ASL signers provide evidence for limits on the degree of modularity for human language processing and thus constrain the theory of cognitive modularity.

ACKNOWLEDGMENTS

This work was supported by NSF grant SBR-9510963 awarded to Karen Emmorey, as well as NIH grants HD13249 and DC00201 awarded to Ursula Bellugi. I thank the following people for invaluable discussions concerning many of the issues addressed here: Ursula Bellugi, Jeff Bettger, Dave Corina, Ed Klima, Steve Kosslyn, and Steve McCullough. Meg Wilson and Ursula Bellugi provided crucial comments on an earlier draft of the chapter.

REFERENCES

Baker-Shenk, C. (1985). The facial behavior of deaf signers: Evidence for a complex language. *American Annals of the Deaf, 130*(4), 297–304.

Bellugi, U., O'Grady, L., Lillo-Martin, D., O'Grady, M., van Hoek, K., & Corina, D. (1990). Enhancement of spatial cognition in deaf children. In V. Volterra & C. J. Erting (Eds.), *From gesture to language in hearing and deaf children* (pp. 278–298). New York: Springer-Verlag.

Bertenthal, B. I. (1993). Infants' perception of biomechanical motions: Intrinsic image and knowledge-based constraints. In C. Granrud (Ed.), *Visual perception and cognition in infancy* (pp. 75–214). Hinsdale, NJ: Lawrence Erlbaum Associates.

Bertenthal, B. I., Proffitt, D. R., Kramer, S. J., & Spetner, N. B. (1987). Infants' encoding of kinetic displays varying in relative coherence. *Developmental Psychology, 23,* 171–178.

Benton, A. L., Hamsher, K., Varney, N. R., & Spreen, O. (1983). *Facial recognition: Stimuli and multiple choice pictures.* New York: Oxford University Press.

Bettger, J. (1992). *The effects of experience on spatial cognition: Deafness and knowledge of ASL.* Unpublished doctoral dissertation. University of Illinois, Urbana-Champaign.

Bettger, J., Emmorey, K., McCullough, S., & Bellugi, U. (1997). Enhanced facial discrimination: Effects of experience with American Sign Language. *Journal of Deaf Studies and Deaf Education, 2*(4), 223–233.

Brentari, D. (1993). Establishing a sonority hierarchy in American Sign Language: The use of simultaneous structure in phonology. *Phonology, 10,* 281–306.

Brown, P. (1991). Spatial conceptualization in Tzeltal. Working Paper No. 6, Cognitive Anthropology Research Group, Max Planck Institute for Psycholinguistics.

Chamberlain, C., & Mayberry, R. (1994). Do the deaf 'see' better? Effects of deafness on visuospatial skills. Poster presented at TENNET V, May, Montreal, Quebec.

Chatterjee, S. H., Freyd, J. J., & Shiffrar, M. (1996). Configural processing in the perception of apparent biological motion. *Journal of Experimental Psychology: Human Perception and Performance, 22,* 916–929.

Coats, E. J., & Feldman, R. S. (1995). The role of television in the socialization of nonverbal behavioral skills. *Basic and Applied Social Psychology, 17,* 327–341.

Corina, D. (1990). Reassessing the role of sonority in syllable structure: Evidence from a visual-gestural language. *Chicago Linguistics Society, 26,* 33–44.

Eimas, P. (1975). Auditory and phonetic coding of the cues for speech: Discrimination of the [r–l] distinction by young infants. *Perception & Psychophysics, 18,* 341–347.

Emmorey, K. (1996). The confluence of space and language in signed languages. In P. Bloom, M. Peterson, L. Nadel, & M. Garrett (Eds.), *Language and space* (pp. 171–209). Cambridge, MA: MIT Press.

Emmorey, K., & Corina, D. (1990). Lexical recognition in sign language: Effects of phonetic structure and morphology. *Perceptual and Motor Skills, 71,* 1227–1252.

Emmorey, K., & Corina, D. P. (1993). Hemispheric specialization for ASL signs and English words: Differences between imageable and abstract forms. *Neuropsychologia, 31,* 645–653.

Emmorey, K., Klima, E., & Hickok, G. (1997). Mental rotation within linguistic and nonlinguistic domains in users of American Sign Language. Manuscript under review.

Emmorey, K., & Kosslyn, S. (1996). Enhanced image generation abilities in deaf signers: A right hemisphere effect. *Brain and Cognition, 32,* 28–44.

Emmorey, K., Kosslyn, S., & Bellugi, U. (1993). Visual imagery and visual–spatial language: Enhanced imagery abilities in deaf and hearing ASL signers. *Cognition, 46,* 139–181.

Emmorey, K., & McCullough, S. (1997). Recognition of objects from non-canonical views: Evidence for enhanced imagery abilities in ASL signers. Manuscript in preparation. The Salk Institute.

Engberg-Pedersen, E. (1993). *Space in Danish Sign Language: The semantics and morphosyntax of the use of space in a visual language.* International studies on sign language research and communication of the deaf, Vol. 19, Hamburg, Germany: Signum-Verlag.

Farah, M., Hammond, K., Levine, D., & Calvanio, R. (1988). Visual and spatial mental imagery: Dissociable systems of representation. *Cognitive Psychology, 20,* 439–462.

Farah, M., Wilson, K., Drain, H., & Tanaka, J. (1995). The inverted face inversion effect in prosopagnosia: Evidence for mandatory, face-specific perceptual mechanisms. *Vision Research, 35,* 2089–2093.

Fodor, J. A. (1983). *The modularity of mind.* Cambridge, MA: MIT Press.

Goldstein, N., & Feldman, R. S. (1996). Knowledge of American Sign Language and the ability of hearing individuals to decode facial expressions of emotion. *Journal of Nonverbal Behavior, 20,* 111–122.

Grosjean, F. (1981). Sign and word recognition: A first comparison. *Sign Language Studies, 32,* 195–219.

Gumperz, J., & Levinson, S. (Eds.). (1996). *Rethinking linguistic relativity.* London: Cambridge University Press.

Hickok, G., Bellugi, U., & Klima, E. (1996). The neurobiology of signed language and its implications for the neural basis of language. *Nature, 381,* 699–702.

Ilan, A. B., & Miller, J. (1994). A violation of pure insertion: Mental rotation and choice reaction time. *Journal of Experimental Psychology: Human Perception and Performance. 20,* 520–536.

Johansson, G. (1973). Visual perception of biological motion and a model for its analysis. *Perception & Psychophysics, 14,* 201–211.

Klima, E. S., & Bellugi, U. (1979). *The signs of language.* Cambridge, MA: Harvard University Press.

Klima, E. S., Tzeng, O., Fok, A., Bellugi, U., & Corina, D. (1996). From sign to script: Effects of linguistic experience on perceptual categorization. Technical Report #INC-9604, Institute for Neural Computation, University of California, San Diego, CA.

Kosslyn, S. M. (1980). *Image and mind.* Cambridge, MA: Harvard University Press.

Kosslyn, S. M. (1987). Seeing and imagining in the cerebral hemispheres: A computational approach. *Psychological Review, 94,* 148–175.

Kosslyn, S. M. (1994). *Image and brain: The resolution of the imagery debate.* Cambridge, MA: MIT Press.

Kosslyn, S., Brunn, J., Cave, K., & Wallach, R. (1985). Individual differences in mental imagery ability: A computational analysis. *Cognition, 18,* 195–243.

Kosslyn, S., Cave, C., Provost, D., & Von Gierke, S. (1988). Sequential processes in image generation. *Cognitive Psychology, 20,* 319–343.

Kosslyn, S. M., Maljkovic, V., Hamilton, S. E., Horwitz, G., & Thompson, W. L. (1995). Two types of image generation: Evidence for left- and right-hemisphere processes. *Neuropsychologia, 33,* 1485–1510.

Kuhl, P. (1991). Human adults and human infants show a 'perceptual magnet effect' for the prototypes of speech categories, monkeys do not. *Perception & Psychophysics, 50,* 93–107.

Lane, H., Hoffmeister, R., & Bahan, B. (1996). *A journey into the Deaf-World.* San Diego, CA: Dawn Sign Press.

Levinson, S. (1996). Frames of reference and Molyneux's Question: Crosslinguistic evidence. In P. Bloom, M. Peterson, L. Nadel, & M. Garrett (Eds.), *Language and Space* (pp. 109–170). Cambridge, MA: MIT Press.

Liddell, S. (1990). Four functions of a locus: Re-examining the structure of space in ASL. In C. Lucas (Ed.), *Sign language research: Theoretical issues* (pp. 176–198). Washington, DC: Gallaudet College Press.

Lillo-Martin, D., (1991). *Universal grammar and American sign language: Setting the null argument parameters*. Dordrecht: Kluwer.

Lucy, J. (1992). *Language diversity and thought: A reformulation of the linguistic relativity hypothesis*. London: Cambridge University Press.

McCullough, S., & Emmorey, K. (1997). Face processing by deaf ASL signers: Evidence for expertise in distinguishing local features. *Journal of Deaf Studies and Deaf Education*, 2(4), 212–222.

McKee, D. (1987). *An analysis of specialized cognitive functions in deaf and hearing signers*. Unpublished doctoral dissertation, University of Pittsburgh, Pittsburgh, PA.

Milner, B. (1971). Interhemispheric differences in the localization of psychological processes in man. *British Medical Bulletin, 27,* 272–277.

Mooney, C. M. (1957). Age in the development of closure ability in children. *Canadian Journal of Psychology, 11,* 219–226.

Neville, H. (1991). Whence the specialization of the language hemisphere? In I. G. Mattingly & M. Studdert-Kennedy (Eds.), *Modularity and the motor theory of speech perception* (pp. 269–294). Hillsdale, NJ: Lawrence Erlbaum Associates.

Neville, H., & Lawson, D. (1987a). Attention to central and peripheral visual space in a movement detection task: An event-related potential and behavioral study: I. Normal hearing adults. *Brain Research, 405,* 253–267.

Neville, H., & Lawson, D. (1987b). Attention to central and peripheral visual space in a movement detection task: An event-related potential and behavioral study: II. Congenitally deaf adults. *Brain Research, 405,* 268–283.

Neville, H., & Lawson, D. (1987c). Attention to central and peripheral visual space in a movement detection task: An event-related potential and behavioral study: III. Separate effects of auditory deprivation and acquisition of a visual language. *Brain Research, 405,* 284–294.

Parasnis, I., Samar, V., Bettger, J., & Sathe, K. (1996). Does deafness lead to enhancement of visual spatial cognition in children? Negative evidence from deaf nonsigners. *Journal of Deaf Studies and Deaf Education, 1,* 145–152.

Pederson, E. (1995). Language as context, language as means: Spatial cognition and habitual language use. *Cognitive Linguistics, 6,* 33–62.

Pinxten, R., van Dooren, I., & Harvey, F. (1983). *Anthropology of space: Explorations into the natural philosophy and semantics of the Navajo*. Philadelphia, PA: University of Pennsylvania Press.

Poizner, H. (1981). Visual and 'phonetic' coding of movement: Evidence from American Sign Language, *Science, 212,* 691–693.

Poizner, H. (1983). Perception of movement in American Sign Language: Effects of linguistic structure and linguistic experience. *Perception & Psychophysics, 33,* 215–231.

Poizner, H., Bellugi, U., & Lutes-Driscoll, V. (1981). Perception of American Sign Language in dynamic point-light displays. *Journal of Experimental Psychology: Human Perception and Performance, 7,* 430–440.

Poizner, H., Fok, A., & Bellugi, U. (1989). The interplay between perception of language and perception of motion. *Language Sciences, 11,* 267–287.

Poizner, H., Klima, E. S., & Bellugi, U. (1987). *What the hands reveal about the brain*. Cambridge, MA: MIT Press/Bradford Books.

Reilly, J. S., McIntire, M., & Bellugi, U. (1991). Baby face: A new perspective on universals in language acquisition. In P. Siple & S. Fischer (Eds.), *Theoretical issues in sign language research: Psychology* (pp. 9–24). Chicago, IL: University of Chicago Press.

Roth, J., & Kosslyn, S. M. (1988). Construction of the third dimension in mental imagery. *Cognitive Psychology, 20,* 344–361.

Shepard, R. N., & Cooper, L. A. (1982). *Mental images and their transformations.* Cambridge, MA: MIT Press.

Shepard, R., & Metzler, J. (1971). Mental rotation of three-dimensional objects. *Science, 171,* 701–703.

Shiffrar, M., & Freyd, J. J. (1990). Apparent motion of the human body. *Psychological Science, 3,* 96–100.

Shiffrar, M., & Freyd, J. J. (1993). Timing and apparent motion path choice with human body photographs. *Psychological Science, 4,* 379–384.

Siple, P. (1978). Visual constraints for sign language communication. *Sign Language Studies, 19,* 97–112.

Slobin, D. I. (1991). Learning to think for speaking: Native language, cognition, and rhetorical style. *Pragmatics, 1,* 7–26.

Slobin, D. (1996). From 'thought and language' to 'thinking for speaking.' In J. J. Gumperz & S. C. Levinson (Eds.), *Rethinking linguistic relativity* (pp. 70–96. London: Cambridge University Press.

Supalla, T., & Newport, E. (1978). How many seats in a chair? The derivation of nouns and verbs in American Sign Language. In P. Siple (Ed.), *Understanding language through sign language research* (pp. 91–132). New York: Academic Press.

Talbot, K. F., & Haude, R. H. (1993). The relationship between sign language skill and spatial visualization ability: Mental rotation of three-dimensional objects. *Perceptual and Motor Skills, 77,* 1387–1391.

Vandenberg, S. G., & Kuse, A. R. (1978). Mental rotations, a group test of three-dimensional spatial visualization. *Perceptual and Motor Skills, 47,* 599–604.

van Hoek, K., Bellugi, U., and Fok, A. (1986). Phonology in Chinese Sign Language. Unpublished manuscript, The Salk Institute for Biological Studies.

Warrington, E. (1984). *Recognition Memory Test.* England: NFER-NELSON Publishing Company, Ltd.

Werker, J. (1994). Cross-language speech perception: Developmental change does not involve loss. In J. Goodman & H. Nusbaum (Eds.), *The development of speech perception: The transition from speech sounds to spoken words* (pp. 95–120). Cambridge, MA: MIT Press.

Werker, J., & Tees, R. C. (1983). Developmental changes across childhood in the perception of non-native speech sounds. *Canadian Journal of Psychology, 37,* 278–286.

Wilson, M. (1997). The influence of sign language expertise on perceived path of apparent motion. Manuscript under review.

Wilson, M., Bettger, J., Niculae, I., & Klima, E. (in press). Modality of language shapes working memory: Evidence from digit span and spatial span in ASL signers. *Journal of Deaf Studies and Deaf Education.*

Yau, S-C. (1987). Chinese Sign Language. In J. van Cleve (Ed.), *Gallaudet Encyclopedia of Deaf People and Deafness, Vol. 3* (pp. 118–120). New York: McGraw-Hill.

Yin, R. K. (1969). Looking at upside-down faces. *Journal of Experimental Psychology, 81,* 141–145.

3

Mental Representation and Memory in Deaf Adults and Children

Marc Marschark
National Technical Institute for the Deaf—Rochester Institute of Technology

Thomas S. Mayer
American University

If one examines the research literature relating to individuals who are deaf, perhaps the most dominant single research theme over the past 100 years has been *memory*. Central to understanding memory is how information is encoded, that is, brought into memory from outside and stored there in some metaphorical, if not literal, sense. In this regard, investigations of the forms (or formats) of mental representation in people who use visual–spatial languages as compared to those who use oral–aural languages have provided important information concerning basic cognitive processes in people who are deaf and yielded key theoretical evidence with regard to human cognition in general.[1] That literature also *should* have a

---

[1] A variety of investigators in this area have contrasted spoken and signed languages in terms of an apparent difference between sequential and nonsequential (or *parallel*) modalities. Although vision most obviously involves parallel processing and hearing most obviously involves sequential processing, this comparison between languages is spurious. Spoken languages include information transmitted in parallel (e.g., prosodic, semantic, and syntactic information) and signed languages also have a temporal–sequential structure, even if they have more flexible lexical ordering constraints (see Marschark, 1993; Marschark, 1997, for discussion).

significant impact on methods of educating deaf children, although the lines of communication between basic research and application are not yet as effective as they should be.

To a large extent, the popularity of memory studies involving deaf adults and children has derived from questions about the development of memory codes in the absence of spoken language, long thought to be the medium of short-term, if not long-term, memory. The assumption that deaf individuals do not have available the acoustic, articulatory, or phonological codes that underlie memory functioning in hearing individuals raises the question of whether there are alternative language codes that can support retention over brief intervals equally well. Studies described here suggest that the answer to that question is clear, even if it is not as simple as a single yes or no and even if some of the initial assumptions turn out not to be entirely correct.

Marschark (1993) provided a comprehensive review of memory research involving deaf children, and we omit consideration of most of the studies he described. Several issues emerge from analyzing earlier research in this area, however, and it is worthwhile acknowledging three of them from the outset. One difficulty evident in a variety of studies involving deaf children is the faulty assumption that nonverbal materials (e.g., nonsense shapes or pictures) provide evidence for nonverbal memory coding by deaf (or hearing) individuals. In fact, both children and adults seek to label nonlinguistic stimuli, and those labels clearly influence memory (e.g., Glucksberg & Krauss, 1967). The more interesting issues, for us anyway, are when linguistic coding of nonlinguistic materials actually benefits memory and the extent to which such coding is influenced by language fluency or other factors. Also at issue is the extent to which deaf individuals make use of sign language or spoken language in linguistic coding and the relative reliance of sign language on hypothesized working memory systems (i.e., verbal or visuospatial stores).

Beyond the question of how deaf people might encode verbal or nonverbal information, studies of how deaf adults and children organize information in long-term memory promise insight into the psychological and academic differences observed between deaf and hearing individuals and a better understanding of whether or not those differences are of any real significance. Marschark (1993), for example, suggested that differences in early experience and early exposure to language might result in deaf and hearing individuals having somewhat different ways of organizing their experience (i.e., categorization or classification). This is not to suggest that any particular memory code or way of organizing information is necessarily any better or worse than another; different memory codes and different memory strategies presumably have differing strengths for different kinds of information. The important point here is that such differences might both reflect and effect differences in other domains that can have both theoretical and applied implications (Marschark, Siple, Lillo-Martin, Campbell, & Everhart, 1997).

In the following review, we focus on recent research, separating long-term memory and short-term memory. *Long-term memory* in this context refers to our permanent memory stores—our knowledge of the world or *semantic memory*. New information either must pass into long-term memory or be forgotten; and it is from long-term memory that information is retrieved as the need arises. *Short-term memory* is considered primarily in the context of the *working memory* scheme proposed by Baddeley and Hitch (1974). Working memory, in their view, consists of a *central executive* that controls two slave systems: the *articulatory loop*, which holds approximately as much information as can be articulated in 2 s, and the *visuospatial scratch pad*. The central executive transmits and regulates information within working memory, thus controlling the inputs to the slave systems, as well as having some computing power of its own (see Logie, 1996). It is also responsible for retrieving information from long-term memory. The articulatory loop is specialized for processing verbal information, whereas the visuospatial scratch pad is specialized for processing visual and spatial material—a contrast that should make memory for sign language a most interesting topic for working memory investigators.

This chapter is intended to provide an integration of diverse research findings in order to arrive at a coherent and current understanding of memory and mental representation in deaf individuals and to use this integration to provide direction for application of research findings in educational and other settings. We begin the discussion with long-term memory. Ultimately, we consider in some detail the possible relations between memory and language fluencies in deaf students (see Marschark et al., 1997, for the larger discussion of relations of language and cognition in deaf children).

Semantic Memory

Long-term, semantic memory is of interest here both as it relates to how knowledge affects *online* processes (including working memory) and in terms of the associations among concepts and knowledge domains. Unfortunately, relatively few studies have investigated the relation between the memory performance of deaf individuals and the breadth and organization of their conceptual knowledge. Tweney, Hoemann, and Andrews (1975) provided one such study in their comparison of the performance of deaf and hearing high-school students' sorting sets of common nouns, pictures, and onomatopoeic words. Analyses of the sorting data indicated that the two groups differed only in minor ways when they sorted familiar stimuli. With the unfamiliar sound words, in contrast, the two groups showed very different organizations, presumably reflecting differing or less consistent underlying organization in memory (see McEvoy, Marschark, & Nelson, submitted).

Koh, Vernon, and Bailey (1971) investigated memory for related and unrelated word lists by 13 to 14 and 18 to 20 year old deaf and hearing students. With unrelated lists, they found greater recall by the hearing than the deaf students at both age levels and more semantic clustering in recall by the older hearing students than by the other groups. Deaf students showed no differences in the extent of their clustering as a function of age. With categorized lists, there were no hearing or age differences in recall (apparently due to ceiling effects), but the hearing students showed greater clustering than the deaf students at both age levels. Koh et al. attributed the lower recall with uncategorized lists by deaf students to the considerable variability in clustering observed in their recall of all lists. Importantly, the observed differences in organization at recall were not linked to differences in the amount remembered. Similar findings were obtained by Hoemann, Andrews, and DeRosa (1974), using release from proactive inhibition (PI) as their indicator of spontaneous use of taxonomic information. They used a single categorical shift from the familiar category of animals to other common objects (e.g., tree, airplane, house) and found clear evidence of release from PI in both deaf and hearing children aged 8 to 12 years using pictures.

In a related study, Liben (1979) examined free recall of taxonomically related line drawings by groups of deaf and hearing children, aged 9 to 13 years. After a baseline memory trial, half of the children at each age level were trained in a semantic clustering strategy, and all were told the category labels and sizes after the second trial. Liben found that training and category labels independently contributed to memory performance at all ages. Deaf children showed just as much semantic clustering in recall as hearing children even before training, but their recall was still lower than that of hearing children. Liben concluded that although deaf children can recognize and attempt to use the categorical nature of a list to improve memory, they might lack either flexibility in item classification or sufficient categorical knowledge. Although she did not address the differences between her study and the Hoemann et al. (1974) study, as compared to the Koh et al. (1971) study, the contradictory results might reflect their use of pictorial and printed English stimuli, respectively. That is, the attempted use of organizational strategies for recall (as well as recall per se) may be more likely or more successful with more familiar material.

Alternatively, deaf and hearing children may have similar conceptual organizations for familiar stimuli but different organizations for unfamiliar stimuli (see Tweney et al., 1975). Parallel findings might also emerge as a function of age: With increasing age there may be convergence in the utilization or success in applying conceptual knowledge to memory tasks both within and between the populations of deaf and hearing children (Bebko & Metcalfe-Haggert, 1997).

This last suggestion is consistent with a study by Marschark and Everhart (submitted). They explored the strategy use by deaf and hearing students aged 7 to 14 years and college age in the context of playing a form of the *Twenty Questions* game in which a target has to be selected from an array of 42 pictures. Marschark and Everhart found that hearing students were more likely to solve the task than deaf students at all ages. Analyses of questions asked by the students revealed that at the younger ages, hearing students tended to ask constraint-seeking category organization questions (e.g., "is it an animal?") whereas deaf students tended to make specific guesses (e.g., "is it the cow?"). Constraint questions eliminate more alternatives on each turn than guesses and are seen as indicating a more planful strategy. Although the task could have been successfully completed using constraint questions other than those involving taxonomic information (e.g., perceptual similarity or location in the array), deaf students generally did not employ any constraint strategies and, correspondingly, were unsuccessful in task solution within the allotted 20 questions. Even among the college-age deaf students, constraint questions were significantly less frequent than among hearing peers. These findings could reflect differences in memory organization, retrieval strategies, problem solving, or even game-playing experience between deaf and hearing individuals.

In a study related to the first possibility, McEvoy et al. (submitted) examined deaf and hearing college students' organization through the use of a controlled, single-word association paradigm. They compared the responses of 136 deaf college students to responses obtained from hearing students. Overall, the responses of the two groups were remarkably similar, although measures of the strength of relations from a concept to other words within its associative set, the size of the associative set, and the degree to which the associates of a given word were interconnected all indicated that deaf students' verbal concepts were less homogeneous than those of hearing students. There was significantly less consistency in associations across deaf than hearing subjects, and deaf subjects had significantly smaller and less well-defined associative sets linked to particular concepts.

The similarity in deaf students' memory organizations for words that are sound-related and those that are not sound-related may seem odd, but it is consistent with a study by Marschark and Cornoldi (in preparation). They used two relative judgment tasks to determine the nature of semantic memory representation for sound-related words in deaf individuals. Marschark and Cornoldi first had groups of deaf and hearing college students rate a set of 80 words for relative loudness, using a 1 to 7 scale. Surprisingly, the ratings from deaf and hearing subjects correlated .97, and there was a high degree of consistency in ratings across the deaf subjects for all of the items. Deaf students' knowledge of the relative loudness of things was also indicated by the results of a symbolic comparison task in which they had to judge which of two things, presented as words on a computer screen, would be louder in real life. Deaf and hearing subjects showed identical functions in their *symbolic distance effects* (i.e., decreasing response times with increasing magnitude differences), but the deaf students took significantly longer to make the comparisons than did hearing students. Although these findings suggested that deaf and hearing individuals both have semantic memory representations that retain sound information in some analog sense, it is unclear whether the difference in response times in the comparison task are related to retrieval (i.e., memory) or comparison (i.e., an executive function). It appears unlikely that the comparisons of loudness have any unique status for deaf individuals, however, because Epstein, Hillegeist, and Grafman (1994) obtained similar findings in relative judgments of number magnitude. Epstein et al. also found that deaf subjects slower latencies in a probed short-term memory task, suggesting that there may be some general, memory-related difference in processing speed between deaf and hearing students.

Taken together, these findings indicate that there may be differences in both semantic memory organization and the strategies involved in accessing that knowledge between deaf and hearing students. Although there is considerable overlap in their semantic structures for concepts varying widely in familiarity, there also appears to be a tendency of deaf students not to apply categorical knowledge in some task situations that would benefit from such application. Whether that situation is related to depth or breadth of semantic memory knowledge; a failure to apply such knowledge strategically and spontaneously; or the use of alternative, nonobvious strategies is yet to be determined. In any case, to the extent that conceptual information from semantic memory is needed but is not used successfully in any particular task, the learning and academic performance of deaf (or hearing) students will suffer. Research into these questions is just beginning, and it will be some time before we have a complete understanding of the content and structure of deaf students' semantic memories, the influences of individual differences (e.g., educational histories, degree of hearing loss and age of onset), and the reasons why deaf students sometimes may not transfer their knowledge across contexts.

Working Memory

Scores of articles on short-term memory have been published concerning short-term and working memory in deaf children and deaf adults. Studies in this area have been conducted both by investigators primarily interested in mainstream cognitive psychology and by others interested specifically in cognitive processes of deaf individuals. For both groups, much of the earliest research in this area appears to have derived from the faulty assumption that deaf individuals allowed the study of memory in the absence of language. With a strong emphasis on verbal learning and memory during the 1960s and early 1970s, the expectation was that studies involving deaf children in particular would shed light on the role of language in memory. The error, of course, was the equation of *language* with *spoken language*.[2]

Despite some mistaken goals for this research at the outset, studies of working memory among deaf individuals with different educational and language backgrounds proved enlightening for those interested in both theoretical and applied questions. Several issues have emerged from this research, including (a) differences observed between serial recall and free recall relating to sequential–linguistic versus visual–spatial information/coding, (b) the form of working memory codes among deaf adults and children in terms of spoken language versus sign language, and (c) the implications of observed differences in working memory of deaf and hearing individuals as a possible contributor to the reading difficulties frequently encountered by deaf children.

Implicit in most of this research was the assumption that deaf and hearing individuals might have qualitatively different ways of parsing incoming information. Hearing people, by virtue of their dependence on spoken language, have been assumed to use verbal–sequential coding to remember short lists of simple stimuli. This code is variously seen as phonological, articulatory, or acoustic in nature (see Baddeley, 1986, for discussion). Deaf people, in contrast, by virtue of their relative lack of oral–aural language experience and their use of visual–gestural language, have been assumed to rely more heavily on visuospatial short-term memory codes. In his review of findings involving both visual stimuli and

---

[2]Although pioneering work on the linguistics of American Sign Language by William Stokoe and others began to be published in 1960, its impact did not reach cognitive psychology until the mid-1970s.

linguistic stimuli, Marschark (1993) concluded that visual and verbal–sequential codes appear to be equally effective for deaf individuals in memory tasks that involve visual presentation of 3 to 5 stimuli (i.e., below memory span). At the same time, the bulk of the literature he reviewed indicated that deaf children are more likely to depend on visual than verbal–sequential coding in such tasks, although the two strategies often lead to similar quantitative performance.

Moving beyond subspan tasks, there is a long history of empirical demonstrations showing that deaf children and deaf adults have shorter memory spans and tend to remember less in other short-term memory tasks than hearing peers. Although the reason for such findings are just now becoming clear, studies from Mott (1899) and Pintner and Patterson (1917) to Marschark (1996) and Wilson and Emmorey (1997a) provided overwhelming evidence for quantitative differences in memory for a variety of linguistic and nonlinguistic materials (see also Hanson, 1982; Klima & Bellugi, 1979; Krakow & Hanson, 1985; Waters & Doehring, 1990; Wilson & Emmorey, 1997b), and we do not belabor the point here. Rather, we consider the more interesting question of why that difference occurs and the implications of reliance on alternative working memory codes for performance in other domains (see Marschark & Harris, 1996; Todman & Seedhouse, 1994).

One study with implications for several issues we discuss next is that of Krakow and Hanson (1985). They examined written serial recall for printed, signed, and fingerspelled words by deaf college students who either had deaf parents and learned American Sign Language (ASL) as their first language or who had hearing parents and learned ASL in school. A group of hearing students was tested with printed words only. Analyses of recall by the deaf subjects showed no differences due to language history. On printed word trials, however, serial recall by the deaf participants was significantly lower than that of the hearing participants; and their serial-position curves for fingerspelling and ASL signs showed that recall in both modes was better than recall of words for the last two serial positions but worse for the first two serial positions. These and other results indicated that deaf individuals use both sign-based and speech-based coding in working memory. Krakow and Hanson concluded that deaf individuals do not necessarily recode printed materials into a sign-based code, and concurred with the long-standing conclusion that speech-based working memory codes are particularly facilitative for serial recall. The questions of interest then become the extent to which coding preference is under strategic control, the characteristics of individuals who tend toward one code or the other, and the way in which coding may differ as a function of the information presented.

Studies by Hanson and Lichtenstein (1990) and others found that good deaf readers tend to use phonetic codes in processing printed words, and one would expect a strong link between those skills and performance in memory tasks that benefit from speech coding. Lichtenstein (1998), for example, reported that deaf students with better speech skills tend to rely primarily on speech recoding as a strategy in both memory tasks and reading, whereas deaf students with low to moderate speech coding abilities tend to use both speech and sign strategies (see Marschark, 1993, for a review of earlier developmental studies). Lichtenstein showed that there was a high correlation between *speech skill* and memory span, concluding that the slower rate of signing relative to speech might be linked to shorter memory spans in deaf individuals (cf. Bebko, Lacasse, Turk, & Oyen, 1992; Marschark, 1996).

Important support for Lichtenstein's (1998) conclusions with regard to speech coding comes from Campbell and Wright's (1990) study of memory for pictures in deaf 7- to 9-year-olds and 13- to 15-year-olds exposed only to spoken language. In that study, deaf subjects showed *word-length effects* in memory. That is, they showed better memory for pictures for which the spoken names would take less time to pronounce than pictures that would take more time to label, presumably because more of them fit into the 2-second articulatory loop. Campbell and Wright and others (e.g., Wilson & Emmorey 1997b) suggested that those results indicated that deaf subjects have an English-based phonological code available to them in working memory. Campbell and Wright found their result paradoxical, however, given that their subjects did not appear to make use of available rhyme cues paired with the pictures during learning. This apparent contradiction may indicate that deaf children have available a phonologically based memory code but that they are less likely to use that code strategically and spontaneously (Bebko & McKinnon, 1990). Alternatively, the Campbell and Wright findings may indicate that phonological codes have different characteristics and privileges of occurrence in hearing and deaf children (Kyle, 1981). For her part, Campbell (1992; Marschark et al., 1997) argued that the ability to use a phonological code in memory is not a direct function of having sign language or spoken language as a primary mode of communication, but is determined by a variety of early experiences and individual characteristics.

Intuitively as well as empirically, it makes sense that individuals with congenital or early onset hearing losses would have more difficulty in phonological processing than hearing peers and would be less likely to employ phonological (speech-based) codes in memory or other information-processing tasks. Among deaf individuals, it also makes sense that we would find a continuum of utilizing phonological coding related to proficiency in English (or some other spoken language) which, in turn, is influenced by a variety of factors including degree of hearing loss, early language exposure, reading experience, and so on. Some earlier investigators suggested that deaf individuals used some kind of veridical visual imagery code in place of verbal coding, but more recent studies have shown no greater visual imagery ability or nonverbal imaginal coding among deaf than hearing persons (e.g., Bonvillian, 1983; Conlin & Paivio, 1975; but see Marschark, 1993, p. 173). In this light, a reasonable alternative is that deaf individuals might make use of sign language-based memory codes, and there have been a variety of studies demonstrating that lists of signs made with similar handshapes tend to disrupt memory performance (e.g., Bellugi, Klima, & Siple, 1974; Hanson, 1982; Klima & Bellugi, 1979; Krakow & Hanson, 1985; Poizner, Bellugi, & Tweney, 1981). Such codes are surely verbal in the sense that Paivio (1971) and Baddeley (1986) use the term in discussions of memory, but the question of whether they are visual, kinesthetic, some combination, or something else altogether remains unclear (cf. Wilson & Emmorey, in press).

Kyle (1981) reported that speech and sign rehearsal differentially affect serial memory, with sign rehearsal producing significant decrements relative to speech coding, presumably due to some kind of modality-specific interference (cf. Marschark, 1996). He concluded that visual or kinesthetic codes may not work in the same way as articulation-based codes. In a related study, Hamilton and Holtzman (1989) presented deaf and hearing students who varied in signing and speech skills with phonologically similar, formationally similar, or control word lists. Their primary question was whether deaf individuals with more residual hearing, better speech, or greater reading ability were more likely to use phonological coding in short-term memory, or whether all deaf subjects would tend to recode printed materials into some sign-based code (Hanson & Lichtenstein, 1990; Shand, 1982). The materials were presented through spoken language, sign language, or through both simultaneously. Results showed that although the mode of early language experience influenced coding of words presented simultaneously in sign and speech, spoken words tended to be remembered using a phonological code and those presented in sign tended to be remembered using a sign code.

Bonvillian, Rea, Orlansky, and Slade (1987) obtained convergent findings in their examination of the effects of rehearsal on memory. They had deaf college students overtly rehearse the sign equivalents of a list of English words prior to immediate and delayed recall tasks. Recall increased as a function of rehearsal frequency, but no recency or negative recency effects were found, a finding later replicated by Novak and Bonvillian (1996) in a study of fingerspelling and signing as coding strategies in memory (cf. Bebko et al.'s, 1992, probe recall task). The lack of a recency effect in immediate recall and of a negative recency effect in delayed recall lends support to Kyle's (1981) observation of possible interference from signing at encoding as well his general conclusion about divergence in the functioning of phonologically based and sign-based memory codes (see also Campbell & Wright, 1990; Engle, Cantor, & Turner, 1989). Alternatively, Chalifoux (1991) proposed adding an articulatory *sign unit* to Baddeley's working memory model. In principle, she argued that the sign unit would account for both sign and (oral) articulatory coding for people who are raised with sign as a first language. Results from empirical studies like those of MacSweeney, Campbell, and Donlan (1996), Marschark (1996), and Wilson and Emmorey (1997a), described below, however, suggest that the results reviewed by Chalifoux are better explained in terms of an articulatory loop that is not modality specific, an alternative also favored by Baddeley (personal communication, July, 1994).

Evidence relevant to these issues can be provided by studies of the relation between memory and the ease or difficulty of making a sign, the relative availability of a sign (i.e., whether or not there is a lexicalized sign for a concept), and ways that sign-based memory codes function in standard working memory paradigms. To date, we have not seen any studies involving the first kind, varying the relative ease or difficulty of making a sign. Introspection suggests that there are some more difficult or complex signs such as FEEDBACK or AMONG and some simpler, or less complex signs, such as SPEECH or BETWEEN.[3] The extent to which sign complexity versus the time required to produce a sign or some other variable directly affects memorability remains to be determined.

Several studies have examined the effects on memory of *signability*, but only in terms of the relative availability of a sign. Odom, Blanton, and McIntyre (1970) were among the first to demonstrate a *signability effect*. They tested children in a paired-associate learning task, hypothesizing that deaf children might use a sign-based code for short-term memory when task demands permitted. Consistent with their expectation, they found that digits paired with words having familiar signs were better remembered than those paired with words not having familiar signs. Conlin and Paivio (1975), Bonvillian (1983), and others replicated the signability effect with deaf adults (see also Siedlecki, Votaw, Bonvillian, & Jordan, 1990); and Novak and Bonvillian (1996) found that deaf college students recalled words better in a signing condition than in a fingerspelling condition. Such findings to the interesting prediction that

---

[3]Capital letters denote the approximate English translations of signs in American Sign Language.

just as variation in English fluency affects the frequency of phonologically based coding, variation in sign language fluency should affect the frequency of sign-based coding. Precisely this result was reported by Marschark (1996) in his study of word- and sign-length effects in working memory, a study that is described below. Additional studies are clearly necessary, however, and an examination of relations between sign language acquisition and memory in deaf children (see Bebko & McKinnon, this volume) would be particularly enlightening.

Let us return to the question of whether the signability effect is a consequence of visual coding or of kinesthetic coding.[4] Poizner et al. (1981) offered some indication from their study of memory coding by deaf persons with ASL as their primary language. They tested serial recall of lists of signs that differed in their level of formational similarity, semantic similarity, and iconicity (the representational value of the sign in relation to the object that it represents). Compared to lists of random signs, formationally similar signs had a significantly debilitating effect on the serial ordered recall of items, but no effects were found for semantically similar or iconic lists, suggesting that the effect is more a function of the way that a sign is made than the way that it looks. Similar interference effects from formationally similar signs were obtained by Hanson (1982), who also observed subjects using overt signed rehearsal.[5]

Siedlecki et al. (1990) examined the effects of manual interference (squeezing rubber balls) and reading level on recall of lists of words. Immediate and delayed free recall revealed a small interference effect for deaf individuals and none for hearing individuals. Although a signability effect was obtained for all deaf subjects, the effect of manual interference was not found to vary with whether deaf subjects used their dominant or nondominant hands to squeeze the balls, and the interference effect disappeared in delayed recall. Siedlecki et al. (1990) therefore concluded that the interference effect was "not related to the use of a kinesthetic sign-based coding strategy" (p. 192) in the college students they tested. MacSweeney et al. (1996), in contrast, found that both two-handed sign production and a simple hand-tapping task reduced memory span in British deaf 11- to 15-year-olds who were exposed to both spoken and

[4]The way that a sign is made and the way that it looks are obviously highly correlated physically, but they are not fully redundant psychologically. For example, we expect that there are memory differences that follow from making a sign versus seeing a sign (i.e., kinesthetic versus visual information), and there may well be memory differences depending on whether or not signs include a facial component in addition to hand characteristics (Marschark, LePoutre, & Bement, in press).

[5]Such findings do not necessarily indicate that signs are processed holistically. Bellugi et al. (1974), Klima and Bellugi (1979), Wilson and Emmorey (in press), and others showed similarity of handshape to affect memory, but we have not yet disentangled possible effects of movement and orientation. Wilbur (1987) also described memory findings that reveal the separation of morphological inflections of signs in ASL from the lexical items themselves.

sign language. Those subjects also showed effects of phonological coding, indicating that deaf students of that age had multiple coding strategies available for memory.

Marschark (1996) obtained evidence for articulatory coding in working memory by deaf students at the National Technical Institute for the Deaf, using both oral and manual articulatory interference tasks. All of the students used sign language as their primary form of communication, although they came from diverse educational–linguistic backgrounds; the mean average hearing loss in the better ear was 91 dB. In two memory span experiments, he had deaf and hearing college students remember digit strings presented either via computer (Arabic numerals) or in sign and then sign them or write them, respectively. Each subject received one block of trials with no interference; one block in which they had to repeatedly mouth "lalala" during presentation; and one block in which they had to drum the fingers of both hands on a table, from index fingers outward to the little fingers (somewhat less automatic than the reverse direction). Overall, hearing subjects showed significantly longer digit spans than deaf subjects, and their memories were reduced by the oral articulatory suppression task but not the manual articulatory suppression task. Deaf subjects were affected by both interference tasks.

Marschark's subjects also read through a matrix of 120 digits (excluding the two-syllable digits 7 and 0) twice prior to testing. Deaf subjects signed the digits and hearing subjects said the digits as quickly as possible without making mistakes. Total articulation time was longer for deaf than hearing subjects,[6] and Marschark therefore divided his subjects' digit spans by their average digit production times, yielding what were essentially the lengths of their articulatory loops. Consistent with the findings of Baddeley and his colleagues, Marschark found an articulatory loop about 2s in length, which did not differ for deaf and hearing subjects. He concluded that deaf and hearing subjects have the same working memory capacity, but that because digit production is faster in speech than in sign, hearing subjects who use speech-based coding can fit more information into their limited-capacity articulatory loops than can deaf subjects (who use sign-based coding; see Ellis & Hennelly, 1980).

Consistent with that conclusion, Marschark found that among deaf students, sign language skill was strongly and inversely related to memory span in the no-interference and manual interference conditions, whereas speech skill was strongly and positively related to memory in both conditions. Neither skill correlated significantly with recall in the oral interference condition. The finding of mixed coding strategies by the deaf

[6]It is well established that although individual signs generally take longer to articulate than individual words, the rate of information exchange in discourse is essentially equivalent because signs can carry more information than words.

students was replicated in a third experiment where Marschark found word-length effects for both deaf and hearing subjects. Deaf subjects but not hearing subjects showed *sign-length effects*, as signs that take less time to produce were remembered better than signs that take more time to produce.

In contrast to Marschark's (1996) results, Chincotta and Chincotta (1996) did not find oral or manual (tapping) interference for Chinese children in Hong Kong exposed primarily to spoken language, although oral articulatory suppression interfered with hearing subjects. The authors suggested that there may be something about the Chinese language compared to other language systems that prevented the finding of articulatory suppression in the deaf subjects, who had lower recall than the hearing subjects in all three conditions. Wilson and Emmorey (in press), however, used long and short signs matched on other dimensions, similar to those of Marschark (1996), and found that deaf college students showed both sign-length and manual articulatory supression effects. They argued that the results suggest that verbal and visuospatial working memories might better be viewed as linguistic and nonlinguistic working memories.

Wilson and Emmorey (1997b) provided evidence of a storage buffer accessed directly by sign presentation and indirectly by picture presentation, the latter mediated by what appeared to be a manual articulatory rehearsal process. Examining serial recall for lists of similar and dissimilar signs, they found both sign similarity interference in memory and a sign articulatory suppression effect. These results suggested the disruption of some kind of active rehearsal or maintenance system (cf. Chalifoux, 1991). They concluded that the articulatory loop of fluent signers is like that of fluent speakers in having a buffer that retains information based on the phonological structure of the language and an active rehearsal process involving the articulators. The visuospatial articulatory loop is then presumed to refresh information in the working memory buffer (rehearsal process) and to be involved in the verbal labelling of information presented in other forms (e.g., as pictures; see Logie, 1996).

This conclusion is consistent with findings of Wilson, Bettger, Niculae, and Klima (1997), who compared the memory performance of deaf children who were native ASL signers with that of hearing children. In forward and backward digit span tasks, the deaf children were equally proficient, suggesting that encoding of serial information in ASL does not entail any directional dominance (cf. Blair, 1957). The deaf children also showed better memory than hearing children on a nonlinguistic, visuospatial task involving Corsi blocks. Taken together, the results of Marschark, Mac Sweeney et al., and Wilson and her colleagues all suggest that mental representation in deaf individuals who are fluent in sign language may have different characteristics than in hearing individuals who rely on spoken language. Depending on the nature of the task and to-be-remembered materials, those differences can lead to deaf individuals having better, equal, or worse memory as compared to hearing individuals.

Further research will clarify the extent to which such findings relate to hearing individuals who are fluent users of sign language (e.g., Marschark & Shroyer, 1993) and deaf individuals who rely on spoken language. At that juncture, we can better understand how language and hearing loss influence memory and other cognitive processes. Research of this sort also should contribute to improved methods for educating deaf children, as we can structure learning situations according to their preferred encoding and organizational strategies or provide transitions between contexts that normally demand particular kinds of organization. Clearly, one of the most important areas for consideration is reading, a domain in which deaf children typically face significant challenges. Given the central role of memory processes with reading and the suggestion that deaf and hearing individuals may differ in their memories for printed English materials, it is worth considering this issue in some detail.

Memory and Reading

Perfetti and Goldman (1976), using a probe digit memory task, showed that good and poor readers did not differ on that task, but skilled readers were better on a discourse memory task. Further, discourse memory was related to reading comprehension, whereas the digit memory was not. They argued that a language specific memory function, and not just short-term memory capacity, is an essential component of reading comprehension. Daneman and Carpenter (1980) later provided specific evidence on this issue and showed that *reading span* or *complex memory span* tasks that involve both the articulatory loop and the central executive provided a much better predictor of comprehension than simple memory span tasks (but see Engle, 1996). Daneman, Nemeth, Stainton, and Huelsmann (1995) found that reading span and a visual shape span test were good predictors of reading achievement in deaf 5- to 14-year-olds, whereas degree of hearing loss was not. However, the children in that study actually had listening spans higher than the normal hearing children, so it is doubtful that this study tells us anything about the relations of memory and reading to hearing loss in deaf children.

At a different level of analysis, several studies demonstrated that deaf students were less likely than hearing students to remember information that they read as coherent sequences of events (Banks, Gray, & Fyfe, 1990;

Gaines, Mandler, & Bryant, 1981). Similar results were obtained when students watched a signed story (Griffith, Ripich, & Dastoli, 1990). Although some educators and investigators have attributed such findings to limitations on working memory, per se, others have cited poorer initial language comprehension or inadequate knowledge or use of discourse structures (see Marschark, 1993). Marschark, Mouradian, and Halas (1994) provided evidence against the latter alternative, demonstrating that deaf and hearing 7- to 15-year-olds showed comparable use of discourse structures in their writing, even though the grammatical and lexical character of deaf children's writing lagged behind that of their hearing peers.

Although research has not yet explicitly examined the intuitively obvious link between text comprehension and memory among deaf students, the pattern of findings observed in deaf children's memory for texts led to a study by Marschark, De Beni, Polazzo, and Cornoldi (1993). They presented simple paragraphs to groups of hearing and deaf high-school students matched either on age or reading ability. Free recall of two passages was scored for the number of relations recalled and the number of individual concepts recalled. Overall, the deaf children recalled significantly less than their hearing age-mates but more than the younger, reading-matched children. Most importantly, the deaf students remembered proportionally fewer relations than individual concepts, whereas the reverse was true for both groups of their hearing peers.

The fact that their finding was obtained with both age- and reading-matched hearing peers means that the *relational-item specific* difference cannot be ascribed to any kind of overall reading deficiency on the part of deaf students. Rather, Marschark et al. concluded that deaf children may attend to and thus remember different things when they read (see also, Marschark, 1993, chapter 7, for related differences in verbal and nonverbal classification skills). Similarly, Cumming and Rodda (1985) suggested that deaf readers can take advantage of *successive processing* during reading, but that there is a bias toward more spatial organization than temporal organization that results in decreased emphases on sequentially related information, including syntax (see also Mayberry & Fischer, 1989; Mayberry & Waters, 1991).

Although that notion has not been tested explicitly in the context of reading, there are several sources of information consistent with the view that lesser fluency with English may lead deaf students to rely on alternative coding strategies involving signs rather than English words, and to emphasize spatial rather than sequential information. Importantly, these two characteristics are not necessarily directly linked. Those investigators who argue that sign-based memory codes are more visuospatial than spoken–written language are obviously correct, but that does not imply that sign language is in any sense less sequential than spoken language. ASL may have more flexible ordering constraints than English, but there are other spoken languages that are as order-flexible as ASL (Marschark et al., 1997). ASL and other sign languages also have regular sequentially related morphological and syntactic rules, even if ordering of subjects, verbs, and objects appears more flexible. At the same time, sign languages tend to acquire the SVO-ordering tendency of the spoken language of their host societies, so there are a variety of confounds that need to be disentangled empirically in order to understand the functioning of memory during reading.

Akamatsu and Fischer (1991), for example, examined memory for lists of randomly selected words, semantically related words, and syntactically related words as well as scrambled or normally ordered sentences by deaf college students with higher or lower levels of English language skills. They found that students who had greater English fluency were better able to make use of semantic and syntactic relations among words, thus improving memory. The difference with regard to semantic relations is particularly interesting for two reasons. First, it clearly relates to attempts to understand better the organization of memory among deaf individuals, as discussed earlier. Whether by virtue of underlying organizational structure or the tendency or ability strategically to make use of such structure, English skill is clearly linked to the use of semantic associations in remembering. Second, and in related fashion, Akamatsu and Fischer's findings indicate the importance of memory in *word-finding* or *lexical look-up* during reading, a subskill that appears to be a most difficult hurdle for young deaf readers (Marschark & Harris, 1996).

Bonvillian and his colleagues (e.g., Bonvillian et al., 1987; Novak & Bonvillian, 1996) cited deaf students' difficulties with committing printed English to memory as a reason for their strategic use of fingerspelling (cf. Treiman and Hirsh-Pasek, 1983) or signing in memory for letters or words. That linkage is consistent with the findings, discussed previously, indicating that signability facilitates memory among deaf individuals. Novak and Bonvillian (1996) further found no negative recency effect (see also Bonvillian, 1983) in recall of signed words, suggesting that the limited capacity buffer normally implicated in the lower recall for the last few items of a list may depend on some kind of echoic, auditory-based system not implemented by the deaf students in this study. One valuable experiment in this area would be an extension of the Novak and Bonvillian paradigm to include deaf and hard-of-hearing subjects in a spoken language condition, but until such a study is done, it is difficult to be sure of the precise locus for their findings.

In their extensive study of memory and reading, Waters and Doehring (1990) examined the memory spans of severely and profoundly deaf children ranging in age from 7 to 20 years enrolled in programs with a spoken-language emphasis. Using printed and spoken versions of memory span tasks for digits, words, and sentences, Waters and Doehring found that deaf children scored well behind hearing peers according to standardized norms, suggesting that deaf children are at a disadvantage on tasks that depend on sequential short-term memory. Short-term memory for phonological information was unrelated to reading ability, leading Waters and Doehring to suggest that phonological processes in deaf readers might involve *whole-word* codes rather than the phonological assembly.

Garrison, Long, and Dowaliby (1997), however, pointed out that simple memory span never has been a good predictor of reading ability, at least not relative to complex memory span tasks, like those of Daneman and Carpenter (1980), which include a processing component as well as a simple memory component. Garrison et al. therefore examined the relations among functional working memory capacity, vocabulary knowledge, content knowledge, and inferencing ability among deaf readers in seventh grade and college. They found that complex memory span performance was reliably correlated with reading comprehension ability, whereas simple memory span performance was not—a finding comparable to those obtained with hearing subjects. Further, Garrison et al. showed that reading comprehension depended heavily on vocabulary and content knowledge. Insofar as deaf readers generally have been found to have more difficulty than hearing peers with word finding, they may tend to depend more heavily on content and world knowledge than hearing readers, a finding consistent with findings of Banks et al. (1990), Gaines et al. (1981), and Griffith et al. (1990). Still to be determined are the ways in which memory processes interact with English and sign language fluencies or preferences during the acquisition of reading. Extensive developmental studies are clearly necessary in this regard and can be expected to pay off handsomely in contributing to improved methods for reading instruction.

Language Fluency and Memory

At the simplest level, a variety of early studies by Conrad (1970, 1979) and others suggested that memory for letters and words by deaf children was closely linked to their spoken language skill and, not coincidentally perhaps, inversely linked to their degree of hearing loss. Given that most of those studies involved children who did not have significant exposure to sign language, it is difficult to know whether those findings suggest some preeminent status for speech coding in memory (see Marschark,

1996). More interesting is the question of when one kind of coding strategy might be more beneficial and how those might be related to learner characteristics, particularly with regard to language fluency. Marschark (1993) noted that language fluency and the availability of effective communication during childhood could have an influence on the structure and contents of long-term, semantic memory and other cognitive skills insofar as children with better communication skills would be more likely to have interactions with others from whom memory strategies and memory-relevant content knowledge could be learned, either explicitly or implicitly. They also are more likely to have interactions with diverse individuals with whom remembering things might be important. Several studies have explored the likelihood of deaf students' adopting strategic approaches to long-term memory. Liben (1979) and other investigators during the 1970s provided evidence that deaf children used spontaneous memory strategies just as frequently as hearing peers, but those strategies often did not facilitate performance equally. Liben and Drury (1977), for example, examined memory for pictures, nonsense shapes, fingerspelling, and printed words in 6- and 8-year-old deaf children. In contrast to their hypothesis that deaf children might not use memory rehearsal because they lack verbal labels for stimuli, their subjects rehearsed spontaneously using both spoken language and sign language, even though there was no reliable relationship between overt rehearsal and memory.

Bebko (1984) examined the extent of spontaneous rehearsal and the success of rehearsal training in profoundly deaf children aged 5 to 15 years. He found that overt, spontaneous rehearsal emerged later in both deaf groups relative to hearing controls, appearing at 7 to 8 years for hearing students, 10 to 11 years for deaf students exposed primarily to spoken language, and 12 to 13 years for students in total communication programs. Overall, the hearing rehearsers recalled more than the deaf rehearsers, but this effect likely resulted from the fact that there were three times as many inconsistent rehearsers among the deaf as among the hearing subjects. In fact, after training in overt cumulative rehearsal, the deaf subjects were as good or better than their hearing peers. Bebko et al. (1992) thus argued that the greatest discrepancies found in recall tasks between deaf and hearing children are those most amenable to spontaneous cumulative rehearsal strategies. Because hearing children appear more skilled in the application of such strategies, particularly in serial recall, Bebko et al. suggested that memory strategies rather than the modality of any particular memory code may have the greatest influence on deaf children's recall performance.

That expectation followed from a study by Bebko and McKinnon (1990), who examined the relationship between strategic memory rehearsal and serial recall performance in deaf and hearing children aged 5 to 15 years. All of the deaf children had profound hearing losses and were enrolled in a total communication program. Bebko and McKinnon presented the children with sequences of three to five colored squares. After each sequence, there was an unfilled delay before the children attempted to put a series of colored blocks in the same order that they had seen in presentation. During stimulus presentation and the pretest interval, children were observed for evidence of cumulative rehearsal either orally or through repeated hand, head, or body movements.

Bebko and McKinnon found that the deaf children lagged behind the hearing children in their spontaneous use of rehearsal, as 58% of the hearing children and 22% of the deaf children were observed to rehearse. More importantly, perhaps, they found that children's language experience was the best predictor of rehearsal use. Using the number of years of effective exposure in children's preferred language modality as a measure of language experience, Bebko and McKinnon found that in both deaf and hearing samples, language experience accounted fully for the age differences observed in the emergence of rehearsal (see also Bebko & Metcalfe-Haggert, 1997). This finding not only emphasizes the need to consider the language backgrounds of deaf individuals involved in memory research, but also demonstrates that approaching deaf children's reading as being amenable to teaching methods identical to those used with hearing children may be a gross oversimplification.

CONCLUSIONS

The evidence reviewed here indicated that deaf children generally reveal shorter memory spans than hearing children. Most early demonstrations in this regard, however, used digits or other stimuli liable to verbal coding. Although most child-related studies have considered only English-based verbal coding, there is considerable evidence that sign language coding is used in memory tasks by adults (e.g., Bellugi et al., 1975; Hanson, 1982; Krakow & Hanson, 1985). As yet there have been no assessments of when sign language coding in working memory becomes available to younger deaf children, whether or not they know when and how to use it effectively. Recent studies, however, have demonstrated that working memory involving sign language coding functions in an apparently identical manner to working memory involving spoken language coding, indicating that *articulatory* processes are essential to memory and other cognitive processes, independent of the kind of articulators involved. The demonstration that digit span is positively related to speech skill and negatively related to sign skill among deaf students also points to the importance of structuring both laboratory tasks and classroom situations in ways that appropriately map onto students' cognitive structures.

Understanding the structure of world and content knowledge should be one of the highest priorities of investigators interested in memory and educators who seek to know how such knowledge interacts with learning situations. Before drawing any strong conclusions about the effects of hearing loss and sign language use on long-term memory, we need to distinguish possible effects on recall due to differences in memory organization or memory strategies from differences due to linguistic coding per se. One would expect, for example, that gross differences in stimulus familiarity would affect memory, and such differences may well be a factor when deaf and hearing persons are tested in tasks requiring memory for printed stimuli. Whorfian hypotheses about language and cognition seem to be making a bit of a comeback in this regard, as we explore ways in which signed and spoken language may make different cognitive structures more or less accessible or available (e.g., Marschark et al., 1997). Further, the experiential differences of deaf, as compared to hearing, students might well make for differences in motivation and cognitive styles (see Marschark, 1993), semantic memory organization, or their approaches to learning situations. All of this should not be taken to indicate that either we have not progressed far from the memory studies of 100 years ago nor that the problem is too complex for solution in the near future. Rather, we see great strides being made in the area and see grand opportunities for bridging basic research, applied research, and real-world needs of deaf learners. This is an occasion we would not want to miss, and we look forward to imminent discoveries.

REFERENCES

Akamatsu, C. T., & Fischer, S. D. (1991). Using immediate recall to assess language proficiency in deaf students. *American Annals of the Deaf, 136*, 428–434.

Baddeley, A. (1986). *Working memory*. New York: Oxford University Press.

Baddeley, A. D., & Hitch, G. J. (1974). Working memory. In G. Bower (Ed.), *The Psychology of learning and motivation*, (Vol. 8, pp. 47–89). New York: Academic Press.

Banks, J., Gray, C., & Fyfe, R. (1990). The written recall of printed stories by severely deaf children. *British Journal of Educational Psychology, 60*, 192–206.

Bebko, J. M. (1984). Memory and rehearsal characteristics of profoundly deaf children. *Journal of Experimental Child Psychology, 38*, 415–428.

Bebko, J. M., Lacasse, M. A., Turk, H., & Oyen, A. -S. (1992). Recall performance on a central–incidental memory task by profoundly deaf children. *American Annals of the Deaf, 137*, 271–277.

Bebko, J. M., & McKinnon, E. E. (1990). The language experience of deaf children: Its relation to spontaneous rehearsal in a memory task. *Child Development, 61*, 1744–1752.

Bebko, J. M., & Metcalfe-Haggert, A. (1997). Deafness, language skills, and rehearsal: A model for the development of a memory strategy. *Journal of Deaf Studies and Deaf Education, 2,* 133–141.

Bellugi, U., Klima, E., & Siple, P. (1975). Remembering in sign. *Cognition, 3,* 93–125.

Blair, F. X. (1957). A study of the visual memory of deaf and hearing children. *American Annals of the Deaf, 102,* 254–263.

Bonvillian, J. D. (1983). Effects of signability and imagery on word recall of deaf and hearing students. *Perceptual and Motor Skills, 56,* 775–791.

Bonvillian, J. D., Rea, C. A., Orlansky, M. D., & Slade, L. A. (1987). The effect of sign language rehearsal on deaf subjects' immediate and delayed recall of English word lists. *Applied Pscyholinguistics, 8,* 33–54

Campbell, R. (1992). Speech in the head? Rhyme skill, reading, and immediate memory in the deaf. In D. Reisberg (Ed.), *Auditory imagery* (pp. 73–94). Hillsdale, NJ: Lawrence Erlbaum Associates.

Campbell, R., & Wright, H. (1990). Deafness and immediate memory for pictures: Dissociation between "inner speech" and "inner ear." *Journal of Experimental Child Psychology, 50,* 259–286.

Chalifoux, L. M. (1991). The implications of congenital deafness for working memory. *American Annals of the Deaf, 136,* 292–299.

Chincotta, M., & Chincotta, D. (1996). Digit span, articulatory suppression, and the deaf: A study of the Hong Kong Chinese. *American Annals of the Deaf, 141,* 252–257.

Conlin, D., & Paivio, A. (1975). The associative learning of the deaf: The effects of word imagery and signability. *Memory and Cognition, 3,* 333–340.

Conrad, R. (1970). Short-term memory processes in the deaf. *British Journal of Psychology, 61,* 179–195.

Conrad, R. (1979). *The deaf school child: Language and cognition.* New York: Harper & Row.

Cumming, C., & Rodda, M. (1985). The effects of auditory deprivation on successive processing. *Canadian Journal of Behavioural Science, 17,* 232–245.

Daneman, M., & Carpenter, P. A. (1980). Individual differences in working memory and reading. *Journal of Verbal Learning and Verbal Behavior, 19,* 450–466.

Daneman, M., Nemeth, S., Stainton, M., & Huelsmann, K. (1995). Working memory as a predictor of reading achievement in orally educated hearing-impaired children. *Volta Review, 97,* 225–241.

Ellis, N. C., & Hennelly, R. A. (1980). A bilingual word-length effect: Implications for intelligence testing and the relative ease of mental calculation in Welsh and English. *British Journal of Psychology, 50,* 449–458.

Engle, R. W. (1996). Working memory and retrieval: An inhibition–resource approach. In J. T. E. Richardson, R. W. Engle, L. Hasher, R. H. Logie, E. R. Stoltzfus, & R. T. Zacks, *Working memory and human cognition* (pp. 89–119). New York: Oxford University Press.

Engle, R. W., Cantor, J., & Turner, M. L. (1989). Modality effects: Do they fall on deaf ears? *Quarterly Journal of Experimental Psychology: Human Experimental Psychology, 41,* 273–292.

Epstein, K. I., Hillegeist, E. G., & Grafman, J. (1994). Number processing in deaf college students. *American Annals of the Deaf, 139,* 336–347.

Gaines, R., Mandler, J., & Bryant, P. (1981). Immediate and delayed story recall by hearing and deaf children. *Journal of Speech and Hearing Research, 24,* 463–469.

Garrison, W. M., Long, G., & Dowaliby, F. (1997). Working memory capacity and comprehension processes in deaf readers. *Journal of Deaf Studies and Deaf Education, 2,* 78–94.

Glucksberg, S., & Krauss, R. M. (1967). What do people say after they have learned how to talk? Studies of the development of referential communication. *Merrill-Palmer Quarterly, 13,* 309–316.

Griffith, P. L., Ripich, D. N., & Dastoli, S. L. (1990). Narrative abilities in hearing-impaired children: Propositions and cohesion. *American Annals of the Deaf, 135,* 14–19.

Hamilton, H., & Holtzman, T. G. (1989). Linguistic encoding in short-term memory as a function of stimulus type. *Memory & Cognition, 17,* 541–550.

Hanson, V. (1982). Short-term recall by deaf signers of American sign language: Implications of encoding strategy for order recall. *Journal of Experimental Psychology: Learning, Memory, and Cognition, 8,* 572–583.

Hanson, V. L. & Lichtenstein, E. H. (1990). Short-term memory coding by deaf signers: The primary language coding hypothesis reconsidered. *Cognitive Psychology 22,* 211–224.

Hoemann, H., Andrews, C., & DeRosa, D. (1974). Categorical encoding in short-term memory by deaf and hearing children. *Journal of Speech and Hearing Research, 17,* 426–431.

Klima, E., & Bellugi, U. (1979). *The signs of language.* Cambridge, MA: Harvard University Press.

Koh, S. D., Vernon, M., & Bailey, W. (1971). Free-recall learning of word lists by prelingual deaf subjects. *Journal of Verbal Learning and Verbal Behavior, 10,* 542–547.

Krakow, R. A. & Hanson, V. L. (1985). Deaf signers and serial recall in the visual modality: Memory for signs, fingerspelling, and print. *Memory & Cognition, 13,* 265–272.

Kyle, J. G. (1981). Signs and memory: The search for the code. In B. Woll, J. Kyle, & M. Deuchar (Eds.), *Perspectives on British Sign Language and Deafness* (pp. 71–88). London: Croom Helm.

Liben, L. S. (1979). Free recall by deaf and hearing children: Semantic clustering and recall in trained and untrained groups. *Journal of Experimental Child Psychology, 27,* 105–119.

Liben, L. S., & Drury, A. M. (1977). Short-term memory in deaf and hearing children in relation to stimulus characteristics. *Journal of Experimental Child Psychology, 24,* 60–73.

Lichtenstein, E. (1998). The relationships between reading processes and English skills of deaf college students. *Journal of Deaf Studies and Deaf Education, 3,* 80–134.

Logie, R. H. (1996). The seven ages of working memory. In J. T. E. Richardson, R. W. Engle, L. Hasher, R. H. Logie, E. R. Stoltzfus, & R. T. Zacks (Eds.), *Working memory and human cognition* (pp. 31–65). New York: Oxford University Press.

MacSweeney, M., Campbell, R., & Donlan, C. (1996). Varieties of short-term memory coding in deaf teenagers. *Journal of Deaf Studies and Deaf Education, 1,* 249–262.

Marschark, M. (1993). *Psychological development of deaf children.* New York: Oxford University Press.

Marschark, M. (1996). *Influences of signed and spoken language on memory span.* Paper presented at annual meetings of the Psychonomic Society, Chicago, November.

Marschark, M. (1997). *Raising and educating a deaf child.* New York: Oxford University press.

Marschark, M., De Beni, R., Polazzo, M. G., & Cornoldi, C. (1993). Deaf and hearing-impaired adolescents' memory for concrete and abstract prose: Effects of relational and distinctive information. *American Annals of the Deaf, 138,* 31–39.

Marschark, M., & Cornoldi, C. (in preparation). *Mental representation of auditory information by deaf adults.*

Marschark, M., & Everhart, V. S. (submitted). *Problem solving by deaf and hearing students.*

Marschark, M., & Harris, M. (1996). Success and failure in learning to read: The special case of deaf children. In C. Cornoldi & J. Oakhill (Eds.), *Reading comprehension disabilities: Processes and intervention* (pp. 279–300). Hillsdale, NJ: Lawrence Erlbaum Associates.

Marschark, M., LePoutre, D., & Bement, L. (1998). Mouth movement and signed communication. In R. Campbell & B. Dodd (Eds.), *Hearing by eye: The psychology of lipreading and audiovisual speech* (pp. 243–264). London: Taylor & Francis.

Marschark, M., Mouradian, V., & Halas, M. (1994). Discourse rules in the language productions of deaf and hearing children. *Journal of Experimental Child Psychology*, *57*, 89–107.

Marschark, M., & Shroyer, E. (1993). Hearing status and language fluency as predictors of automatic word and sign recognition. *American Annals of the Deaf*, *138*, 370–375.

Marschark, M., Siple, P., Lillo-Martin, D., Campbell, R., & Everhart, V. (1997). *Relations of language and thought: The view from sign language and deaf children*. New York: Oxford University Press.

Mayberry, R. I. & Fischer, S. D. (1989). Looking through phonological shape to lexical meaning: The bottleneck of non-native sign language processing. *Memory & Cognition*, *17*, 740–754.

Mayberry, R. I., & Waters, G.S. (1991). Children's memory for sign and fingerspelling in relation to production rate and sign language input. In P. Siple & S. S. Fischer (Eds.), *Theoretical issues in sign language research, Volume 2: Psychology* (pp. 211–229). Chicago: University of Chicago Press.

McEvoy, C., Marschark, M., & Nelson, D. (submitted). *Comparing the mental lexicons of deaf and hearing individuals.*

Mott, A. (1899). A comparison of deaf and hearing children in their ninth year. *American Annals of the Deaf*, *44*, 401–412.

Novak, L. L., & Bonvillian, J. D. (1996). Word recall in deaf students: The effects of different coding strategies. *Perceptual and Motor Skills*, *83*, 627–639.

Odom, P. B., Blanton, R. L., & McIntyre, C. K. (1970). Coding medium and word recall by deaf and hearing subjects. *Journal of Speech and Hearing Research*, *13*, 54–58.

Paivio, A. (1971). *Imagery and verbal processes*. New York: Holt, Rinehart, and Winston.

Perfetti, C. A., & Goldman, S. R. (1976). Discourse memory and reading comprehension skill. *Journal of Verbal Learning and Verbal Behavior*, *15*, 33–42.

Pintner, R., & Patterson, D. (1917). A comparison of deaf and hearing children in visual memory for digits. *Journal of Experimental Psychology*, *2*, 76–88.

Poizner, H., Bellugi, U., & Tweney, R. D. (1981). Processing formational, semantic, and iconic information in American Sign Language. *Journal of Experimental Psychology: Human Perception and Performance*, *7*, 1146–1159.

Shand, M. A. (1982). Sign-based short term coding of American sign language signs and printed English words by congenitally deaf signers. *Cognitive Psychology*, *14*, 1–12.

Siedlecki, T., Jr., Votaw, M. C., Bonvillian, J. D., & Jordan, I. K. (1990). The effects of manual interference and reading level on deaf subjects' recall of word lists. *Applied Psycholinguistics*, *11*, 185–199.

Todman, J., & Seedhouse, E. (1994). Visual-action code processing by deaf and hearing children. *Language and Cognitive Processes*, *9*, 129–141.

Treiman, R., & Hirsh-Pasek, K. (1983). Silent reading: Insights from second-generation deaf readers. *Cognitive Psychology*, *15*, 39–65.

Tweney, R. D., Hoemann, H. W., & Andrews, C. E. (1975). Semantic organization in deaf and hearing subjects. *Journal of Psycholinguistic Research*, *4*, 61–73.

Waters, G. S., & Doehring, D. G. (1990). Reading acquisition in congenitally deaf children who communicate orally: Insights from an analysis of component reading, language, and memory skills. In T. H. Carr & B. A. Levy (Eds.), *Reading and its development* (pp. 323–373). New York: Academic Press.

Wilbur, R. (1987). *American Sign Language: Linguistic and applied dimensions, Second Edition*. Boston: Little, Brown.

Wilson, M., Bettger, J. G., Niculae, I., & Klima, E. S. (1997). Modality of language shapes working memory: Evidence from digit span and spatial span in ASL signers. *Journal of Deaf Studies and Deaf Education, 2,* 152–162.

Wilson, M., & Emmorey, K. (1997a). Working memory for sign language: A window into the architecture of the working memory system. *Journal of Deaf Studies and Deaf Education, 2,* 121–130.

Wilson, M., & Emmorey, K. (1997b). A "phonological loop" in visuospatial working memory: Evidence for American Sign Language. *Memory & Cognition, 25,* 313–320.

Wilson, M., & Emmorey, K. (in press). A "word length effect" for sign language: Further evidence on the role of language in structuring working memory. *Memory & Cognition.*

4

Development of Theories of Mind in Deaf Children

Cyril Courtin
Anne-Marie Melot
Laboratoire de Psychologie du Développement de l'Enfant
CNRS & Université Paris V–René Descartes

It is generally assumed that second-generation deaf children are compa-rable to hearing children in terms of their psycho-affective, intellectual, linguistic, and psychosocial development (Marschark, 1993) and are neurologically healthy (Wolff & Thatcher, 1990). For these reasons, some authors consider this deaf group to be the only one accurately paired with hearing children (e.g., Courtin, 1996), and believe that comparing the results of these children in cognitive tasks to those of deaf children born to hearing parents could provide information on the impact of several factors, such as communication mode and maternal control on the development of deaf children. One could be tempted to adopt this model when working on theories of mind and to consider the performance of second-generation deaf children to be directly comparable—and simi-lar—to those of hearing children. However, we believe this to be an error, for it is quite hard to claim, theoretically, that deaf children of deaf parents, and hearing children are in a similar position when faced with theories of mind tasks.

AN OVERVIEW OF THEORIES-OF-MIND
RESEARCH IN A DEVELOPMENTAL PERSPECTIVE

Research on the so-called *theories of mind* in developmental psychology has a very broad objective: to gain insight into children's comprehension of mental entities and phenomena. The basic idea in this framework is to determine whether and how children call on mental entities such as intentions, desires, and beliefs, to describe, explain, and predict human behavior. Another aim is to define the potential conditions under which representations of mental entities and phenomena are constructed, and the processes by which they evolve in the course of child development.

From the data gathered over the past 15 years, it appears quite clear that very young children have representations of the human mind. By about the age of 3, such representations allow children to distinguish mental entities from physical entities (Wellman & Estes, 1986), to attribute a variety of mental states to human beings, including themselves (Moses & Flavell, 1990; Wellman, 1990), to use various expressions to refer to different mental states (Bretherton & Beeghly, 1982; Shatz, Wellman, & Silber, 1983), and to explain and predict certain actions and/or emotions related to mental states (Astington, Harris, & Olson, 1988; Lewis & Mitchell, 1994). However, the representations a child of this age can manipulate are not conceptualized as products of mental activity. It is not until approximately the age of 4 or 5 that a child's knowledge undergoes a reorganization process through which he or she moves away from a conception of the mind as a container of mental states and begins conceiving of the mind as a mediator and generator of mental representations (Wellman, 1988, 1990). In this view, the 5-year-old is considered to be capable of grasping the idea that mental representations are constructions, interpretations, transformations, or even distortions of information about a given state of the world or a given state of reality. Access to the notions of metarepresentation and misrepresentation allow the child to understand a whole new set of phenomena, such as the fact that not all individuals have the same perspectives, understandings, and beliefs about one and the same reality, that one's own knowledge and beliefs can change, and that one can have several representations, perhaps contradictory, of the same reality.

The term *theory of mind* is employed in a narrower sense by researchers who consider the mind-related knowledge and representations of mental life built by the child to be theoretical constructions resulting from the elaboration of naive theories. Such naive theories, which differ from typologies and empirical generalizations (Gopnik & Wellman, 1992), are made up of abstract, interdependent entities (a central core of coherent beliefs; Perner, 1991; Wellman, 1990) that provide a causal framework for explaining, interpreting, and predicting the observable human behaviors that constitute the referent of the theory. It is postulated that these naive theories have certain features in common with scientific theories. One such feature is the fact that the vocabulary used to express the explanations and predictions made on the basis of a naive theory differs from that used to describe phenomena themselves. For example, a subject explaining why individuals who want to find an object will look for it in a place where the object cannot objectively be found, might say that it is because they *think* or *believe* the object is there, or because they do not *know* the object was moved.

Another feature is the fact that as in science, naive theory-based predictions are not confined to previously observed behaviors. As such, subjects can make a whole set of predictions, even ones about new and unknown events. For example, without having observed a given individual's behavior or feelings about a tube of Smarties in front of him, a subject might predict that the *individual will be happy*, based on the mental states attributed to her/him in that situation (desires, beliefs, intentions), that *the individual wants Smarties*, based on the assumption that she/he likes Smarties, that *the individual will want Smarties*, or that *she/he thinks the tube actually does contain Smarties*, and so forth. A third feature is that predictions based on a theory can be false. For example, if in the naive theory, beliefs are considered to be exact replicas of reality and not products of mental activity about that reality, then a subject may make an erroneous prediction about the actions of an individual whose beliefs differ from his or her own. Finally, naive theory-based predictions and explications are highly diverse. Thus, the same event or behavior may be interpreted, for instance, in terms of *desires, beliefs, a combination of desires and beliefs, or false beliefs*, depending on the type of theory of mind the subject has at the time about the situation in question.

It is also postulated that naive theories evolve in the same way as scientific theories do, especially when they are challenged or invalidated by the facts. For scientific and naive theories alike, counter-examples are first treated as noise or artifacts and as such, are ignored; then auxiliary, *ad hoc* hypotheses are formed to account for facts that come up in a given context; finally, an alternative theory is constructed—via a restructuration process—to incorporate both the facts accounted for by the initial theory and the counter-evidences that contributed to its destabilization (Gopnik & Wellman, 1992).

The transition from a rudimentary mentalist theory (Wellman, 1988, 1990) to a representational theory of mind (Perner, 1991) constitutes a major change in children's comprehension of the mind, "for they now understand that a mental state can be a representation, which is the essence of the human mind. In particular, they understand that because an object or event is different from its mental representation, there may not be a single, accurate representation. Rather, a specific real-world thing can be mentally represented in different ways, some of which may be false" (Flavell, Miller, & Miller, 1993, p. 106). In this respect, many authors consider false belief tasks (Wimmer & Perner, 1983) to be the litmus-test (Wellman, 1988) of a representational theory of mind. In these experiments, the child is required to predict and/or explain the behavior of a character who holds a false belief. For example, Maxi (a little boy) puts some chocolate in a drawer and leaves the room. While Maxi is away, his mother removes the chocolate and puts it in a cupboard. Then, Maxi comes back, wanting his chocolate. The child is asked: "Where will Maxi look for his chocolate?" It is assumed that children who say that Maxi will look in the drawer understand the causes and consequences of a person's having a false belief. Note that other tasks have been studied widely in this framework, including level-2 visual perspective-taking tasks (Flavell, Everett, Croft, & Flavell, 1981), appearance–reality distinction tasks (Flavell, Flavell, & Green, 1983; Flavell, Green, & Flavell, 1986), representational change tasks (Gopnik & Astington, 1988), and so on. In the level-2 visual perspective taking tasks, the child and the experimenter sit facing each other. A sideview of an object (a turtle, for example) is placed flat between them. Though the turtle appears right side up (standing on its feet) to the child, it appears upside down (lying on its back) to the experimenter. The child is then asked two questions, namely: "Do you see the turtle right side up or upside down?" and "And me, do I see the turtle right side up or upside down?" One can assume that, when they succeed in the task, children understand that two people can have two conflicting representations of one and the same reality. As for the appearance–reality distinction tasks, the child is presented with illusory objects (e.g., a sponge that looks like a rock; a stone that looks like an egg, etc.). After having experienced the two aspects of the object, subjects are asked several questions about the appearance of the object ("Does it look like a rock, or does it look like a sponge?") and about its reality ("Really and truly, is it a rock or is it a sponge?"). Once again, when children successfully answer the two questions, such as, when they distinguish appearance and reality, they understand that one and the same object may be represented simultaneously in multiple, even contradictory, ways.

One can indeed assume that in order to perform these tasks correctly, the child must also understand the fact that one and the same object or event can be represented in different ways, depending on how it was processed mentally. Moreover, these different tasks appear to be mastered at about the same age, and to be strongly correlated with each other: (a) correlation between appearance–reality and level-2 visual perspective taking (Flavell et al., 1986); (b) between appearance–reality, false belief, and representational change (Gopnik & Astington, 1988); and (c) between level-2 visual perspective taking, appearance–reality, and false belief (Melot, Houdé, Courtel, & Soenen, 1995).

However, despite the strong correlations between these tasks, certain developmental lags appear systematically. Melot et al. (1995) had 3- to 5-year-old subjects perform several level-2 visual perspective-taking tasks, appearance–reality distinction tasks, and false-belief attribution tasks, and were able to show that success on level-2 visual perspective taking always precedes success on the other tasks. Moreover, success on the appearance–reality and false-belief tasks implies success on level-2 visual perspective taking (Melot et al., 1995). The results reported by Gopnik, Slaughter, and Meltzoff (1994) also showed that visual perspective taking is mastered before false-belief attribution. For some authors, this earlier comprehension of perceptual misrepresentation suggests that "children might use perceptual misrepresentation as a model for false belief" (Gopnik et al., 1994, p. 166). At a more general level, we consider perception to be one of the domains in which children begin to understand that representations are not pure and simple reflections of reality, and may therefore be misleading. "Later, the idea would be available to be much more widely applied to all cases of belief" (Gopnik et al., 1994, p. 166).

A second type of developmental lag noted in the literature (Flavell, 1988) concerns children's earlier ability to manipulate pretend representations. Three-year-olds indeed appear to be able to distinguish correctly between several different representations in pretense–reality tasks (Flavell, Flavell, & Green, 1987), yet fail to make those same distinctions in appearance–reality tasks or in level-2 visual perspective-taking tasks, which according to Flavell (1988) can be regarded as appearance–appearance distinction tasks. The debate about the metarepresentational status of pretend representations remains unresolved. On the other hand, it is almost unanimously agreed that children's ability to manipulate nonserious representations during pretend play by age 2, is "a likely precursor to the understanding of belief" (Gopnik et al., 1994, p. 158) and hence to the understanding of metarepresentations and misrepresentations.

Most developmental theorists who consider that the child develops a theoretical knowledge about mental life (theory-theorists) believe that the processes governing the acquisition and development of naive theories of mind are similar to those governing the evolution of scientific theories. However, as Perner, Ruffman, and Leekam (1994) said, "In science, one thing is fairly clear; new theories and insights do not simply mature but need hard work and devotion. Only scientists who immerse themselves in creating and contemplating relevant data are likely to make significant contributions to their field" (p. 1228). Extending this analogy raises the question of what conditions permit and/or favor the collection and processing of the data involved in the construction and evolution of theories of mind during childhood. Several authors have stressed the crucial role played by social interactions and communication within the family (Brown & Dunn, 1991; Dunn, 1994; Dunn, Bretherton, & Munn, 1987; Perner et al., 1994), and by the development of the various dimensions of language (syntactic, semantic, and pragmatic; Baldwin & Moses, 1994; Jenkins & Astington, 1996; Shatz, 1994).

It appears in particular that between the ages of 2 and 3, references to mental states and their causes and effects increase considerably in the pragmatic context of mother–child interactions, as the mother directs her child's attention to the mental states of others in a way that is not related to satisfying the child's immediate needs or controlling his or her behavior. In addition to focusing the child's attention on internal, nonobservable states that are potentially different from those he or she experiences, social interactions have an explanatory component that enables the child to achieve an understanding of intentional states. As Gray and Hosie (1996) stated in regards to Harris' (1996) analysis, "Information-bearing conversations, which involve a continual back-and-forth shuttling from one viewpoint to the other, serve as a constant demonstration that partners in a conversation differ in what they know and believe about a shared topic, from which it eventually becomes clear that people differ in what they know and think" (p. 228).

WHY SHOULD DEAF CHILDREN DIFFER FROM HEARING CHILDREN ON THEORIES OF MIND DEVELOPMENT: A FIRST APPROACH

Given the preceding analyses, it appears that several variables need to be taken into account when working on theories of mind in deaf children: communication mode (e.g., sign language or oral), its quality (unrestrained vs. externally controlled), and the number of potential communicative partners; but also the developmental achievement of the precursors, of cognitive flexibility, of impulse control, and so forth.[1] We

---

[1] Flexibility is defined as the ability to change one's criterion or viewpoint when analyzing a task or a problem.

first present the most important variables, that is, those related to communication and to the theories of mind precursors. We address cognitive flexibility and impulse control when discussing our preliminary results.

Given the great diversity of backgrounds in which deaf children are raised, we consider in this chapter, a few cases and opt for a rather radical dichotomy, considering only profoundly deaf children, two communication modes (sign language or oral), and two parental hearing groups: parents being both deaf or both hearing.

The communication mode used by deaf children and their parents has to be carefully considered, because of sign language properties that, unlike French or English oral ones, could promote *visual perspective taking* mastery.

Sign languages are, as any other language, fully developed languages, made of sublexical structures that are, for signs, the hand configuration, place of articulation, and movement (Klima & Bellugi, 1979). Sign languages also have rules that specify how signs are bound to each other (grammar) in the three-dimensional space to express well-organized sentences. In the present study, the one property of sign languages considered is *syntax*.

Three main points have to be highlighted on this issue. First, the referential perspective of a message is generally understood from the signer's viewpoint. Thus, there is a need for a visual perspective change; the addressee has to reorient the linguistic space according to the angle existing between himself and the signer. Second, there exist inflectional verbs that require a division of the material space into subspaces, each one referring to a single item (subject or object) that will be part of the signed *scene*—this linguistic process is called spatial mapping. The connections made among these subspaces correspond to the conjugation of those verbs. Third, sign languages make use of spatial shiftings of the referential frame of discourse, when signing from the viewpoint of one of the protagonists of the signed story, or when confronting opposite ideas (for a development on this third point, see Poulin & Miller, 1995). It is noteworthy that these three features require the addressee to understand the fact that there exist multiple visual perspectives of one and the same entity, at least of the signed scene.

Referential shiftings, involving multiple representations of a unique reality, have many things in common with visual perspective taking. As the latter is considered to be a precursor to theories of mind representation, it is possible that sign language promotes its development, provided that this communication mode be used from a very early age and its effects not thwarted by other variables. It is important to note that, in the case of sign language, perspective-taking training is longer and more intense than in Flavell's experiment (Flavell et al., 1981), where the training of hearing children proved to be useless. In fact, as sign language is acquired from birth by deaf children born to signing deaf parents, they are much more used to perspective shiftings compared to the hearing children tested by Flavell et al.—these authors conducted an experimental training procedure on 13 children 3-years-old, using no more than two or three tasks.

At what age do children understand these features of sign language?[2] According to Marschark (1993), 2-year-old deaf children of deaf parents "give all appearances of understanding [inflected verb signs]" (p. 117) and, according to Lillo-Martin, Bellugi, Struxness, & O'Grady (1985), spatial mapping is understood by the age of 3. It seems we can maintain that deaf children of deaf parents have acquired an understanding of linguistic space rotation, spatial mapping, and spatial shifting by the age of 3 (Bellugi, O'Grady, Lillo-Martin, O'Grady Hynes, VanHoek, & Corina, 1990; Lillo-Martin et al, 1985; Petitto & Bellugi, 1988; Wilbur, 1987). Thus, as soon as they reach the age of 3, signing deaf children of deaf parents may differ from hearing children, as well as from oral deaf ones, in their visual perspective-taking abilities. Therefore, it is important to separate children according to their communication mode, considering it not only from the message transmission point of view, which we address next.

An idea that has already been stated concerning theories of mind development is that they are acquired in part through interpersonal exchanges between children and their parents (or, by and large, with any other person), leading to a conflict between cognitive representations of each one, what results in a possible awareness from the child of the existence of multiple representations. It is thus conceivable that a deaf child whose parents do not devote enough quality time to talking with him or her as early and as much as they would with an average child, or a deaf child who does not have access to an appropriate communication mode may encounter developmental difficulties, particularly in theories of mind acquisition.[3]

As signs are easier to perceive and to distinguish from each other, compared to oral words, for a profoundly deaf child, we consider that deaf children exposed to sign language have an easier access to and better understanding of communication than deaf children exposed to spoken language only. Harris (1978) showed that deaf children of hearing parents are not exposed to communication at the same time as deaf children of

---

[2]Note that we use the term *understand* and not *master*, implying that we take into account the age at which children are able to understand those features, but are not, however, able to use them correctly.
[3]The term *talking* should be understood as meaning either *signing to* or *speaking to*.

deaf parents, because deaf parents sign to their child, be the latter deaf or not—note that there exist deaf children of oral deaf parents, but they are rare and they have not been sufficiently studied in order to be included here. One could think that Harris' results do not reflect the actual situation any more, as intervention programs are beginning earlier and earlier. However, Mayberry (1989) observed that out of 24 deaf children of hearing parents, one third have no one to communicate with, and a second third communicate only with their mother, because of a lack of sign language knowledge in the family. This shows that even if deafness is detected at an early stage, hearing parents do not necessarily choose to learn sign language. Besides, as they become aware of their child's deafness, hearing parents may tend to initiate an educational relationship with their child instead of the common playful one.

Thus, hearing parents begin to communicate effectively later in the development of their deaf child, compared to deaf parents, and their communication style also does not seem to be optimal. For example, it was proved to be less effective than that of a hearing mother of hearing children (Cross, Johnson-Morris, & Nienhuys, 1980; but on a small sample, see also Gregory, 1976). However, parental auditory status is not the only factor that influences communication quality—communication mode is another such factor: Greenberg (1980) noted, in 28 dyads communicating orally or in simultaneous communication, a trend (.07) of a higher communication competence in simultaneous communication dyads over oral ones. Their linguistic interactions are longer and more complex. It is worth noting that this poor linguistic environment is observed in familial (Mather, 1990) as well as in most educational milieus (Harrison, Layton, & Taylor, 1987).

It is generally assumed that hearing mothers of deaf children are more directive and intrusive than deaf mothers and hearing mothers of hearing children in their verbal and nonverbal interactions (Bonkowski, Gavelek, & Akamatsu, 1991; Marschark, 1993; Meadow-Orlans, 1990).[4] This higher level of control also tends to be coupled with a weaker adjustment to the child's ongoing activities. Hearing mothers of 2-year-old deaf children refer more often to their own behavior and less to that of their child, less to their attentional focus, than do hearing mothers of hearing children (Cross et al., 1980; Spencer & Gutfreund, 1990). Now, in order to change the focus of attention, one has to inhibit his/her ongoing

---

[4]See Lederberg (1993), who maintains that hearing mothers of hearing children are not more intrusive when child linguistic competency is controlled. Let us note that in young children, deaf children of Deaf parents have a higher linguistic achievment (and competency) than deaf children born to hearing parents. Thus, with an average sample of children, there are more intrusive mothers in the group of hearing mothers of deaf children as compared to the other groups.

cognitive activity and processes, then to redirect his/her attention and cognitive processes, a task that may be difficult for young children. This process for attentional recentration requires some energy from the child's working memory. This energy will finally not be available to go as deeply into the new activity and into communication as when the children are left alone with the one and same former activity.

Let us finally note that the communication mode chosen by hearing parents of deaf children is combined with uncertainty (albeit unconscious) as to which of their child's skills to promote (Musselman & Churchill, 1991). These authors have observed, in 17 hearing mother–deaf child oralist dyads and 17 hearing mother–deaf child total communication dyads, that for oralist dyads, maternal input seems to be related to the child's oral skills. Yet, for total communication dyads this maternal input seems to be related to the child's social development. The hearing mothers who use total communication (unconsciously) supply their deaf children with a reference frame for social actions, a frame with which to modulate their desires, actions, and so forth, inducing the children to inhibit their own thoughts in order to consider those of others.

Thus, deaf children of hearing parents have a late access to communication compared to deaf children of deaf parents—and, for deaf children of hearing parents, the oralists compared to the signers. Besides, this communication is poorer (with a weak activation of metacognition), more restrained (henceforth less creative, in relation to flexibility, shown later), and less optimal. The deaf children of hearing parents finally receive, for these reasons, fewer explanations about emotions, or on action motives (an idea already stated by Peterson and Siegal, 1995; see also Harris, 1992; Marschark, 1993 who have noted fewer conversations about imaginary or unobservable topics in hearing parents–deaf child dyads), which should on principle have an influence on theories of mind development (Dunn, 1994; Dunn et al., 1987; Jenkins & Astington, 1996; Perner et al., 1994).

Pretense and visual perspective taking are considered to be precursors of theories of mind. We addressed previously the possible interest of sign language on visual perspective taking in that children (be they deaf or hearing) who are accustomed early to sign language could master perspective taking earlier than nonsigning children.

Concerning pretense, the linguistic modality *per se* does not seem to matter as much as communication quality and maternal style. As long as a code is easily and fully accessible to the children, they can have access to behavior that is part of higher constituents of pretend play, for example, preplanning, substitution, and so forth. (Spencer, 1996; Spencer & Deyo,

1993). In fact, Spencer (1996) noted that linguistic competency is associated with sequenced and preplanned play.

Children whose actions are constrained—because of the directiveness of the mother or because she engages in an educational relationship with her child centered on her own interests instead of a playful relationship tuned to the child's activity—may be delayed in pretend play development. This idea is supported by individual differences reported by Spencer, Deyo, & Grindstaff (1990): They note that the mother of the child who demonstrated the highest amount of symbolic play engaged herself fully in the play, and "never tried to redirect [her daughter's] attention to a new toy while she was already engaged with a toy" (p. 402). In contrast, the mother of the child who demonstrated the lowest amount of pretend play "rarely participated fully" in the play, she "frequently interrupted her child's play" and finally tried to engage her child in an educational activity.

Thus, deaf children of deaf parents could attain higher levels of mastery on pretend play compared to deaf children of hearing parents, due to maternal tuning,[5] deaf parents being better tuned to their deaf child than hearing parents are. Furthermore, Pretend play, could be influenced by maternal adjustment in another way, as the latter is related to child cognitive flexibility (Calderon, Greenberg, & Kusché, 1991, on 10-year-old subjects). In addition, sign language usage could be related to cognitive flexibility, as noted by Courtin (1997) on a cognitive categorization task in which deaf children of deaf parents proved to be more flexible than hearing children. It should be noted that flexibility is important for pretend play, in order to go from one cognitive representation to another—for example, a telephone to a banana. In this case the flexibility is a creative one, which depends on the child, and could be compared to creative flexibility observed in sign language by Marschark and West (1985), and by Marschark, West, Nall, and Everhart (1986). This creative flexibility could lead to an analytical one, in which the child selects, among the whole ideas and/or linguistic expressions generated, those that may be suited for solving the one and same task, question, thus depending on the task demands; this analytical flexibility has been exemplified elsewhere (Courtin, 1997). One can think that the latter flexibility is involved in theories of mind.

---

[5]Note that this effect was not observed by Spencer (1996). However, deaf subjects were not quite homogeneously selected concerning their level of deafness (moderate to profound, unaided). Now deaf children of hearing parents could be less deaf than second generation ones. Besides, the use of hearing aids could differ between the two groups as Deaf parents, being part of the Deaf community, may be reluctant to use these aids at home, during play periods.

THEORIES OF MIND IN DEAF CHILDREN

Little research has been carried out on deaf children's theories of mind. The first published test (Peterson & Siegal, 1995; see Gray and Hosie, 1996; Steeds, Rowe and Dowker, 1997, for a presentation) was performed on 24 deaf children ages 8 to 13, in total communication settings. The authors reported that most of these children failed to complete a task usually achieved by most of the 4-year-old hearing children, which has since been confirmed on a wider sample (Peterson & Siegal, 1996). However, each child was tested on only one false belief task and was then said to master or fail on theories of mind on this sole base, which seems to be quite a premature conclusion. Besides, this study does not provide much information on which factors are responsible for success and failure on these tasks.

An Experimental Study

We are now working on theories of mind development in deaf children with profound hearing losses. Given the previous analyses on the effects of early communication, on parental hearing status, and on precursors such as visual perspective taking (but also given the possible importance of impulse control and flexibility on this development), we have formed six deaf subject groups: deaf children of deaf parents communicating in sign language *versus* orally, deaf children of hearing parents with deaf siblings communicating in sign *versus* oral language, deaf children of hearing parents communicating in sign language *versus* orally, and a seventh group, a control, of hearing children. All deaf children were diagnosed audiologically as profoundly deaf (i.e., losses of pure tone receptivity of more than 90 dB in the better ear). They were drawn from public and private schools for deaf children throughout France. No subject had any known associated physical or mental disability. In each of these seven subject groups, five age classes were formed (from 4 to 8 years of age).

Each group was observed on 11 to 14 theories of mind tasks (3 tasks for testing visual perspective-taking abilities, 6 for appearance–reality distinction, 3 for first-order false beliefs, 1 for second-order false beliefs, 1 for conceptual perspective taking) as well as on three to five executive function tasks (trail-making test, matching familiar figure test, go–no go task, competing motor program test, conditional competing-motor program test), the exact number depending on the child's age. Our results are presented on first-order false beliefs as these are the tasks that have been studied by other researchers (Peterson & Siegal, 1995, 1996; Steeds, Rowe, & Dowker, 1997).

First, it is relevant that the hearing control children were chosen from the lower socioeconomic class in order to match the class that is, unfortunately, often the one of adult Deaf signers in France. Second, the results presented here are those of children who were able to understand the instructions of at least all but three theories-of-mind tasks. Thus, a rather large group of the children tested by the Deaf researcher (C.C.) was excluded, coming from both the oral and the signing group—but it is worthy of note that no second generation deaf child had to be excluded. Our results may then not reflect the real skills of an average deaf population. Third, unlike some authors, we report only the results of children who have correctly passed the different control questions, to be sure that any error from the child is due to theories of mind misunderstanding and not to a mere linguistic or memory matter. No second-generation deaf child has been excluded for this reason, though 5 signing and 12 oralist children born to hearing parents had to be excluded.

The results presented in this chapter concern 102 children, divided into four main auditory status groups:

- 23 hearing children (fourteen 4-year-olds and nine 5-year-olds)
- 13 second-generation signing deaf children (eight 5-year-olds and five 6-year olds)
- 22 signing deaf children born to hearing parents (three 6-year-olds, nine 7-year-olds, and ten 8-year-olds)
- 44 oral deaf children born to hearing parents (fifteen 6-year-olds, nineteen 7-year-olds, and ten 8-year-olds)

Given the small sample size of some age groups, we first tested the possible effect of age in each one of the four main groups. In the hearing children group, there is only a trend for better performances in the 5-year-old (mean age: 5;5 years) subgroup, compared to the 4-year-old one (mean age: 4;5 years); 28.6% of the 4-year-old children—4 out of 14—succeeding on at least two out of the three tasks, compared to 66.7%—six out of nine—of the 5-year-olds. We consider these two subgroups separately in the next analysis.

For deaf children, performance analyses always failed to reveal an effect of age on false-belief performances. Data has therefore been combined in each group, leading to one group of 13 five-year-old deaf children of deaf parents (mean age: 5;4 years), a second group of 22 seven-year-old signing deaf children of hearing parents (mean age: 7;5 years), and a third one of 44 seven-year-old oral deaf children born to hearing parents (mean age: 7;0 years).

The percentages of children passing at least two out of the three false-belief tasks are presented for each group in Fig. 4.1. It is noteworthy

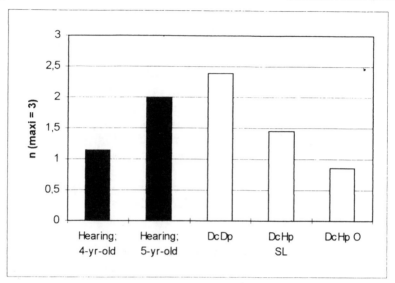

FIG. 4.1. Success in false beliefs using the 2 out of 3 criteria, according to subject group. (With DcDp = 5-year-old deaf children of deaf parents; DcHp SL = 7-year-old signing deaf children of hearing parents; DcHp O = 7-year-old oral deaf children of hearing parents.)

that more 5-year-old deaf children of deaf parents attained the success criterion (indeed, all these deaf children succeeded) compared to any other subject group. They thus differ from 4-year-old hearing children as well as from 5-year-old ones. They also outperform 7-year-old deaf children of hearing parents, whether these children communicate in sign language or orally. Five-year-old hearing children are only slightly more numerous in attaining the success criterion than 7-year-old signing deaf children of hearing parents, but much more numerous than 7-year-old oral deaf children. When comparing 7-year-old deaf children of hearing parents, we note that more children using sign language succeeded in attaining the criterion compared to children communicating orally. Finally, 4-year-old hearing children do not notably differ from 7-year-old signing and oral deaf children of hearing parents.

Thus, when considering the number of children succeeding on at least two out of three false-belief tasks, it appears that 5-year-old deaf children of deaf parents outperform 5-year-old hearing children. The latter tend to surpass 7-year-old signing deaf children of hearing parents, themselves, tending to outperform 4-year-old hearing children. Four-year-olds do not differ from 7-year-old oral deaf children of hearing parents.

When analyzing the mean number of tasks succeeded by each subject group (see Fig. 4.2), it appears that 5-year-old deaf children of deaf parents again achieve the higher mean number of success, followed by the 5-year-old hearing children. However, the two subject groups will not be considered further to differ from each other, as the observed performance differences appear to be rather slight. Concerning the other performance comparisons, analysis of the mean number of tasks achieved by subject groups supports the hierarchy of success obtained from the preceding analysis (on the number of children passing at least two out of the three false-belief tasks).

DISCUSSION AND CONCLUDING REMARKS

One could first be surprised by the relatively low success rate on false-belief tasks of hearing children, as they are generally said to succeed on these tasks by 4 years of age. However, this is not the first time that such results have been noted in a French sample (e.g., Melot et al., 1995). Furthermore, it is important to keep in mind the fact that the hearing children we tested are not from the usual socioeconomic middle class. It is possible that the social milieu also mediates the development of theories of mind.

A more important point concerning our results is that 5-year-old signing deaf children of deaf parents give similar—or even better, depend-

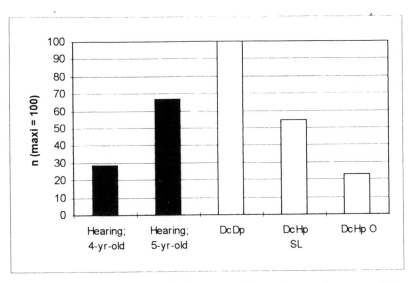

FIG. 4.2. Mean number of tasks succeeded out of 3, according to subject group (with DcDp = 5-year-old deaf children of deaf parents; DcHp SL = 7-year-old signing deaf children of hearing parents; DcHp O = 7-year-old oral deaf children of hearing parents).

ing on the comparison mode chosen—performances than 5-year-old hearing children. Because of the small number of subjects in each, it seems safest to conclude that these two subject groups do not differ from each other. This prevents us for the moment from confirming or excluding the idea of a promoting role that sign language could have on theories of mind development, as presented later in this chapter. Four-year-old signing deaf children of deaf parents should be tested in order to compare their performances on false beliefs with those of hearing children. This would be a difficult project to carry out in France, and we hope that American researchers will take up the challenge.

It clearly emerges from our results that 5-year-old second-generation deaf children outperform 7-year-old deaf children born to hearing parents and, in this latter group, that signing children outperform oral ones. To know what may engender such performance differences, we have worked on the impulse control and cognitive flexibility and their relation to false beliefs. Impulse control, as part of cognitive inhibition abilities in general, is important for false-belief success, as found by Perner (1991). The young child may be prone to respond immediately to the experimenter's question, leading to a wrong answer, though the child does succeed in a similar task when a *stop and think* condition is introduced just before asking him or her for his or her response.

Impulse control is estimated here with a test similar to the matching familiar figure test (Kagan, Rosman, Day, Albert, & Phillips, 1964), in which each subject is asked to select the one out of six drawings that is the same as the model. We compared times for first responses on the nine items of our test between the three deaf subject groups. Contrary to some authors (e.g., Harris, 1978), we did not note any difference of impulse control between the three groups, though 7-year-old oral deaf children did make more errors than the two other groups. At first, it seemed that the differences of false-belief performances observed between these three groups could not be ascribed to a higher impulsivity of 7-year-old deaf children born to hearing parents. However, an identical swiftness in response from deaf children of deaf parents *versus* those of hearing parents may be due to different cognitive processes. In the former, given their mastery on false beliefs, the task may appear to be quite easy and thus not to require a long reflection time. In deaf children of hearing parents, impulsivity may be caused by a weaker cerebral maturation (see Wolff & Thatcher, 1990, for cerebral development of deaf children, and Pascual-Leone & Baillargeon, 1994, for cerebral "localization" of cognitive inhibitory processes). The children may thus not be able to inhibit their propensity for immediate response and thereafter forget to analyze the experimenter's statements or the task itself, leading to more errors on the matching familiar figure test (and false-belief tasks) with the identical swiftness of response. Besides, these experimenter's statements may be more difficult to understand for the deaf children of hearing parents as compared to those born to deaf parents, requiring more effort from working memory in order to be studied, using energy which is no longer available for inhibition processes. Introducing a stop-and-think condition could be most useful here.

We note that on an individual level, impulse control and false-belief successes do not correlate with each other for 5-year-old deaf children of deaf parents nor for 7-year-old signing deaf children of hearing parents, but do correlate for 7-year-old oral deaf children of hearing parents ($r_{43} = .50, p = .001$). A difficulty is that for the latter deaf children all measures (false beliefs, time, and errors on the matching familiar figure test, and trail-making test) correlate with each other, as discussed later.

Another point to study is the relationship between false beliefs and cognitive flexibility. Failure on a false-belief task is generally assumed to be proof of the child's inability (or difficulty) to consider the conceptual perspective of someone who knows less than the child him/herself about a given critical fact. The question remains of whether this is an inability or a difficulty. One idea is that the child cannot admit another perspective than his or her own, and that there exists only one conception of reality, one knowledge, and thus only one way to act; for this reason succeeding on a false-belief task is impossible for the child. Another idea is that the child does admit multiple perspectives for the same fact, but has difficulty in going back and forth from one perspective to the other in harmony with the task demands; for this reason succeeding on a false-belief task is difficult for the child. It is worth noting that this cognitive flexibility required for success on false-belief tasks is based on activating and inhibitory processes acting on the adequate variables.[6]

Flexibility has been estimated with a version of the trail making test (Reitan, 1958) that we adapted for preschoolers. Because age had no effect on success in this task, results were combined according to subject group. It appeared that 5-year-old deaf children of deaf parents were only slightly more flexible than 7-year-old signing deaf children of hearing parents but were much more flexible than 7-year-old oral ones. Similarly, 7-year-old signing deaf children of hearing parents were more flexible than oral ones. Thus, a similar success pattern was observed in flexibility and in false beliefs, and one could be inclined to conclude that the former is partly the cause of the latter.

---

[6]This idea has been proposed by Melot & Houdé (in press) concerning the appearance–reality distinction tasks.

However, one could also think those similar performances on the different tasks were due to children's global ability or inability. Five-year-old deaf children of deaf parents were skillful in all tasks, which resulted in a highly homogeneous group. Given the ceiling effect on each false-belief task, success did not correlate with flexibility: In fact, there is no correlation between the different measures. In the 7-year-old oral deaf children group, there existed a global ability of some of those children, compared with a global difficulty of some of the others, that led to a high heterogeneity. Thus, for the oral group—in which all measures correlate with each other—the relationship between false belief and flexibility reaches the .02 significance rate.

Then, for those two groups, it is quite hard to determine whether flexibility engendered false-beliefs success or whether success on both tasks was due to general cognitive development. Seven-year-old signing deaf children of hearing parents could prove to be useful in clarifying this question, as they formed a rather heterogeneous group that was rather competent. However, given the small subject sample (only 12 subjects were available for computation as the 8-year-old deaf children were not tested on the trail-making test), this correlation failed to reach significance ($r_{11} = .43, p = .093$).

To sum up, deaf children of deaf parents did succeed on false belief tasks at least at the same age as hearing children. Signing deaf children of hearing parents (mean age: 7;5 years) achieved performances falling between those of 4- and 5-year-old hearing children, whereas oral deaf children (mean age: 7;0 years) hardly equaled 4-year-old hearing children's performances—this latter deaf group obtained quite similar results to those obtained by deaf children in the Peterson and Siegal studies (1995, 1996). We failed to confirm the possible relationship between cognitive flexibility and false beliefs; this point is under further investigation on other theories-of-mind tasks and, for false beliefs, on wider samples (however, our results tended to support the suggestion of a promoting role of sign language on cognitive flexibility, expressed by Courtin [1997]). How, then, may one consider the performance differences noted among the three groups of deaf children?

Dividing the children into auditory status groups may lead one to regard communication competence as playing the major role. However, the fact that the performance of the 7-year-old signing deaf children with hearing parents did not improve with age, contrary to their communication skills, did not seem to support this idea. It is a reality that the 7-year-old oral deaf children achieving the highest performances on false beliefs were indeed those having *good* communication skills as estimated by their teachers and by the experimenter. However, it is worth noting that these same oral deaf children's success on false-belief tests often originated from the highest socioeconomic backgrounds. This social factor should not be neglected, as the performance of hearing children reminds us (see, for example, Geers & Moog, 1989, for a relation between socioeconomic status and deaf children's oral skills).

Furthermore, all deaf children born to hearing parents tested were capable of communication, as we have excluded any child who did not understand the oral or signed instructions as well as those children failing on false belief control questions—but some differences in ease of understanding are still possible, with some potential consequences on inhibitory processes; a stop-and-think condition would once again be useful. It would thus not be justifiable to ascribe the performance differences on false beliefs solely to linguistic competence differences. Concerning communication, in addition to the mode, only its early use may really have differed between deaf children groups, as noted earlier. This would then imply a rather frozen situation, in which the success of deaf children in false-belief tasks (and on theories-of-mind in general) would be predictable from the age of their first exposure to language. This seems to be a quite simplistic and pessimistic suggestion.

It is noteworthy that some of the deaf children born to hearing parents we tested, who were exposed to sign language after failing to develop oral skills, succeeded on false-belief tasks (note that the results obtained by those children are not taken into account in the data analyses presented in this chapter). It is thus possible that some of the deaf children who failed on false beliefs in the present study will nevertheless subsequently develop some theories-of-mind skills. The fact that, on the whole, the performance of deaf children does not improve with age, at least for the age range examined here, is quite disconcerting, but does not go against the precedent idea, as our present study employs a cross-sectional method. Only longitudinal research could clarify this point.

It seems that success in false belief tasks—and certainly on all other theories of mind tasks—is a function of a crossing-over, a combination between communication mode and *parental variables*, that is, according to a contextualist–interactionist model, such as that proposed by Clark (1993). Communication mode has an effect on early communication fluency and certainly, for sign languages, on visual perspective taking and flexibility. Parental variables include hearing status (and then communication mode); this is the major variable that leads to maternal tuning toward the child (and the child's pretend play quality), desires and wills concerning the child's development. Deaf children born to signing deaf parents are in an optimal position in this regard, as they stand at the golden mean of this crossing. Deaf children of hearing parents are, for a certain period of time, deprived of sign language and stand at the bottom of the parental variables scale. Oral children remain in this situation—some parents may nevertheless develop a better sense of tuning, their position is not necessarily fixed—whereas signing ones are then introduced to sign language, which may finally lead to improvement in maternal tuning, in visual perspective taking, and progressively the child could master theories-of-mind. Thus the observed hierarchy in theories-of-mind achievement, estimated through false-beliefs success, among deaf children.

Once this hierarchy is established, it would be useful to study atypical children, such as hearing children born to signing deaf parents. Those children are accustomed to visual perspective taking because of their deaf parents signing to them; they thus should outperform average hearing children, as long as our hypotheses are correct. They may also, however, outperform second-generation deaf children, because hearing children can attend to discussions (and conflicts) not directed toward them, contrary to deaf children who have to be in eye-contact with others in order to perceive conversations. These conversations the hearing child hears—though not being the intended addressee—may provide information on representational conflicts, hence promoting conceptual perspective taking and theories-of-mind in general—but this latter factor does not seem to be a very important promoting one, as our present results on false beliefs in 5-year-old hearing *versus* second generation deaf children are not in favor of the first ones. Yet, this remains an idea to be explored.

It would also be worthwhile to determine the performances of oral second generation deaf children (this is part of our ongoing work) as they lack sign language, but are quite equal in every other way to second generation signing deaf children. These two populations would permit further investigations into the role of sign language on children's cognitive development.

REFERENCES

Astington, J. W., Harris, P. L., & Olson. D. R. (Eds.). (1988). *Developing theories of mind.* New York: Cambridge University Press.

Baldwin, D. A., & Moses, L. J. (1994). Early understanding of referential intent and attentional focus: Evidence from language and emotion. In C. Lewis & P. Mitchell (Eds.), *Children's early understanding of mind: Origins and development* (pp. 133–156). Hillsdale, NJ: Lawrence Erlbaum Associates.

Bellugi, U., O'Grady, L., Lillo-Martin, D., O'Grady Hynes, M., Van Hoek, K., & Corina, D. (1990). Enhancement of spatial cognition in deaf children. In V. Volterra & C. Erting (Eds.), *From gesture to language in hearing and deaf children* (pp. 278–299). Berlin: Springer-Verlag.

Bonkowski, N., Gavelek, J., & Akamatsu, T. (1991). Education and the social construction of mind: Vygotskian perspectives on the cognitive development of deaf children. In D. S. Martin (Ed.), *Advances in cognition, education, and deafness* (pp. 185–194). Washington, DC: Gallaudet University Press.

Bretherton, I., & Beeghly, M. (1982). Talking about internal states: The acquisition of an explicit theory of mind. *Developmental Psychology, 18*, 906–921.

Brown, J. R., & Dunn, J. (1991). "You can cry Mum": The social and developmental implications of talk about internal states. *British Journal of Developmental Psychology, 9*, 237–256.

Calderon, R., Greenberg, M. T., & Kusché, C. A. (1991). The influence of family coping on the cognitive and social skills of deaf children. In D. S. Martin (Ed.), *Advances in cognition, education and deafness* (pp. 195–200). Washington, DC: Gallaudet University Press.

Clark, M. D. (1993). A contextual/interactionist model and its relationship to deafness research. In M. Marschark & M. D. Clark (Eds.), *Psychological perspectives on deafness* (pp. 353–362). Hillsdale, NJ: Lawrence Erlbaum Associates.

Courtin, C. (1996). Pour une relecture critique des travaux de Pierre Oléron sur les enfants sourds. *Bulletin de Psychologie, 50*(1), 57–62.

Courtin, C. (1997). Does sign language provide deaf children with an abstraction advantage? Evidence from a categorization task. *Journal of Deaf Studies and Deaf Education, 2*, (3), 161–171.

Cross, T. G., Johnson-Morris, J. E., & Nienhuys, T. G. (1980). Linguistic feedback and maternal speech: Comparisons of mothers addressing hearing and hearing-impaired children. *First Language, 1*, 163–189.

Dunn, J. (1994). Changing minds and changing relationships. In C. Lewis & P. Mitchell (Eds.), *Children's early understanding of mind: Origins and development* (pp. 297–310). Hillsdale, NJ: Lawrence Erlbaum Associates.

Dunn, J., Bretherton, I., & Munn, P. (1987). Conversations about feeling states between mothers and their young children. *Developmental Psychology, 23*, 132–139.

Flavell, J. H. (1988). The development of children's knowledge about the mind: From cognitive connections to mental representations. In J. W. Astington, P. L. Harris, & D. R. Olson (Eds.), *Developing theories of mind* (pp. 244–267). New York: Cambridge University Press.

Flavell, J. H., Everett, B. A., Croft, K., & Flavell, E. R. (1981). Young children's knowledge about visual perception: Further evidence for the level 1–level 2 distinction. *Developmental Psychology, 17*, 99–103.

Flavell, J. H., Flavell, E. R., & Green, F. L. (1983). Development of the appearance–reality distinction. *Cognitive Psychology, 15*, 95–120.

Flavell, J. H., Flavell, E. R., & Green, F. L. (1987). Young children's knowledge about the apparent–real and pretend–real distinction. *Developmental Psychology, 23*, 816–822.

Flavell, J. H., Green, F. L., & Flavell, E. R. (1986). Development of knowledge about the appearance–reality distinction. *Monographs of the Society for Research in Child Development, 51* (1, serial No. 212).

Flavell, J. H., Miller, P. H., & Miller, S. (1993). *Cognitive Development*. (3rd Ed.). Englewood Cliffs, NJ: Prentice-Hall.

Geers, A., & Moog, J. (1989). Factors predictive of the development of literacy in profoudly hearing-impaired adolescents. *Volta Review, 91*, 69–86.

Gopnik, A., & Astington, J. W. (1988). Children's understanding of representational change and its relation to the understanding of false belief and the appearance-reality distinction. *Child Development, 59*, 26–37.

Gopnik, A., Slaughter, V., & Meltzoff, A. (1994). Changing your views: How understanding visual perception can lead to a new theory of mind. In C. Lewis & P.

Mitchell (Eds.), *Children's early understanding of mind: Origins and development* (pp. 157–181). Hillsdale, NJ: Lawrence Erlbaum Associates.

Gopnik, A., & Wellman, H. M. (1992). Why the child's theory of mind really *is* a theory. *Mind and Language, 7,* 145–172.

Gray, C. D., & Hosie, J. A. (1996). Deafness, story understanding, and theory of mind. *Journal of Deaf Studies and Deaf Education, 1,* 217–233.

Greenberg, M. T. (1980). Social interaction between deaf preschoolers and their mothers: The effects of communication method and communication competence. *Developmental Psychology, 16,* 465–474.

Gregory, S. (1976). *The deaf child and his family.* New York: Halsted.

Harris, M. (1992). *Language experience and early language development.* Hove, UK: Lawrence Erlbaum Associates.

Harris, M. (1996). Desires, beliefs, and language. In P. Carruthers & P. K. Smith (Eds.), *Theories of theories of mind* (pp. 200–220). London: Cambridge University Press.

Harris, R. I. (1978). The relationship of impulse control to parent hearing status, manual communication, and academic achievement in deaf children. *American Annals of the Deaf, 123,* 52–67.

Harrison, M. F., Layton, T. L., & Taylor, T. D. (1987). Antecedent and consequent stimuli in teacher–child dyads. *American Annals of the Deaf, 132,* 227–231.

Hoffmeister, R., & Wilbur, R. B. (1980). Developmental: the acquisition of sign language. In H. Lane & F. Grosjean (Eds.), *Recent perspectives on American Sign Language* (pp. 61–78). Hillsdale, NJ: Lawrence Erlbaum Associates.

Jenkins, J. M., & Astington, J. W. (1996). Cognitive factors and family structure associated with theory of mind development in young children. *Developmental Psychology, 32,* 70–78.

Kagan, J., Rosman, B. L., Day, L., Albert, J., & Phillips, W. (1964). Information processing in the child: Significance of analytical and reflective attitudes. *Psychological Monographs, 78,* No. 578.

Klima, E. S., & Bellugi, U. (1979). *The signs of language.* Cambridge, MA: Harvard University Press.

Lederberg, A. (1993). The impact of deafness on mother–child and peer relationships. In M. Marschark & M. D. Clark (Eds.), *Psychological perspectives on deafness* (pp. 93–119). Hillsdale, NJ: Lawrence Erlbaum Associates.

Lewis, C., & Mitchell, P. (Eds.). (1994). *Children's early understanding of mind: Origins and development.* Hillsdale, NJ: Lawrence Erlbaum Associates.

Lillo-Martin, D., Bellugi, U., Struxness, L., & O'Grady, M. (1985). The acquisition of spatially organized syntax. *Papers and Reports on Child Language Development, 24,* 70–78.

Marschark, M. (1993). *Psychological development of deaf children.* New York: Oxford University Press.

Marschark, M., & West, S. A. (1985). Creative language abilities in deaf children. *Journal of Speech and Hearing Research, 28,* 73–78.

Marschark, M., West, S. A., Nall, L., & Everhart, V. (1986). Development of creative language devices in signed and oral production. *Journal of Experimental Child Psychology, 41,* 534–550.

Mather, S. M. (1990). Home and classroom communication. In D. F. Moores & K. P. Meadow-Orlans (Eds.), *Educational and developmental aspects of deafness* (pp. 232–254). Washington DC: Gallaudet University Press.

Mayberry, R. I. (1989). *Deaf children's reading comprehension in relation to sign language structure and input.* Paper presented at the Biennial Meeting of the Society for Research in Child Development, Kansas City, MO.

Meadow-Orlans, K. P. (1990). Research on developmental aspects of deafness. In D. F. Moores & K. P. Meadow-Orlans (Eds.), *Educational and developmental aspects of deafness* (pp. 283–298). Washington, DC: Gallaudet University Press.

Melot, A. M., & Houdé, O. (in press). Categorization and theories of mind: The case of the appearance/reality distinction. *Current Psychology of Cognition*.

Melot, A. M., Houdé, O., Courtel, S., & Soenen, L. (1995). *False beliefs attribution, distinction between appearance and reality, and visual perspective taking: Do they develop simultaneously?* Paper presented at the 25th Annual Symposim of the Jean Piaget Society. Berkeley.

Moses, L. J., & Flavell, J. H. (1990). Inferring false beliefs from actions and reactions. *Child Development, 61*, 929–945.

Musselman, C., & Churchill, A. (1991). Conversation control in mother–child dyads. Auditory–oral versus total communication. *American Annals of the Deaf, 136*, 5–16.

Pascual-Leone, J., & Baillargeon, R. (1994). Developmental measurement of mental attention. *International Journal of Behavioral Development, 17*, 161–200.

Perner, J. (1991). *Understanding the representational mind*. Cambridge, MA: MIT Press.

Perner, J., Ruffman, T., & Leekam, S. R. (1994). Theory of mind is contagious: You catch it from your sibs. *Child Development, 65*, 1228–1238.

Peterson, C. P., & Siegal, M. (1995). Deafness, conversation and theory of mind. *Journal of Child Psychology, Psychiatry and Allied Disciplines, 36*, 458–474.

Peterson, C. P., & Siegal, M. (1996). *The domain-specificity of knowledge in normal, autistic and deaf children: Differentiation between the biological, physical and psychological thinking*. Paper presented at the 14th Biennial Meetings of ISSBD, Quebec City, Canada.

Petitto, L. A., & Bellugi, U. (1988). Spatial cognition and brain organization: Clues from the acquisition of a language in space. In J. Stiles-Davis, M. Kritchevsky, & U. Bellugi (Eds.), *Spatial cognition: Brain bases and development* (pp 299–326). Hillsdale, NJ: Lawrence Erlbaum Associates.

Poulin, C., & Miller, C. (1995). On narrative discourse and point of view in Quebec Sign Language. In K. Emmorey & J. Reilly (Eds.), *Language, gesture, and space* (pp. 117–131). Hillsdale, NJ: Lawrence Erlbaum Associates.

Reitan, R. M. (1958). Validity of the Trail Making test as an indication of organic brain damage. *Perceptual and Motor Skills, 8*, 271–276.

Shatz, M. (1994). Theory of mind and the development of social–linguistic intelligence in early childhood. In C. Lewis & P. Mitchell (Eds.), *Children's early understanding of mind: Origins and development* (pp. 311–329). Hillsdale, NJ: Lawrence Erlbaum Associates.

Shatz, M., Wellman, H. M., & Silber, S. (1983). The acquisition of mental terms: A systematic investigation of the first reference to mental state. *Cognition, 14*, 301–321.

Spencer, P. E. (1996). The association between language and symbolic play at two years: Evidence from deaf toddlers. *Child Development, 67*, 867–876.

Spencer, P. E., & Deyo, D. A. (1993). Cognitive and social aspects of deaf children play. In M. Marschark & M. D. Clark (Eds.), *Psychological perspectives on deafness* (pp. 65–91). Hillsdale, NJ: Lawrence Erlbaum Associates.

Spencer, P. E., Deyo, D., & Grindstaff, N. (1990). Symbolic play behavior of deaf and hearing toddlers. In D. F. Moores & K. P. Meadow-Orlans (Eds.), *Educational and developmental aspects of deafness* (pp. 390–406). Washington, DC: Gallaudet University Press.

Spencer, P. E., & Gutfreund, M. K. (1990). Directiveness in mother-infant interactions. In D. F. Moores & K. P. Meadow-Orlans (Eds.), *Educational and developmental aspects of deafness* (pp. 350–365). Washington, DC: Gallaudet University Press.

Steeds, L., Rowe, K., & Dowker, A. (1997). Deaf children's understanding of beliefs and desires. *Journal of Deaf Studies and Deaf Education, 2* (3), 185–195.

Wellman, H. M. (1988). First steps in the child's theorizing about the mind. In J. Astington, P. Harris, & D. Olson (Eds.), *Developing theories of mind* (pp. 64–92). New York: Cambridge University Press.

Wellman, H. M. (1990). *The child's theory of mind.* Cambridge, MA: MIT Press: Bradford Books.

Wellman, H. M., & Estes, D. (1986). Early understanding of mental entities: A reexamination of chidlhood realism. *Child Development, 57,* 910–923.

Wilbur R. (1987). *American Sign Language: Linguistic and applied dimensions.* Boston: Little, Brown.

Wimmer, H., & Perner, J. (1983). Beliefs about beliefs: Representation and constraining function of wrong beliefs in young children's understanding of deception. *Cognition, 13,* 103–128.

Wolff, A. B., & Thatcher, R. W. (1990). Cortical reorganization in deaf children. *Journal of Clinical and Experimental Neuropsychology, 12,* 209–221.

5

Effects of Phonetically Augmented Lipspeech on the Development of Phonological Representations in Deaf Children

Jacqueline Leybaert
Laboratoire de Psychologie Expérimentale, Université Libre de Bruxelles

It is now widely recognized that deafness is compatible with normal language development, provided that deaf children are reared in a linguistic environment suitable for their sensory possibilities. This generally implies that language could be perceived through the visual modality. This is the case for visual-manual sign languages. A number of studies showed strong similarities between the formal characteristics, acquisition, and breakdowns of sign languages and spoken languages (see e.g., Bellugi, Poizner, & Klima, 1989; Pettito & Marentette, 1991; Poizner, Klima, & Bellugi, 1987). Native signers also appear to rely on mental representations of signs in situations in which hearing subjects rely on speech phonological representations (see Marschark, chap. 3, this volume). For example, native signers use sign representations in a task of ordered recall of signed stimuli (Hanson, 1982). Finally, the presentations of signed stimuli elicit electrophysiological responses in native signers similar to those elicited by written words in hearing subjects (Neville, 1991; Neville, Coffey, Lawson, Fischer, Emmorey, & Bellugi, 1997). Taken together, these data suggest that there are strong constraints on acquisition and processing of formal languages, and that these constraints are independent of the modality through which language is acquired.

In light of the linguisitic and cognitive skills achieved by deaf children reared with sign language, the linguistic and cognitive abilities of deaf children in oral language are surprisingly poor. Speech onset is delayed and the rate of speech development is slow (Quigley & Kretschmer, 1982). Phonological development is delayed and even deviant (Dodd, 1976), with deaf children making some errors that are atypical of hearing children. Lexical and morpho-syntactical development also is strongly delayed and limited, as Griswold and Cummings (1974) reported that at 4 or 5 years of age, deaf children had an expressive vocabulary of under 500 words, compared to the 3,500 words of hearing children. Why is it so, given the fact that deaf children have an intact potential of linguistic development, as demonstrated by their ability to acquire a sign language?

Spoken languages have evolved to be heard, not seen (Studdert-Kennedy, 1988). Lipreading, although providing information about some phonological contrasts, does not allow the perception of all. Lip movements give some clues about place of articulation, but no clues at all about features like nasality and voicing (Erber, 1969; Walden, Prosek, Montgomery, Scherr, & Jones, 1977). For example, visual information allows the discrimination of consonants articulated in the front from those articulated in the back of the mouth, but does not permit differentiation of consonants produced at the same articulation point (e.g., /b/, /p/, and /m/). The amount of information perceivable through the lips likely varies from language to language. For example, liprounding distinguishes back vowels from front vowels in English, but not in language such as French that has both front- and back-rounded vowels (e.g., the back /y/ and the front /u/ are both rounded in French). Moreover, the visibility of consonants varies in function of the vocalic context. Studies showed that in French as well as in English the visual intelligibility of consonants is higher in the /a/ context, intermediate in the /i/ context, and low in the /u/ or /y/ contexts (Auer, Berstein, Waldstein, & Tucker, 1997; Benoît, Mohamadi, & Kandel, 1994). The lip rounding for /u/ is likely responsible for the low identification accuracy in the /u/ environment. The visual speech information is thus fragmentary. Deaf children trying to perceive (or to produce) spoken language are thus "striving to interpret a facial sign language, as it were, of which the gestures are partially obscured by an arbitrary grid" (Studdert-Kennedy, 1988, p. 256). Deaf children thus receive an inconsistent and phonetically underspecified language signal. This results in incomplete encoding of phonetic distinctions based on spoken language. To give a hint of the difficulties resulting from experience with the lipread input, we consider two problems. The first problem is that lexical development requires relatively systematic relationships between referents and the corresponding phonological sequences. Lipreading cannot provide this. Because lipreading is intrinsically underspecified at the phonological level, there is a large number of referents with similar lipread images. For example, the French words papa /papa/ and maman /mamã/ that are among the earliest referential items, are identical at lipreading. The second problem is that a single word may lead to different perceptual images. Suppose that children perceive the word ouvrir /uvrir/ (to open) through lipreading. What phonemes would they be able to grasp? The phoneme /u/ has a similar lipread image to /y/; the phoneme /v/ has the same visual image as /f/; the phoneme /r/ has no perceptible visual correlate. Thus for the single word ouvrir, deaf children may have different perceptual images: /uvir/, /uvi/, /ufir/, /ufi/, /yvrir/, /yvri/, /yvir/, and /yvi/. The fact that each phoneme does not lead to an unambiguous percept hinders deaf children's phonological, lexical, and morpho-syntactic development in oral language.

　　Does this mean that the child born with profound hearing loss is condemned to have only a fragmentary perception of spoken language, with all the cognitive consequences associated with this? The recent theoretical perspectives on the cross-modal perception of speech (see next section) and empirical data on speech perception and cognitive functioning of deaf children reared with augmented lipspeech allow the answer no to this question.

CROSS-MODAL PERSPECTIVE
IN SPEECH PERCEPTION

That speech perception is not a purely auditory phenomenon is demonstrated by the long known fact that optic information contributes to speech perception in difficult conditions (Erber, 1969; Reisberg, McLean, & Goldfied, 1987). Perhaps a stronger argument is the fact that hearing people integrate optic and acoustic information precategorically, and arrive at a categorical phonetic percept that they could not achieve from either vision or audition alone. Seeing a face saying "ga" while hearing the syllable "ba" leads to a compound percept, like "da" (McGurk & Mac-Donald, 1976). The influence of visual speech on the perception of acoustic speech information has also been demonstrated in serial recall experiments (Campbell & Dodd, 1980). These pioneering studies were later largely confirmed (see e.g., the collection of articles edited by Dodd & Campbell, 1987 and by Stork & Hennecke, 1996). These audio-visual interactions arise because the auditory and visual forms of speech share a common metric (Summerfield, 1987).

The integration of auditory and visual speech information seems already established during the first weeks of life. Infants 5- to 6-months old prefer to look to faces pronouncing the same syllable as that delivered acoustically than to faces pronouncing a different syllable (Kuhl & Meltzoff, 1982). Moreover, these amodal representations of speech seem to be already located in the left hemisphere at 4 to 5 months of age. Indeed, when the two faces are presented to left and right of an infant's central gaze, the preference for the auditory–visual match was evident only when the infants were looking at the right-side display (MacKain, Studdert-Kennedy, Spieker, & Stern, 1983). These studies showed that infants can match auditory and visual speech information. An even stronger demonstration of audio-visual integration in infants was provided by Burnham and Dodd (1996), who showed that 4-month-old children were sensitive to the McGurk effect. Infants habituated to repetitions of an audio /ba/ presented simultaneously as a visual /ga/ looked more often, in a test phase, to a face pronouncing /da/ than to a face pronouncing /ba/. This suggests that infants have combined, in the habituation phase, the auditory and the visual information and arrived at a percept not provided either acoustically or visually.

Precategorical, cross-modal integration seems also to occur between haptic and auditory information. Fowler and Dekle (1991) set up an auditory–haptic McGurk effect. Their hearing participants listened to syllables drawn from a /ba/–/ga/ continuum while holding their fingers against the lips of the experimenter, who was silently mouthing either /ba/ or /ga/ in synchrony with the auditorily presented syllables. Subjects had to report on each trial what they heard and what they felt. The reports of heard syllables was influenced significantly by the felt syllable, and vice-versa. This demonstrates that cross-modal integration is not limited to the visual and auditory speech information. Subjects seemed to integrate information perceived through different modalities when these came from the same event, that is the talker's gestures.

This cross-modal perspective has important consequences regarding speech perception in deaf children. A first implication, underlined by Dodd 20 years ago, is that lipreading may constitute a primary input to sustain perception of phonological information in deaf children. The information perceived through lipreading may entail the development of speech phonological representations (Dodd, 1976, 1987; Dodd & Hermelin, 1977; Dodd, McIntosh, & Woodhouse, 1996). The second implication is at least as important: If one adds to the speechread signal, which is fragmentary by essence, complementary information perceivable through an unimpaired sensory modality (e.g., the visual one, or the tactile one), deaf children could integrate these different informations into a unique speech percept. In other words, if the speech module is ready to process and integrate informations of different sensory modalities, provided that they come from the same event, the talker's gestures, it should be possible to bypass the ineffective auditory system and to provide the deaf child with a completely unambiguous speech signal.

CUED SPEECH: A SYSTEM PROVIDING WELL-SPECIFIED INFORMATION ABOUT SPEECH CONTRASTS

Preliminaries

Deaf children's unsatisfactory linguistic development in oral language has frequently led speech therapists and teachers of the deaf to add systematic signals, usually visual but sometimes tactile, to lipreading to reduce its ambiguity. Several such systems have been designed (see Plant & Spens, 1995, for a recent review of tactile aids). The existence of such systems provides a unique opportunity to examine the validity of the hypotheses discussed here. If the acquisition of a phonological system does not depend in any necessary sense on the auditory modality, but rather on the delivery of accurate information about phonological contrasts, one should predict that the use of systems that deliver well-specified phonological information, by adding visual or tactile information to the lipread signal, would improve the development of phonological skills in deaf children.

Over the past several years, our group has explored the consequences of exposure to one such system, namely Cued Speech (CS; Alegria, Leybaert, Charlier, & Hage, 1992; Alegria, Charlier, & Mattys, submitted; Charlier, 1994; Charlier & Leybaert, submitted; Hage, 1994; Leybaert, in prep.; Leybaert & Alegria, 1994; Leybaert & Charlier, 1996; Leybaert, Alegria, Hage, & Charlier, 1997). The remainder of this chapter summarizes what we know about the effects of CS on deaf youngsters' perception of speech, on their development of phonological representations, and on the use of such representations for reading and spelling. Before describing the results observed with CS, a caveat should be made. These data should be considered as highlighting the potential of development of accurate phonological representations in profoundly, prelinguistically deaf children. This development seems more shaped by the linguistic experience deaf children made early in life than by the lack of auditory experience per se. One should not conclude, though, that the results described here are specific to the use of CS. It is likely that other systems transmitting accurate information about phonological contrasts by the visual or the tactile channel would entail similar results. Future research should explore this point.

Description of Cued Speech

CS was devised by Cornett (1967). In CS, the speaker complements lip gestures of speech with manual cues. A cue is made of two parameters: hand shape and position of execution around the mouth (see Fig. 5.1). The hand can adopt several shapes (eight in the French version of CS) at different positions around the mouth (five in French). Handshapes disambiguate the consonants and hand positions the vowels. The phonemes are grouped together in such a way that those easy to discriminate by lipreading share a handshape (or a hand position), whereas those difficult to discriminate from each other belong to different groups. For example, a particular handshape is shared by /p, d, ʒ/, another one by /b, n/. For the vowels, one place is shared by /i, ɔ̃, ɑ̃/, a second one by /a, o, œ/. Each time a speaker pronounces a Consonant–Vowel (CV) syllable, a cue (a particular handshape at a specific position) is produced simultaneously. By doing so, the speaker is giving visually unambiguous information about this syllable and its constituent phonemes. For example, suppose that the word /pɔ̃/ is presented in lipreading alone. This word has a similar lipread image as the syllables /pɔ/, /bɔ/, /mɔ/, /bɔ̃/, and /mɔ̃/; and it is thus impossible to know which of these six words has been presented. When the manual cues are added, the six words are clearly distinguishable one from each other (the reader should pronounce them by adding the manual cues displayed in Fig. 5.1). To complete the description, it should be added that syllabic structures other than CV are produced with additional cues. For example, a V syllable is represented by the neutral handshape (the same one as that used for /f, t, m/) placed at the position corresponding to that vowel. Syllables with several consonants, such as CVC and CCV are coded using the handshape corresponding to the additional consonant at the neutral hand position (the same one as that used for /a, o, œ/).

The consonants

The vowels

[p] p (pas)
[d] d (dis)
[ʒ] j (je)

[k]
[v] k (cou)
[z] v (vu)
     z (maison)

[s] s (sur)
[r] r (rit)

[b]
[n] b (bon)
[ɥ] n (non)
     w (cuisine)

[m] m (maman)
[t] t (tout)
[f] f (feu)
     *

[l] l (loup)
[ʃ] ch (chat)
[w] w (oui, quoi)
[ɲ] gn (cogne)

[g] g (gui)

[j] y (fille)
[ŋ] ng (parking)

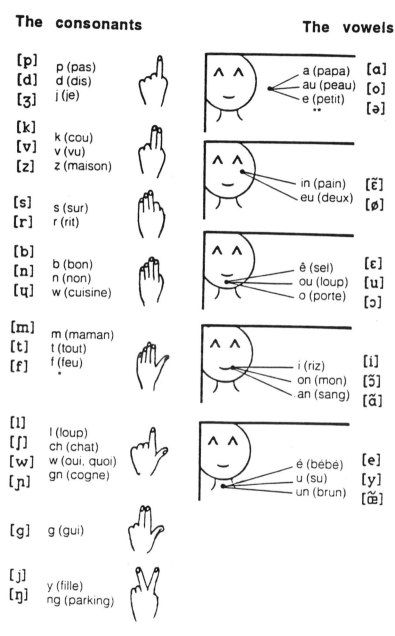

a (papa)   [a]
au (peau)   [o]
e (petit)   [ə]
**

in (pain)   [ɛ̃]
eu (deux)   [ø]

ê (sel)   [ɛ]
ou (loup)   [u]
o (porte)   [ɔ]

i (riz)   [i]
on (mon)   [ɔ̃]
an (sang)   [ɑ̃]

é (bébé)   [e]
u (su)   [y]
un (brun)   [œ̃]

* and any vowel not preceded by a consonant (arrête)

** and any isolated consonant (sec, prof) or followed by a silent e (lune)

FIG. 5.1. CS lip gestures and manual cues. Reproduced with the permission of the A. L. P. C. (Belgium).

Lip gestures are ambiguous, and so are the manual cues. The basic idea of CS is that the integration of labial and manual information points to a single, unambiguous, phonological percept that deaf children could not have achieved from either source alone. Deaf children are thus in a situation in which they can interpret the oral input as a reliable facial sign language in which the gestures (i.e., the combination of lip movement and manual cue) are now entirely specified, both at the syllabic and at the phonemic levels. At each syllable (and at each phoneme) corresponds one (and only one) combination of labial and manual information, and vice-versa. This made CS information processing a quite effortless task, at least for the children who have been exposed early and intensively to it.

Although the system may appear somewhat complex and artificial to uninitiated persons, it is possible to learn it in about 10 hours of exercises. With some practice, normal-hearing adults succeed at using it while speaking at a natural rate. This makes CS a potentially powerful system of communication with deaf children. If educators use CS systematically, that is, each time they speak to the deaf child, and even in linguistic exchanges between hearing persons, and if they code everything (i.e., not only content words, but also function words, grammatical morphemes), the deaf child will be immersed in a visual linguistic bath, in the same way as the hearing child is immersed in audio-visual linguistic information. From this linguistic supportive environment, a deaf child will be able to extract the phonological, morphological, semantic, and syntactic regularities and use them to develop its own language. For example, the phonological contrast between /e/ and /ɛ/, which is not visible on the lips, is possible to grasp when the words are coded in CS. This contrast distinguishes minimal pairs like *été* /ete/ (summer) and *étais* /etɛ/ (was). It is also a carrier of the morphological distinction between two forms of past tense in French (e.g., *j'ai mangé* /m ã ʒe/; *je mangeais* /m ã ʒɛ/). The perception of accurate information about phonological contrasts thus may have consequences on lexical and morpho syntactical development.

EFFECTS OF CUED SPEECH ON PHONOLOGICAL PROCESSING

Initially, CS was aimed at improving deaf children's speech reception skills. This improvement has been evaluated both for English- and French-speaking children. Nicholls and Ling (1982) studied a group of profoundly deaf Australian children taught at school with CS for at least

3 years. They found that the speech reception scores of these youngsters increased from about 30% for both syllables and words in the lipreading condition to more than 80% in the lipreading + cues condition. They emphasized that the children's average scores in the lipreading + cues condition were within the range of normal hearing listeners' reception scores of similar material through audition.

Périer, Charlier, Hage, and Alegria (1988) investigated the effect of the French version of CS on deaf children's reception of oral language. The authors also wished to determine whether children's linguistic backgrounds influenced the benefit gained from the addition of cues to lip gestures. Two groups were identified: The children who were exposed to CS early and intensively, because their parents used CS (either exclusively or in combination with Signed French, see Charlier, 1992) to communicate with them at home (the Home group), and the children who benefited from CS later, and only at school, usually from the age of 6 (the School group). The children had to identify sentences presented either by lipreading or by lipreading + cues. Although both groups showed better understanding for sentences presented in the lipreading + cues than in the lipreading condition, the advantage provided by the addition of cues was greater in the Home group (from 39% correct responses in the lipreading to 72% in the lipreading + cues condition) than in the School group (from 37% to 53%).

A more recent experiment (Alegria, Charlier, & Mattys, submitted) replicated and extended this result. Alegria et al. compared early CS-users (children reared with CS at home, at least before the age of 2 years) and late CS-users (children educated with CS at school after the age of 3 years) in written spelling of words and pseudowords, presented either by lipreading or by lipreading + cues. They showed that the addition of cues improved spelling accuracy significantly for words as well as for pseudowords in the early group (words: 41.5% of correct responses in the lipreading vs. 73.6% in the lipreading + cues condition; pseudowords: 17.9% in the lipreading vs. 54.9% in the lipreading + cues condition) as well as in the late group (words: 47.3% in the lipreading vs. 67.4% in the lipreading + cues condition; pseudowords: 9.4% in the lipreading vs. 32.9% in the lipreading + cues condition). The improvement induced by the cues was significantly larger in the early (32.1% for words and 37% for pseudowords) than in the late group (20.1% for words and 23.5% for pseudowords). This not only confirmed Périer et al.'s (1988) data for the processing of words, but extends it to the processing of pseudowords. This is important because the fact that early CS-users benefit more from the addition of cues than late CS-users for word processing might be explained by difference of familiarity with the material, the former being more familiar with words presented in CS than the latter. By contrast, pseudowords are unfamiliar for both subject groups.

The differences between early and late CS-users might arise for several, nonexclusive reasons. One reason could simply be that early users decode the cues better than late CS-users. For example, one could imagine that the decoding of lipreading + cues signal has become automatic for early CS-users but not for late CS-users who have to pay more attention to phonological processing. Another reason could be that early CS-users have developed more efficient processing of phonological information because they have encoded the phonemic distinctions based on spoken language more completely. Following that view, early and intensive use of CS might provoke the development of a mental phonological space where the identity of each phoneme is well defined visually. In this phonological space, each phoneme could be defined by a particular combination of lip movement and manual cue, allowing ready identification of speech stimuli. On the other hand, the late CS-users who had to rely mainly on lipreading during their first years to understand spoken language likely also have developed a mental phonological space, in which the different phonemes (or some of them) are still underspecified. Their phonological system is probably more similar to that of orally educated deaf children, characterized by absence of certain phonemes and deviance (Dodd, 1976). The fact that the late CS-users performed more poorly than early CS-users on identification of pseudowords delivered with the cues (Alegria et al., submitted) may be explained by this hypothesis. Early CS-users seem to be able to assign a segmental structure readily because they have refined prototypes of those segments to which the input must be compared. By contrast, the late CS-users who have less stable representations for lexical items also have greater difficulty in assembling a new representation for nonlexical items.

The conjecture that early use of CS allows deaf children to develop a mental phonological system in which the different phonemes are assigned to different places leads to several hypotheses. A first hypothesis would be that early CS users become able to extract more information from speech information delivered *without* the cues (i.e. auditory information, or lipread information). To date, this hypothesis apparently has not been tested. Another hypothesis would be that children educated with CS could benefit more from auditory information when this has been restored through cochlear implants. The motivation of such an idea is that children reared with CS would have developed already, preoperatively, a complete mental representation of the phonological contrasts used in a particular language. Their postoperative task would consist of learning to identify in the acoustic signal the distinctive features corresponding to each phoneme. On the other hand, non-CS-users would have to learn to discriminate in the acoustic stream phonemes for which they do not have any preoperative awareness. Clinical observations about the predictive factors of postimplant evolution support this conjecture: Children who had benefited preoperatively from CS evolve rapidly and in a favorable way in speech perception as well as in speech production (Busquet, in press).

EFFECTS OF CUED SPEECH ON THE DEVELOPMENT OF PHONOLOGICAL REPRESENTATIONS

The Development of Phonological Representations in Hearing and Deaf Children

To put the effects of CS in a broader perspective, it might be useful to refer to recent theoretical ideas about how phonological representations develop in young hearing children. During the last years, several authors argued that, even for hearing children, phonological representations are not "a preset immutable part of language" (Fowler, 1991, p. 112). Rather, these representations seem to evolve during preschool and even the first school years (from 1 to 8 years, approximately). A child's first words would not be represented as a sequence of phonemes, but rather as holistic patterns. With linguistic development, the scope of the representations narrows, giving salience first to syllable and then to subsyllabic units (onset and rime, then phonemes).

Fowler argued that the factors triggering the development of phonological representations are both biological and environmental. On the biological side, the expanding phonological lexicon exerts an increasing pressure toward a segmental mode of organization. As Nittrouer, Studdert-Kennedy, and McGowan (1989) proposed:

> the initial domain of perceptuomotor organization is a meaningful unit of one or a few syllables. As the number and diversity of the words in a child's lexicon increase, words with similar acoustic and articulatory patterns begin to cluster. From these clusters there ultimately precipitate the coherent units of sound and gesture that we know as phonetic segments. Precipitation is probably a gradual process perhaps beginning as early as the second to third year of life when the child's lexicon has no more than 50–100 words. But the process is evidently going on in at least some regions of the child's lexicon and phonological system as late as 7 years of age. (p. 131)

On the environmental side, metalinguistic factors like language games and alphabetic instruction may play a large role in developing phonological representations. Exposure to language play (e.g., nursery rhymes) enables the child to become aware of phonemic units. Besides, the conscious task of segmenting speech stream into segments for the purpose of reading and writing an alphabetic script likely provokes changes in the underlying phonological representations.

This evolution of the child's phonological representations is assumed to be mirrored in the changes in performance in metaphonological tasks. Indeed, although 4-year-old children can note similarities in sound only when a syllable is shared by two words (e.g., *entreat–retreat*), 5-year-old children are able to group words either on the basis of a shared onset or a shared rime (Treiman & Zukowski, 1991). In the process of refining of phonological representations, those representations corresponding to highly familiar words may be reorganized in terms of phonetic segments first, whereas the representations of less familiar words, or more complex words, may be defined in terms of segments later. These hypotheses proved successful in explaining the deficits of hearing children who are dyslexic (Swan & Goswami, 1997).

The hypothesis of a developmental change of phonological representations may also have significant implications for the understanding of deaf children's phonological abilities. Deaf children's first representations likely are holistic, but less accurate than those of hearing children because these representations are developed on the basis of the lipread, fragmentary input. The pressure toward a development of these representations, although existent, may be less strong in the deaf than in the hearing for different reasons. One reason is that the phonological lexicon expands at a slower rate in the deaf because of the lack of distinctness of the words in lipread images. The number and the quality of utterances stored may be insufficient to allow deaf children to appreciate structural regularities of spoken language at the phonological level. The fact that less utterances are stored also means that the pressure toward a segmental mode of organization is less strong than in hearing children of the same age. Another reason is that deaf children likely are less in contact with language games in spoken language because of the limitations of linguistic interactions in that modality. Therefore, one could reasonably think that deaf children's phonological representations are less likely to evolve toward syllabic, subsyllabic, and finally a segmental mode of organization before learning to read. Reading and writing instructions of an alphabetic orthography might thus play a larger role in refining and redefining phonological representations in the deaf.

Given that CS allows deaf children to perceive visually the same amount of phonological information about speech as that perceived through audition by hearing children, a strong effect of exposure to CS on the acquisition of phonological representations might be expected. The receptive phonological lexicon of deaf children educated early and intensively with CS develops rapidly during their early years (Charlier, 1992; Cornett, 1973; Nash, 1973). These children thus develop phonological representations based on visual information (i.e., lipreading + manual cues), which are numerous and well specified. This affords them the possibility to discern the structural regularities between stored representations at the phonological level. Their expanding phonological lexicon might exert a pressure toward a more economic form of storage, based on units smaller than the whole word. Children educated precociously and intensively with CS might thus develop phonological representations that change from a holistic through a syllabic, subsyllabic, and finally segmental mode of organization. These changes may occur in response to the same biological and environmental pressures as in hearing children. Therefore, access to syllable, rhyme, and phoneme units may occur at approximately the same age as in hearing children.

Effects of Cued Speech on Rhyme Awareness

As a first step, we decided to explore whether deaf children educated with CS could perform rhyme judgments and rhyme-production tasks with pictures and words as targets. These tasks require access to lexical phonological representations and comparison of the words' final vowel (or vowel + coda). It was established that rhyming sensitivity emerges in hearing children as soon as 3 or 4 years of age (Read, 1978; Slobin, 1978), and that this ability is well developed at 5 years (Treiman & Zukowski, 1991). The type of information taken into account for rhyming judgment seems, however, to be different for preliterate than for literate children: Whereas preliterate hearing children seem to detect rhyme on the basis of a global phonological similarity, first graders pay attention to segments (Cardoso-Martins, 1994; Lenel & Cantor, 1981).

Asking whether deaf children could identify rhymes might seem a silly question. The very notion of rhyme may seem based inherently on sound patterns, which are unavailable to deaf children. However, literate deaf youngsters have been found to be able to perform rhyme judgment tasks (Campbell & Wright, 1988; Charlier & Leybaert, submitted; Hanson & Fowler, 1987; Hanson & McGarr, 1989; Sterne, 1996). The rhyming ability of deaf children or young adults is generally lower than that of hearing children matched for reading level. Deaf children mainly rely on word spelling to judge whether two words rhyme, even when pictures are presented as targets. For example, in Campbell and Wright's (1988) study of rhyming judgment about pictures, deaf teenagers achieved about 75%

of correct responses when the word spelling gave a reliable clue about rhyming (e.g., *dog–frog*), but only 55% when the word spelling gave no clue about rhyming (e.g., *hair–bear*). However, using a forced-choice paradigm in which participants had to choose which of two pairs of orthographically similar written words do rhyme (e.g., *bribe–tribe* vs. *touch–couch*), Hanson and Fowler (1987) showed that in such a situation, young deaf adults can escape the orthographic criterion and base their judgment on a phonological code, although with a lower accuracy than that of hearing controls. From this overview, three points must be underlined. First, the absence of useful hearing does not preclude deaf children from developing a sensitivity to rhyme. However, their rhyming ability is not as efficient as that developed by hearing children. Second, the development of rhyming ability is not only delayed in deaf children, but also qualitatively different. Indeed, deaf youngsters rely on orthographic information in situations (i.e., picture-rhyming judgment) in which hearing children do not. This qualitative difference seems to be a long-lasting one: even deaf adults are more influenced by spelling than their hearing peers (Hanson & McGarr, 1989). Third, until now, studies showing rhyme sensitivity in deaf subjects have not made the difference between phonological genuine rhyme and lipread similarity. Two rhyming words of course share the same lipread image; but two words sharing the same lipread image do not necessarily rhyme. When deaf subjects decide that two words rhyme, it is impossible to know whether they detect the real rhyme, or whether they simply detect the similarity between lipread images. This problem was tackled in our study described in the following.

In one of our experiments (Charlier & Leybaert, submitted), deaf children were asked to make rhyme judgments about pairs of pictures belonging to four conditions. In the rhyming pairs, the pictures represented either words with similar spelling (e.g. *train* /trɛ̃/- *main* /mɛ̃/) or words with different spelling (e.g., *lit* /li/–*riz* /ri/). The second variable was similar in lipreading. To distinguish between sensitivity to rhyme and sensitivity to lipread similarity, performance for nonrhyming pairs in which the names of the pictures have similar lipread images when spoken (e.g., *lit* /li/–*nez* /ne/) was compared with performance for nonrhyming pairs with different lipread images (e.g., *lune* /lyn/–*fleur* /flør/). Subjects who believe that rhyme and similar lipread images are the same thing were expected to judge erroneously that nonrhyming pairs with similar lipread patterns do rhyme.

Children were presented with pairs of drawings. For each pair, they had to say whether the pictures were friends or not. In a pretest, the notion of *friend*, that is, rhyme, was assessed for each child, and only children who showed a comprehension of this notion were included as subjects.

Groups of hearing children, children educated with CS early at home and at school (the CS Home group), children educated with CS only at school after 3 years of age (CS School group), and children educated in spoken language only (the Oral group) were enrolled. In addition, to control for the effects of having a full language early in life, two groups of signers were tested. One group consisted of children of deaf parents, who were exposed to sign language both at home and at school (SL Home). The other group consisted of children from hearing parents who were exposed to sign language only at school (SL School).

In the two conditions in which spelling gives a reliable clue about rhyming, all groups achieved a high level of performance (at least 80% correct responses in the rhyming pictures with similar spelling condition; at least 90% in the nonrhyming control condition). The two other experimental conditions affected the groups of participants differently. First, rhyming pairs with different spelling significantly deteriorated the performance of all groups of deaf subjects, but the CS Home one. This indicated that the participants educated with CS only at school, those educated orally, and those educated with sign language used their knowledge of spelling to support rhyme judgment, probably because their phonological representations were not detailed enough. The fact that the CS Home children did not show any sensitivity to word spelling, like the hearing participants, differentiates them clearly from the other groups of deaf children tested in the experiment as well as from the deaf subjects evaluated in the literature.

Second, nonrhyming pairs with similar lipread patterns induced more errors than the nonrhyming control condition in all groups of deaf children. However, the effect of lipread similarity was significantly lower in the CS Home group than in the other groups. The effect of lipread similarity may be accounted for by two explanations. The first one is that deaf children develop their phonological representations from articulatory patterns given to them by eye. Nonrhyming words with similar lipread images would thus have very similar representations, which may induce children to judge erroneously that they do rhyme. This explanation might hold in the case of deaf children who are not early CS-users. But it does not seem plausible in the case of early CS-users because the CS signal corresponding to words with similar lipreading is clearly different (the reader should pronounce words like *lit* and *nez* and add the manual cues displayed in Fig. 5.1 to appreciate this). The second explanation is that the lipread similarity effect is an "inner speaking effect." Indeed, words similar in lipreading also share a high degree of articulatory similarity. Subjects often pronounce the items before making their decision about rhyming; they thus may be mislead by the similarity at the articulatory level. Although the distinction between the perceptual and the production explanation of the effect of lipread similarity is interesting in its own right, the conclusions produced are fundamentally the same: this effect indicates that the rhyme unit is not easily or always perceivable. If we consider that the magnitude of this effect is an indicator that the phonological representations are not detailed enough, the data indicate that the degree of specification is lower in deaf children who are not early CS-users than in those who are early CS-users. The performances achieved by children reared with CS at home suggest that their representations are sufficiently detailed to allow the perception of phonological commonalities between words, like the rhyme. However, their representations may be less detailed than those of hearing children.

The next question was whether this ability appears naturally through language development. The alternative hypothesis is that rhyming ability emerges only in response to environmental pressures, such as those involved in reading and writing an alphabetic code. An attempt was thus made to test deaf prereaders from all groups with the same material. Only children educated early with CS turned out to be able to understand the notion of rhyme assessed in the pretest. A group of CS Home prereaders was compared to a control group of hearing children. Both groups showed the same pattern of results: There was a high level of performance in the four conditions, no effect of spelling, but a significant effect of lipread similarity. The lipread similarity effect displayed by both groups is compatible with the notion that the representations of prereaders are less specified at the phonological level than those of readers. Prereaders may be misled by articulatory similarity, because they detect rhyme on the basis of a global phonological similarity rather than on the basis of detailed segmental information that still remains unavailable for them (Cardoso-Martins, 1994).

In summary, early exposure to phonetically augmented lipspeech seems to induce the development of rhyming ability similar to that of hearing children and different from that displayed by other deaf children. In early CS-users, the notion of rhyme seems to emerge naturally in the course of primary language development, before any contact with written language. This indicates the intervention of a mechanism of structure analysis that decomposes the phonological word representations that have been acquired and that locates recurring elements across utterances, such as the rhyme. The activation of such a process is likely due to the fact that early CS-users have stored a large sample of good-quality phonological representations in the first years of their life. By contrast, in non-early CS-users the onset of the mechanism of phonological analysis of spoken language utterances seems delayed at least until the acquisition of the written code.

This mechanism of analysis is less efficient at detecting phonological similarity independently of lipread and orthographic similarity. These specific characteristics are likely due to the fact that the phonological representations stored by the non-early CS-users are less numerous, and of poor quality. Note that the natural emergence of rhyming ability in early CS-users may not be attributed to the fact that these children have had an experience of linguistic stimulation early in life. Indeed, the SL Home children, who certainly have benefited from a supportive linguistic environment in sign, do not show the same sensitivity to rhyme between spoken words (of course, these children have probably developed a sensitivity to rhyme in sign language).

Effects of Cued Speech on Phonemic Awareness

The next question addressed is whether children educated with CS can develop phonological representations that are organized on a segmental mode. Reading and writing an alphabetic script requires that the child be able to segment the speech stream to establish the correspondences between the phonological segments and the letters or letter groups that represent them. Is it possible for deaf children educated with CS to decompose the previously stored phonological forms into segments, and do they do that better than other deaf children? Remember that a manual cue most of the time corresponds to a CV syllable. The phonological segments (consonants, vowels) although clearly represented in the CS system, are never produced alone. There is thus no clue in the CS signal itself that may facilitate the development of phonemic awareness. CS differs on this point from fingerspelling. In fingerspelling, each manual configuration represents one letter of the alphabet, a fact that likely enhances the discovery of phonemic segments in speech. The phonemic awareness that could develop in children educated with CS cannot be ascribed to the CS signal; it would thus be the product of an internal mechanism of analysis of the stored phonological representations, triggered by internal (i.e., necessity of a more economical storage system) and external (i.e., alphabetic instruction) pressures.

Again, asking the question whether deaf children may become aware of phonemes may seem curious, if one thinks that phonemes belong exclusively to spoken languages. However, previous studies have demonstrated that literate deaf children can use phoneme-to-grapheme rules when spelling words (see, e.g., Dodd, 1987), indicating that they are able to isolate phonemic units in their mental representations of speech. If the mechanism of analysis of phonological forms depends on the quantity and quality of the representations previously stored, one may predict a large effect of language input on the rate of development and efficiency of this mechanism. Deaf children who have been exposed to a lipread, poorly specified input will be delayed in the development of phonemic awareness. Their awareness of phonemes may also be qualitatively different from that of hearing children, because some phonemic distinctions have no visual correlate and some phonemes are not visible at all in certain phonetic contexts (e.g., the /r/ and the /l/ as second consonant of a cluster, as in *fleur* or *pluie*). By contrast, children exposed to phonetically augmented lipspeech should experience a development of phonemic awareness similar to that of hearing children.

Until now, phonemic awareness has not been tested at all in deaf children. Therefore, the hypotheses discussed here will be evaluated in the light of results of two experiments on the development of spelling abilities in deaf children. In these experiments, children are asked to write down words in response to pictures. The analysis of errors constitutes a good source of information about the structure of the phonological representations. Phonologically accurate errors (e.g., "trin" or "trein" for *train*) reveal two interesting facts: that children's representations are accurate and that they are detailed at the segmental level. In a first study (Leybaert & Alegria, 1995), we found that orally educated children made a certain amount of phonologically accurate errors, but in a lower proportion than the hearing controls. Interestingly, whereas the proportion of phonological substitutions remained constant for hearing children, this proportion was higher for the older deaf children than for the younger ones, indicating that orthographic experience led deaf children to develop more accurate phonological representations for highly familiar words. We also observed that part of the errors not compatible with the words' standard pronunciation were consistent with the lipread image of the words. For example, for the regular word *ouvrir*, children made errors like "oufrir," "oufir," "ouvi," and "uvi." These spelling errors suggest that some phonemes are misrepresented in deaf children's lexical representations (i.e., /f/ and /v/), whereas others may be not represented at all. These errors remain compatible with the hypothesis of a segmental mode of organization of the phonological representations. Other errors, however, reveal a much more important inaccuracy of the phonological representations. For example, some children spelled "escorlr" for *escalier*, "atouse" for *attention*. In these productions, there is little evidence, if any, that children possess representations detailed at the level of segments. Taken together, these data suggest that deaf children's awareness of phonemes is hindered by the poor quality of the phonological representations they developed from the lipread, fragmentary input.

This conclusion led us to study, in a recent experiment, the effect of linguistic input on deaf children's spelling. Three groups of subjects, matched for general spelling level, were compared: deaf children educated with CS at home and at school (the CS Home group), deaf children exposed to CS only at school (the CS School group), and hearing children (Leybaert, in prep.). Children were asked to spell the names of pictures representing concrete words of high and low frequency. The analysis of the type of errors showed that most of the errors (92.9%) of the hearing group were phonologically accurate (e.g., "sigarette" for *cigarette*; "trin" for *train*). A predominance (74.3%) of phonologically accurate errors was also observed in the CS Home group, although less marked than in the hearing group. By contrast, the CS School children made, besides phonologically accurate misspellings (30.5%), a large amount (32.1%) of errors that contain the same number of phonemes as the target but do not respect the word pronunciation (e.g., "copat" for *copain*, "jou" or "zus" for *jus*). This analysis thus supports the expectation that the phonological representations of CS Home children are well specified in terms of phonological segments.

Given this, CS Home children should be able to transcribe accurately phonologically complex words, such as words containing phonological clusters. Consonant clusters like *br, tr, gr* are difficult to spell for young hearing children who frequently omit the liquid in their written productions (Bruck & Treiman, 1990; see also Sprenger-Charolles & Siegel, in press, for similar observations in French). Consonant clusters provoke persistent difficulties in spelling for deaf children educated orally, probably because the two consonants do not have distinct images on the lips (Leybaert & Alegria, 1995).

The delivery of precise phonological information by CS should play a positive role on spelling consonant clusters, because each consonant is indicated by a distinct manual cue (the reader should try to pronounce words like *green* while making the cues displayed in Fig. 5.1). In the same study (Leybaert, in prep.), the spelling of *r* and *l* either in a consonant cluster (e.g., *train, fleur, trompette*) or at the beginning of a syllable (e.g., *lapin, rouge, revolver*) was compared in the three groups of subjects. A correct response was scored if the *r* or the *l* was present in the subject's response. The data of the Hearing beginners showed that words containing consonant clusters (90% correct responses) entailed slightly more errors than control words (100% correct responses), and that word frequency did not have an impact on performance. The CS Home group, although achieving slightly lower performance for the clusters (85% correct responses), showed the same pattern as the Hearing group. This indicates that they are able, most of the time, to isolate in their phonological representations the two consonant segments. The CS School children were more challenged by consonant clusters, especially for rare words, and showed a stronger effect of word frequency (Frequent words: Clusters: 81%; Controls: 97%—Rare words: Clusters: 56%; Controls: 81%). The data of the CS School children confirm the difficulty experienced by these children in developing phonological representations detailed in terms of segments on the basis of the lipread input. This difficulty is at the origin of the effects of phonological complexity and of frequency. The phonological representations of words containing consonant clusters and of low frequency words are not accurately detailed in terms of segments. By contrast, the limited effects of phonological complexity and word frequency in CS Home children indicate that they have developed, for words of high and low frequency, representations that are sufficiently detailed at the level of phonological segments.

DISCUSSION AND PERSPECTIVES

According to recent theories, speech perception is crossmodal. The listener arrives at a categorical, unique phonetic percept after having precategorically integrated informations provided by different sensory modalities (audition, vision, and haptic sense in some situations). This cross-modal perspective opens interesting perspectives for deaf children's perception of speech. From that point of view, the communication systems aimed at clarifing ambiguous lip shapes by adding information in an unimpaired sensory modality (visual or tactile) takes a new sense. These systems may allow deaf children to arrive at unique, unambiguous speech percepts that are not provided by either modality. Accurate speech perception may trigger the development of phonological representations, from a holistic to a syllabic and subsyllabic organization, and finally a segmental mode. Such representations may be used in cognitive activities to the same extent as the representations developed by hearing children from audio-visual speech.

The results observed when deaf children are educated early and intensively with Cued Speech supported that view. The addition of the manual cues to the lip shapes had a strong effect on their ability to perceive speech. These children thus seemed to interpret the input delivered by CS as a reliable facial language in which the different gestures (i.e., the combination of lip movement and manual cue) pointed to different, unambiguous, phonological percepts. Further research is needed to establish whether the integration between labial shapes and manual cues occurs precategorically, as it seems to be the case for integration of audio-visual information, or later. Further research would also detail the structure of the representations developed by deaf children from the CS signal. Are these representations completely abstract, or do they include visual speech parameters? A preliminary study indicates that words produced in CS activate representations coding the visual dimensions (i.e., lipreading and manual cues) of speech (Leybaert & Marchetti, 1997).

The representations developed from the CS signal seem to fulfil the same functions as those developed by hearing children from the audio-visual input. These representations are used in mental operations often thought to depend on audition. For example, these youngsters judged accurately whether two words rhymed, independent of the word spelling. They were able to use accurately phoneme–grapheme correspondences for spelling. They also used a phonological loop to retain information during a task of ordered recall of pictures (Charlier, 1994; Leybaert & Charlier, 1996). These data showed that the developmental course of phonological representations in deaf children may be similar to that occurring in hearing children, provided that children have acquired a large number of well-specified phonological representations. Further consequences in this causal chain should be studied. It is likely, for example, that the extended phonological knowledge acquired by these children helps them in learning to read and spell. Preliminary data indicate that CS Home children may achieve the same spelling level and the same reading level as hearing controls with a delay of less than 1 year (Leybaert, in prep.; Leybaert & Charlier, 1996). This position contrasted with the well-known, age-relevant lag in reading generally observed in deaf children (Conrad, 1979; Marschark, 1993). Similarly, the enhanced reception of spoken language provided by systems like CS likely favors the acquisition of morphosyntactical abilities. Indeed, certain features of morphology such as inflections and function words are difficult to perceive in lipreading because they are short, unaccentuated morphemes. Deaf speakers of languages like English or French often fail to perceive and encode these morphological markers. Because CS visually transmits all the phonetic information of spoken language, it likely enhances the development of morphological knowledge (Hage, 1994; Hage, Alegria, & Périer, 1991; see also Leybaert et al., 1997).

To summarize, deafness per se does not entail a breakdown in the process of acquisition of phonology and of development of phonological representations. What seems to be the critical factor is the delivery of accurate, well-specified information about the phonological contrasts of spoken language, independent of input modality. This conclusion needs to be validated by studies on the effects of other systems that disambiguate lipreading by adding either manual or tactile cues.

In the view developed so far, the emergence of internal speech is strongly dependent on the quality of the phonological input provided to the deaf child. This view differs from Conrad's (1979) hypothesis on the origin of internal speech. Conrad reported a significant relationship between degree of hearing loss and use of internal speech. However, the presence of internal speech was even more strongly associated with deaf youngsters' speech intelligibility. This led Conrad to propose a causal model in which speech intelligibility and nonverbal intelligence determined the emergence of internal speech. Conrad's theory was invalidated by the observation that anarthric and dysarthric persons did show rhyme effect in a short-term memory task, which indicates that external speech is not a prerequisite to the development of internal speech (Bishop & Robson, 1989).

In a recent paper, Gathercole and Martin (1996) proposed that phonological representations developed from the speech *perception* process, not from the speech *production* mechanisms, formed the basis for performance in memory and rhyme judgment tasks. Our data showed a strong effect of the quality of the input on the presence of internal speech, and were thus more compatible with Gathercole and Martin's theory than with Conrad's. Conrad's data may be reinterpreted by postulating that speech intelligibility provides an index of the degree to which the deaf child has been able to develop an accurate phonological system. Consistent with that view, speech intelligibility is strongly determined by degree of hearing loss. The close relationship between speech intelligibility and use of internal speech in memory could thus reflect a common influence on both abilities of a third factor, i.e. the quality of the phonological representations of speech (but see Marschark & Mayer, this volume).

These data led to the conclusion that the quality of the linguistic input should be high among the priorities of deaf children's educational programs. An important constraint seems to be that the phonetically augmented lipspeech should be used early and intensively in order to improve significantly the development of the child's phonological skills. Indeed, children educated with CS only at school after 3 years of age did not show the same benefit from the addition of cues in speech perception as those educated with CS at home. Moreover, they did not achieve a high level of rhyming ability, nor use of phoneme-to-grapheme correspondences for spelling. Children educated with CS at home may differ from those educated with CS only at school in several aspects: *quantity* of language addressed to the child, *quality* of the language addressed to the child, and *precociousness* of the exposure to the phonological input.

Regarding the *quantity* of language, it is obvious that children educated with CS at home benefit from a larger number of linguistic interactions in CS than those who use CS only at school. On the other hand, the distinction between Home and School groups is certainly not fine-grained enough. There might also exist large differences among parents claiming that they use CS at home: Although some of them may use it every time they speak to their child, others may have used it extensively when the child was young, but limited the use of CS to lexical or syntactically difficult structures as the child grew older. Future research should examine whether there is an association between the degree of parental use of CS and the degree of development of phonological skills. The fact that the CS Home children differed slightly from the hearing controls in some respects (the effect of lipread similarity on rhyme judgment; the amount of spelling errors compatible with the word's pronunciation; more difficulties with the consonant clusters) may indicate that, even for the CS Home children, the language-learning situation may not be the same as that of a hearing child. Hearing people who use CS may only do so when directly addressing the child, cutting down the amount and variety of language exposure and the opportunity for incidental learning. On the other hand, *quality* of linguistic stimulation may also be important; for example, it is possible that teachers use CS mainly for informing and asking direct questions, and less for social interactions than do parents.

A third factor that may determine variability in linguistic development may be the *precocity* of exposure to CS. Parents who use CS to communicate with their child generally begin to do so before the child is 2 years old; on the other hand, the age of starting exposure of children to CS at school is at least 3 years, and generally 6. Research on sign language demonstrated the existence of a sensitive period for language acquisition. Mayberry and Eichen (1991) showed that age of acquisition of sign language affected significantly the different levels of linguistic ability of deaf adults who have used sign language for more than 40 years. Late learners (i.e., people who learned sign language after 6 years of age) did not understand the meaning of ASL messages as well as the early learners (who learned sign language before they were 6 years old). Mayberry (1995) argued that the phonological processing of signs may be less automatic for late signers than for early signers, a fact that may affect the development of other linguistic structures, such as morphology and syntax. It seems reasonable to transpose these conclusions to the data described here: Children educated late with CS do not seem as proficient as those educated early in the decoding of CS stimuli, a fact that may have consequences on all aspects of lingusitic development.

The evidence in favor of a sensitive period in sign language acquisition raises the questions of which mechanism(s) develop during this period and why they do not develop any more when children are exposed to language later. Detailed hypotheses about the nature and the timing of such mechanisms were proposed by Locke (1997) in his "theory of neurolinguistic development." Although a fair report of this theory is beyond the scope of the present chapter, it is interesting to pinpoint that one critical phase of linguistic development, extending from around 18 months to 3 or more years, is

> analytical and computational. Previously stored forms are decomposed into syllables and segments, a process that facilitates discovery and subsequent application of grammatical rules. This phase is active for a finite period and is largely served by left hemisphere mechanisms that make possible phonology, morphology, and syntax. . . .Children who are delayed in the second phase have too little stored utterance material to activate their analytic mechanism at the optimum biological moment, and when sufficient words have been learned, this modular capability has already begun to decline. (p. 266)

The data described in this paper may be interpreted in this kind of framework. The early use of systems like CS may allow the deaf child to store a large amount of utterances on which the analytical process may operate later. On the other hand, children educated with CS only at school could be assimilated to children delayed in the phase of utterances storage that precedes the analytic and computational phase. This would explain, for instance, that early CS-users develop a rhyming ability at the same age and with nearly the same efficiency as hearing children, whereas late CS-users, and other deaf children do not achieve the same accuracy, even at a later age. In this perspective, use of systems like CS would constitute the environmental factor needed to allow biological processes to become operational.

ACKNOWLEDGMENTS

The research described here was supported by grants from the Fondation Van Goethem-Brichant in 1989, and from the Fondation Houtman in 1993. The writing of this paper was partly supported by a ARC grant from the Belgian Ministry of Scientific Policy ("The structure of the mental lexicon: A multilevel approach to the multiple representations of words.")

REFERENCES

Alegria, J., Charlier, B., & Mattys, S. (submitted). The role of lipreading and Cued Speech in the processing of phonological information in French-educated deaf children. Manuscript submitted for publication.
Alegria, J., Leybaert, J., Charlier, B., & Hage, C. (1992). On the origin of phonological representations in the deaf: hearing lips and hands. In J. Alegria, D. Holender, J.

Morais, & M. Radeau (Eds), *Analytic Approaches to Human Cognition*. (pp. 107–132). New York: North-Holland.

Auer, E. T., Bernstein, L. E., Waldstein, R. S., & Tucker, P. E. (1997). Effects of phonetic variation and the structure of the lexicon on the uniqueness of words. In C. Benoît & R. Campbell (Eds.), *Proceedings of the ESCAM workshop on audio-visual speech processing* (pp. 21–24).

Bellugi, U., Poizner, H., & Klima, E. S. (1989). Language, modality and the brain. *Trends in Neurosciences, 12*, (10), 380–388.

Benoît, C., Mohamadi., T., & Kandel, S. (1994). Effects of phonetic context on audio-visual intelligibility of French. *Journal of Speech and Hearing Research, 37*, 1195–1203.

Bishop, D. V. M., & Robson, J. (1989). Unimpaired short-term memory and rhyme judgement in congenitally speechless individuals: implications for the notion of "articulatory coding." *The Quarterly Journal of Experimental Psychology, 41A*, 123–140.

Bruck, M., & Treiman, R. (1990). Phonological awareness and spelling in normal children and dyslexics: The case of initial consonant clusters. *Journal of Experimental Child Psychology, 50*, 156–178.

Burnham, D., & Dodd, B. (1996). Auditory–visual speech perception as a direct process: The McGurk effect in infants and across languages. In D. G. Stork & M. E. Hennecke (Eds.), *Speechreading by humans and machines: Models, systems and applications* (pp. 103–115). Berlin: Springer.

Busquet, D. (in press). Language Parlé Complété et Implants cochléaires. *Bulletin d'audiophonologie*.

Campbell, R., & Dodd, B. (1980). Hearing by eye. *Quarterly Journal of Experimental Psychology, 32*, 85–99.

Campbell, R., & Wright, H. (1988). Deafness, spelling and rhyme: How spelling support written words and picture rhyming skills in deaf sujects. *The Quarterly Journal of Experimental Psychology, 40A*, 771–788.

Cardoso-Martins, C. (1994). Rhyme perception: Global or analytical? *Journal of Experimental Child Psychology, 57*, 26–41.

Charlier, B. L. (1992). Complete signed and cued French: An original signed language-cued speech combination. *American Annals of the Deaf, 137*, 331–337.

Charlier, B. L. (1994). Le développement des représentations phonologiques chez l'enfant sourd: Etude comparative du Langage Parlé Complété avec d'autres outils de communication. Unpublished doctoral dissertation, Brussels: U.L.B.

Charlier, B. L., & Leybaert, J. (submitted). The rhyming skills of deaf children educated with phonetically augmented lipspeech.

Conrad, R. (1979). *The deaf school child*. London: Harper & Row.

Cornett, O. (1967). Cued speech. *American Annals of the Deaf, 112*, 3–13.

Cornett, O. (1973). Comments on the Nash case study. *Sign Language Studies, 3*, 92–94.

Dodd, B. (1976). The phonological system of deaf children. *Journal of Speech and Hearing Disorders, 41*, 185–198.

Dodd, B. (1987). Lip-reading, phonological coding and deafness. In B. Dodd & R. Campbell (Eds.), *Hearing by eye: The psychology of lip-reading* (pp. 163–175). Hillsdale, NJ: Lawrence Erlbaum Associates.

Dodd, B., & Campbell, R. (Eds.), (1987). *Hearing by eye: The psychology of lip-reading*. Hillsdale, NJ: Lawrence Erlbaum Associates.

Dodd, B., & Hermelin, B. (1977). Phonological coding by the prelinguistically deaf. *Perception and Psychophysics, 21*, 413–417.

Dodd, B., McIntosh, B., & Woodhouse, L. (1996). Children with hearing loss: Speechreading skills. In D. G. Stork & M. E. Hennecke (Eds.), *Speechreading by humans and machines: Models, systems and applications* (pp. 27–43). Berlin: Springer.

Erber, N. P. (1969). Interaction of audition and vision in the recognition of oral speech stimuli. *Journal of Speech and Hearing Research, 12*, 423–425.

Fowler, A. E. (1991). How early phonological development might set the stage for phoneme awareness. In S. Brady & D. Shankweiler (Eds.), *Phonological processes in literacy: A tribute to Isabelle Y. Liberman* (pp. 97–117). Hillsdale, NJ: Lawrence Erlbaum Associates.

Fowler, C. A., & Dekle, D. J. (1991). Listening with eye and hand: Cross-modal contributions to speech perception. *Journal of Experimental Psychology: Human Perception and Performance, 17*, 816–828.

Gathercole, S. E., & Martin, A. J. (1996). Interactive processes in phonological memory. In (Eds). pp. 73–100)

Griswold, L. E., & Cummings, B. A. (1974). The expressive vocabulary of pre-school deaf children. *American Annals of the Deaf, 119*, 16–28.

Hage, C. (1994). *Développement de certains aspects de la morpho-syntaxe chez l'enfant à surdité profonde: Rôle du Langage Parlé Complété.* Unpublished doctoral dissertation, Brussels, Free Université Libre de Bruxelles.

Hage, C., Alegria, J., & Périer; O. (1991). Cued speech and language acquisition: The case of grammatical gender morpho-phonology. In D. S. Martin (Ed.), *Advances in cognition, education and deafness* (pp. 395–399). Washington, DC: Gallaudet University Press.

Hanson, V. L. (1982). Short-term recall by deaf signers of American Sign Language: Implications of encoding strategy for order recall. *Journal of Experimental Psychology: Learning, Memory and Cognition, 8*, 572–583.

Hanson, V. L., & Fowler, C. A. (1987). Phonological coding in word reading: Evidence from hearing and deaf readers. *Memory and Cognition, 15*, 199–207.

Hanson, V. L., & McGarr, N. S. (1989). Rhyme generation by deaf adults. *Journal of Speech and Hearing Research, 32*, 2–11.

Kuhl, P. K., & Meltzoff, A. N. (1982). The bimodal perception of speech in infancy. *Science, 218*, 1138–1141.

Lenel, J. C., & Cantor, J. H. (1981). Rhyme recognition and phonemic perception in young children. *Journal of Psycholinguistic Research, 10*, 57–67.

Leybaert, J. (in prep.). *The effect of early exposure to Cued Speech on the development of deaf children's spelling procedures.*

Leybaert, J., & Alegria, J. (1994). Cued Speech and the acquisition of reading by deaf children. *Cued Speech Journal, 4*, 24–36.

Leybaert, J., & Alegria, J. (1995). Spelling development of spelling in hearing and deaf children: Evidence for use of morpho-phonological regularities in French. *Reading and Writing, 7*, 89–109.

Leybaert, J., & Charlier, B. (1996). Visual speech in the head: The effect of Cued Speech on rhyming, remembering and spelling. *Journal of Deaf Studies and Deaf Education, 1*, 234–248.

Leybaert, J., Hage, C., Charlier, B., & Alegria, J. (1997). The effect of exposure to phonetically augmented lipspeech in the prelingual deaf. In R. Campbell, B. Dodd, & D. Burnham (Eds.), *Hearing by eye II* (pp. 287–299). Psychology Press.

Leybaert, J., & Marchettti, D. (1997). Visual rhyming effects in deaf children. In C. Benoît & R. Campbell (Eds.), *Proceedings of the ESCAM workshop on audio-visual speech processing* (pp. 13–16).

Locke, J. L. (1997). A theory of neurolinguistic development. *Brain and Language, 58*, 265–326.

MacKain, K. S., Studdert-Kennedy, M., Spieker, S., & Stern, D. (1983). Infant intermodal speech perception is a left hemisphere function. *Science, 219*, 1347–1349.

Marschark, M. (1993). *Psychological development of deaf children.* New York: Oxford University Press.

Mayberry, R., & Eichen, E. (1991). The long-lasting advantage of learning sign language in childhood: Another look at the critical period for language acquisition. *Journal of Memory and Language, 30,* 486–512.

Mayberry, R. (1995). Mental phonology and language comprehension, or what does that sign mistake mean? In K. Emmorey & J. Reilly (Eds.), *Language, gesture, and space* (pp. 355–370). Hillsdale, NJ: Lawrence Erlbaum Associates.

McGurk, H., & MacDonald, J. (1976). Hearing lips and seeing voices. *Nature, 264,* 746–748.

Nash, J. E. (1973). Cues or signs: A case study in language acquisition. *Sign Language Studies, 3,* 80–91.

Neville, H. J. (1991). Whence the specialization of the language hemisphere? In I. G. Mattingly & M. Studdert-Kennedy (Eds.), *Modularity and the motor theory of speech perception* (pp. 269–295). Hillsdale, NJ: Lawrence Erlbaum Associates.

Neville, H. J., Coffey, S. A., Lawson, D. S., Fischer, A., Emmorey, K., & Bellugi, U. (1997). Neural systems mediating american sign language: Effects of sensory experience and age of acquisition. *Brain and Language, 57,* 285–308.

Nicholls, G., & Ling, D. (1982). Cued Speech and the reception of spoken language. *Journal of Speech and Hearing Research, 25,* 262–269.

Nittrouer, S., Studdert-Kennedy, M., & McGowan, R. S. (1989). The emergence of phonetic segments: Evidence from the spectral structure of fricative-vowel syllables spoken by children and adults. *Journal of Speech and Hearing Research, 32,* 120–132.

Périer, O., Charlier, B. L., Hage, C., & Alegria, J. (1988). Evaluation of the effects of prolonged Cued Speech practice upon the reception of spoken language. In I. G. Taylor (Ed.), *The education of the deaf: Current perspectives,* Vol.1, 1985 International Congress on Education for the Deaf. London: Croom Helm.

Pettito, L. A., & Marentette, P. F. (1991). Babbling in the manual mode: Evidence for the ontogeny of language. *Science, 251,* 1493–1496.

Plant, G., & Spens, K. E. (1995). Profound deafness and speech communication. London: Whurr Publishers.

Poizner, H., Klima, E. S., & Bellugi, U. (1987). *What the hands reveal about the brain.* Cambridge, MA: MIT Press.

Stork, D. G., & Hennecke, M. E. (1996). *Speechreading by humans and machines: Models, systems and applications.* Berlin: Springer Verlag.

Quigley, S. P., & Kretschmer, R. E. (1982). *The education of deaf children: Issues, theory and practice.* Baltimore, MD: University Park Press.

Read, C. (1978). Children's awareness of language, with an emphasis on sound systems. In A. Sinclair, R. Jarvella, & W. Levelt (Eds.), *The child's conceptions of language* (pp. 65–82). New York: Springer-Verlag.

Reisberg, D., McLean, J., & Goldfield, A. (1987). Easy to hear but hard to understand: A lip-reading advantage with intact auditory stimuli. In B. Dodd & R. Campbell (Eds.), *Hearing by eye: The psychology of lip-reading* (pp. 97–113). Hillsdale, NJ: Lawrence Erlbaum Associates.

Slobin, D. (1978). A case study of early language awareness. In A. Sinclair, R. Jarvella, & W. Levelt (Eds.), *The child's conceptions of language* (pp. 45–54). New York: Springer-Verlag.

Sprenger-Charolles, L., & Siegel, L. S. (in press). A longitudinal study of the effects of syllabic structure on the development of reading and spelling skills in French. *Applied Psycholinguistics.*

Sterne, A. (1996). Phonological awareness, memory, and reading in deaf children. Unpublished doctoral dissertation, University of Cambridge.

Studdert-Kennedy, M. (1988). Reading gestures by light and sound: A comment on lipreading by Ruth Campbell. In A. W. Young & H. D. Ellis (Eds.), *Handbook of research on face processing* . New York: North Holland.

Summerfield, Q. (1987). Some preliminaries to a comprehensive account of audio-visual speech perception. In B. Dodd & R. Campbell (Eds.), *Hearing by eye: the psychology of lip-reading* (pp. 1–51). Mahwah, NJ: Lawrence Erlbaum Associates.

Swan, D., & Goswami, U. (1997). The relationship between picture naming and phonological awareness in developmental dyslexia. *Journal of Experimental Child Psychology.*

Swan, D., & Goswami, U. (in press). Phonological awareness deficits in developmental dyslexia and the phonological representations hypothesis.

Treiman, R., & Zukowski, A. (1991). Levels of phonological awareness. In S. A. Brady & D. P. Shankweiler (Eds.), *Phonological processes in literacy: A tribute to Isabelle Liberman.* Hillsdale, NJ: Lawrence Erlbaum Associates.

Walden, B. E., Prosek, R. A., Montgomery, A. A., Scherr, C. K., & Jones, C. J. (1977). Effects of training on the visual recognition of consonants. *Journal of Speech and Hearing Research, 20,* 130–145.

6

Play as "Window" and "Room": Assessing and Supporting the Cognitive and Linguistic Development of Deaf Infants and Young Children

Patricia Elizabeth Spencer
Gallaudet University

Jan Christian Hafer
Gallaudet University

Several years ago, we requested support from an administrator of a school for deaf children for a study of play behaviors of the infants and toddlers in their early intervention program. According to reports, the administrator (who rejected our request) asked, "Why on earth should we waste resources studying play anyway? We need to use all our energy teaching our deaf children language skills!"

After considerable mulling over of this response, we concluded that it was based on two possible assumptions. The first was that the play of young children is of little developmental importance. The second was that, even if play has some role in development, it does not differ for deaf and hearing children: It is necessary only to refer to existing literature about hearing children's play to know about deaf children's development. We disagree to some extent with both assumptions. At long last, here is our reply to the administrator's comments.

PLAY AS A "WINDOW" ON DEVELOPMENT

Young children's play is treated with considerable respect in literature devoted to early development, early childhood education, and even development of early literacy skills of hearing children (e.g., Christie, 1991; Hall, 1991). One important use for knowledge of young children's development of play is in assessment of cognitive–symbolic skills. Play behavior, especially play involving objects, has been characterized as providing a *window* through which these abilities can be observed (McCune, DiPane, Fireoved, & Fleck, 1994).

The majority of scales and procedures used to assess play of infants and toddlers is based either directly or indirectly on the work of Piaget (1952, 1962), which has been further documented and defined by a number of researchers (e.g., Belsky & Most, 1981; Fenson & Ramsay, 1980; Lowe, 1975; McCall, 1974; McCune, 1995; McCune-Nicolich, 1981). Piaget's now well-known reports of his own children's initial explorations and actions with objects provided a description of infants' journeys from the sensorimotor world of the here-and-now to a world in which symbolic representation and symbolization is commonplace. (See Table 6.1.)

During the first year of life, infants typically engage in simple explorations of single objects and repetitive actions on objects. These play actions at the level of *Manipulation* are similar initially, regardless of object characteristics but, as the first birthday approaches, become increasingly refined to take advantage of specific object characteristics. Early on, infants presented with a toy car will tend to mouth it, visually examine it, or perhaps tap it on a table top or the floor. Later, they attend more carefully to the car's unique attributes—perhaps spinning its wheels, opening doors or manipulating other moving parts, even rolling it across the floor. Infants may combine exploration of the car with use of other objects in *Relational* play—tapping on the car with a block, placing the car in and out of a box or bucket. Only later do they, as they approach

TABLE 6.1.
Cognitive Levels of Play During Infant and Toddler Ages

Prerepresentational Play
Manipulation—Oral and manual examination and manipulation of single objects.
Relational—Examination and manipulation of more than one object in an intentional or coordinated fashion.
Representational Play
Simple—Single acts of pretense with realistic toys.
Sequenced—A combination or series of thematically related acts of pretense.

Symbolic Play
Preplanned—Play at the Representational level that shows evidence of having been planned in advance. Evidence of planning can include specific search for object to use, arranging objects to ready for play, or verbal announcement that play acts are to occur.
Substitutional—Using an object in a way to show that it is substituting for another perceptually dissimilar object.

toddlerhood, begin to make "motor" noises or give evidence of *Representational* play in which they pretend that the toy is a real car.

Toddlers may engage in a sequence or combination of pretend activities with the car—"driving" it across the floor, running into an obstacle, perhaps sitting a toy doll on top of the car to give it a ride. Somewhat older toddlers, functioning at the *Symbolic* level of play, may use a block or other such object as a substitute "car" or may show through preparation or search activities that they plan to engage in a pretend activity involving a car or riding in a car. Finally, preschool children may engage in play that is related to a car but that includes many associated activities recreating a "real-life" story or script. These changes in degree of specificity and the degree of symbolism or pretense in object use, as well as in the degree of organization and coordination of play themes, reflect progressive growth in cognitive abilities. Because these play behaviors can occur and be recognized without the children's use of language, play-based assessments are often used to estimate a level of general cognitive development for infants and young children who are not yet producing much language expressively.

The advent of play involving pretense or pretend at the representational level gives evidence of emerging abilities to engage more generally in the use of symbols. For hearing children, this advance typically occurs at about the same time as production of the first spoken words (Bates, 1976; Kelly & Dale, 1989; McCune-Nicolich, 1982). Sequences or combinations of pretend activities with toy objects immediately precede or co-occur with the production of linguistic combinations (emerging syntax; Bates, Benigni, Bretherton, Camaioni, & Volterra, 1979; McCune-Nicolich & Bruskin, 1982). Demonstration of preplanning and "scripts" or elaborate thematic play sequences, which demonstrate symbolic-level play, tend to occur as children develop more complex syntactic and discourse abilities. Engaging in script-like play is thought to provide support for emerging literacy skills (Christie, 1991).

These play–language connections have prompted the use of play-based assessments to estimate cognitive readiness for the emergence and development of early language skills. Such assessments are thought to be especially helpful for children who are experiencing an apparent delay in the acquisition of language (Lowe, 1975; McCune-Nicolich & Carroll, 1981) or for children who are "reluctant" to speak during an assessment (Sigman & Sena, 1993, p. 38). Evidence of cognitive–symbolic abilities as shown through play behaviors can indicate sufficient cognitive abilities to support a specific level of language development—even if specific language delays or lack of sufficient exposure to a language system have interfered with language development. In contrast, an absence of play at that level can suggest that more than linguistic development is delayed and that more general developmental difficulties should be investigated.

Given the richness of the array of skills and abilities that can be observed in children's play, their inherent motivation to engage in play activities, and the fact that play may give evidence of cognitive–symbolic skills in children with language delay, play may provide a useful context for assessment of children who are deaf. Before this can be done with confidence, however, it is important to ascertain that the view through the play *window* can be expected to be the same for deaf and hearing children, and that there are no important differences in the progression of development of play skills by the two groups. This information is needed to determine whether existing descriptions of the timing and order of acquisition of play skills based on studies of hearing children should be used as a metric to assess cognitive and symbolic abilities of deaf children. Do observations of play provide an unbiased assessment of the developing cognitive skills and linguistic readiness of a group of children who experience a high rate of language delay and who, more than hearing children, must depend on vision for communication as well as for exploring and monitoring the play environment?

Some of the existing studies of play behaviors of deaf children suggest, in fact, that language skills can impact the level of play demonstrated. For example, deaf children with delayed language have been reported to engage in less "make believe" and less substitutional play than is usual for hearing children (with typical rates of language development) at the same age (Darbyshire, 1977; Schirmer, 1989). Gregory and Mogford (1983) found that deaf toddlers with significantly delayed language were deficient in higher levels of symbolic play, including play with imaginary objects, play coordinating more than one object, and play showing evidence of advance planning. Others have reported that the degree of delay in symbolic levels of play is directly associated with levels of language performance (Casby & McCormack, 1985; Vygotsky, 1978). To the degree that language delay hampers demonstration of age-appropriate play skills, the presumed ability to measure underlying cognitive potential and ability by observing play is compromised.

More recently, Spencer (1996) investigated the relation between expressive language and symbolic play of two groups of 2-year-old deaf children. One group of 10 children (DD) had deaf parents; another group of 10 children (DH) had hearing parents. A third group comprised of 10 hearing children (HH) with typical developmental rates was also included for comparison. Despite a strong tendency for higher language levels in groups DD and HH compared to group DH, there was diversity within each group in the language levels that were demonstrated. Three language groups were identified based on lexical size and typical length of linguistic expressions (single words or signs or multiword/sign utterances). Data were collected during a 30-minute mother–child play session at home. The first 20 minutes of each play session were coded to determine the amount of time the children engaged in representational and symbolic play. Play behaviors were categorized as single acts of representational-level play, sequences of representational play acts, and abstract symbolic play (characterized by advance planning and/or object substitutions).

Analyses indicated that language level was associated positively with duration as well as frequency of sequenced play in which the play acts were produced in a logical or "canonical" order. (Canonical play sequences replicate the order of acts in a "real" scenario.) Language level also appeared to be related to the prevalence of play that was "preplanned." Substitution play occurred too rarely for analysis. Thus, this study, like most earlier ones, indicated a relation between level of language development and the production of symbolic or abstract play. Further analysis focusing only on the DH group found this association even when the children's language development was delayed because of lack of exposure to a language model and apparently not because of other social or organic developmental problems. Such a relation suggests that, instead of play developing at typical rates when children's language development is delayed, there is a reciprocal delay in at least *selected* aspects of symbolic or abstract play that involve complex sequencing or preplanning. Observations of play may not, therefore, provide the hoped-for unbiased estimate of underlying cognitive–symbolic ability.

In both the Spencer (1996) and Gregory and Mogford (1983) studies, simpler representational play was observed in equal amounts from children with and without language delay. Thus it is possible that at least at this level, play can inform about cognitive–symbolic functioning and cognitive readiness for language in children with language delays. However, both of these studies included only children (15 months and older) who were already past the chronological age at which representational play typically emerges. Do findings from these two studies indicate that language (or the lack of it) has no effect on development of representational level play? Or might it be that initial delays in representational play had been experienced by these children with delayed language but had been resolved by the time the children had entered their second year of life?

Spencer and Meadow-Orlans (1996) investigated this question with a younger cohort of deaf and hearing children. A longitudinal study assessed the play behaviors of three groups of infants at the ages of 9, 12, and 18 months. The infants were videotaped in a laboratory setting during 15 to 20 minutes of interaction with their mothers, although only 10 minutes of the interactions were coded. The subjects included 13 deaf children with deaf parents (DD), 15 deaf children with hearing parents (DH), and 15 hearing children with hearing parents (HH). Beginning at this early age allowed the observation of play during transitions from primarily manipulation and relational play to representational and, finally, symbolic play.

Language levels were characterized in this study based on the children's expressive language performance during the play session. At 9 months, no expressive language was observed. At 12 months, the language measure was dichotomous: Infants were categorized as using or not using language expressively. (60% of HH, 54% of DD, and only 1 [6%] DH infant produced expressive language at this age.) At 18 months, language levels were categorized as "emerging single-word/sign production," "established single-word/sign production," or "emerging syntax production." Although language levels were generally higher for HH and DD than DH children, there was again considerable diversity within groups.

At 9 months, the infants engaged in manipulation and relational play only. Regression analyses indicated that language level was not a significant predictor of time in simple or sequenced representational play at 12 months. (No symbolic-level play occurred at that age.) At 18 months, language was a marginally significant contributor ($p=.06$) to the full regression equation predicting preplanned (symbolic) play. These findings are consistent with a hypothesis that the development of language and play occur independently during the first year or so of life but become intertwined to a greater degree during the second year of life. (Interdependence of play and language skills may be observed only after language skills are developed to a degree sufficient to aid in storage and retrieval of symbolic "memories.") Given the relative lack of association between language and play at the earliest developmental levels, it would at first appear that play assessments of development before and around 1 year of age can provide unbiased measures of cognitive–symbolic abilities for young deaf children even when language acquisition is delayed. It is important, though, to consider other findings from the study before making that judgment.

The same set of analyses produced another finding that greatly surprised the researchers: Infant hearing status itself was related to the amount of representational play produced at the 12-month session. Hearing infants engaged in more representational play than did either group of deaf infants, regardless of parent hearing status or the rate of the deaf child's acquisition of language. This initial lag in representational play for DD and DH children was no longer significant by 18 months. At this age, the play of HH and DD children was highly similar. However, although DH children no longer trailed DD and HH children on production of representational play, the DH children produced less symbolic-level play than the other two groups. Thus, DH children, who tended more than the other groups to have delays in language development, continued to show a pattern of delay in development of play. (See Figs. 6.1 and 6.2.)

In this study, being deaf was associated with a lag in expression of representational play at around 12 months of age. Although this lag resolved by 18 months for deaf children whose language was developing at a normal rate, a continuing delay was noticed for deaf children who continued to lag in language development. As a result, play levels demonstrated at 12 months by deaf children in both groups failed to predict significantly their levels of play at 18 months, although 12- and 18-month levels were associated for hearing children. Findings from this study raise significant questions about the validity of assessments of play behaviors of deaf infants around 1 year of age if comparison is made with data from hearing children. Will such observations give a misleading view of the symbolic abilities of deaf children during the second year of life even when language is developing at a typical rate? What might be different in the situation for deaf and hearing infants at this important developmental juncture that results in the play differences observed?

The Spencer and Meadow-Orlans (1996) study included an additional factor that had been reported previously to influence the level of play demonstrated by hearing children. This factor was a measure of maternal responsiveness during the play interaction. The measure used was derived from a scale developed by Meadow-Orlans and Steinberg (1993) and was

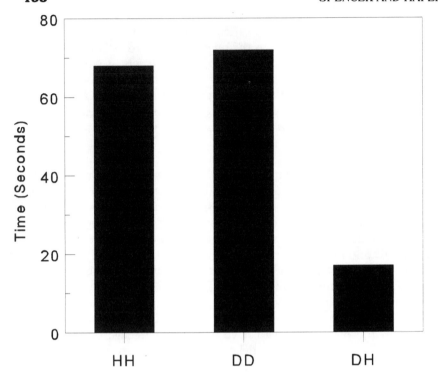

HH = Hearing Infant, Hearing Mother
DD = Deaf Infant, Deaf Mother
DH = Deaf Infant, Hearing Mother

FIG. 6.1. Time (seconds) in Symbolic play at 18 months (during 10 minutes of dyadic play).

a composite of ratings from three of the dimensions included in the original scale: (a) Sensitivity (High rating—Mother responds to child's interests and is willing to continue activity initiated by the child; Low rating—Mother intrudes on child's attention or self-initiated exploration or activity); (b) Flexibility (High rating—Mother is willing to bend rules at times and will accept child's expression of disinterest in her proposed activity; Low rating—Mother is rigid and unwilling to change a routine that has begun); and (c) Consistency (High rating—Mothers' affect, flexibility–rigidity, and responsiveness–nonresponsiveness are not subject

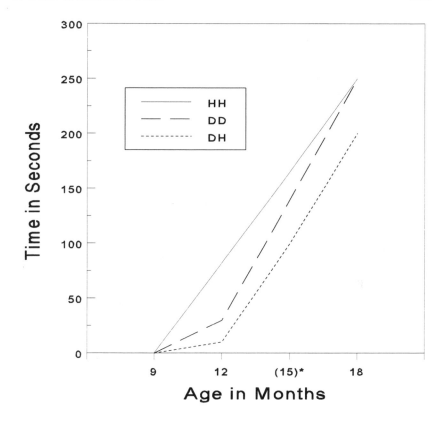

Age in Months

HH = Hearing Infant, Hearing Mother
DD = Deaf Infant, Deaf Mother
DH = Deaf Infant, Hearing Mother

12 Months: HH > DD, DH

* Interpolated

FIG. 6.2. Time in Representational play: 9, 12, and 18 months.

to quick changes; Low rating—Frequent abrupt and unpredictable changes in the preceding characteristics).

Previous studies indicated that maternal responsiveness tends to decrease in dyads of hearing mothers and deaf children. This was again found by Spencer and Meadow-Orlans (1996). In addition, maternal responsiveness was associated positively with the production of higher-level, symbolic play at 18 months for the children in the study, regardless of hearing status. Thus, maternal responsiveness appears to have similar effects on deaf and hearing toddlers' play. The tendency toward less responsiveness from mothers of DH children, however, suggests that the environment in which those dyads interact may provide less support for DH children's play than is typically experienced by DD and HH dyads.

What do these studies suggest about the use of observations of play for assessing general cognitive–symbolic levels of deaf infants and toddlers? Should one expect the view through the play "window" to look the same for deaf and hearing infants and toddlers who are developing at typical rates? We definitely do not want to discourage the use of play-based assessments for children who are deaf. We continue to be impressed with the amount of information available about cognitive, social, linguistic, and motor development in a dyadic play situation and are well aware of the difficulties obtaining valid information from structured testing of infants and toddlers, especially those who are deaf. However, available data suggest that the rate of development of play differs between young deaf and hearing children. To date, three areas of concern have been raised: (a) Being deaf may result in production of fewer representational play acts at around one-year of age when compared to the play of same-age hearing infants; (b) From about the age of 18 months or so, when children typically begin to produce signed or spoken utterances greater than one unit in length and complexity, significant delays in language development may be reflected in deficits in production of logically or realistically ordered sequences of play actions centered on a theme, and on play that is obviously preplanned; (c) By about the same age, differences in maternal interactive responsiveness, frequently reported to be a problem in DH dyads, may be reflected in deficits again in the higher, symbolic levels of play sequencing and preplanning.

Given that play-based assessments may be most helpful for children at these young ages, it is critical that expectations be established for deaf children that do not result in negatively biased conclusions about their development. Current information is limited in that studies are few, and those available include relatively few participating children. In addition, there is little diversity in the racial, ethnic, socioeconomic status, and rate of overall development in the children who have been studied thus far. Clearly, additional research is needed both to replicate and expand existing studies.

PLAY AS A "ROOM" OR CONTEXT
IN WHICH DEVELOPMENT OCCURS

In addition to providing a view of a young child's current developmental level, play is thought to be a particularly conducive context for *promoting* further development in cognitive and linguistic skills. Even when a child is playing alone, the freedom and positive affective characteristics of a play context encourage experimentation, flexible application of known behaviors to new objects, and practice and reinforcement of emerging skills and behaviors. Chance (1979), summarizing discussions among leading investigators of children's play, described a "play–competence spiral" in which "learning leads to more sophisticated play, and play provides a kind of mastery that leads to more learning, which leads to more sophisticated play… " (pp. 23–24). Although the benefits of play are often thought of in relation to concepts about objects and general cognition, the participants in these discussions pointed out that the practice–improve play spiral is also typical of language development. (See also Weir, 1962, who documented her child's experimentation and "practice play" with babbling and emerging linguistic structures.) Thus, we propose that a play situation can be conceived of as a "room" in which freedom to practice, experiment, and extend current skills in a number of domains is available.

Note, however, that findings of studies summarized previously suggest that the "room" looks different when viewed through the window of observations of play of deaf children compared to the view for hearing children. How might these differences impact the degree to which a play context can support cognitive and linguistic development of deaf and hearing children?

If play can be thought of as a room in which development is supported, young children are rarely in that room alone. We know from observations of dyadic play of hearing infants and children with hearing mothers that the potential value of play in promoting development is enhanced by the involvement of a more experienced play partner (O'Connell & Bretherton, 1984; Slade, 1987a). However, the mere presence of an expert partner (whether older child, parent, or other caregiver) does not serve this function. Instead, fairly specific maternal behaviors and interactive characteristics promote development in the play setting.

General affective aspects of mother–child interaction are associated with young children's play sophistication: Affectively positive interactions in which mothers are warm and responsive to the children's interests are associated with higher levels of children's play (Vibbert & Bornstein, 1989). Thus, it is not surprising that secure attachment (which is thought to result from positive, sensitive parenting behaviors) is associated with higher levels of toddler play (Slade, 1987b). In fact, Slade found that maternal involvement facilitated a child's play only when secure attachment had been established, and Fiese (1990) reported that children's play levels decreased rather than increased after intrusive attempts by mothers to redirect play. Although there is no evidence of differences in the warmth or security of attachment between deaf or hearing children and their mothers (Koester & MacTurk, 1991; Lederberg & Mobley, 1990), dyads of hearing mothers and deaf children experience problems establishing reciprocal, mutually responsive interactions (Meadow, Greenberg, Erting, & Carmichael, 1981; Meadow-Orlans, 1997; Power, Wood, Wood, & MacDongall, 1990; Wedell-Monnig, & Lumley, 1980). These difficulties may result in dyadic play providing a less conducive environment for acquisition of play and language skills by children in this group.

In addition to general interactive characteristics, specific maternal behaviors have been found to be supportive of hearing infant–toddler play. These behaviors include soliciting and demonstrating or modelling play (Fiese, 1990) as well as stimulating play by pointing toward or highlighting objects in the environment or by suggesting or naming objects and activities verbally (Belsky, Goode, & Most, 1980). Although it would seem that similar strategies support play of deaf children, there have been no published reports yet of the effects of specific maternal behaviors on their play.

Part of the value to children of engaging in dyadic play accrues to language development, which benefits from the language model presented to the child while he or she engages in play. In HH dyads, language produced by mothers seems to support child language acquisition most effectively when it directly relates to an object or action with which the child is already engaged and interested (Tomasello, 1988). Such language can take the form of mirroring or imitation of the child's utterances, commenting on the child's actions, describing mother's own actions when the child is attending to her, and (with children who are showing the ability to produce connected or multiword utterances) asking open-ended questions and expanding on the child's utterances (Linder, 1993). In reports of hearing children's development, there are also indications that the sheer quantity of maternal language during interactions is associated with rate of language acquisition. There is one recent report that the degree to which deaf mothers' language is responsive, or semantically related to deaf infants' current focus of attention is associated with deaf children's language level (Wilson & Spencer, 1997). This suggests that responsiveness of mothers' language influences the development of deaf, as well as hearing, children.

Although linguistic responsiveness appears to be distributed similarly for HH and DD mothers, this is not the case for DH dyads. Clearly, some hearing mothers provide highly responsive language models for their deaf children, although this is less frequently accomplished than in dyads in which hearing status of mothers and children are matched (Jamieson, 1994; Spencer, Bodner-Johnson, & Gutfreund, 1992). Thus, again, environmental characteristics may interfere or at least fail to provide support for development in the DH group equivalent to that experienced by other children. Maternal responsiveness and dyadic reciprocity and mutual understanding do not, however, tend to differ between DD and HH mothers. Thus, these factors do not explain the difference found between HH and DD children at 12 months. Are there other factors that might result in the differences in representational play observed near 12 months for hearing children and deaf children regardless of language level and parent hearing status? What might this difference indicate about the play "room" as providing an optimal context for learning and development of deaf compared to hearing children? Given that we have as yet no data-based reports on differences in specific play behaviors of deaf and hearing mothers, we must turn to information available about communication behaviors of these mothers to look for differences that might relate to their support of play.

One striking difference between deaf mothers who sign and hearing mothers who speak (even when they are accompanying some of that speech with signs) is in the quantity of language produced during interactions with their infants. It is now recognized that deaf mothers tend to produce far less language during toy-play interactions with deaf infants than is typical for hearing mothers (Mohay, Luttrell, & Milton, 1991). Furthermore, this difference is greater with infants at 12 than at 18 months (Spencer, Lederberg, & Waxman, 1996.; Waxman & Spencer, 1997). Could it be that deaf mothers of deaf infants are less likely to prompt or "boost" play with language than are hearing mothers of hearing infants? Unfortunately, we were unable to locate any data regarding deaf mothers' nonlinguistic prompting of play. However, the language data as well as other reports of deaf mothers waiting frequently for their children's attention before signing to them (Spencer et al., 1992) raise the possibility that deaf mothers are generally less likely to try to prompt their infants' play at this age than are hearing mothers. This may be due to differences in turntaking and communication patterns necessitated by reliance on visual communication.

Unlike hearing persons, who can receive language directed to them while looking away from the speaker, deaf children and their mothers must split their visual attention between animate and inanimate aspects of the play situation (Wood, 1989). Attention to objects must be broken frequently in order to attend to communicative messages. Of course, deaf mothers who are experienced visual communicators utilize a variety of well-adapted strategies (one of which is apparently a decrease in quantity of language produced) to accommodate this need in their infants. The following transcript of a deaf mother and her 12-month-old deaf infant during almost 2 minutes of play illustrates a variety of these strategies:

> 12 Months: (Signs are shown in all capital letters.) M (mother) and D (infant) are seated on the floor with toys scattered about. D reaches out and tries to pick up a plastic shape-sorting bowl with a lid that has different shape cut-outs. M reaches across and brings the bowl closer to D. Reaching down to sign within D's visual field (where D is already looking), M signs OPEN OPEN with large, slow movements. D tries to pull off the lid but is unsuccessful. D looks up at M who nods and signs OPEN OPEN. D appears to imitate the sign, moving his hands together and quickly apart. He is looking up at mother who signs OPEN YES. D picks up the bowl and drops it. The lid pops off. M signs WELL, and claps her hands in a congratulatory manner. The signs are made in D's peripheral visual field. D looks up, then back down at the bowl. M moves the bowl closer to D, who replaces the lid. M moves her hands down to sign PUT–ON in D's visual field. D looks up at M, who then signs GOOD. While D continues to look up at M, she gives another congratulatory hand-clap and signs YOUR (apparently meaning "you did it"). D then looks back down at the toy and explores it visually and tactually for some time while M looks on quietly and attentively.

This deaf mother has produced far less language during this period of time than would be expected from a hearing mother with a hearing child. However, the deaf mother's language appears to be highly responsive not only semantically (following the infant's interest and actions) but also visually. She tends to sign within the visual field where the infant is already looking, although once signing in his peripheral visual field as Swisher (1992) reported does occur sometimes. Mother also tends to sign every time the infant looks up at her but is willing, especially at the end of this segment, to sit quietly while the infant explores the toy. Mother's signs are noticeably large and produced slowly compared with signing to an adult. The sign OPEN is produced with a repeated movement. These characteristics probably cause the signing to be more visually salient and processed more easily than adult-like signing would be.

In the interaction just recounted, the mother makes few play suggestions and apparently focuses her attention on responding to her infant's demonstrations of interest. The next excerpt of interaction occurred when the same child was 18 months old. It is notable that although this interaction lasted only a little longer than that at 12 months, the transcript is much longer. This change in length reflects a more active communication style from both mother and child and is typical of developmental changes seen in other DD dyads between 12 and 18 months (Spencer, Lederberg, & Waxman, 1996).

> 18 Months: (Signs are shown in all capital letters.) D kneels and looks at three dolls M has placed in a row on the floor. D looks up at M who then

signs BOY GIRL INDEX (point to)-boy doll INDEX (point to)-girl doll. D reaches for one of the dolls and M moves it closer to him, signing DOLL. D has not seen the sign. M picks up another doll, moves it toward D, and taps D on the shoulder. D immediately looks up at M and she signs DOLL. D looks down at doll, then back up to M with no prompting. M signs BOY with several repeated movements, POINTS to boy doll, then signs BOY again. D visually follows the point then follows M's hand back up to her face to observe the "boy" sign. M then POINTS to the girl doll, and signs GIRL (movement for sign is repeated quickly—at least 6 times). Again D follows her hand movements and is able to see the doll, then look back up to see the sign. D then points to a monkey toy and looks up at M, who immediately signs MONKEY with several repeated movements. D looks back down at the dolls and monkey. M straightens out the boy doll to make him "lie down" then taps on D's shoulder. D looks up immediately and M signs SLEEP/BED on the side of her face. M reaches to D's left and picks up a small piece of felt cloth and another piece of cloth. With the cloths in her hands, she signs BLANKET and places each cloth over a doll like a blanket. D visually follows these movements. He puts a finger to his mouth as if to sign SHHH and looks at M. M leans in toward D and signs SHHHH SLEEP/BED. D watches as M covers another doll, then D reaches out, pulls up the cloths with a quick movement, and looks up at M while smiling. M sits quietly and smiles back at D, watching his actions. D POINTS to the boy doll, then looks up at M who immediately signs BOY and picks up the doll, moving it toward D. D reaches out and touches/points at the doll's eye, then looks up at M who immediately signs EYE. M then POINTS to each of the doll's eyes and to her own. D looks back at the dolls and picks up the girl doll. M signs EYE. As her hand moves toward her own eye, D looks up at her. He then looks back down at the dolls, signs SLEEP/BED (making the sign with only one hand brought to the side of his face) and arranges the three dolls as if to put them to bed. D looks around and finds another doll which he puts with the others, again signing SLEEP/BED. Turning away from the dolls and back to M, D signs SLEEP/BED. M signs WHERE SLEEP/BED BLANKET? SLEEP/BED INDEX (point to)-cloth as she indicates the cloths behind D. D turns around to look but does not immediately see the cloths. M taps on the side of D's arm and again POINTS toward the cloths. D visually follows the point and picks up the cloths, puts them on the dolls, and looking up with an impish grin, signs SLEEP/BED. This time D makes the sign with both hands but with one on each side of his face. He acts as though he thinks this is funny. M smiles and signs SLEEP/BED YES (giving an exaggerated head nod) SLEEP/BED.

Although even at 18 months this deaf mother used less language than is characteristic of hearing mothers, she has increased not only the quantity but the speed of her language production since the 12-month session. Despite, or perhaps because of, these changes in her language production the mother provides numerous, quickly made repetitions of signs while the child is looking. In addition, she is taking a more active role than before in prompting play and redirecting the child's visual attention: The mother now suggests a symbolic play act when the child is merely gazing at the toys; she actively redirects the child's visual attention from objects back to herself and her communications. It is noticeable also that the child is very visually alert and responds readily to mother's signals (taps, points, moving objects toward herself) to redirect attention.

The language and attention-related strategies used by this deaf mother are characteristic of those shown by most of the deaf mothers we have observed. Deaf mothers, like hearing mothers, differ in the degree to which they successfully modify their communication behaviors to match their infants' needs. However, visually sensitive interactive behaviors including modifying the location, speed, size, and frequency of signing to accommodate their children's attending skills, as well as tapping on the child to redirect attention are common (e.g., Erting, Prezioso, & Hynes, 1994; Harris, 1992; Mohay et al., 1991; Waxman & Spencer, 1997). Deaf mothers' own experiences as visual communicators may allow them to employ these strategies intuitively (Koester, 1992), without conscious planning, and to readily modify their own behaviors as their children mature as communication partners. Their experience with signing and visual communication may also give deaf mothers comfort with and confidence in their ability to parent deaf children and thus indirectly lead to high levels of responsiveness and flexibility during interactions with the children.

Observations of the communicative behaviors of deaf mothers interacting with deaf infants lead us to conclude that a "room" providing deaf children a play context optimally facilitative of cognitive and linguistic development may be furnished a bit differently from one that best fits the needs of hearing children. That these differences are adaptive is shown by the evidence that symbolic play as well as communication skills of deaf children with deaf parents match those of hearing children at 18 months and beyond (Spencer, 1996; Spencer & Lederberg, 1997; Spencer & Meadow-Orlans, 1996).

Is this typically the case for deaf children with hearing parents? It certainly can be. We have observed such children who, either because of amplification and maximal use of residual hearing or because of parents' abilities to accommodate their needs for visual communication, have achieved developmental stages at ages typical for hearing peers and deaf peers with deaf parents. Unfortunately, these examples remain infrequent. Many hearing parents apparently find the task of learning signs and adapting to visual communication to be daunting. Adopting signals for visual turntaking and knowing how to help their deaf infants and children hone visual attention skills is not second nature, or intuitive, for persons who depend primarily on auditory-based communication. Confusion about the basic communicative rules and attention needs for a visually based communication system may be one factor that interferes with hearing parents' comfort and abilities to provide a responsive communicative and play environment for deaf children.

Hafer and Topolosky (1995) noted that providing a maximally supportive context for deaf children's acquisition of skills requires a *combination* of two different sets of parenting behaviors. One set appears to be critical regardless of communication modality. This set includes responsive communication, modeling of play and language behaviors, and providing a secure environment for learning. Parents, hearing or deaf, may be more or less skilled in this area. The other set is of special importance for parents of deaf children. This is the set of behaviors mentioned previously that are specific to visual communication: (a) modifying signs to attract attention to them by signing slowly, rhythmically, with large movements and many repetitions; (b) modifying the location of signs to produce them on or near an object to which the child is already attending; (c) using attention-directing signals including tapping on the child and waving in the visual field; and (d) waiting to allow the child to attend sequentially to an object or event and then to the communication partner. Again, both deaf and hearing parents will vary in their abilities to employ these strategies effectively, but hearing parents can be expected to have more difficulty with this set of behaviors.

Until *both* sets of interactive or communicative strategies are used consistently, parents and deaf infants or children will face difficulties in interactions—and these difficulties may be particularly noticeable during play when objects compete with the communication partner for the child's attention. It is doubtful that dyadic play interactions can provide the expected comfortable "room" for development when these two sets of interactive skills or strategies are not readily employed by the parent. Of course, this is also true when the child's interaction partner is another adult like a teacher or therapist or even an older child.

How "learnable" are these two sets of skills? And what is the most effective way to increase adults' effective use of the skills? Available evidence is primarily anecdotal. We have seen effective instruction in these strategies employed by gifted teachers and therapists in parent-infant and early education programs. At least one formal curriculum has been developed (Mohay, Milton, & Turner, 1993) and other programs are actively engaged in helping parents improve their use of these behaviors and strategies (Scuyler, 1993; Topolosky, personal communication, May 2, 1994). However, to our knowledge, there has been no controlled study to provide evidence about effects of various lengths and types of training on behaviors of parents and children's cognitive and linguistic development. Results of systematic studies of interventions are necessary to help programs make informed decisions about the types of training and parent support that provide the best outcome for effort expended.

In addition, it is important to determine whether employing the combined responsiveness- and visually-oriented strategies discussed previously will influence assessment results. Will deaf children show higher levels of play and associated skills when assessment specialists (or parents who serve as partners in the assessment process) are experienced in the combined responsive and visually sensitive techniques? If this turns out *not* to be the case, might direct elicitation of higher-level play behaviors effectively increase the level of play shown by deaf infants and young children? If so, use of an elicitation context as well as more naturalistic dyadic play contexts may be necessary to avoid misleading results. On the other hand, it is possible that the apparent lag in representational play found for deaf children (regardless of parent hearing status and child language level) at 12 months by Spencer and Meadow-Orlans (1996) reflected actual competence differences at that age. If neither free play in a setting more conducive to visual communication nor elicited play formats result in deaf infants' play levels consistently matching those of hearing infants, it may be necessary to establish expectations for performance specific to deaf children if bias in assessment results is to be avoided.

SUMMARY

Studies of hearing children's play have provided interventionists and caregivers with (a) a picture of play as a readily observed behavior that gives evidence of a child's cognitive and social skill development and readiness for language and (b) a description of characteristics of the social context that promote optimal opportunities for young children to practice and elaborate their cognitive and linguistic skills. We believe that play can provide equal opportunities for assessment of existing skills and facilitation of further development for deaf children. However, evidence was presented that suggests a potential for bias if existing expectations for development of play which have been derived from observations of hearing infants and toddlers are applied indiscriminately to assessment of deaf children.

At least around the age of 12 months, deaf and hearing children show different amounts of representational play during interaction with mothers, even when (as for most deaf children with deaf parents) the children's language is developing at a normal rate. This may indicate an underlying difference in play competence at that developmental juncture, perhaps reflecting differences for deaf and hearing toddlers in the importance of, and developmental energy used to support, acquisition of flexible visual attention skills. Alternatively, the difference found at 12 months may merely reflect a difference in the degree to which mothers actively support and encourage specific play behaviors, with deaf mothers tending to be less active in that regard. If this is the case, the play of deaf children with deaf mothers may be more consistent with independent than with supported levels of play at around 1 year of age. Whatever its source, the difference in play disappears by 18 months of age for deaf and hearing children when levels of language skills and maternal responsiveness are similar.

The developmental pattern is more complicated for deaf children for whom language development is delayed and maternal responsiveness is relatively low during interactions. In this case, delays in representational play at 12 months lessen by 18 months, but a deficit in higher-level symbolic play is then seen (and continues to be seen at 2 years of age) relative to hearing children and deaf children with more optimal language development and interactive experiences. It is unclear to what degree this continuing delay in play levels observed during assessments reflects differences in supportiveness in the play context or, alternatively, gives evidence of actual immaturity in cognitive–symbolic development. It seems reasonable to assume that patterns of mother–child interaction that result in decreased evidence of higher-level play over time are also failing routinely to provide optimal support during play for developing cognitive, language, and social skills.

Given the important role of play experiences in promoting development, and the frequent use of play observations to assess development of infants and toddlers, we believe that play experiences and performances of young deaf children need further investigation. Systematic investigation and comparison of interventions are needed to determine ways to assure that play experiences provide a comfortable, supportive "room" in which deaf (like hearing) infants and toddlers can experiment with and enhance their emerging skills: linguistic, cognitive, and social. Finally, interventionists need more information about what to expect when they look through the "window" provided by deaf children's play to assess their development and the effects of programming efforts. We hope that program administrators, interventionists, and parents of deaf children will recognize that play is, in fact, serious business. Perhaps then they will be more willing to support investigations to assure that deaf children have opportunities for effective learning through the medium of play.

REFERENCES

Bates, E. (1976). *Language and context: The acquisition of pragmatics*. New York: Academic Press.

Bates, E., Benigni, L., Bretherton, I., Camaioni, L., & Volterra, V. (1979). *The emergence of symbols: Cognition and communication in infancy*. New York: Academic Press.

Belsky, J., & Most, R. (1981). From exploration to play: A cross-sectional study of infant free play behavior. *Developmental Psychology, 17*, 630–639.

Belsky, J., Goode, M., & Most, R. (1980). Maternal stimulation and infant exploratory competence: Cross-sectional, correlational, and experimental analyses. *Child Development, 51*, 1163–1178.

Casby, M., & McCormack, S. (1985). Symbolic play and early communication development in hearing-impaired children. *Journal of Communication Disorders, 18*, 67–78.

Chance, P. (1979). *Learning through play*. New York: Gardner Press.

Christie, J. (1991). Psychological research on play: Connections with early literacy development. In J. Christie (Ed.), *Play and early literacy development* (pp. 27–43). Albany, NY: State University of New York Press.

Darbyshire, J. (1977). Play patterns in young children with impaired hearing. *Volta Review, 79*, 19–26.

Erting, C. J., Prezioso, C., & Hynes, M. (1994). The interactional context of deaf mother–infant communication. In V. Volterra & C. J. Erting (Eds.), *From gesture to language in hearing and deaf children*. Washington, DC: Gallaudet University Press.

Fenson, L., & Ramsay, D. (1980). Decentration and integration of the child's play in the second year. *Child Development, 51*, 171–178.

Fiese, B. (1990). Playful relationships: A contextual analysis of mother–toddler interaction and symbolic play. *Child Development, 61*, 1648–1656.

Gregory, S., & Mogford, K. (1983). The development of symbolic play in young deaf children. In D. Rodgers & J. Sloboda (Eds.), *The acquisition of symbolic skills* (pp. 221–231). New York: Plenum.

Hafer, J., & Topolosky, A. (1995, June). Facilitating language through play. Paper presented at Conference of American Instructors of the Deaf. Minneapolis MN.

Hall, N. (1991). Play and the emergence of literacy. In J. Christie (Ed.), *Play and early literacy development* (pp. 3–25). Albany, NY: State University of New York Press.

Harris, M. (1992). *Language experience and early language development: From input to uptake*. Hillsdale, NJ: Lawrence Erlbaum Associates.

Jamieson, J. (1994). Teaching as transaction: Vygotskian perspectives on deafness and mother–child interaction. *Exceptional Children, 60*, 434–449.

Kelly, C., & Dale, P. (1989). Cognitive skills associated with the onset of multiword utterances. *Journal of Speech and Hearing Research, 32*, 645–656.

Koester, L. (1992). Intuitive parenting as a model for understanding parent–infant interactions when one partner is deaf. *American Annals of the Deaf, 137*, 362–369.

Koester, L., & MacTurk, R. (1991). Attachment behaviors in deaf and hearing infants. In K. Meadow-Orlans, R. MacTurk, P. Spencer, & L. Koester, *Interaction and support: Mothers and deaf infants*. Final report to Maternal and Child Health Research Program, Bureau of Maternal and Child Health and Resources Development, HRSA, PHS, DHHS. Grant MCJ-110563.

Lederberg, A., & Mobley, C. (1990). The effect of hearing impairment on the quality of attachment and mother-toddler interaction. *Child Development, 61*, 1596–1604.

Linder, T. (1993). *Transdisciplinary play-based assessment*. Baltimore: Brookes.

Lowe, M. (1975). Trends in the development of representational play in infants from one to three years—An observational study. *Journal of Child Psychology and Psychiatry, 16*, 33–47.

McCall, R. (1974). Exploratory manipulation and play in the human infant. *Monographs of the Society for Research in Child Development, 39* (2, Serial No. 155).
McCune, L. (1995). A normative study of representational play at the transition to language. *Developmental Psychology, 31,* 198–206.
McCune, L, DiPane, D., Fireoved, R., & Fleck, M. (1994). Play: A context for mutual regulation within mother–child interaction. In A. Slade & D. P. Wolf (Eds.), *Children at play: Clinical and developmental approaches to meaning and representation* (pp. 148–166). New York: Oxford University Press.
McCune-Nicolich, L. (1981). Toward symbolic functioning: Structure of early pretend games and potential parallels with language. *Child Development, 52,* 785–797.
McCune-Nicolich, L. (1982). Play as prelinguistic behavior: Theory, evidence, and applications. In D. McClowry, A. Guilford, & S. Richardson (Eds.), *Infant communication development, assessment, and interaction* (pp. 55–81). Philadelphia, PA: Grune & Stratton.
McCune-Nicolich, L., & Bruskin, C. (1982). Combinatorial competency in play and language. In K. Rubin & D. Pepler (Eds.), *The play of children: Current theory and research* (pp. 30–40). Basel, Switzerland: Karger.
McCune-Nicolich, L., & Carroll, S. (1981). Development of symbolic play: Implications for the language specialist. *Topics in Language Disorders,* 1–15.
Meadow, K., Greenberg, M., Erting, C., & Carmichael, H. (1981). Interactions of deaf mothers and deaf preschool children: Comparisons with three other groups of deaf and hearing dyads. *American Annals of the Deaf, 126,* 454–468.
Meadow-Orlans, K. (1997). Effects of mother and infant hearing status on interactions at twelve and eighteen months. *Journal of Deaf Studies and Deaf Education, 2*(1), 26–36.
Meadow-Orlans, K., & Steinberg, A. (1993). Effects of infant hearing loss and maternal support on mother–infant interactions at eighteen months. *Journal of Applied Developmental Psychology, 14,* 407–426.
Mohay, H., Luttrel, R., & Milton, L. (1991, January). How much, how often and in what form should linguistic input be given to deaf infants? *Proceedings,* Australian and New Zealand Conference for Educators of the Deaf. Queensland, Australia.
Mohay, H., Milton, L., & Turner, K. (1993, September). Teaching hearing mothers of deaf children the communication strategies used by deaf mothers. Paper presented at the Developmental Psychology Conference. Birmingham, U.K.
O'Connell, B., & Bretherton, I. (1984). Toddlers' play, alone and with mother: The role of maternal guidance. In I. Bretherton (Ed.), *Symbolic play: The development of social understanding* (pp. 337–368). Orlando, FL: Academic Press.
Piaget, J. (1952). *The origins of intelligence in children.* New York: Norton.
Piaget, J. (1962). *Play, dreams, and imitation in childhood.* New York: Norton.
Power, D., Wood, D., Wood, A., & MacDougall, J. (1990). Maternal control over conversations with hearing and deaf infants and young children. *First Language, 10,* 19–35.
Schirmer, B. (1989). Relationships between imaginative play and language development in hearing-impaired children. *American Annals of the Deaf, 134,* 219–222.
Scuyler, V. (1993). *Promoting early communication II: The role of the family.* Portland, OR: Infant Hearing Resource, Portland Center for Speech and Hearing.
Sigman, M., & Sena, R. (1993). Pretend play in high-risk and developmentally delayed children. In M. Bornstein & A. Watson O'Reilly (Eds.), *The role of play in the development of thought* (pp. 29–42). San Francisco: Jossey-Bass.
Slade, A. (1987a). Quality of attachment and early symbolic play. *Developmental Psychology, 23,* 78–85.
Slade, A. (1987b). A longitudinal study of maternal involvement and symbolic play during the toddler period. *Child Development, 58,* 367–375.

Spencer, P. (1996). The association between language and symbolic play at two years: Evidence from deaf toddlers. *Child Development, 67*, 867–876.

Spencer, P., Bodner-Johnson, B., & Gutfreund, M. (1992). Interacting with infants with a hearing loss: What can we learn from mothers who are deaf? *Journal of Early Intervention, 16*, 64–78.

Spencer, P., & Lederberg, A. (1997). Different modes, different models: Communication and language of young deaf children and their mothers. In L. Adamson & M. Romski (Eds.), *Research on communication and language disorders: Contributions to theories of language development* (pp. 203–230). Baltimore: Brookes.

Spencer, P., Lederberg, A., & Waxman, R. (1996, April). Language mode and communication models. Paper presented at Conference of International Society for Infant Studies. Providence, Rhode Island.

Spencer, P., & Meadow-Orlans, K. (1996). Play, language, and maternal responsiveness: A longitudinal study of deaf and hearing infants. *Child Development, 67*, 3176–3191.

Swisher, M. V. (1992). The role of parents in developing visual turn-taking in their young deaf children. *American Annals of the Deaf, 137*, 92–100.

Tomasello, M. (1988). The role of joint attentional processes in early language development. *Language Sciences, 10*, 69–88.

Vibbert, M., & Bornstein, M. (1989). Specific associations between domains of mother-child interaction and toddler referential language and pretense play. *Infant Behavior and Development, 12*, 163–184.

Vygotsky, L. (1978). *Mind in society: The development of higher psychological processes.* Cambridge, MA: MIT Press.

Waxman, R., & Spencer, P. (1997). What mothers do to support infant visual attention: Sensitivities to age and hearing status. *Journal of Deaf Studies and Deaf Education, 2* (2), 104–114.

Wedell-Monnig, J., & Lumley, J. (1980). Child deafness and mother–child interaction. *Child Development, 51*, 766–774.

Weir, R. (1962). *Language in the crib.* The Hague, Netherlands: Mouton.

Wilson, S., & Spencer, P. (1997, April). Maternal topic responsiveness and child language: A cross-cultural, cross-modality replication. Poster presented at Conference of Society for Research in Child Development. Washington, DC.

Wood, D. (1989). Social interaction as tutoring. In M. Bornstein & J. Bruner (Eds.), *Interaction and human development* (pp. 59–80). Hillsdale NJ: Lawrence Erlbaum Associates.

7

Deaf Young People: Aspects of Family and Social Life

Susan Gregory
University of Birmingham, England

This chapter is concerned with the young deaf person, considering the period of secondary schooling, leaving school and entering work, training or higher education, the period of adolescence, and the transition to adulthood. It focuses on social aspects of development, including family relationships, peer relationships, and developing partner relationships.

This period in the transition from child to adult is generally characterized by developing independence from parents, making decisions about work and training, and establishing an adult social life. It is a critical period both in terms of assuming adult roles and establishing a sense of identity. During this time of transition, the role of the parents is usually eclipsed by that of the peers in constructing and maintaining an adult identity, and one of the tasks of this period for the young person is to develop adult social competence and acceptance by peers. There are also tasks for the family, and MacKeith (1973) suggested it is one of the four major periods of adjustment for families. Many parents who have accepted the deafness of their child now find they have to reflect further as they come to recognize their son or daughter as an adult deaf person. There is also the need for the family to establish more adult forms of communication (Kluwin & Gaustad, 1994).

In all of these areas, language and communication are of paramount importance. Adolescence can be a time of strained relationships and the ability to communicate in order to resolve issues is critical. Morrison and Zetlin (1988) showed that families with high degrees of cohesiveness have more positive communication patterns. In addition, language is an important element in establishing, maintaining, and sustaining social relationships. Language is significant in a more general sense, as much of the understanding of the rules of social interaction comes through incidental, overheard, or overseen communication. Yet, language and communication competence, taken for granted in most young people, cannot be assumed in the same way for the young deaf person.

Language mediates culture. The cultural transmission that occurs though family conversation may be inaccessible to a deaf child in a hearing family. Neither can deaf children easily assimilate cultural knowledge through the media or through incidental learning. In terms of the development of cultural identity and group membership, the issues for the deaf young person may be different. Although most deaf young people grow up in hearing families, some will choose to identify with deaf people and the deaf community and its culture. It is an issue both for young people and their families and has implications for the communication choices made by the family.

Although much has been written about the social development of the young deaf child and the impact of deafness on the mother, particularly around the time of diagnosis, less attention has been paid to aspects of the social life of the deaf adolescent and young person. As has been pointed out (Moores, 1987), this area is one that receives comparatively little attention in the literature about the psychological development of deaf children and young people. In terms of family relationships, Lederberg (1993) noted in a previous volume of this book, "We know little about the impact of deafness on the mother–child relationship for older children. There are no published studies on the effect of deafness on the mother–child relationship past the preschool years" (p. 108). In fact, the research literature that concerns social life and friendship in this period more often focuses on aspects of education and educational choices, and much of our understanding of a deaf young person's social world comes through studies of the implications of different educational settings.

LANGUAGE AND COMMUNICATION

The Language of Deaf Young People

In most discussions of the social development and social relationships of young people, language is the given, the taken-for-granted element. There may be discussions of communication, of possible breakdowns in inter-action due to different attitudes, different perceptions, or problems within the relationship but language itself is not usually seen as a factor. The situation is not the same when we consider deaf young people. Language, the very bedrock of relationships, is an issue. Language competence may be limited and the choice of mode or language may change the interaction or affect the dynamics of the situations in which communication takes place.

The development of communication in young deaf children is well documented. The extent of the delay for deaf children of hearing parents, the relationship with hearing loss, the impact of using sign language is well known. Yet, although delays in the language of young deaf people are recognized, less is documented about their language competence, their use of language, and their communication strategies. Most studies of language of deaf young people either concern literacy or have been designed to look at the efficacy of different approaches to language and communication. Few have focused on language preference or competence.

Gregory, Bishop, and Sheldon (1995) conducted a study comprised of interviews with 82 hearing families and 61 of their deaf sons and daughters, all in their late teens or early 20s. The research looked at aspects of family life including language and communication. The families were the same as in a previous research study carried out when these young people were under 6 years, an unselected sample based on all children diagnosed in a particular region of the UK at the time of that research. In the follow-up study, the interviews with the young people were carried out in the preferred language of the deaf young person, based on a number of questions asked in the parent interviews and checked at the time with the interviewee. The majority of these interviews were carried out by the deaf researcher. However, she was accompanied to every interviewer by a notetaker who would take over as interviewer if changes needed to be made at the time. Different notetakers were used for different interviews based on an assessment of the likely language of the interview.

The young people were born in the 1970s and were educated, initially at least under the oral system. However, as young people, 38% (31) had British Sign Language (BSL) as their preferred language, 37% (30) used spoken English, 16% (13) used sign-supported English (SSE, also de-scribed as manually coded English) and 10% (8) had severely limited skills in any language. The researchers were generous in their attribution of language, and the category does not imply fluency in the language but the use of a recognizable linguistic form. A significant number of those who were oral, or used SSE, were starting to learn to sign although they were not yet fluent. At the time of the interview, 44 (54%) were bilingual in the sense that they used two languages actively in their day-to-day lives, although this description does not imply fluency in either or both of the languages.

As might be expected, there was some relationship between preferred language and hearing loss (see Table 7.1). There was also a significant relationship between preferred language and gender (Table 7.1). The proportions adopting BSL were similar (17/48, 35% of men; 14/34, 41% of women). However, although the numbers using English-based communication were similar (23/48 [48%] young men and 20/34 [59%] young women who communicated using a form of English), young men were more likely to be oral and young women more likely to use SSE. It seems that young women who use English were more likely to accompany it with signs taken from BSL. Other findings in the study, particularly relating to friendship patterns, discussed later, indicated a higher priority for communication among the young women, and their use of signs to support their English may be a further indication of this gender difference.

The young people who grew up to use BSL or SSE were more likely to have families who used gesture and who approved of the use of gesture when they were young. The type of school and attitude to signing at school showed a relationship with preferred language. Not surprisingly, preferred language related to a number of social aspects of the young people's lives. Those who went to deaf club, identified with the deaf community, and had mainly deaf friends were more likely to be BSL users. Those who had mostly hearing friends and socialized within the hearing world were more likely to be oral. Other factors, the degree of independence, personality factors, obtaining and staying in work, and extent of their social life did not show a relationship.

As well as their preferred language, the communication skills of the young people are a critical issue, and we endeavored to get some measure of their skills and their abilities to answer the interview questions. As a measure of how well the interview schedule as a whole was understood,

TABLE 7.1
Preferred Language, Hearing Loss, and Gender

	BSL	SSE	Oral	Limited Language Skills
Profound	17	7	2	5
Severe	12	5	12	1
Moderate	2	1	8	2
Partially hearing	0	0	8	0
Young men	17	2	21	8
Young women	14	11	9	0

the proportion of the interview questions that had to be rephrased at each interview for those young people included in the quantitative analysis was checked. For one third of the interviewees, no questions or only a few questions had to be rephrased, but it was disturbing that for one quarter of the group, over half the schedule had to be rephrased. Even then, questions were not always understood or responded to appropriately. For example, nearly half the sample could not answer the question: "Do you think your school expected too much of you?"

The study also looked at their ability to give detailed answers using four selected questions for each scale. About one third (31%) gave detailed answers to most of the questions on the scale, and a further third (38%) gave detailed answers some of the time. Overall, the level of language used for those who were oral was similar to those using BSL. However, in similar measures of the comprehension of questions, both simple and complex, BSL users scored less well than those who were oral or who used SSE, although the range of scores was the same. This finding cannot be taken as endorsement of the view that the oral approach was more successful. The two languages did not have equal status in the lives of the young people, all of whom were only offered the oral approach in their early lives, and it was often those who failed who, in later life, started to use BSL.

A study of a group of 39 deaf young people born in the late 1960s in the United States, thus educated under an oral system, found that at 15 to 17 years many were using some form of signed communication. Of the group, 16 used English, either signed or spoken, which they termed *strict English* and 23 mixed languages, such as, not strict English. There was a strong relationship with educational history, and whereas those with strict English performed better on a number of subtests of an intelligence test, they showed no substantial difference on a number of conversational ratings (Lou, Strong, & De Matteo, 1991). Thus it seems that in the United Kingdom and the United States, even when early education is within the oral tradition, significant numbers elect to use some form of sign language as adults. However, the linguistic competence that is developed is variable and cannot be assumed for all.

Language Choice of the Families

The variety of language and modes available to the young person means that for parents and other family members there is an issue about their own language and communication. It is generally accepted that difficulties in communication in the family can have consequences for identity and social relationships. Leigh and Stinson (1991) suggested that problems of family integration can be magnified by problems in communication, and as Kluwin and Gaustad (1991) stated: "In the absence of a shared communication system there is a general sense of isolation of family members" (p. 28).

Those studies that have attempted to specify the language use within families with one deaf member showed that the possible combinations and permutations are enormous when one considers the different modes and languages used by the various members of the family. Moores, Kluwin, and Mertens (1985) reported 176 unique patterns of communication in the families of 185 high-school students. Kluwin and Gaustad (1994) discussed 20 different possibilities in their study of 325 adolescents in terms of who communicated in which language in the family. There were three basic configurations: where all spoke (28.9%), where all signed (21.6%), and the various combinations, about one quarter. For 23% there was not adequate data on all members. In our study, 39% (32) of the parents attempted to learn to sign. Interestingly, nearly one quarter of those who learned to sign (7/32, 22%) did so, not because they needed it to communicate with their own child, but to communicate with their children's friends. As their child got older and began bringing home deaf friends, signing became essential for some parents in order to enter the social life of their sons and daughters.

In the case of parents, factors affecting language choice and use are numerous and diverse. Some are related to early advice; for example, until recently, the positive choice to sign with deaf infants was rare and unsupported by professional advice. Karchmer, Milone, and Wolk (1979) showed a relationship with the degree of hearing loss of the child. Lerman (1984) showed socioeconomic status to be a factor, whereas Kluwin and Gaustad (1991) showed that the degree of hearing loss, the preschool mode of communication, and the mother's level of education were related. In terms of the father, the greatest effect was the mother's mode, although for siblings it was both the mother's mode and the degree of hearing loss of the deaf family member.

The choice of language is more than a pragmatic one relating to ease of communication. Inherent within the choice is also the attitudes to deafness within the family and the perceived status of the deaf person. Some studies related family language use to the self-esteem of the deaf member. Moores (1987) suggested that rejecting sign language is rejecting the child, whereas accepting sign language should produce greater self-esteem. A study by Desselle (1994) of deaf teenagers with hearing parents revealed more positive self-esteem where families *could* sign. In addition they found that parents who were most able to communicate with their children by using sign language had children whose self-esteem scores were higher than those of children whose parents were less skilled. In our study (Gregory et al., 1995), most young people welcomed attempts by their parents to learn to sign even if the level they achieved was poor. More often the benefit of parents signing was as much in the recognition it gave to the deafness as to the actual communication.

Family cohesion has also been found to be related to the use of sign language. Kluwin and Gaustad (1994) in their study of 325 deaf students found that "The strongest predictor of family cohesion was the mother's mode of communication. The direction of the relationship means that mothers who signed tended to have more cohesive families than those who used speech or other means of communication" (p. 333).

However, many studies show that even when parents or other members learn to sign, they do not necessarily acquire high levels of competency but rather more basic day-to-day communication (Foster, 1996). Language choice is not itself simple. One of the main issues facing families is that the choice to sign, which may enhance communication, may also marginalize some family members.

FAMILY RELATIONSHIPS

Relationships With Individual Family Members

As implied in the previous section, there are differences in communication with different family members. Such variations in ease of communication are clearly likely to affect relationships within the family. These differences are probably most marked in the differential relationship between the young person and his or her father and mother. Lerman (1984) suggested that the mother is the primary communicator in half of families and a sibling is primary in the other half.

In the study by Gregory et al., (1995), the young people were asked a number of questions about the person in the family with whom they communicated best. Whereas in many families, communication was similar with all members (38%)—where a family member was best it was most often the mother (25%), or a sibling (20%). The father was cited only by 5% of the sample. An additional 7% said there was no one in the family with whom they could communicate. The general impression gained from the interviews was that communication with the father was, in many instances, difficult. Although there was no specific question on this topic, almost all of those who mentioned spontaneously that a family member was being particularly difficult specified the father (16/61, 26%, one quarter of the total sample). Meadow-Orlans (1990) reported that communication satisfaction for the father declined during adolescence. This imbalance in communication is likely to create some stress in families where the father withdraws or communication is mediated by the mother. Luterman (1987) pointed out that because the mother is the best communicator, she may often assume the role of interpreter. This is likely to have consequences for the dynamics of the family.

Another factor that may affect the relationship with parents may be issues around dependency. The late teens and early 20s are the period when most people establish independence from their families, both financially and in terms of setting up their own homes. However, deaf young people may be more dependent on their parents than are their hearing counterparts (Luterman, 1984); Morgan-Redshaw, Wiglosh, & Bibby, 1990). The two factors of language–communication and access to information are significant here. Parents may be asked to facilitate communication or assist in arrangements with colleagues of the young person. They can take a major role in obtaining employment. They may need to explain financial and other matters when such information is not readily available in an accessible form elsewhere. Most of these are necessary because the hearing world is not adapted to the requirements of deaf people, and young people have less access to the information they need about the world in order to manage their own affairs. Gregory et al. (1995) considered those who were 20 to 21 years, and of the 40 in this group, most (28/40, 70%) were living in the family home and although 36 had their own bank account, only half could manage their finances without help. Although most could cope with travelling, 38 went on public transport alone and nearly three quarters could drive, or were learning to; less than half (16) were able to go to the doctor alone at an age when it might be assumed that privacy in medical matters was important.

Another role that parents may have in their son or daughter's social life is in assisting in contacting friends and making arrangements. Many deaf young people have friends at a distance, and although contact can be maintained through prearranged meetings, parents may mediate or take responsibility for making arrangements through assisting with telephone conversations or passing on messages. Gregory et al. (1995) reported that many parents felt they had a greater role in social arrangements than they would have had their son or daughter been hearing, a situation that was not always satisfactory for either party, and in some cases was a cause of concern for the parents.

In social development, sibling relationships may also be a crucial factor. Dunn (1995), reporting on the Colorado Sibling study—one of the few major studies of hearing sibling relationships—concluded "early relationships between siblings show not only concurrent associations with children's social cognitive development, but long term associations with children's later relationships, patterns that link pre-school and adolescent periods on development" (p. 346).

Luterman (1987), in discussing the issue of deaf and hearing sibling relationships, noted:

> Siblings form the first social laboratory for the individuals's experiments with peer relationships. Within the sibling system, children can learn how to resolve conflicts and support one another. They learn how to negotiate among equals or near equals. (They learn how to deal with authority in their relationships with their parents.) The sibling system teaches them how to make friends and allies, how to save face while losing, and how to achieve recognition for their skills. In the sibling world, children learn how to negotiate, co-operate and compete. The jockeying for position within the family system shapes and moulds children into their adult roles. When children come into contact with the world outside the family, they take with them the knowledge they learned from their siblings to form their peer relationships. (p. 73)

The study of sibling relationships is a neglected area, for both hearing/hearing and hearing/deaf relationships. Despite their perceived importance, relatively little is known about them. It is hardly surprising that they are little understood because of their diversity, depending on family structure, relative position of siblings, gender, and age difference. Dunn (1995), reporting on the Colorado Adoption Project, pointed out there can be difference in treatment by mothers and fathers and different experiences within the sibling relationship itself. In families with deaf and hearing siblings these can be compounded by further differences. The language choices and use may be different for different siblings; the deaf child may have been educated in a different educational setting from the other siblings and even have been sent away to a residential school for some of the period. Some studies suggested that there is a particular negative impact for older, hearing female siblings of deaf children (Israelite, 1986).

Gregory et al. (1995) in their study of deaf young people considered sibling relationships. Of the 82 young people for whom the parents were interviewed, 79 had siblings and 20% specified siblings as the easiest with whom to communicate. Of these, five had deaf siblings. Even if they were not deaf, siblings were often felt to have a special sort of understanding with the deaf young people. Overall the relationship with the siblings was described in positive terms, with 23 (42%) of them describing themselves as getting on very well with their siblings, 19 (32%) quite well, 11 (20%) differentiated between siblings, and only 2 (4%) said they did not get on well at all.

Despite this generally positive picture, there are a number of potential causes for concern reported in the literature. Luterman (1987) suggested that a negative impact on sibling relationships can occur when hearing siblings turn outside the family for relationships because they are unable to communicate with a deaf sibling. A further issue is the need to spend more time with the deaf son or daughter, both as a child and as an emerging adult (Morgan-Redshaw, Wilgosh, & Bibby, 1990), which some parents have reported as a cause of sibling resentment (Gregory et al., 1995). It also seems that stress can be induced if the deaf child has to attend boarding school part of the week, and this situation could be very disruptive to family relationships. For much of the time, life goes on without them, but often when they are there all attention is focused on them.

Gregory et al. (1995) suggested that where relationships between siblings were close and positive, when the children were young the mother had tried to discuss feelings with the hearing sibling about having a deaf child. This finding has parallels in the Colorado study where as Dunn reported "emotional experiences, family talk, and the quality of close relationships may play a significant role in the development of this sophisticated understanding (about social worlds)" (p. 346).

Communication and Family Life

Regardless of the means of communication, there are issues relating to the dynamics of communication in the family. Although one-to-one communication may be relatively straightforward, group or family communication can be more difficult. Whether or not individual family members can sign, signing is unlikely to be used as a way of family communication, although signing members may interpret during or after the conversation.

In the study by Gregory et al. (1995), the young people reported feeling left out of family gatherings or alternatively, feeling embarrassed by attempts to involve them. A critical issue in general for deaf people is access to information, particularly that which is part of general conversation that could be a factor in family affairs. Often parents assumed that the deaf person was aware of information that was generally known in the family, even though they were not. The young people were asked whether there were important family matters that had not been communicated to them. Of the 49 who understood and could answer the question, 39 (80% of those responding) said this lack of communication had happened to them. The events included such major family occurrences as deaths in the family, pregnancy, and marital breakdown.

Many parents experienced difficulty in communication, described in terms of a loss of immediacy or difficulty in explaining issues they felt needed explaining. Often, the stress came about, not through reluctance to communicate, but because families wanted to discuss things with each other. Communication within the group could be an effort, and some family members could feel excluded. Sometimes extra attention was given to managing social situations, and often the mother assumed significant responsibilities for communication. Sometimes specific plans were made and implemented to allow deaf young person to join in. Often parents were aware of a responsibility in conveying information and took steps to do so consciously. These difficulties are not a consequence of deafness per se but arise at the interface between communication in the deaf and hearing worlds.

FRIENDSHIPS, RELATIONSHIPS, AND SOCIAL LIFE

Friendship Patterns

Most research into the friendships of deaf young people has been carried out in the context of examining the consequences of different educational settings, in particular comparing mainstream and special settings for both school and college. Overall, from the literature it seems that some young deaf people enjoy a rich and varied social life, for some involving traveling significant distances to meet their deaf friends. However, some are extremely lonely at times, feel isolated, and have difficulty making friends and sustaining friendships.

In the research by Gregory et al. (1995), a positive pattern emerged overall, with the majority of the sample (young people report 77%, parents report 57%) having a special friend or a stable group of friends. However, parents and the young people differed in the way in which friendship patterns were described. In the interviews, the parents of the young people tended to focus on the problems that they felt their sons and daughters had in their social lives, whereas the young people themselves presented a more positive picture. For example, 39 (64%) of the young people described themselves as seeing their friends often, and a further 19 (31%) as seeing them sometimes. Overall, they felt themselves to be in regular contact and conveyed a generally positive view. However, the parents seemed conscious of many more problems and described the majority of the young people as having difficulty in making friends. This discrepancy may be because the young people saw things differently or, alternatively, because they chose not to elaborate on their difficulties. Alternatively it may be that the parents had a more conventional understanding of friendship patterns and a different view of what constituted a good social life. For the most part, the parental concept of social life was a hearing view, involving regular contact with a number of people, most of whom were likely to live locally. Many of the deaf young people saw their friends less regularly but travelled all over the country to meet up with people, and belonged to a vast network of relationships. Many compared their own experience favorably with their perception of the relationships of hearing young people, which they saw as being more limited.

Loneliness was an issue, but for a minority. Five young people (6%) were described by their parents as having no friends at all. Although it was rare for the young people interviewed to describe such total isolation, many young people experienced periods of loneliness or feelings of not belonging or not knowing how to make friends. One young woman actually asked her mother about how to make friends.

Of the sample, 20% (16/82) were said by their parents to make friends easily. Because our research involved families that had been involved in an earlier study, when the young people were 6-years-old and younger (Gregory, 1976, 1995), we were able to look at the relationship between early experience and later friendship patterns. The early interviews included questions relating to the sociability of the child. A scale of social skills was devised based on whether or not they made themselves understood easily with other children, whether or not they were able to share toys, the extent to which they understood about taking turns, and their understanding of games that had a winner. Good skills were classified as a positive response to three or four of the questions, whereas poor skills were indicated by two or fewer positive responses. Table 7.2 shows the relationship between early social competence and the ability as young people to make friends, based on the 60 of the sample who were 3½ years or older at the first interview, and parental report of later friendship patterns.

Thus, the majority of those who made friends easily as young adults had good skills as a child, although those who did not make friends easily as adults varied in their skills as a child. This is statistically significant

TABLE 7.2
Social Skills as Child and Young Person

	Good skills as child	Poor skills as child
Makes friends easily as young person	11	2
Some difficulty as young person	16	4
Does not make friends easily as young person	14	13

($c = 6.240, p > .05$). However, the amount that the young people played with other children as a child, whether their parents felt they were left out of games when young, and whether or not they were submissive or bossy with other children did not show statistical relationships with patterns of friendships as an adult, either those reported by the parents or by the young people themselves.

Meeting and Making Friends

For most hearing young people, most of their friends are made at school or at college or through work, leisure activities, and casual social contacts. For deaf young people it could be expected to be the same, although for some of them, their informal contacts include friends made through deaf organizations.

A number of studies reviewed the impact of educational setting on social life. Many studies of mainstream settings suggested that deaf students experience social difficulties in these settings (Davis, 1986; Foster, 1989) whereas only a few studies showed a positive effect for mainstream, either in terms of some students (Lynas, 1986) or when special arrangements are made (Ladd, Munson, & Miller, 1984). Many students described feelings of loneliness, isolation, and social rejection (Foster, 1988; Holcomb, 1996). Mertens (1989) suggested that students attending residential school had a more positive social experience than those in mainstream settings. It seems somewhat paradoxical that special provision, which aims to provide an education appropriate for deaf pupils, is often deemed inadequate in this regard, yet positive in the social environment it provides. Integrated/mainstream settings, while aiming at social integration, are often more successful in the access to the curriculum that they achieve.

One aspect of the problem for relationships in mainstream settings is similar to those described in family interactions—communication in groups. In our study, of the 34 of the young people who included hearing people among their friends and could answer the question, 19 said they had great difficulty in the group situation, 5 had some difficulty, and only 10 could converse easily. Although the primary effect is the difficulty of participating in interactions because of the difficulty in following group conversations, a secondary consequence is that much informal information that is transmitted in such interactions relating to social conventions and social life is missed. Foster (1996) noted that "Failure to access the conversations of those around them can result in social as well as professional separation from hearing colleagues" (p. 128).

Conventionally, one's place of work or one's college is a source of potential friends. In our study it was apparent that some of the young people were isolated, and around one third were considered by their parents to have no friends at work or at college. In addition, whereas nearly two thirds of young people were felt to have made friends at work or at college, about half of these friendships were confined to the workplace or the college only and these friends were not met outside. Parents, however, proffered a number of explanations for this limitation; some focused on the difficulties deaf people have in carrying on conversations at the same time as doing their work. Parents also described the reluctance their sons and daughters felt to join groups of hearing people because of the high likelihood of their being excluded, no matter how good the intentions of their colleagues.

Even when friends were seen outside work or college, it was for more formal, rather than casual events. Parents noted that when with hearing people the deaf young people had to be doing something. When the young people were invited out, it was to more structured social occasions; for the young women, frequent mention was made of invitations to engagement parties, weddings, makeup parties, whereas the young men were invited to darts matches and snooker games. It may be that more unstructured gatherings were difficult as the procedures were less predictable and would inevitably involve more verbal negotiation; a wedding or a sports match has its own prescribed rules and deaf people can follow established protocol. In less formal gatherings it is not so easy to follow the crowd or rely on remembered routine.

Deaf and Hearing Friends

For many deaf young people their source of friends is not work or college as it is for hearing people. Some of the young people will be more likely to find all or some of their social life with other deaf people, and they will meet with other deaf people in special settings or at informal gatherings. Deaf centers or clubs are often used as meeting places, and many deaf young people travel widely to meet their friends. For many of them, an advantage of being deaf is the feeling they belong to a group throughout the country and, for some, throughout the world.

However, it is not so for all deaf young people. For oral deaf young people, it can be difficult to integrate into the deaf community, as the language used is sign language and some places are not welcoming to them. Some young deaf people are discouraged by their schools from integrating with the deaf community, and other young people's parents are reluctant for them to attend. There is of course a real issue here for parents, for association with deaf people may seem to be the beginning of their son or daughter moving away from the family, not in the usual adolescent way of establishing a new life where the parents assume a different, known role, but it is a move into a world that is unknown, unpredictable; and inaccessible.

Many studies have shown that the preference for deaf or hearing friends relates to language use. Leigh and Stinson (1991), in a study of 64 deaf students, showed that those who were oral assigned higher ratings to the need for closer relationships with hearing peers whereas those who used ASL or simultaneous communication assigned higher ratings to deaf peers. In our study too, a preference for deaf or hearing friends showed a significant relationship with their preferred communication. In our study, most of those who used BSL (23/31) had all or mostly deaf friends, whereas most of those who were oral (22/30) had all or mostly hearing friends. More interesting is the finding that there were gender differences in friendship patterns as shown in Table 7.3.

All of those with no friends were young men, the majority of these (4/5) being drawn from the group with limited language skills. Young women were significantly more likely to have deaf friends than were young men, as shown in Table 7.3, a finding that may reflect a greater significance given to communication by young women as was suggested by their language preference.

One of the crucial features for these years is the establishment of partnerships of boyfriends or girlfriends and later, marriage or cohabitation. Cole and Edelman (1991) suggested the establishment of boy–girl relationships are perceived by deaf young people to be a problem area. Of the 48 young people over 21 years in our study, 18 (38%) were reported by their parents as never having had a boyfriend or girlfriend. In the sample as a whole, young women were more likely to have partners, or have had partners (29/34, 85%) than young men (20/48, 42%). For those involved in a stable relationship, it was more often with a deaf than with a hearing person. As with friendships, young women were more likely to have and to prefer a deaf partner than a hearing one and more likely to emphasize the need for communication in a relationship. Seventeen of the young women had partners, of whom 16 were deaf and one was hearing, whereas seven of the young men had partners, of whom three

TABLE 7.3
Gender Differences in Friendship Patterns

	Men	Women
Equal deaf and hearing	6	5
All/mostly deaf	15	23
All/mostly hearing	22	6
No friends	5	0

were deaf and four hearing. This bias was also reflected in expressed partner preferences.

Thus, in choice of both partners and friends, young women were more likely to prefer deaf people, seemingly indicating a higher priority being given to communication. In contrast, some young men appeared more instrumental in their preferences. In terms of friendship, this may reflect different social activities of men and women, the women preferring to engage in conversation, and the men seemed more likely to take part in group activities where the communication demands were more predictable and less complex. In partnerships, however, young men were often more pragmatic, and some suggested explicitly that a hearing partner was more desirable as she could interface with the hearing world.

CONCLUSIONS

As this chapter illustrates, the social development of deaf young people is affected by a number of complex interrelated issues, reflecting the great variety of circumstances, family structures, and language choices in which their relationships occur. At the core is the issue of communication. Although the research findings indicate benefits for families choosing sign as a means of communication, the issue is complex. Family relationships are affected by other factors that act as barriers to the independence of the deaf young person.

In terms of friendship patterns as described by the deaf young person and their parents, social life varies from rich and complex relationships to feelings of loneliness. However, the perception of the young person may differ from that of the parent. The description and evaluation of the deaf young person's social relationships as given by the parents and young people themselves are not always identical. The same social behavior may be given a different meaning in the two accounts, perhaps indicating differing expectations and evaluations in the deaf and hearing worlds.

It is at the interface between deaf and hearing cultures that problems arise for the deaf young person wishing to participate in the hearing world, problems consequent upon lack of ease of communication in the language of hearing people. Not only does this linguistic barrier affect interpersonal face-to-face communication, but it may also deny access to information vital for participation in the hearing world, for example the incidental information that hearing people pick up as a matter of course through overhearing the conversations of others, through the radio and television. Thus, the deaf young person's cultural knowledge of hearing society, the kind of knowledge that is transmitted verbally during the routine interactions of everyday life, may be restricted and limited to what they are able to acquire in direct face-to-face communication. They may miss some of the vital information that promotes participation in the hearing world through being restricted to information that has been explicitly articulated and directed at them.

Although there are deaf young people isolated from relationships by poor language or by the inability of the hearing world to adjust to their needs, it would be a mistake to see these features as an inevitable consequence of deafness. As seen here, most deaf children are born into hearing families. Had it been a discussion of aspects of family and social life for deaf young people in deaf families, the conclusions could have been very different although certain barriers to interaction with the hearing world would remain.

It would be simplistic to suggest that the issues addressed in this chapter could be resolved easily if families learned to sign. It seems that few hearing family members are likely to achieve competence in signing, and the burden of communication often falls on one family member and may marginalize others. It is important to remember that although the use of sign language may facilitate communication, its use by the young deaf person in a hearing family represents an aspect of that person's emerging deaf cultural identity. The consequent and inevitable biculturalism that develops within the family is likely to have profound effects on family dynamics and social relationships, effects that remain largely unexplored.

REFERENCES

Cole, S. H., & Edelman, R. J. (1991). Identity patterns and self and teacher perceptions of problems for deaf adolescents. *Journal of Child Psychology and Psychiatry, 32,* 1159–1165.

Davis, J. (1986). Academic placement in perspective. In D. Luterman (Ed.), *Deafness in perspective* (pp. 205–224). San Diego: College Hill Press.

Desselle, D. D. (1994) Self-esteem, family climate and communication pattern in relation to deafness. *American Annals of the Deaf, 139,* 322–328.

Dunn, J. (1995). Studying relationships and social understanding. In P. Barnes (Ed.), *Personal, social and emotional development of children* (pp. 336–347). Oxford, England: Milton Keynes, The Open University Press in association with Basil Blackwell.

Foster, S. (1988). Life in the mainstream: Reflection of deaf college freshmen on their experiences in the mainstreamed high school. *Journal of Rehabilitation of the Deaf, 22,* 37–56.

Foster, S. (1989). Social alienation and peer identification. A study of the social construction of deafness. *Human Organisation, 48,* 226–235.

Foster, S. (1996). Communication experiences of deaf people: An ethnographic account. In I. Parasnis (Ed.), *Cultural and Language Diversity* (pp. 117–135). Cambridge, England: Cambridge University Press.

170   GREGORY

Gregory, S. (1976, 1995). *The deaf child and his family*. London, George Allen and Unwin, republished as *Deaf Children and their Families*. Cambridge, England: Cambridge University Press.

Gregory, S., Bishop, J., & Sheldon, L. (1995). *Deaf young people and their families*. Cambridge, England: Cambridge University Press.

Holcomb, T. K. (1996). Social assimilation of deaf high school students: The role of the school environment. In I Parasnis (Ed.), *Cultural and language diversity and the deaf experience* (pp. 181–198). Cambridge, England: Cambridge University Press.

Israelite, N. K. (1986). Hearing impaired children and the psychological functioning of their normal hearing siblings. *Volta Review, 88*, 47–54.

Karchmer, M. A., Milone, M. N., & Wolk, S. (1979). Educational significance of hearing loss at three levels of severity. *American Annals of the Deaf, 124*, 97–109.

Kluwin, T. N., & Gaustad, M. G. (1991). Predicting family communication choices. *American Annals of the Deaf, 136*, 28–34.

Kluwin, T. N., & Gaustad, M. G. (1994). The role of adaptability and communication in fostering cohesion in families with deaf adolescents. *American Annals of the Deaf, 139*, 329–335.

Ladd, G. W., Munson, J. L., & Miller J. K. (1984). Social integration of deaf adolescents in secondary level mainstreaming programmes. *Exceptional Children, 50*, 420–429.

Lederberg, A. (1993). The impact of deafness on mother–child and peer relationships. In M. Marschark & D. Clark (Eds.), *Psychological Perspectives on Deafness* (pp. 93–119). London: Lawrence Erlbaum Associates.

Leigh, I. W., & Stinson, M. S. (1991). Social environments, self-perceptions and identity of hearing impaired adolescents. *The Volta Review, 93*, 1–22.

Lerman, A. (1984). Survey of Hispanic hearing impaired students and their families in New York City. In G. Delgado (Ed.), *The Hispanic deaf* (pp. 72–79). Washington, DC: Gallaudet University Press.

Lou, M. W., Strong, M., & DeMatteo, A. (1991). The relationship of educational background to cognitive and language development among deaf adolescents. In D. Martin (Ed.), *Advances in cognition, education and deafness* (pp.). Washington, DC: Gallaudet University Press.

Luterman, D. (1984). *Counselling the communicatively disordered and their families*. Boston, Mass: Little, Brown.

Luterman, D. (1987). *Deafness in the family*. Boston: College Hill Press.

Lynas, W. (1986). *Educating the handicapped in mainstream schools*. London: Croom Helm.

MacKeith, R. (1973). The feelings and behaviour of parents of handicapped children. *Developmental Medicine and Child Neurology, 15*, 524–527.

Meadow-Orlans, K. P. (1990). Research on developmental aspects of deafness. In D. F. Moores & K. P. Meadow-Orlans (Eds.), *Educational and developmental aspects of deafness* (pp. 283–298). Washington DC: Gallaudet University Press.

Mertens, D. (1989). Social experiences of hearing impaired high school youth. *American Annals of the Deaf, 134*, 15–19.

Moores, D. (1987). *The education of the deaf: Psychology, principles and practices*. (3rd edition). Boston: Houghton Mifflin.

Moores D. F., Kluwin T., & Mertens D. (1985). High school programmes for deaf students in metropolitan areas. *Gallaudet Research Institute Monograph No. 3*. Washington, DC: Gallaudet University.

Morgan-Redshaw, M., Wilgosh, L., & Bibby, M. A. (1990). The parental experience of mothers of adolescence with hearing impairment. *American Annals of the Deaf, 135*, 293–298.

Morrison, G., & Zetlin, A. (1988). Perceptions of communication, cohesion and adaptability in families of adolescents with and without learning handicaps. *Journal of Abnormal and Child Psychology, 16*, 675–685.

8

Psychopathology

Robert Q. Pollard, Jr.
University of Rochester Medical Center

The psychological and psychiatric professions have long pathologized the characteristics and life experiences of deaf individuals, frequently advancing erroneous or exaggerated theories of causal relationships between hearing loss and mental disorder (Lane, 1992; Pollard, 1992b). Yet, mental disorders (psychopathology) certainly do affect deaf and hard-of-hearing persons, just as they do the rest of the population. This chapter addresses the identification, diagnosis, incidence, and treatment of psychopathology when it happens to affect deaf and hard-of-hearing people. It also touches on topical issues in treatment and examines recent service and legislative initiatives.

NORMALCY, DEVIANCE, AND CROSS-CULTURAL PSYCHOLOGY

The past decade has seen an explosion of professional and popular literature describing the unique linguistic and sociocultural characteristics of the American Deaf community (Dolnick, 1993; Lane, Hoffmeister, & Bahan, 1996; Moore & Levitan, 1993; Padden & Humphries, 1988). Although all people, deaf and hearing, share commonalities of physical and psychological development and function, our language and sociocultural differences can affect pivotal aspects of our behavior, values, and manners of thinking and interacting with others. Because the definition, evaluation, and treatment of psychopathology are largely interpersonal processes that are deeply rooted in normative expectations about people's psychosocial and communicative characteristics, differences in these characteristics between clinician and patient can introduce error or bias into the evaluation and treatment process. The recently evolved field of cross-cultural psychology recognizes such risks (Comas-Diaz & Griffith, 1988). Across the mental health disciplines, there has been a marked increase in teaching and research efforts directed toward the complex and delicate situation where practitioner and patient are from different sociocultural and/or linguistic backgrounds. Recent literature in the deafness and mental health field reflects this trend (Glickman & Harvey, 1996; Harvey, 1993; Henwood & Pope-Davis, 1994; Pollard, 1992a).

Because the overwhelming majority of professionals in the mental health field are hearing persons who are not knowledgeable about deafness, American Sign Language (ASL), or Deaf community sociocultural characteristics, it is no surprise that "normally different" characteristics of deaf persons can sometimes be mislabeled as psychopathology (e.g., dysfluent English writing misjudged as reflecting psychosis or mental retardation, or fluent and animated signing misjudged as reflecting labile affect). Equally disturbing is the risk that the same lack of information might lead hearing professionals to overlook signs and symptoms of psychopathology that may be manifested by deaf persons in ways that are somewhat different from hearing persons (e.g., the nature of English vs. ASL distortions caused by psychosis). The term "shock-withdrawal-paralysis" was coined by Schlesinger and Meadow (1972) to describe yet another source of cross-cultural bias, where otherwise talented hearing professionals fail to use their clinical skills to the fullest because of competency fears when attempting to serve deaf patients. This, too, can lead to underdiagnosis and other errors. Language and sociocultural differences not only complicate the identification and diagnosis of psychopathology, they can affect dramatically the psychotherapy process and outcome and even patterns of referral and treatment service utilization. All of these biases have been identified in research examining hearing clinicians serving deaf patients (Dickert, 1988; Goldsmith & Schloss, 1986; Pollard, 1994).

These circumstances have led many to call for specialized education and service programs better to meet the mental health needs of the deaf population, and the recent growth in specialized services has been remarkable (Levine, 1977; Pollard, 1996). Yet, the number of deaf and hard-of-hearing individuals served by specialists remains only a small fraction of those who receive mental health care, and an even smaller fraction of those who could benefit from such services but do not receive them. Estimates are that over 40,000 deaf Americans suffer from serious mental illness (Goulder, 1977). If the hard-of-hearing population is included, the figure jumps to over 2,000,000 (Trybus, 1987), and this does not include deaf and hard-of-hearing people with less serious forms of mental illness who might still benefit from treatment. Despite this tremendous need, only 2% of deaf people with serious mental illness are actually thought to receive treatment (Vernon, 1983). Moreover, it is nonspecialist clinicians who provide the bulk of assessment and treatment services to this population. How well they do so, especially when cross-cultural issues are significant, is yet another matter.

THE CLINICAL INTERVIEW IN CONTEXT

For the most part, diagnosis and treatment planning flows from the observations made and conclusions drawn from the initial clinical interview, especially in the current fiscal and public policy climate favoring rapid diagnosis, disposition, and short-term treatment. If the linguistic or sociocultural characteristics of deaf or hard-of-hearing patients can impact differentially certain aspects of the clinical interview, and if these differences are not recognized and appreciated by the clinician, serious misperceptions and oversights can result. Table 8.1 lists major components of the standard clinical interview and mental status examination (MSE), noting aspects of the interview where special considerations or observations pertaining to deaf patients *may* be pertinent. It must be emphasized that the deaf population is a heterogeneous one, and that the considerations noted in Table 8.1 and discussed here are not always relevant. However, experience in serving the deaf *patient* population suggests that the issues described are often important.

Initial Presentation

Given the frequency with which deaf persons are inadequately or inappropriately served in mental health care settings, some may present in these settings with an understandable degree of trepidation, defensiveness, or vigilance. Such observations or even direct inquiry by deaf patients regarding the nature and quality of planned communication and clinical intervention strategies should not be pathologized. There have been occasions when deaf patients' requests for communication accommodations required by the Americans with Disabilities Act (ADA) were labeled egregiously as evidence of paranoia or obstinacy. At a more subtle

TABLE 8.1
Special Considerations in the Clinical Interview and MSE With Deaf Individuals

Topic	Special Considerations
Initial presentation	Prior negative experiences in hearing medical care settings; majority–minority dynamics; fluent signing and children's nonverbal communication increase behavioral "feel"
Presenting complaint	Deafness rarely the focus but colors many issues; broad or specific caretaking requests; discrimination and service inaccessibility; fund of information factors
Language/Communication	Speechreading and writing rarely adequate; learn communication tips; frequent limitations in English proficiency; variability in sign methods and fluency; variable interpreter sign and especially voicing skills (distortions, additions, deletions); seek interpreter overview
Affect	Distinguish from fluent sign characteristics; interpreter voicing critical; depression more likely with recent-onset deafness; anxiety in hearing settings reasonable
Psychosis	Auditory hallucinations less common; disorganization and delusions more typical; psychotic disruption of signing possible but hard to identify; paranoia not expected
Orientation	Names of persons and places may involve sign names or descriptors
Sensation/Perception	Voice skills do not predict hearing ability; communication data more important than hearing acuity data; visual impairment associated with some hearing disorders and is always important
General Cognition	Incidence of developmental disorders and learning disabilities considerable; seek etiology information (often unknown); testing is specialized
Intelligence	Normally distributed; difficult to judge from communication, factual knowledge base, or education; testing is specialized
Fund of Information	Commonly limited and no indicator of intelligence; broad impact for treatment recommendations
Abstract reasoning	Not necessarily limited by deafness or use of sign; developmental impoverishment more significant; do not judge from proverbs or fund of information
Judgment/Insight	No assumed differences but note impact of developmental history; fund of information relevant but more easily addressed; watch Deaf culture and lifestyle variations

level, majority–minority sociocultural dynamics can impact the initial clinician–patient interaction. The clinician and the deaf patient are often virtual strangers from very different power and privilege backgrounds. As Lane (1992) described, hearing persons have exerted an enormous degree of control over the lives of deaf persons for centuries; perceptions of actual oppression are not uncommon. That deaf persons are entrusting so much to the hearing clinician and service system, including at times, their civil liberties and very lives, a degree of caution and testing in the initial clinical interview is both normal and appropriate.

Finally, the initial presentation of deaf patients often feels very "behavioral" to the hearing clinician unfamiliar with the physical nature of sign language or the sound of deaf persons' speech. The active behavior and facial expressions associated with signing, especially when fluent or impassioned, can be misread by hearing clinicians as reflecting mania, disinhibition, lability, or other problems of excess. In contrast, active signing behavior can mislead clinicians to overlook depressed affect. Apart from signing, the comprehensibility of a deaf individual's speech (if they choose to use it) varies greatly from person to person and is no indicator of intellectual ability, personality, or even hearing acuity. No offhand assumptions about cognition or affect should be made on the basis of physical observations of signing or speech alone, due to the confound between these behaviors, the communication process itself, and the communication demands of the particular environment the person is in. Similarly, the active behavior of deaf children, especially those for whom signed or oral communication is not highly effective in their regular living environments, should not be misconstrued. Such children often must communicate with and explore their world through active physical behavior. Judgments of attentional or behavioral disorder should not be made hastily.

Presenting Complaint

Deaf and hard-of-hearing persons are subject to the full range of mental disorders and problems in living that impact the general population. Presenting complaints should not be expected to be of any particular sort, especially not focused necessarily on the hearing loss itself. An exception is late-onset hearing loss, whether gradual or sudden, which often is a presenting concern to those who experience it. When the deafness onset was early in life, it is rarely a presenting concern to adults, though it may color the nature of other presenting complaints, such as identity concerns in young adulthood or parent–child conflicts at a later age. Some deaf persons were raised in family and/or school environments where excessive degrees of caretaking and paternalism were experienced. Such persons may look to the clinician to provide broad or specific forms of help that would otherwise be considered inappropriate to the mental health setting (e.g., "I need a girlfriend/job/apartment"; "Please call my mother and tell her to stay out of my life"). Of course, job or social discrimination and inaccessibility to any number of services may well be experienced by deaf and hard-of-hearing persons and these may arise as presenting complaints, especially if fund of information limitations (see below) lead such individuals to the mental health service system simply because more appropriate resources are not known or accessible to them.

Language, Communication, and Translation

Most hearing persons' judgments of the effectiveness of speechreading are grossly overblown. It is a laborious, usually inadequate process that depends far more on the characteristics of the hearing speaker and the physical environment than the deaf person's talents. Most agencies serving deaf individuals can provide communication tip sheets that explain how to optimize the speechreading situation. Yet, unless specifically preferred by the deaf or hard-of-hearing patient, speechreading should never be the primary mode of communication employed. Writing, too, has serious limitations, especially if the deaf individual has limited English proficiency, as many do, particularly in the clinical population. Though preferable to speechreading, writing is also laborious and comprehensively risky.

Because deaf individuals' knowledge of English vocabulary and syntax is frequently limited, written communication, if essential, must be kept at very modest difficulty levels. Idioms and expressions are particularly to be avoided, as these are frequently the last and most difficult aspects of language usage to master. The most extreme caution should be exercised in conjecture about the person's education, intelligence, and thought processes on the basis of their writing. The risk of overpathologizing is very great, even when writing samples appear to be severely limited or disorganized. This is not at all uncommon and usually, but not always, evidence of educational or experiential limitations, not psychopathology.

In regard to sign communication, hearing clinicians must appreciate the tremendous variability in ASL proficiency that exists among deaf individuals. Many deaf individuals never learn ASL at all. Some are raised in speech-only environments. Others are exposed to non-ASL forms of signing that are only used in educational settings or in their families. Others are exposed to a variety of communication modalities but too briefly or ineffectively to learn any of them well. The resulting distribution of ASL (or English or other communication modality) proficiency in the deaf population is far greater than the distribution of English or other preferred language (e.g., Spanish) proficiency in the hearing population. Hence, evidence of communication dysfluency (in sign or otherwise) cannot be as readily construed as symptomatic of neuropathology or psychopathology as communication dysfluency is in hearing persons.

Essentially, disrupted communication fluency in hearing persons is indicative of psychosis, aphasia, dysphasia, or related serious mental disorder. Yet, the majority of deaf patients who demonstrate gross limitations in communication fluency (in ASL, English, or other modalities) do so for reasons other than neuro- or psychopathology. Expert consultation is needed to identify neuro- or psychopathology based on communication impairment in deaf people. Interpreters are not typically qualified to render such opinions, as their education does not address the nature of psychotic or aphasic disruptions of sign language.

Not only do deaf patients present with highly variable communication proficiencies, sign language interpreters do as well. Thus, there are two potential sources of dysfluent communication in an interpreted clinical interview. Voicing for deaf patients is typically a much more challenging skill for interpreters than signing for hearing clinicians. Interpreter errors made during voicing can include: failing to voice or sign communication content, distorting the intended content, or adding content that was unintended by either party. "Cleaning up" the communication of a deaf patient manifesting gross disruptions in sign fluency is a particular risk, and may obfuscate evidence of developmental or psychiatric disorder. Although interpreters who are certified, especially those certified at the highest level by the Registry of Interpreters for the Deaf (RID), can usually be regarded as skilled professionals, one's proficiency in interpreting on a given day or with a given patient naturally varies. Unfortunately, interpreters might not give clinicians direct feedback about how difficult or successful *they* judged the communication exchange to be. Inviting conversation with the interpreter on this topic (but not during the interpreted interview) can be invaluable. The employment of uncertified interpreters is to be avoided, even though some talented persons have not gone through the RID certification process. The use of family members or nonprofessionals as interpreters is improper except in the most dire of circumstances.

In summary, whether through speechreading, writing, or a sign language interpreter, the likelihood that communication between the clinician and the deaf patient has included gaps and misunderstandings is so high as to be regarded as a given and, depending on the quality of the communication arrangements employed and the importance of the communication content or observations to the clinical issues at hand, an according degree of caution should be exercised in reaching diagnostic and treatment decisions.

Affect

As noted, one should not expect depressed affect to accompany deafness per se, except in cases of recent onset or increasing hearing loss. Otherwise, deaf and hard-of-hearing persons may present with a full range of affect, normal or otherwise. Cautions regarding misreading or overlooking affect as a function of the behavioral nature of signed communication, including facial expressions, were noted previously. So, too, were cautions regarding the difficult challenge interpreters face in voicing for deaf patients who sign. One of these challenges is choosing the best English equivalent for the much wider range of affective concepts that can be expressed in ASL. Another challenge is to reflect the patient's affect (as best as the interpreter can discern it) in their voicing style. As both judgments are difficult and somewhat subjective, interpreters' renditions of affective words and tone should be scrutinized through direct inquiry with the patient. A certain degree of patient anxiety as a function of being in the "hearing" health care system, as well as in relation to the majority–minority dynamics noted earlier should also be allowed for as appropriate to the situation.

Psychosis

The incidence and nature of psychotic symptoms in deaf patients differ to some degree from that manifested by hearing patients, primarily because symptoms of psychosis are so often expressed through auditory or speech anomalies in hearing people. That deafness, and signed versus spoken communication in particular, might result in changes in the nature or expression of such symptoms makes intuitive sense but is not a topic that has received much attention in the literature. Evans and Elliott (1981) identified differences in the frequency pattern of schizophrenia symptoms in deaf versus hearing patients, including a reduced incidence of auditory hallucinations. Yet, others have reported similar incidence rates of hallucinations in deaf and hearing patients (Rainer, Abdullah, & Altshuler, 1970). The sheer frequency with which mental health professionals ask the question, "Do you hear voices?" when evaluating patients (hearing or deaf), and the possibility that an affirmative answer might be spurious or even learned, could play a significant role in such situations. The voices question, unelaborated, is not recommended. Instead, more open-ended investigation of atypical perceptual and ideational experiences is preferred.

The limited research evidence suggests that when auditory hallucinations are reported, they are usually experienced by patients with partial hearing loss or late-onset deafness and sometimes involve perceptual distortion of tinnitus sounds (ringing in the ears), common in some forms of hearing loss. Auditory hallucinations involving the perception of music have been described in a number of publications. This probably just reflects authors' curiosity at the phenomenon; it is not a common psychotic symptom in deaf or hard-of-hearing patients. Musical hallucinations may well be organic, not psychiatric in nature (Berrios, 1991; Hammeke, 1983; Murata, Naritomi, & Sawada, 1994). A related question is whether command hallucinations (perceptions of being told to do something), ideas of reference, or other delusions involving communication reflect sensory experiences, either auditory or visual, in deaf persons. Visual hallucinations of an individual who is signing, though reported (Evans & Elliott, 1981; Vernon & Andrews, 1990), are probably quite rare, although signing to oneself is rather common in deaf psychotic patients. Whether such signing is in response to a visually hallucinated signer or merely a response to internal thought stimuli cannot readily be known but is likely the latter.

Another class of psychotic symptoms manifested by some deaf patients involves disruptions of sign communication. Very few publications have addressed this topic (Thacker, 1994). Just as hearing patients may manifest neologisms, "clang associations," loss of goal, poverty of content, and other communication symptoms, deaf patients can, but the detection of such symptoms in persons who use sign language is much more difficult. Unless the clinician is *fluent* in ASL *and* experienced in the detection of such language and communication symptoms, such symptoms are likely to be overlooked or misattributed to limited sign fluency when present. The presence of an interpreter usually does not diminish the likelihood of this error, because few are knowledgeable about the nature of psychotic communication anomalies (in speech or in sign). Furthermore, the great variability of ASL fluency in deaf patients, noted previously, presents a confound when judging the nature and significance of dysfluent signing.

Dysfluent speech in hearing people is so noticeable and meaningful precisely because the assumption of speech fluency in the absence of mental or neurological impairment is a valid one. This assumption cannot be made in regard to the deaf population, especially that portion of the deaf population that typically presents in mental health service settings. Whereas dysfluent signed communication *may* reflect psychopathology, educational and experiential limitations that limit or distort sign fluency are much more common. Deteriorations in a deaf individual's sign fluency or sign proficiency that is grossly poorer than their (signing) educational and social history would suggest are observations that should heighten concern regarding the potential contribution of psychopathology (including neurological disorder). Expert consultation by *clinicians* who are fluent (not just conversant) in ASL is usually needed to identify definitively psychopathology-based sign language disruptions.

Consultation with certified, experienced interpreters, including deaf "relay" interpreters, may assist such diagnostic considerations but should not be relied on too heavily. When interpreters have difficulty understanding or voicing for deaf patients, the nature of the difficulty should be scrutinized in a private discussion with the interpreter. Although the difficulty may have been "theirs" (e.g., fatigue, lack of receptive ASL fluency, or voicing skill) it may instead have been the patient's. If so, psychopathological contributions must be considered. When interpreters have difficulty understanding or voicing for psychotic deaf patients, they may erroneously blame themselves for communication impasses, which may be marked by periods of silence (while the patient is still signing), frequent requests for the patient to repeat, or other obvious indications of their struggle to understand.

Exploring with the interpreter (in privacy) what they *saw* (even if they could not fully understand or voice it) and how the problematic aspects of the patient's signing compare to normal signing can yield critical information. "She kept using signs that don't exist in ASL and I'm sure they weren't 'home signs' or regional sign variations; He was putting together sentences with signs I understood, but the sentences made no sense; She put together three signs in a row that didn't make sense, plus they all used the same handshape." Although such comments do not definitively diagnose sign-based neologisms, "word salad," or clang associations respectively, they certainly raise the possibility, especially if confirmed by another skilled interpreter. Each of these phenomena can be manifested by psychotic deaf patients who are otherwise fluent ASL signers, as can most other forms of communication disruption that hearing patients manifest. Thacker (1994) documented similar observations with psychotic British Sign Language users. In summary, the more the patient's problematic signing deviates from common patterns of educational or experiential-based sign dysfluency (with which many interpreters will be familiar) the more likely a psychopathological contribution may be present, especially if the patient's sign communication history is also inconsistent with poor signing.

The topic of psychosis must include mention of paranoia, if only because of the common misperception that deafness frequently leads to it. This is not the case, despite continued pronouncements of a deaf-ness–paranoia link by the American Psychiatric Association (1994). Much of the literature supporting a relationship between deafness and paranoia is based on studies of hearing subjects who were made to wear noise-inducing devices that prevented their hearing, then asked to respond to psychological tests that documented feelings of paranoia. This is hardly a valid approach for making psychological conjectures about deaf people. There is a more sizable literature, though, on paranoid symptoms manifested by elderly patients who have lost some or most of their hearing. The term *late paraphrenia* has been used to refer to a constellation of paranoid and other psychotic symptoms that have their onset in this geriatric patient population (Eastwood, Corbin, Reed, Nobbs, & Kedward, 1985; Holden, 1987; Prager & Jeste, 1993). It is not yet clear how hearing loss contributes to this symptom cluster versus the coincident potential contributions of dementia, memory loss, and other forms of neuropathology.

Cognitive Functions and the Mental Status Exam

The remainder of Table 8.1 lists several subcategories of cognitive functioning that are typically investigated during the mental status exam (MSE). The MSE is an interview procedure often conducted by psychiatrists, psychologists, and other mental health professionals when assessing new patients. Although somewhat varied in its depth and methodology, the MSE generally involves questions and observations pertaining to a hierarchy of mental, emotional, and psychosocial functions, from matters as basic as awareness of one's surroundings, to emotional features, to intelligence, to social judgment. Conducting the MSE with deaf persons usually requires special considerations.

Difficulties in orientation are not hard to identify, though it should be noted that the names of buildings and even people may not be as readily known to some deaf patients, for reasons unrelated to disorientation. *Sign names*, rather than repetition of English proper nouns, are often used in ASL to refer to familiar places and people. Less familiar places and people may be remembered and referred to in descriptive rather than nominal terms.

When descriptions of sensory and perceptual abilities are part of the MSE, the variability of hearing loss severity and communication preferences in the deaf population should be appreciated as well as the frequency of coincident visual impairment in some deafness etiologies (e.g., Usher's syndrome). Impairments in vision are very important to document due to the obvious significance of the visual modality in the lives of deaf and hard-of-hearing people. Hearing loss severity cannot be reliably judged from a person's speech skills, communication modality, English or sign fluency, or speechreading ability. More important than the degree of hearing loss per se is to document the individual's preferred mode of communication and, if possible, their proficiencies across various modes of communication.

Many deafness etiologies are associated with additional physical and neurological impairments (e.g., rubella, cytomegalovirus infection, prematurity, meningitis, anoxia, and various genetic syndromes). In fact, medical research that has resulted in the prevention of hearing loss as a singular condition (e.g., fewer ototoxic medications), and advancements in neonatal and pediatric medicine that increase the viability of children with multiple disabilities, both result in an increase in the frequency of situations where hearing loss coexists with neurological disorder. In the more narrowly defined deaf *patient* population, general or specific difficulties in cognitive functioning are therefore common. Although knowledge of the cause of the patient's hearing loss may be valuable in this regard, often the cause is unknown—either truly unknown or simply unknown to the patient. The identification of cognitive impairment, especially when subtle (e.g., some learning disabilities) or when limited to verbal functions (meaning language, not voice) requires special expertise. Psychological and neuropsychological testing with deaf persons is a specialized practice area; the presence of an interpreter is not sufficient in many cases to allow nonspecialist psychologists to test deaf persons validly.

No single category of misdiagnosis has been so pervasive in the history of psychology, psychiatry, and deafness as that involving mental retardation (Pollard, 1992b; Vernon & Andrews, 1990). Intelligence cannot be gauged reliably through a clinical interview with a deaf or hard-of-hearing individual. Neither education nor language proficiency (in English or in sign) nor fund of information (see the following) should be used to estimate intelligence. Even psychological testing is unreliable, except when conducted by professionals who are well-versed with the literature and procedures in this area. When questions regarding mental retardation or other aspects of general intellectual ability are raised, a specialist should be contacted to conduct a formal assessment. Frequently, valid psychological evaluations can be found in deaf patients' educational or vocational service records, but caution is always necessary in considering such data, as many psychologists, even those who are hired to test deaf individuals by schools or vocational rehabilitation agencies, are nevertheless unqualified to do so.

Although intelligence is distributed normally in the deaf population, the clinical interview often reveals limitations in fund of information, that is, the number of facts one knows, especially when persons have been deaf most of their lives. This usually has nothing to do with cognitive limitations or psychopathology. Limitation in fund of information is a natural consequence of several factors associated with deafness. Limited English reading proficiency, very common in deaf individuals, impairs access to factual information contained in most books, magazines, and newspapers. Although television programs and videotapes that are closed captioned have increased the deaf population's access to information, the captions themselves (if present at all) are in English, which may not be fully comprehended. Information from the radio is inaccessible to deaf and many hard-of-hearing people. Overheard conversation, a large and effortless source of factual information for hearing people, is generally inaccessible. For these and other reasons, access to information simply requires more effort and is harder to acquire when one is deaf or hard-of-hearing, especially given society's general malaise in rectifying information access inequities that deaf and hard-of-hearing people face. Thus, although many deaf and hard-of-hearing people do pursue and acquire normal or above normal funds of information, findings of limitations in this area during the clinical interview are common and should not be pathologized or used to gauge intelligence. This is not to say that limitations in factual knowledge are unimportant. Very often, the provision of factual information is a critical aspect of a good treatment plan, just as it is with hearing people.

Another common misconception is that deafness, or sign language itself, is associated with concrete thought processes. Neither is true. ASL is a rich and complex language that in no way limits conceptualization or conversation about abstract topics (Valli & Lucas, 1992). Similarly, there is nothing inherent in deafness that sets limits on cognitive capacity and reasoning. Yet, impoverished cognitive abilities are observed in some deaf patients. When not attributable to mental retardation or other developmental or neurological disorders, these are usually a function of educational and experiential restrictions, especially unstimulating communication and thinking environments during childhood (Braden, 1994; Schlesinger, 1992).

Unfortunately, in the deaf *patient* population, it is common to find individuals who suffered such environmentally induced deficits, including severe cases of early and prolonged neglect by families or institutions that left them with serious and permanent cognitive deficits that were otherwise entirely preventable. The clinical interview should always seek information regarding communication and learning history, in both family and school contexts; the information is often relevant to current cognitive skills findings. Requesting explanations of the meaning of proverbs, however (a common MSE interview procedure), is not recommended. Proverbs and idioms are among the most advanced and culture-bound elements of a language. Persons who are not *very* fluent in English and familiar with American (hearing) culture should not have their abstraction skills, intelligence, or other advanced cognitive functions judged on such a basis.

The final topics in the MSE, judgment and insight, raise no particular considerations in relation to deaf and hard-of-hearing patients that are not extensions of the issues already discussed. Fund of information limitations and developmental or educational impoverishment, if present, can certainly impact judgment and insight. When judgment or insight limitations have their basis in informational gaps, educational and counseling interventions can be very effective. Clinicians must be very cautious not to misattribute Deaf community sociocultural variations to problems in these more subjective MSE areas. As already noted, social norms, values, and behavior can differ between Deaf and hearing people (Moore & Levitan, 1993; Padden & Humphries, 1988). Failure to understand and appreciate these differences can easily lead to bias and error in the assessment of Deaf persons, with subsequent negative impact on the treatment process (Glickman & Harvey, 1996).

MENTAL DISORDERS AND THE ADULT DEAF POPULATION

Far more attention has been paid to psychological development and disorder in deaf children than to psychopathology in deaf adults. A review of the psychological literature on deaf children, even if limited to cognitive, behavioral, and other mental disorder topics, is beyond the scope of this chapter. In addition to other chapters in this volume, readers interested in mental health and deaf children may find the following authors' texts useful: Braden (1994), Marschark (1997), Meadow (1980), and Schlesinger and Meadow (1972). The remainder of this chapter focuses on topics pertaining to mental disorders in the adult deaf and hard-of-hearing populations.

Epidemiology

There have been few empirical studies of the incidence of various types of psychopathology in the adult deaf and hard-of-hearing population. Epidemiological research is one of the greatest needs in the field of deafness and mental health but is costly and challenging to do well. The few studies that have been conducted focused on individual hospital, clinic, or regional patient populations, contrasting deaf and hard-of-hearing patients' diagnostic patterns with those of hearing patients. One of the larger epidemiological studies to date used data collected over a 5-year period by 18 public mental health agencies in Rochester, New York, home of the largest per capita deaf and hard-of-hearing population in the world (Pollard, 1994). Over 500 case records pertaining to deaf and hard-of-hearing patients were identified. Proportional analyses of their diagnostic patterns found only a few significant variations from those identified for hearing patients served in the same time period. Comparable diagnostic rates for adjustment disorders, mood disorders, organic disorders, psychotic disorders, anxiety disorders, and personality disorders were found between the two samples. The few discrepancies that did emerge, such as lower frequencies of childhood disorders and substance use disorders in the deaf and hard-of-hearing sample, lower prevalence of the less common mental disorders (i.e., a restricted range of mental illnesses; also reported in a study by Vanderbosch, 1991), and a greater frequency of missing or deferred diagnoses, were judged to arise from clinician error (specifically shock-withdrawal-paralysis) and differential patterns of mental health service access and utilization between deaf and hearing people, not real differences in mental disorder prevalence rates. The study also found a higher mental retardation prevalence rate in the deaf and hard-of-hearing sample, as did an earlier study by Trybus (1983). Misdiagnosis of mental retardation is always a risk, yet this finding may be valid, especially given other reports (Evans, no date; Vanderbosch, 1991) that deaf persons with the most severe needs (e.g., mentally ill and developmentally disabled) are often overrepresented in clinical populations.

The opinions presented in this and other reviews of epidemiological data, and descriptions of long-term clinical experience in serving deaf people (Corker, 1994; Elliott, Glass, & Evans, 1987; Glickman & Harvey, 1996; Lane, 1992; Pollard, 1994; Vernon & Andrews, 1990), suggest that the full range of mental disorders appears with approximately equal frequency in the deaf and hearing populations, but that inequities in service access and problems of cross-cultural evaluation bias lead to the significant occurrences of misdiagnosis, overdiagnosis, and underdiagnosis with deaf patients. Neurological impairment and developmental disorders may be somewhat more prevalent in that portion of the deaf clinical population whose hearing loss results from certain high-risk etiologies. Lane's (1992) pointed critique of the psychiatric literature has underscored the need for high-quality, socioculturally appropriate epidemiological and treatment efficacy research. "Heaven help the deaf man or woman who really is mentally ill," he lamented. "Such diagnostic mayhem not only leads to irresponsible characterizations of deaf people; it prevents effective planning of the services deaf people need" (p. 55).

Disorders of Current Special Interest

Although a review of each of the many mental disorder categories and the literature that exists in relation to deaf and hard-of-hearing persons cannot be presented here, some disorders have been the focus of particular research or intervention strategies recently.

Alzheimer's Disease and Other Dementias. Several studies have found an association between hearing loss and Alzheimer's disease or other dementias (Gold, Lightfoot, & Hnath-Chisolm, 1996; Ives, 1995; Uhlmann, 1986), yet a causal attribution between deafness and the decline of memory and other cognitive functions cannot be inferred. Although this attribute has been suggested by some authors, other studies suggest that a common central nervous system mechanism may underlie both the dementia and the hearing loss (Almeida, 1993; Gates et al., 1995).

A particularly difficult aspect of the evaluation of memory decline and other symptoms of dementia in deaf adults is how to evaluate verbal (linguistic) memory functions in persons whose primary language is ASL. Often, verbal fluency and memory functions are the first to decline in Alzheimer's disease. Without ASL-based verbal measures, diagnosis of this and other types of dementia in deaf patients is likely to be delayed. One ASL-based test of verbal memory, the Signed Paired Associates Test, has been developed and its clinical utility demonstrated (DeMatteo, Pollard, & Lentz, 1987; Rediess, Pollard, & Veyberman, 1997).

Later-Onset Hearing Loss and Depressive Disorders. The onset of hearing loss in later life may well be associated with at least a mild degree of depressive symptoms (Eastwood et al., 1985; Falconer, 1985; Jones & White, 1990; Larew, Saura, & Watson, 1992; Trychin, 1991), although the presence of additional disabling conditions may be a confounding factor (Jones, 1984; Steinberg, 1991). The concurrent experience of tinnitus may aggravate depressive symptoms and contribute to the development of sleep and other disorders (Alster, Shemesh, Ornan, & Attias, 1993; Attias et al., 1995; Sullivan, Katon, Dobie, Sakai, Russo, & Harrop-Griffiths, 1988). Scant attention has been paid to the mental health needs of late-deafened and hard-of-hearing adults, even though diagnostic and treatment issues with this population can differ markedly from those impacting the Deaf population (Larew et al., 1992; Luey & Glass, 1995; Trychin, 1991). A new research and training center at the California School of Professional Psychology in San Diego is addressing the mental health needs of the late deafened and hard-of-hearing populations specifically.

Substance Use Disorders. Alcohol abuse and dependence has received a considerable degree of attention in the general field of deafness and mental health. Other forms of drug abuse have not. Alcoholism incidence rates are judged to be similar to that found in the hearing population (Isaacs, Buckley, & Martin, 1979), yet sociocultural and especially service system barriers restrict diagnosis and the provision of effective treatment (Lane, 1989; Moser & Rendon, 1992; Pollard, 1994; Rendon, 1992; Steinberg, 1991). Although a considerable number of alcohol treatment services for deaf and hard-of-hearing people exist (Rochester Institute of Technology [RIT], 1993), the Minnesota Chemical Dependency Program for Deaf and Hard-of-Hearing Individuals is the most well known. This Minneapolis-based program has disseminated a number of products and publications stemming from their extensive experience serving deaf inpatients (Guthmann, Lybarger, & Sandberg, 1993). They have reported a high incidence of comorbid psychiatric and developmental disorders in their patient population, again suggesting that those with multiple, severe difficulties are the most likely to overcome treatment referral barriers. The Minnesota program has developed and employed a variety of specialized tools and practices for use with deaf patients, including educational videos and classes in ASL, art and drama therapies, and homework packets modified for deaf readers. Outcome research available from the program indicates that successful sobriety postdischarge is most strongly associated with regular 12-step meeting attendance, employment, and the ability to communicate with one's family regarding sobriety maintenance.

Trauma and Abuse. Although not mental disorders per se, trauma and abuse can certainly lead to mental illness, including posttraumatic stress disorder, other anxiety disorders, depression, or even dissociative identity disorder (multiple personality). Like substance abuse, these dangerous societal problems are the focus of increasing attention by mental health professionals and the Deaf community (Elder, 1994; Swartz, 1995). A specialized trauma center for deaf women in Seattle (Merkin & Smith, 1995) is rapidly becoming a national model. A specialized treatment program serving sexually abused deaf children exists at the Boys Town National Research Center in Omaha, Nebraska (Sullivan, 1990) and has documented the effectiveness of its treatment approaches in a controlled study (Sullivan, Scanlon, Brookhouser, & Schulter, 1992).

TREATMENT AND THE SERVICE
DELIVERY SYSTEM

Psychotherapy and Other Treatment Approaches

The literature addressing specific methodologies of psychotherapeutic treatment with deaf and hard-of-hearing adults typically consists of individual therapist's reflections, case studies, or reports of small treatment programs (Gerstein, 1988; Halgin, 1986; Hittner & Bornstein, 1990; Quedenfeld & Farelly, 1983; Sarlin, 1984; Speer, 1994; Swink, 1985). Such reports typically describe successful applications of existing treatment approaches to deaf patients, adapted to accommodate their communication needs. Empirical studies of treatment outcome are rare (Cook, 1993, 1994; Nickless, 1993; Sullivan et al., 1992). These circumstances likely reflect a general assumption that treatment methods appropriate for hearing persons are also appropriate for deaf and hard-of-hearing individuals. Although this may be the case as a general rule, differing modes of communication, life experiences, and sociocultural characteristics may impact the effectiveness of psychotherapy, especially when rendered by hearing clinicians.

Glickman and Harvey (1996) recently edited a volume regarding psychotherapy methods and issues pertaining to the culturally Deaf population. The text explored Glickman's model of Deaf identity and its relation to psychosocial functioning, the cross-cultural barriers hearing clinicians face in serving this population, and specific complications and treatment approaches relevant in psychotherapy work with Deaf people. Numerous other publications have also addressed cultural and social issues in psychotherapy with deaf and hard-of-hearing people (Corker, 1994; Freedman, 1994; Harvey, 1993; Henwood & Pope-Davis, 1994; Larew et al., 1992; Leigh, 1996; Pollard, 1992b; Trychin, 1991). Some have specifically dealt with issues of deaf versus hearing therapists (Elliott, Glass, & Evans, 1987; Wax, 1990).

Given the significance of family dynamics in the psychological development of deaf children, it is no surprise that family therapy has been one of the more popular topics in the treatment literature (Harvey, 1985, 1989; Sloman & Springer, 1987). In addition to a focus on deaf children in hearing families, the topic of hearing children raised by deaf families has also been addressed by Harvey and others (Frankenburg, Sloman, & Perry, 1985; Preston, 1994).

Clinical hypnosis is a treatment technique that has been investigated with deaf subjects (Isenberg & Matthews, 1995; Matthews & Isenberg, 1995). Generally, the results indicate that deaf persons are hypnotized as readily as hearing persons, despite earlier concerns regarding the importance of speech sounds and closing one's eyes in inducing a hypnotic state. A scale to assess the hypnotic responsivity of deaf subjects has been developed (Repka & Nash, 1995). Reports of the actual use of hypnosis in the treatment of mental disorders in deaf and hard-of-hearing people are rare (Bowman & Coons, 1990).

The impact of sign language interpreters on psychotherapy process and outcome has been the focus of much discussion and debate (Brauer, 1990; Gerber, 1983; Pollard, 1983; Steinberg, 1991). There is little doubt that the presence of this third party alters the dynamics of the typical therapist–patient dyad. Although interpreters provide the obvious benefit of access to mental health treatment that would otherwise be denied to many, perhaps the majority of deaf consumers, some have questioned whether interpreter-facilitated access to psychotherapy should be so readily accepted as satisfactory. At the opposite end of the spectrum, some clinicians feel that the presence of the interpreter allows them to conduct specific, beneficial interventions that would otherwise be impossible (Harvey, 1989). Interpreters themselves have written about the practical and ethical challenges they face in the psychotherapeutic setting (Stansfield & Veltri, 1987; Fritsch-Rudser, no date). Clearly, empirical data is needed to explore further the impact of the interpreter in both assessment and treatment situations.

The Service Delivery System

The modern era of mental health services for deaf people was launched by the opening of a specialized inpatient treatment program at the New York State Psychiatric Institute in 1955 under the direction of Franz Kallman. Although smaller-scale research, teaching, and service initiatives were led previously, especially by Rudolph Pintner in the early 1900s and, later, by Edna Levine, Kallman's program rapidly stimulated the establishment of other treatment programs for deaf patients in Chicago, San Francisco, Washington, DC, and England. The checkered history of the psychological and psychiatric study of deaf individuals, much of which took place in the decades immediately following the establishment of Kallman's program, has been reviewed elsewhere (Elliott, Glass, & Evans, 1987; Lane, 1992; Pollard, 1992b). At present, many large cities have

clinics or private practitioners specializing in mental health care for deaf
and hard-of-hearing people. Some urban locations have a number of such
services (RIT, 1993; Willigan & King, 1992). Yet, access to competent
specialized treatment services, especially for persons in nonurban settings
and those who prefer direct (noninterpreted) sign language communication with their provider, remains hard to come by.

Seeking services from the public mental health system is not a com-
forting alternative to accessing specialized care. Long suspected of leading
to misdiagnosis, underdiagnosis, and inappropriate or iatrogenic treatment, public mental health service inequities experienced by deaf and
hard-of-hearing patients are only beginning to be documented through
empirical research (McEntee, 1995; Pollard, 1994). The aforementioned
Rochester study (Pollard, 1994) indicated a dramatic underrepresentation
of the city's large deaf population in its public mental health system,
especially its large, multiservice community mental health centers
(CMHCs). Deaf children, women, and people of color were particularly
underrepresented. Deaf and hard-of-hearing patients were overrepresented in small programs that were more communicatively accessible,
even though the programs provided fewer services than the CMHCs. It
appeared that communication issues, rather than clinical service needs,
were dictating referral patterns. When they were served by the CMHCs,
deaf and hard-of-hearing patients received more continuing treatment and
case management services and fewer services that would be considered
communicatively demanding, such as assessment and psychotherapy.

ADVOCACY, LAW, AND PUBLIC POLICY

More than all the accumulated research in the deafness and mental health
field, it is legal clout that has advanced treatment initiatives most. From
Section 504 of the Rehabilitation Act of 1973, to the Education for All
Handicapped Children Act of 1975, to the Americans with Disabilities
Act (ADA) of 1990, legislation has brought mental health care to more
deaf people than any other force.

Section 504 required access to and equitable treatment of persons with
disabilities in programs that received federal funding and were of a certain
size. Most state psychiatric facilities and many community mental health
centers fit this definition and were thus open to litigation if deaf patients
could not access or receive appropriate levels of care. *Nancy Doe v. Wilzack*
(1986), filed by the National Association of the Deaf won recognition
that deaf patients in mental hospitals deserved more than just medication
when hospitalized. This and other pre-ADA lawsuits called attention to
the long-neglected rights of deaf patients in institutions for the mentally

ill and mentally retarded. Such litigation initiated the establishment of numerous specialized treatment programs. In some cases, as young deaf patients grew too old for children's programs, or adult deaf patients were preparing for discharge from the hospital, strong legal advocates or family members used the power of Section 504 to assure that new specialized programs were created to receive them. These programs then experienced an influx of other, equally needy deaf patients who did not have tireless advocates fighting on their behalf.

Despite the important victories stemming from Section 504, it is the ADA that has generated the most widespread interest in mental health services to deaf and hard-of-hearing people (O'Keefe, 1993; Raifman & Vernon, 1996a, 1996b). Several ADA rulings have underscored the rights of deaf patients to be provided with interpreter services in inpatient and outpatient mental health settings. Due to the wider applicability and greater public awareness of the ADA (as opposed to Section 504) many mental health programs have made plans for arranging interpreter services proactively, without the threat of lawsuit. However, in a stunning decision, the U.S. District Court in Florida ruled in *Tugg v. Towey* (1994) that mental health services provided through sign language interpreters are not equivalent in quality to services that hearing people receive and thus violate the ADA. The court required the agency that was sued to hire sign-fluent clinicians with knowledge of the Deaf community and its sociocultural characteristics. It remains to be seen whether this much higher standard withstands further legal scrutiny and spreads to other parts of the country.

Beyond litigation under the ADA or Section 504, lesser-known legal strategies are also available to consumers, family members, and advocates seeking to rectify access and service quality inequities (Herbison, 1986). The consent decree, a legally binding agreement between parties in a lawsuit, which sometimes curtails more protracted class action litigation, has been used effectively in cases involving deaf individuals (Katz, Vernon, Penn, & Gellice, 1992; Raifman & Vernon, 1996b).

Nonlitigious community advocacy efforts on behalf of mental health services for deaf and hard-of-hearing persons are also gaining attention and can be very effective. Regional service planning conferences have stimulated rapid and significant changes (Pollard, 1995). Community needs assessments (Moser & Rendon, 1992; Myers, 1989; Whitehouse, Sherman, & Kozlowski, 1991), model state plans (Gore, 1992; Lawler, 1986; Myers, 1993; Tucker, 1981), and reports of smaller scale approaches (Farrugia, 1989; Rizzo, 1992) provide critical guidance to advocates and service administrators alike. The recently published standards of care document (Myers, 1995) provides welcome specificity in terms of program design and evaluation.

CONCLUSIONS

From gaining initial access to the clinician, to establishing the professional–consumer relationship, to conducting the clinical interview, to rendering a thorough and accurate diagnosis, to treatment planning and execution, to measuring outcome and quality of care, mental health services for deaf and hard-of-hearing people involve complexities of biology, psychology, language, sociology, culture, and society that must be appreciated by specialists and nonspecialists alike. This specialist discipline will continue to grow and mature (Pollard, 1996), but we are a diverse society that can no longer assume that those who use a different language, or who have differences in physical or sociocultural attributes, exist in some separate reality that is not relevant to our own. We share a common humanity and community. We interact with one another, both personally and professionally. In light of this, we have a duty to do so with regard for individual diversity and with all the competence we can bring to bear.

REFERENCES

Almeida, O. P. (1993). Unilateral auditory hallucinations. *British Journal of Psychiatry*, *162*, 262–264.
Alster, J., Shemesh, Z., Ornan, M., & Attias, J. (1993). Sleep disturbance associated with chronic tinnitus. *Biological Psychiatry*, *34*(1–2), 84–90.
American Psychiatric Association. (1994). *Diagnostic and statistical manual of mental disorders.* (4th ed.). Washington, DC: Author.
Attias, J., Shemesh, Z., Bleich, A., Solomon, Z., Bar-Or, G., Alster, J., & Sohmer, H. (1995). Psychological profile of help-seeking and non-help-seeking tinnitus patients. *Scandinavian Audiology*, *24*(1), 13–18.
Berrios, G. E. (1991). Musical hallucinations: A statistical analysis of 46 cases. *Psychopathology*, *24*(6), 356–360.
Bowman, E. S., & Coons, P. M. (1990). The use of hypnosis in a deaf patient with multiple personality disorder: A case report [see comments]. *American Journal of Clinical Hypnosis*, *33*(2), 99–104.
Braden, J. P. (1994). *Deafness, deprivation, and IQ.* New York: Plenum.
Brauer, B. (1990, Spring). Caught in the middle: Does interpreting work in a mental health setting? *Gallaudet Today*, 46–49.
Comas-Diaz, L., & Griffith, E. E. H. (1988). *Clinical guidelines in cross-cultural mental health.* New York: Wiley.
Cook, J. (1993). Psychosocial rehabilitation of deaf persons with severe mental illness: A multivariate model of residential outcomes. Psychology and deafness [Special issue]. *Rehabilitation Psychology*, *38*(4), 261–274.
Cook, J. (1994). Psychosocial rehabilitation of deaf persons with severe mental illness: A multivariate model of residential outcomes: Erratum. *Rehabilitation Psychology*, *39*(1), 72.
Corker, M. (1994). *Counselling—The deaf challenge.* Bristol, PA: Jessica Kingsley.

DeMatteo A. J., Pollard, R. Q, & Lentz, E. M. (1987). Assessment of linguistic functions in brain-impaired and brain-intact prelingually deaf users of American Sign Language: A preliminary report. Paper presented at the biennial meeting of the American Deafness and Rehabilitation Association, Minneapolis, MN.

Dickert, J. (1988). Examination of bias in mental health evaluation of deaf patients. *Social Work, 33*(3), 273–274.

Dolnick, E. (1993, September). Deafness as culture. *Atlantic Monthly, 272,* 37–53.

Eastwood, M. R., Corbin, S. L., Reed, M., Nobbs, H., & Kedward, H. B. (1985). Acquired hearing loss and psychiatric illness: An estimate of prevalence and co-morbidity in a geriatric setting. *British Journal of Psychiatry, 147,* 552–556.

Elder, M. (1994). Deaf survivors of sexual abuse: A look at the issues. (and) Abused because of deafness? *Moving Forward, 2*(5), 1, 12–15.

Elliott, H., Glass, L., & Evans, J. W. (1987). *Mental health assessment of deaf clients: A practical manual.* Boston: Little, Brown.

Evans, J.W. (no date). Mental health treatment of hearing impaired adolescents and adults. Unpublished manuscript. San Francisco: University of California San Francisco, Center on Deafness.

Evans, J. W., & Elliott, H. (1981). Screening criteria for the diagnosis of schizophrenia in deaf patients. *Archives of General Psychiatry, 40,* 1281–1285.

Falconer, J. (1985). Aging and hearing. *Physical & Occupational Therapy in Geriatrics, 4*(2), 3–20.

Farrugia, D. (1989). Practical steps for access and delivery of mental health services to clients who are deaf. *Journal of Applied Rehabilitation Counseling, 20*(1), 33–35.

Frankenburg, F. R., Sloman, L., & Perry, A. (1985). Issues in the therapy of hearing children with deaf parents. *Canadian Journal of Psychiatry—Revue Canadienne de Psychiatrie, 30*(2), 98–102.

Freedman, P. (1994). Counseling with deaf clients: The need for culturally and linguistically sensitive interventions. *Journal of the American Deafness & Rehabilitation Association, 27*(4), 16–28.

Fritsch-Rudser, S. (no date). Interpreters and clinicians: Defining the partnership. Unpublished manuscript. University of California San Francisco, Center on Deafness.

Gates, G. A., Karzon, R. K., Garcia, P., Peterein, J., Storandt, M., Morris, J. C., & Miller, J. P. (1995). Auditory dysfunction in aging and senile dementia of the Alzheimer's type. *Archives of Neurology, 52*(6), 626–634.

Gerber, B. M. (1983). A communication minority: Deaf people and mental health care. The psychiatric care of "minority" groups [Special issue]. *American Journal of Social Psychiatry, 3*(2), 50–57.

Gerstein, A. I. (1988). A psychiatric program for deaf patients. *Psychiatric Hospital, 19*(3), 125–128.

Glickman, N., & Harvey, M. (1996). *Culturally affirmative psychotherapy with deaf persons.* Mahwah, NJ: Lawrence Erlbaum Associates.

Gold, M., Lightfoot, L. A., & Hnath-Chisolm, T. (1996). Hearing loss in a memory disorders clinic: A specially vulnerable population. *Archives of Neurology, 53*(9), 922–928.

Goldsmith, L., & Schloss, P. J. (1986). Diagnostic overshadowing among school psychologists working with hearing-impaired learners. *American Annals of the Deaf, 131*(4), 288–293.

Gore, T. A. (1992). The development of a state-wide mental health system for deaf and hard of hearing persons. *Journal of the American Deafness & Rehabilitation Association, 26*(2), 1–8.

Goulder, T. (1977). Federal and state mental health programs for the deaf in hospitals and clinics. In R. Trybus (Ed.), *The future of mental health services for deaf people:*

Proceedings of the first orthopsychiatric workshop on deafness. Journal of Mental Health and Deafness. Experimental issue No. 1, 13–17.

Guthmann, D., Lybarger, R., & Sandberg, K. (1993). Providing chemical dependency treatment to the deaf or hard of hearing mentally ill client. *Journal of the American Deafness & Rehabilitation Association, 27*(1), 1–15.

Halgin, R. P. (1986). Psychotherapy with hearing-impaired clients. *Professional Psychology—Research & Practice, 17*(5), 466–472.

Hammeke, T. A. (1983). Musical hallucinations associated with acquired deafness. *Journal of Neurology, Neurosurgery & Psychiatry, 46*(6), 570–572.

Harvey, M. A. (1985). Toward a dialogue between the paradigms of family therapy and deafness. *American Annals of the Deaf, 130*(4), 305–314.

Harvey, M. A. (1989). *Psychotherapy with deaf and hard-of-hearing persons: A systemic model.* Hillsdale, NJ: Lawrence Erlbaum Associates.

Harvey, M. A. (1993). Cross cultural psychotherapy with deaf persons: A hearing, White, middle class, middle aged, non-gay, Jewish, male, therapist's perspective. *Journal of the American Deafness & Rehabilitation Association, 26*(4), 43–55.

Henwood, P. G., & Pope-Davis, D. B. (1994). Disability as cultural diversity: Counseling the hearing-impaired. *The Counseling Psychologist, 22*(3), 489–503.

Herbison, P. J. (1986). Legal rights of hearing-impaired children: A guide for advocates. *Health & Social Work, 11*(4), 301–307.

Hittner, A., & Bornstein, H. (1990). Group counseling with older adults: Coping with late-onset hearing impairment. Techniques for counseling older persons [Special issue]. *Journal of Mental Health Counseling, 12*(3), 332–341.

Holden, N. L. (1987). Late paraphrenia or the paraphrenias? A descriptive study with a 10-year follow-up. *British Journal of Psychiatry, 150*, 635–639.

Isaacs, M., Buckley, G., & Martin, D. (1979). Patterns of drinking among the deaf. *American Journal of Drug and Alcohol Abuse, 6*, 463–476.

Isenberg, G. L., & Matthews, W. J. (1995). Hypnosis with signing deaf and hearing subjects. *American Journal of Clinical Hypnosis, 38*(1), 27–38.

Ives, D. G. (1995). Characteristics and comorbidities of rural older adults with hearing impairment. *Journal of the American Geriatrics Society, 43*(7), 803–806.

Jones, D. A. (1984). Hearing difficulty and its psychological implications for the elderly. *Journal of Epidemiology & Community Health, 38*(1), 75–78.

Jones, E. M., & White, A. J. (1990). Mental health and acquired hearing impairment: A review. *British Journal of Audiology, 24*(1), 3–9.

Katz, D., Vernon, M., Penn, A., & Gellice, J. (1992). The consent decree: A means of obtaining mental health services for people who are deaf. *Journal of the American Deafness & Rehabilitation Association, 26*(2), 22–28.

Lane, H. (1992). *The mask of benevolence: Disabling the deaf community.* New York: Knopf.

Lane, H., Hoffmeister, R., & Bahan, B. (1996). *A journey into the Deaf-world.* San Diego, CA: Dawn Sign Press.

Lane, K. E. (1989). Substance abuse among the deaf population: An overview of current strategies, programs & barriers to recovery. *Journal of the American Deafness & Rehabilitation Association, 22*(4), 79–86.

Larew, S. J., Saura, K. M., & Watson, D. (Eds.). (1992). *Facing deafness.* Proceedings of ALDACON III, The Association for Late-Deafened Adults. DeKalb, IL: Northern Illinois University.

Lawler, D. M. (1986). Mental health service planning for deaf persons: A beginning. *Journal of Rehabilitation of the Deaf, 19*(3–4), 1–4.

Leigh, I. W. (1996). Providing psychological services to deaf individuals: A response to new perceptions of diversity. *Professional Psychology—Research & Practice, 27*(4), 364–371.

Levine, E. (1977). The preparation of psychological service providers to the deaf: A report of the Spartanburg conference on the functions, competencies and training of psychological service providers to the deaf. *Journal of Rehabilitation of the Deaf*, Monograph No. 4.

Luey, H. S., & Glass, L. G. (1995). Hard-of-hearing or deaf: Issues of ears, language, culture, and identity. *Social Work, 40*(2), 177–182.

Marschark, M. (1997). *Raising and educating deaf children*. New York: Oxford University Press.

Matthews, W. J., & Isenberg, G. L. (1995). A comparison of the hypnotic experience between signing deaf and hearing participants. *International Journal of Clinical & Experimental Hypnosis, 43*(4), 375–385.

McEntee, M. L. (1995). Deaf and hard-of-hearing clients: Some legal implications. *Social Work, 40*(2), 183–187.

Meadow, K. P. (1980). *Deafness and child development*. Berkeley, CA: University of California Press.

Merkin, L., & Smith, M. J. (1995). A community based model providing services for deaf and deaf-blind victims of sexual assault and domestic violence. Sexuality and deafness [Special issue]. *Sexuality & Disability, 13*(2), 97–106.

Moore, M. S., & Levitan, L. (1993). *For hearing people only*. (2nd ed.). Rochester, NY: Deaf Life Press.

Moser, N., & Rendon, M. E. (1992). Alcohol and drug services: A jigsaw puzzle. *Journal of the American Deafness & Rehabilitation Association, 26*(2), 18–21.

Murata, S., Naritomi, H., & Sawada, T. (1994). Musical auditory hallucinations caused by a brainstem lesion. *Neurology, 44*(1), 156–158.

Myers, P. C. (1989). Deafness mental health needs assessment: A model. *Journal of the American Deafness & Rehabilitation Association, 22*(4), 72–78.

Myers, R. R. (1993). Model Mental Health State Plan (MMHSP) of services for persons who are deaf or hard-of-hearing. *Journal of the American Deafness & Rehabilitation Association, 26*(4), 19–28.

Myers, R. R. (1995). *Standards of care for the delivery of mental health services to deaf and hard of hearing persons*. Silver Spring, MD: National Association of the Deaf.

Nickless, C. (1993). Program outcome research in residential programs for deaf mentally ill adults. *Journal of the American Deafness & Rehabilitation Association, 27*(3), 42–48.

O'Keeffe, J. (Ed.). (1993). Implications of the Americans with Disabilities Act of 1990 for psychologists [Special issue]. *Consulting Psychology Journal: Practice and Research, 45*(2), 1–62.

Padden, C., & Humphries, T. (1988). *Deaf in America: Voices from a culture*. Cambridge, MA: Harvard University Press.

Pollard, R. Q (1983). Comment on the RID code of ethics for interpreters in psychotherapy. *American Annals of the Deaf, 128*, 371–372.

Pollard, R. Q (1992a). Cross-cultural ethics in the conduct of deafness research. *Rehabilitation Psychology, 37*(2), 87–101.

Pollard, R. Q (1992b). 100 years in psychology and deafness: A centennial retrospective. *Journal of the American Deafness & Rehabilitation Association, 26*(3), 32–46.

Pollard, R. Q (1994). Public mental health service and diagnostic trends regarding individuals who are deaf or hard of hearing. *Rehabilitation Psychology, 39*(3), 147–160.

Pollard, R. Q (1995). Mental health services and the deaf population: A regional consensus planning approach [Special issue]. *Journal of the American Deafness & Rehabilitation Association, 28*(3), 1–47.

Pollard, R. Q (1996). Professional psychology and deaf people: The emergence of a discipline. *American Psychologist, 51*(4), 389–396.

Prager, S., & Jeste, D. V. (1993). Sensory impairment in late-life schizophrenia. *Schizophrenia Bulletin, 19*(4), 755–772.

Preston, P. (1994). *Mother father deaf: Living between sound and silence.* Cambridge, MA: Harvard University Press.

Quedenfeld, C., & Farelly, F. (1983). Provocative therapy with the hearing impaired client. *Journal of Rehabilitation of the Deaf, 17*(2), 1–12.

Raifman, L. J., & Vernon, M. (1996a). Important implications for psychologists of the Americans with Disabilities Act: Case in point, the patient who is deaf. *Professional Psychology–Research & Practice, 27*(4), 372–377.

Raifman, L. J., & Vernon, M. (1996b). New rights for deaf patients; new responsibilities for mental hospitals. *Psychiatric Quarterly, 67*(3), 209–220.

Rainer, J. D., Abdullah, S., & Altshuler, K. Z. (1970). Phenomenology of hallucinations in the deaf. In W. Keup (Ed.), *Origin and mechanisms of hallucinations* (pp. 449–465). New York: Plenum.

Rediess, S., Pollard, R., & Veyberman, B. (1997). Assessment of verbal (ASL-based) memory in deaf adults: Clinical utility of the Signed Paired Associates Test. Address presented at the annual meeting of the International Neuropsychological Society, Orlando, FL.

Rendon, M. E. (1992). Deaf culture and alcohol and substance abuse. *Journal of Substance Abuse Treatment, 9*(2), 103–110.

Repka, R. J., & Nash, M. R. (1995). Hypnotic responsivity of the deaf: The development of the University of Tennessee Hypnotic Susceptibility Scale for the Deaf. *International Journal of Clinical & Experimental Hypnosis, 43*(3), 316–331.

Rizzo, A. M. (1992). Strategies for responding to community opposition in an existing group home. *Psychosocial Rehabilitation Journal, 15*(3), 85–95.

Rochester Institute of Technology. (1993). *National directory of alcohol and other drugs prevention and treatment programs accessible to the deaf.* Rochester, NY: Author.

Sarlin, M. B. (1984). The use of dreams in psychotherapy with deaf patients. *Journal of the American Academy of Psychoanalysis, 12*(1), 75–88.

Schlesinger, H. S. (1992). Elusive X factor: Parental contributions to literacy. In M. Walworth, D. F. Moores, & T. J. O'Rourke (Eds.), *A free hand: Enfranchising the education of deaf children* (37–64). Silver Spring, MD: T. J. Publishers, Inc.

Schlesinger, H. S., & Meadow, K. P. (1972). *Sound and sign: Childhood deafness and mental health.* Berkeley, CA: University of California Press.

Sloman, L., & Springer, S. (1987). Strategic family therapy interventions with deaf member families. *Canadian Journal of Psychiatry—Revue Canadienne de Psychiatrie, 32*(7), 558–562.

Speer, D. C. (1994). Group therapy in nursing homes and hearing deficit. *Clinical Gerontologist, 14*(4), 68–70.

Stansfield, M., & Veltri, D. (1987). Assessment from the perspective of the sign language interpreter. In H. Elliott, L. Glass, & J. W. Evans (Eds.), *Mental health assessment of deaf clients: A practical manual* (153–163). Boston: Little Brown.

Steinberg, A. (1991). Issues in providing mental health services to hearing-impaired persons. *Hospital & Community Psychiatry, 42*(4), 380–389.

Sullivan, M. D., Katon, W., Dobie, R., Sakai, C., Russo, J., & Harrop-Griffiths, J. (1988). Disabling tinnitus: Association with affective disorder. *General Hospital Psychiatry, 10*(4), 285–291.

Sullivan, P. M. (1990). Psychotherapy with handicapped sexually abused children. Sexual abuse [Special issue]. *Developmental Disabilities Bulletin, 18*(2), 21–34.

Sullivan, P. M., Scanlon, J. M., Brookhouser, P. E., & Schulter, L. E. (1992). The effects of psychotherapy on behavior problems of sexually abused deaf children. *Child Abuse & Neglect, 16*(2), 297–307.

Swartz, D. B. (1995). Effective techniques in treating survivors of child sexual abuse: Problematic areas in their application to the deaf population. Sexuality and deafness [Special issue]. *Sexuality & Disability, 13*(2), 135–144.

Swink, D. F. (1985). Psychodramatic treatment for deaf people. *American Annals of the Deaf, 130*(4), 272–277.

Thacker, A. J. (1994). Formal communication disorder. *British Journal of Psychiatry, 165*(6), 818–823.

Trybus, R. (1983). Hearing-impaired patients in public psychiatric hospitals throughout the United States. In D. Watson & B. W. Heller (Eds.), *Mental health and deafness: Strategic perspectives* (pp. 1–19). Silver Spring, MD: American Deafness and Rehabilitation Association.

Trybus, R. (1987). Unpublished manuscript. Washington, DC: Gallaudet University.

Trychin, S. (1991). *Manual for mental health professionals, part II: Psycho-social challenges faced by hard of hearing people.* Washington, DC: Gallaudet University Press.

Tucker, B. P. (1981). Mental health services for hearing-impaired persons. *Volta Review, 83*(4), 223–235.

Uhlmann, R. F. (1986). Hearing impairment and cognitive decline in senile dementia of the Alzheimer's type. *Journal of the American Geriatrics Society, 34*(3), 207–210.

Valli, C., & Lucas, C. (1992). *Linguistics of American Sign Language: A resource text for ASL users.* Washington, DC: Gallaudet University Press.

Vanderbosch, J.E. (1991). Prevalence and type of mental disorders in hearing impaired persons seeking outpatient services. Unpublished manuscript. Chicago, IL: Illinois School of Professional Psychology.

Vernon, M. (1983). Deafness and mental health: Emerging responses. In E. Petersen (Ed.), *Mental health and deafness: Emerging responses* (pp. 1–15). Silver Spring, MD: American Deafness and Rehabilitation Association.

Vernon, M., & Andrews, J. F. (1990). *The psychology of deafness: Understanding deaf and hard-of-hearing people.* New York: Longman.

Wax, T. M. (1990). Deaf community leaders as liaisons between mental health and deaf cultures. *Journal of the American Deafness & Rehabilitation Association, 24*(2), 33–40.

Whitehouse, A., Sherman, R., & Kozlowski, K. (1991). The needs of deaf substance abusers in Illinois. *American Journal of Drug and Alcohol Abuse, 17*(1), 103–113.

Willigan, B. A., & King, S. J. (1992). *Mental health services for deaf people.* Washington, DC: Gallaudet University, American Deafness and Rehabilitation Association, University of California San Francisco Center on Deafness.

9

Learning Disabilities, Attention Deficit Disorders, and Deafness

Vincent J. Samar
National Technical Institute for the Deaf, Rochester Institute of Technology
University of Rochester Medical School

Ila Parasnis
National Technical Institute for the Deaf, Rochester Institute of Technology

Gerald P. Berent
National Technical Institute for the Deaf, Rochester Institute of Technology

Since the early 1940s there has been expansive growth in speculation, theorizing, and research on learning disabilities (LD) and attention deficit disorders (ADD) in the general population (Gerber, 1993; Shaywitz, Fletcher, & Shaywitz, 1994).[1] Remarkable progress has been made in the

---

[1] The abbreviation LD is used throughout this chapter to refer to the general class of *learning disabilities* that arise across the whole range of relevant cognitive domains, including language, spatial cognition, social cognition, memory systems, and so on. The abbreviation LLD, for *language learning disabilities*, refers to the subset of learning disabilities that primarily involves disorders of language. The abbreviation ADD is used throughout this paper as the generic label for the entire class of disorders that may predominantly involve inattentiveness, hyperactivity–impulsivity, or a combination of the two, including both behavioral and cognitive domains of dysfunction that might be present separately in an individual to any degree of severity.

development of diagnostic procedures and in understanding the cognitive and neural mechanisms of certain forms of LD and ADD. The field today is burgeoning with commitment, professional interaction, and interdisciplinary research activity due to widespread recognition of the high incidence of these conditions among children and adults (Algozzine & Ysseldyke, 1986; Shaywitz et al., 1994), the significant impact that they have on academic achievement, self-esteem, and career success over the lifespan (Hersh, Stone, & Ford, 1996), and the imminent development of advanced remediation and evaluation technology (Eden, VanMeter, Rumsey, Maisog, Woods, & Zeffiro, 1996; Merzenich, Jenkins, Johnston, Schreiner, Miller, & Tallal, 1996; Tallal et al., 1996).

By contrast, theory and research on LD and ADD in the deaf[2] population have remained a mere backwater, burbling occasionally with statements of quandary and urgency by a few forward-looking commentators but largely bereft of strong conceptual or empirical currents. A few pioneering studies have attempted to establish the incidence of LD and ADD and to deal with the special problems of evaluating and remediating these conditions in a deaf population. However, the topic has remained relatively sheltered from the dynamic climate of debate, empiricism, and paradigm shift raging in the mainstream (Gerber, 1993). The cry for research and high-quality diagnostic and habilitative services to identify and educate deaf children with LD and ADD remains as plaintive in the 1990s (Mauk & Mauk, 1992) as it was over a decade ago (Sabatino, 1983).

This chapter attempts to contextualize and synthesize the small literature on LD and ADD in the deaf population. The educational relevance of studying LD and ADD in the deaf population is addressed first. This is followed by a description of the history of LD and ADD definitions and the role of definitional issues in relegating LD and ADD among the deaf population to the backwater of academic and professional interest. A brief conceptual overview of the neurobiology underlying LD and ADD is presented next to motivate the general understanding that LD and ADD are largely grounded in neurological pathology occurring during prenatal and early postnatal neural development in both hearing and deaf populations. Specific information is then presented on the estimated incidences of LD and ADD in the deaf population and on current approaches to evaluating LD and ADD in deaf individuals. An exposition of fundamental problems for future progress in developing effective LD and ADD evaluation protocols for the deaf population is then presented. It is argued

---

[2]The term *deaf* is used here to refer to all persons with educationally significant hearing losses, including individuals with both hereditary and acquired deafness and hard-of-hearing individuals.

that problems of definition, evaluation, and syndrome complexity peculiar to the deaf population present significant problems for progress in
this field. Finally, a discussion of current and future research directions
for the deaf population based on advanced developments in the mainstream literature on the hearing population is presented. It is shown that
certain problems can be overcome to a significant degree by catching the
currents of contemporary advances in LD and ADD research in the
mainstream.

A novelty of this chapter is the explicit treatment of LD and ADD in
the deaf population as distinct domains of cognitive variation that can
both lead to learning problems. Although the literature on deafness has
tended to conflate the conditions of LD and ADD under the rubric of LD
(e.g., Griffith & Scott, 1985; Karchmer, 1985; Morgan & Vernon, 1994),
the mainstream literature has emphasized their syndrome distinctiveness
(Epstein, Shaywitz, Shaywitz, & Woolstein, 1991). In fact, a large body
of neurobiological, behavioral genetic, and neuropsychological research
indicates that executive neural systems in the brain, especially but not
exclusively frontal-lobe systems, normally control and coordinate the
specific neural subsystems distributed elsewhere throughout cortical and
subcortical brain areas that are responsible for cognitive and social
behavior (Pennington, 1991; Welsh, 1994). ADD results from disorders
of this executive control system whereas LD results from disorders of the
various specific cognitive and social reasoning subsystems. Accordingly,
ADD entails overarching problems in attentional regulation, planning,
self-control, arousal, time management, and other *metacognitive* functions.
By contrast, LD entails specific learning disorders such as dyslexia,
spatial cognition disorders, social intelligence disorders, auditory language processing disorders, and other specific *cognitive* disorders.

Thus, LD and ADD are now generally regarded as hierarchically related
(cognitive versus metacognitive, respectively) but taxonomically distinct
(caused by damage to distinct brain mechanisms). Following this dominant current in the mainstream, ADD in the deaf population is explicitly
regarded in this chapter as entailing a disorder of overarching executive
functions, and LD as entailing a distinct set of disorders related to specific
cognitive and social processing systems. Although they are distinct disorders, LD and ADD often co-occur in the same individual (August &
Garfinkel, 1990; Shaywitz et al., 1994). By treating LD and ADD together
in the same chapter, we simultaneously emphasize their distinctiveness
and their interrelatedness in affecting the learning abilities of many deaf
individuals. LD and ADD in the deaf population are kindred denizens of
the backwater whose neurobiological foundations, methods of evaluation,
implications for learning and academic achievement, and prospects for

remediation await the further attention of researchers and educators concerned with the advancement of deaf children and adults.

EDUCATIONAL RELEVANCE

The need for research and evaluation programs to identify deaf children with LD and ADD has been echoed throughout academic, educational, and government quarters for many years (Davila, Williams, & MacDonald, 1991; Kelly, Forney, Parker-Fisher, & Jones, 1993a, 1993b; Mauk & Mauk, 1992; Shroyer, 1982). Large-scale national surveys revealed strong grassroots recognition among teachers and administrators of a critical educational need for LD assessment of deaf children and of the serious ill-preparedness of teachers and school personnel to serve LD deaf students appropriately (Elliot & Powers, 1988; Elliot, Powers, & Funderburg, 1988; Israelite & Hammermeister, 1986; Powers, Elliot, & Funderburg, 1987). The need for curriculum-based LD evaluation in which deaf students are evaluated on their ability to learn actual materials from the school curriculum is a strong contemporary theme (Roth, 1991). Furthermore, deaf children are particularly vulnerable to the detrimental effects of ADD due in part to the compounded effects of deafness and ADD in producing social isolation (Kelly et al., 1993b); accordingly, the U.S. Department of Education emphasized the need for local and state education agencies to increase teacher awareness of ADD through specialized training programs (Davila et al., 1991).

The proper evaluation of LD and ADD will permit deaf children access to comprehensive and coordinated accommodations and special education services,[3] including classroom and curricular modifications, study

---

[3]These may include modified classroom environments, reduced course loads, individualized instructional assistance and support, modified test instructions and protocols, emphasis on experiential approaches to learning and the use of concrete examples that promote memory, reciprocal teaching techniques, management of the span of work periods, instruction in specific study skills and strategies, use of visually enhanced materials, use of organizational strategies, involvement of children in cooperative learning groups and peer tutoring, coaching in behavior and anger management, specially structured approaches to homework management, family counseling, career counseling, social skills training, advocacy training, extensions for completing noncredit requirements, support groups, and psychostimulant medication (Elliot, Powers, & Funderburg, 1988; Kelly et al., 1993; Rush & Baechle, 1992).

Psychostimulants have been repeatedly shown to improve attentional control and reduce hyperactivity and impulsive behavior in approximately 75% of children with ADD (Barkley, 1990) and to normalize neural indices of selective attention and other executive cognitive processes (Klorman et al., 1990; Klorman, 1991). Importantly, Kelly et al. (1993b) have reported high success rates for Ritalin treatment in a pilot sample of 15 deaf children at the Illinois School for the Deaf. This suggests that pharmaceutical intervention can effectively supplement a well-structured educational environment management program for deaf children with correctly diagnosed ADD.

skills training, testing modifications, counseling, and psychostimulant medication (Elliot, Powers, & Funderburg, 1988; Kelly et. al, 1993b; Rush & Baechle, 1992). Although the actual impact of many of these accommodations on academic performance has rarely been studied quantitatively, limited work shows that certain accommodations commonly provided by universities to LD hearing students, such as special advisement and computer laboratories, do significantly improve their academic success (Keim, McWhirter, & Bernstein, 1996). Additionally, the development of interactive multimedia to remediate language learning disabilities, other forms of LD, and ADD in classroom and home settings is an imminent reality (Campbell, Neill, & Dudley, 1986; Merzenich et al., 1996; Tallal et al., 1996). The extension of these accommodations and technologies to the deaf population and the demonstration of their effectiveness should be a direct focus of future remediation efforts.

DEFINITIONS OF LD AND ADD

Learning Disabilities

Auxter (1971) provided an early warning that LD occurs in the deaf population. However, the original federal definition only referred to children who have a disorder in one or more "basic psychological processes" involved in using and understanding language, including poorly defined constructs such as perceptual handicaps, minimal brain damage, dyslexia, and developmental aphasia. Children whose learning difficulties were primarily caused by deafness or other sensory or motor impairments, mental retardation, or environmental, cultural, or economic disadvantage were excluded explicitly from concomitant classification as LD (PL 94-142; Education for all Handicapped Children Act of 1975). The current federal definition, PL 101-476, preserves the exclusionary language of PL 94-142, although the 1986 Education of the Handicapped Act Amendments broadened the eligibility criteria and definitions, making deaf children with concomitant LD potentially eligible for intervention programs and services (Mauk & Mauk, 1992).

The PL 94-142 definition motivated a turbulent clamor to revise the definition to recognize the heterogeneous conditions that comprise LD and to include adolescents, adults, and populations with sensory and other disabilities such as the deaf population (Gerber, 1993; Hammill, Leigh, McNutt, & Larsen, 1981). Several authors argued that excluding deaf children from the possibility of also having LD would seriously compromise their education (Bunch & Melnyk, 1989; Mauk & Mauk,

1992; Hammill et al., 1981). With gadfly candor, Sabatino (1983) reasoned persuasively that the exclusion of deaf children from concomitant classification as LD was an act of "idiocy" (p. 26).

The 1981 National Joint Committee on Learning Disabilities (NJCLD) published a revised definition that reasserted a core characterization of LD as a heterogeneous class of disorders, eliminated the restrictive population characterizations and theoretically ill-defined references to basic psychological processes and mental conditions, and emphasized the presumed central nervous system cause of LD and the possibility of its co-occurrence with other disabilities (Hammill et al., 1981). The most recent NJCLD (1994, pp. 65–66) definition of LD is as follows:

> Learning disabilities is a general term that refers to a heterogeneous group of disorders manifested by significant difficulties in the acquisition and use of listening, speaking, reading, writing, reasoning, or mathematical abilities. These disorders are intrinsic to the individual and presumed to be due to central nervous system dysfunction. Problems in self-regulatory behaviors, social perception, and social integration may exist with learning disabilities but do not by themselves constitute a learning disability. Even though a learning disability may occur concomitantly with other handicapping conditions (e.g., sensory impairment, mental retardation, social and emotional disturbance) or environmental influences (e.g., cultural differences, insufficient/inappropriate instruction, psychogenic factors), it is not the result of those conditions or influences.

Anticipating the upcoming reauthorization of the Individuals with Disabilities Education Act (IDEA), which supersedes PL 94-142 and related acts, Shaw, Cullen, McGuire, and Brinkerhoff (1995) proposed replacing the current federal definition with the 1994 NJCLD definition and outlined a process for operationalizing the definition to overcome a reliance on aptitude/achievement discrepancy criteria and to link the categorical classification of LD subtypes to criteria of educational relevance and access. At the other extreme, OSEP (U.S. Office of Special Education Programs, 1995, p. 13), noting the importance of curriculum-based evaluation and remediation, proposed an explicitly noncategorical disability definition as follows: "A child with a disability eligible for services under the IDEA would be defined as a 'child who has a physical or mental impairment and who by reason thereof requires special education.'" Coutinho (1995, p. 667) noted that the OSEP proposal substantially worsens the long-standing LD definitional crisis and proposed that "LD research, advocacy, and policy communities move swiftly and in a focused, consensus-driven manner to identify the core purposes a federal definition of learning disabilities should embrace." Whatever the outcome of the IDEA reauthorization, it is clear that tying LD assessment to the curriculum and to goals for a child's academic performance will be a major theme of new legislation and operationalization principles.

Although it has no federal status, Laughton (1989) proposed a definition that comes closest to capturing the construct of an LD deaf individual and explicitly recognizes the complexly interactive influence of deafness and LD on the psychological, academic, and life success of deaf people:

> Learning disabled, hearing impaired individuals have significant difficulty with the acquisition, integration, and use of language and/or nonlinguistic abilities. These disorders are presumed to be caused by the coexisting conditions of central nervous system dysfunction and peripheral sensorineural hearing impairment, and not by either condition exclusively. The condition can vary in its manifestations and degrees of severity and can affect education, communication, self-esteem, socialization, and/or daily living activities throughout life.

Mauk and Mauk (1992, p. 174) note that the federal definition's exclusionary clause has resulted in "minimal general interest in investigations into the possibility that a group of [deaf LD] children ... exists." Granting this historical point, the definitional crisis that began in 1975 is insufficient to explain the paucity of research on LD in the deaf population. Other vexing factors have surely posed major impediments. These include (a) the complicated interaction of LD and deafness in mutually determining English language learning and general academic achievement in the deaf population, (b) the ubiquitous and poorly understood role of cultural, cognitive, and linguistic diversity in determining normative learning patterns in the deaf population, and (c) the long-standing ill-preparedness of professionals in deaf education to deal with LD.

We address these issues further. Nevertheless, notwithstanding the current federal definition, the professional community has affirmed the co-occurrence of deafness with LD.

Attention Deficit Disorders

The definition of ADD has undergone a series of revisions (Shaywitz et al., 1994) since the term was first introduced in the Diagnostic and Statistical Manual of Mental Disorders (3rd ed.)—the DSM-III (American Psychiatric Association, 1980). The DSM-III regarded three constructs as cardinal symptoms of ADD—inattentiveness, impulsivity, and hyperactivity—requiring that attentional difficulties be present for an ADD diagnosis. Specific diagnostic criteria classified individuals into two subtypes, namely, ADD with or without hyperactivity. Curiously, the subsequent Diagnostic and Statistical Manual of Mental Disorders (3rd ed., revised)—the DSM-III-R (American Psychiatric Association, 1987) took a step backward toward classificatory confusion by replacing the cardinal symptoms with a single checklist of 14 items, most of which did not relate to attention difficulties. This scheme resulted in what Shaywitz et al. (1994) called the ADD *paradox*, namely, the possibility that a child could be diagnosed as ADD yet exhibit few psychological or behavioral symptoms of inattention.

Using the DSM-III-R (1987) to apply a monothetic ADD label to research participants who actually have heterogeneous symptoms has compromised the comparability of research and impeded progress toward a useful nosology[4] of ADD symptomatology (Shaywitz et al., 1994). This practice has presumably also compromised the management of children with distinct types of ADD. Fortunately, the Diagnostic and Statistical Manual of Mental Disorders (4th ed.)—the DSM-IV (American Psychiatric Association, 1994) reinstates the distinction between inattention and hyperactivity–impulsivity, allowing classification of individuals into clinical subgroups known to be factorially distinct (Lahey et al., 1988).

The DSM-IV (1994) characterization of ADD is definitional but not definitive. It represents a set of hypotheses that must be empirically verified (Shaywitz et al., 1994) about the discrepancies in behavior and cognition that distinguish ADD from non-ADD populations and that classify individuals into ADD subtypes. Future research on ADD classification in the deaf population should heed the trend set by the DSM-IV toward defining diagnostic criteria that produce cognitively and behaviorally homogeneous subtyping of ADD individuals. Nevertheless, as will become clear, several items on the DSM-IV are culturally problematic for use with a deaf population.

ETIOLOGY AND NEUROBIOLOGY
OF LD AND ADD

LD and ADD are rooted in neurological pathology occurring during prenatal and possibly post-natal development due to genetic and environmental influences (Chase, 1996; Pennington, 1991). Prenatal neural

---

[4]A useful nosology is a classification system that has predictive power because it is based on fundamental principles governing the objects that it classifies. For example, the periodic table of elements is a useful nosology because it is based on the atomic properties of elements that govern their chemical behavior and it can be used therefore to predict which elements will behave chemically in similar ways. It would be possible, for example, to classify the elements according to their colors or smells but this would result in groupings that had no predictive value regarding the chemical behavior of members of the same group. Similarly, a useful nosology of ADD or LD is one that classifies the cognitive and behavioral characteristics of LD subtypes (syndromes) into groupings that have common etiologies and neural foundations.

development proceeds through sequenced stages of cell division, migration, and structural differentiation. Under the regulation of genetic, biochemical, and electrophysiological events, the primitive neural tube burgeons and self-organizes. By birth, it has transmogrified into an elaborate system of highly interconnected and anatomically localized neural processing modules.

The most evolutionarily advanced of these modules provide the child with specialized neural processors that continue to self-organize structurally in response to direct experience during the acquisition of adult cognitive, language, and social behavior. Genetic or environmental factors, including experiential deprivation, can affect the normal course of development of brain systems at various stages in this process. Generally, the earlier damage occurs during development, the more profound is its impact on the adult brain. Damage at the cell migration stage, for example, will propagate into far-flung regions as the full structure of the brain unfolds, establishing abnormally placed concentrations of cells (ectopias) and leaving gaps at the locations originally targeted for those cells under normal development (dysplasias). Ectopias and dysplasias are the anatomical signature of the neural misorganization that leads to developmental dyslexia and presumably other LD (Galaburda, Rosen, & Sherman, 1989).

Prenatal developmental misorganization can interact with abnormal experience or environmental trauma after birth to set up a recursive cascade of brain-environment interactions that leads to abnormal cognitive system development. Biologically active connections among remote brain regions are a necessity for their mutual structural development and survival (Friedlander, Martin, & Wassenhove-McCarthy, 1991), and early experience during critical periods fine-tunes the neural architecture of perceptual and cognitive systems (Kandel, 1985). During normal development, synaptic connections among cells in myriad neural subsystems proliferate to provide early cognitive plasticity and are carefully pruned back by specific types of environmental experience. This structural shaping, in turn, feeds back to regulate the brain's neurotransmitter environments and physiological interactions among subsystems. Anything interfering with this cyclical brain development process, especially at early stages, can result in widespread structural and metabolic anomalies that are ultimately manifested as learning and attention disorders.

This account makes it clear that LD and ADD can result from many different kinds of developmental misorganization and environmental insults. Therefore, LD and ADD constitute heterogeneous classes of disorders both at the behavioral and the neural system level, making the tasks of defining specific syndromes and elucidating their neural bases a daunting affair for any population. Considering that deafness and its developmental consequences, even in the absence of any genetically or environmentally induced learning or attention disorder, can lead to highly adaptive patterns of neural reorganization of cognitive, language, and attentional systems (Neville, 1988; Parasnis & Samar, 1985), understanding the neural foundations of LD and ADD in the deaf population is a significantly more complex challenge than it is for the hearing population.

Nevertheless, the complexity is reduced somewhat because the different neural systems responsible for cognitive, language, and social behavior have different evolutionary histories and cerebral localizations and therefore different susceptibilities to early damage. Accordingly, executive function disorders due to frontal lobe damage, and phonological processing disorders due to localized left hemisphere damage, produce the most common developmental disorders, ADD and dyslexia, respectively (Pennington, 1991), probably even in the deaf population.

Learning Disabilities

The neurobiology of dyslexia has been extensively studied because of its high prevalence and a general societal concern with disorders of language and literacy. Dyslexia has polygenic and major gene etiologies, a heritability rate of approximately 50%, and multiple environmental etiologies including sociolinguistic and socioeconomic factors (Pennington, 1991). Autopsy data (Galaburda et al., 1989), magnetic resonance imaging studies (Larsen, Hoien, Lundberg, & Odegaard, 1990; Semrud-Clikeman & Hynd, 1994; Shaywitz et al., 1995), and behavioral genetic studies (Olsen, Wise, Conners, Rack, & Fulker, 1989) confirm that dyslexia is primarily a phonological processing disorder involving developmental damage to the perisylvian cortex.

The phonological deficit in dyslexia in the hearing population appears to be a common feature of all forms of developmental dyslexia, regardless of any specific etiology (Olsen, 1985; Olsen et al., 1989). This suggests by extension that phonological deficits might be the primary underlying cause of developmental dyslexia in the deaf population as well, regardless of its specific etiology, including possibly auditory language deprivation.

Disruption of visual system transmission mechanisms is also associated with dyslexia in some hearing individuals (Livingstone, Rosen, Drislane, & Galaburda, 1991). However, the phonological coding and visual system anomalies in hearing dyslexics appear to occur jointly and may stem from a more fundamental temporal processing disorder (Eden et al., 1997). If so, dyslexia in the deaf population might be associatedwithboth phonological coding and visual system anomalies. Furthermore, given the high incidence of visual system disorders in the deaf population (Parasnis, 1983a), it is possible on separate grounds that visual pathway pathology may play an etiological role in dyslexia in deaf individuals.

Spatial cognition disorders are rare in the general population, estimated at about 0.1 to 1% (Pennington, 1991). Unlike dyslexia, their heritability and neurobiology are poorly understood. Developmental damage to the right hemisphere is believed to cause spatial cognition disorders (Semrud-Clikeman & Hynd, 1990), although direct localization evidence is lacking. They are manifested on visual perceptual and visual constructive tasks including the Wechsler Intelligence Scale for Children-Revised, the WISC-R (Wechsler, 1974), the mainstay of nonverbal performance evaluation for hearing and deaf children (Levine, 1974). Spatial cognition disorders cause deficits in mathematical reasoning and perceptual aspects of sign language processing (Ratner, 1988; Rourke, 1989; Strang & Rourke, 1985). However, developmental mathematical reasoning and calculation disorders may comprise two subtypes, associated with posterior left and right hemisphere damage respectively and presenting two different neuropsychological profiles (Rourke & Conway, 1997).

Social cognition disorders (autism spectrum disorder) appear to have both genetic and environmental etiologies. Evidence supports an underlying deficit in intersubjectivity; autistic children apparently do not realize that other people have mental states. An executive function deficit component also occurs, although the causal relationships between the intersubjectivity and executive function deficits are murky. Limbic system, orbital frontal lobe structures, and right hemisphere mechanisms have been implicated (Pennington, 1991).

Memory disorders have not been attributed to a genetic etiology. Acquired memory disorders are caused by several factors, including closed head injury, seizure disorders, tumors, anemia, medication, encephalitis, and perinatal anoxia. Damage to temporal lobe structures, especially the hippocampal memory system has been implicated (DeLong, 1992). Acquired memory disorder is associated with "misplacing things, becoming lost, especially in new situations, word-finding problems, difficulty in learning new information in school or forgetting such information overnight, and failure to remember everyday information, such as what happened during the day" (Pennington, 1991, p. 169). Because encephalitis and anoxia are common etiologies of deafness, some individuals in the deaf population might be especially susceptible to acquired memory disorders.

Attention Deficit Disorders

ADD is highly heritable (Gillis, Gilger, Pennington, & DeFries, 1992) and likely to be etiologically independent of LD (Faraone et al., 1993). Evidence for environmental etiologies is weak, but extreme prematurity, fetal alcohol syndrome, lead toxicity, and head injury are implicated (Kelly & Aylward, 1992; Pennington, 1991; Zametkin & Rapoport, 1987).

ADD has both neuroanatomical and biochemical components and is linked to dysfunction of frontal lobes and related subcortical systems (Barkley, Grodzinsky, & DuPaul, 1992; Shue & Douglas, 1992; Swanson, Potkin, Bonforte, Fiore, Cantwell, & Crinella, 1991). Imbalances in related dopamine and noradrenaline neurotransmitter systems have been implicated (Hechtman, 1994; Hynd et al., 1993).

Several processes underlie ADD, including underarousal (Klorman, 1991), sustained and selective attention disorders (Klorman, 1995; Satterfield, Schell, Nicholas, Satterfield, & Freese, 1990), and disorders of inhibitory processes (Ross, Hommer, Breiger, Varley, & Radant, 1994; Westby & Cutler, 1994). These processes are aspects of overarching self-regulatory mechanisms, or executive functions, associated with frontal lobe function. On this view, ADD is a "generalized self-regulatory deficit that affects the organization of information processing, the mobilization of attention throughout information processing, and the inhibition of inappropriate responding" (Pennington, 1991, p. 93). Thus, ADD is basically a metacognitive disorder, producing difficulty in organizing, planning, monitoring, evaluating, and regulating behavior. These executive functions are engaged whenever a person encounters an academic task that is novel and requires critical thinking, judgment, planning, and self-monitoring (Welsh, 1994).

INCIDENCE OF LD AND ADD
IN THE DEAF POPULATION

Learning Disabilities

The primary exogenous etiologies of deafness are also etiologies of LD, including maternal rubella, Rh incompatibility, meningitis, anoxia, complications of prematurity, and cytomegalovirus infection (Mauk & Mauk, 1992). It is therefore common sense to acknowledge that LD and ADD are also likely to be common disabilities within the deaf population. Furthermore, this commonality of etiologies suggests that the incidence of LD might be higher in the deaf population than in the hearing population (Moores, 1996).

The Annual Survey of Deaf and Hard-of-Hearing Children and Youth (Schildroth & Hotto, 1996) lists LD as the highest single category of additional disabilities and the survey noted for the first time an increase in the overall number of children with additional disabilities due to the inclusion of ADD as a new category. Craig and Craig (1987) and Powers et al. (1987) reported large-sample incidences of LD deaf children in the U.S. of 5% to 7% and 6.7%, respectively, although only a 2.5% LD incidence was found in a much smaller Canadian sample of 2,232 children from nine residential schools (Bunch & Melnyk, 1989). The most recent annual survey figures (Gallaudet Research Institute, 1997) based on 44,399 children broken out by ethnic background classification indicate incidences of 8.4% (White), 9.7% (Black/African American), 11% (Hispanic), 10.4% (American Indian), 8.9% (Asian/Pacific), 9.8% (Other), 7.9% (Multiethnic), and 9.1% (Total).

Accurate estimates of the LD incidence in the deaf population have been hampered by definitional problems, inadequate assessment techniques, and poor study design (Bunch & Melnyk, 1989). More accurate estimates must await the development of a valid LD classification system and norm-based evaluation protocols for the deaf population.

Attention Deficit Disorders

Several studies report a high incidence of impulsivity (a cardinal characteristic of ADD) in the deaf population (Altshuler, Deming, Vollenweider, Rainer, & Tendler, 1976; Chess & Fernandez, 1980; Freeman, 1979; Meadow & Trybus, 1979; O'Brien, 1987), although deaf children of deaf parents are less impulsive than deaf children of hearing parents (Harris, 1978). These results could reflect a higher incidence of ADD in the deaf than in the hearing population, partly determined by nonhereditary factors. On the other hand, psychological factors unrelated to ADD could also account for a higher incidence of impulsivity.

Kelly, Kelly, Jones, Moulton, Verhulst, & Bell (1993) provided limited support for the speculation of a high ADD incidence in deaf children due to nonhereditary factors. Teachers and supervisors rated 238 deaf students at the Illinois School for the Deaf on the Conners Parent Rating Scale (Conners, 1990) and the ADD-H Comprehensive Teacher Rating Scale (Ullman, Sleator, & Sprague, 1984). The *at risk* rate for children with acquired deafness was 38.7%, reliably higher than hearing norms, suggesting that exogenous etiologies of deafness may lead to additional neurological problems that underlie ADD. Children with hereditary deafness had an *at risk* rate of 14.1% for ADD. Although apparently higher than the 3 to 5% general population incidence (Shelton & Barkley, 1994), this incidence was not statistically significant.

Given a 62% incidence of hereditary deafness in the U.S. (Marazita, Ploughman, Rawlings, Remington, Arnos, & Nance, 1993), the Kelly et al. (1993) figures imply that the overall *at risk* ADD incidence among deaf people is 22.7% (14.1 × .65 + 38.7 × .35). This figure must be interpreted cautiously due to the potential sampling bias toward residential school populations, the lack of parent ratings, and the lack of objective measures of ADD for diagnostic cross-validation. Note that parent ratings would likely raise the incidence estimates by several times (Achenbach & Edelbrock, 1981).

Recent large-sample figures from the Annual Survey of Deaf and Hard-of-Hearing Children and Youth (Gallaudet Research Institute, 1997) indicate that only 3.4% of the residential school population has been identified as ADD, with an ethnic category breakdown of 4% (White), 3.1% (Black/African American), 1.7% (Hispanic), 3.2% (American Indian), 1.8% (Asian/Pacific), 3.6% (Other), and 5.9% (Multiethnic). However, these figures are probably underestimates because they only represent confirmed cases; most children within the schools have not been carefully evaluated for ADD. Currently, methodological uncertainties and a paucity of studies make it unclear whether a higher ADD incidence occurs in the deaf population.

EVALUATING LD AND ADD IN THE DEAF POPULATION

Current LD Evaluation Practices

Deaf students with LD are most often identified by teacher observation and referral (Elliot, Powers, & Funderburg, 1988; Rush & Baechle, 1992). LD evaluation programs usually depend on a multifaceted approach to identifying individuals with specific cognitive and academic discrepancies in potential/achievement or with other intrinsic processing difficulties. However, operationalizing constructs such as potential/achievement discrepancy is problematic and, in practice, no standard procedures exist to evaluate hearing and deaf individuals. This results in considerable idiosyncratic variation in LD assessment from setting to setting and state to state (Coutinho, 1995).

Morgan and Vernon (1994) recommended obtaining eight categories of evaluation data for deaf children after a referral for LD assessment. These are (a) a thorough medical, developmental, and etiological case history, (b) an educational history, (c) two measures of nonverbal intellectual functioning, (d) a normed measure of educational achievement, (e) a neuropsychological screening, (f) an assessment of adaptive behavior functioning and/or classroom behavior, (g) a current audiological evaluation and vision screening, and (h) information on communication and language skills. In addition, they offered guidelines for specialized procedures and testing modifications, and they evaluated several tests of intelligence, adaptive behaviors, educational achievement, and neuropsychological function. Kelly et al. (1993b) also listed several formal measures for psychoeducational assessment of deaf children's intelligence, processing skills, and behavioral–emotional problems, although no critical commentary on the validity of these measures was given.

Few studies address the characteristics of deaf individuals with LD. Elliot, Powers, & Funderburg (1988) provided teacher survey-based rank orderings of common behavioral and academic characteristics of LD deaf children that differentiate them from other deaf children. From most to least frequent these are memory problems, visual perception problems, attention problems, inconsistent performance, poor organizational skills, achievement/potential discrepancy, atypical language for hearing-impaired individuals, behavior problems, unusual learning styles, and a nondescript "other" category. These categories offer provocative descriptors but provide few clues to the underlying deficits, comorbidity rates, and syndrome distinctiveness of the various characteristics. Notably, teachers ranked achievement/potential discrepancy relatively low on the list, reflecting the general suspicion that accurate assessment of this construct is problematic for deaf children (Powers, Elliot, Fairbank, & Monaghan, 1988).

Powers et al. (1988) compared the results of school professionals' identifications of seven LD deaf students with two instruments that purport to identify LD deaf students. They reported that LD was associated with atypically low language functioning ratings, behavioral/social–emotional problems, difficulty in attending, poor organizational skills, and difficulty in retaining information.

Hill, Luetke-Stahlman, and Kapel (1985) showed that teachers' informal evaluations of deaf children effectively classify them into LD and non-LD groups. Fourth- and fifth-grade children identified as having LD by teachers at a residential school for the deaf were strongly discriminated from non-LD children by their joint performance on spelling and arithmetic computation but not by measures of connotative semantics, time-on-task, oral reading, or sentence and word meaning. Hill et al. suggested that the strong dependence of spelling and arithmetic computation on the visual modality accounts for their predictive power. Berent, Samar, and Parasnis (1997) confirmed that teachers of English to deaf college students identify spelling difficulties as the primary distinguishing characteristic of deaf students with English language learning disabilities.

Plapinger and Sikora (1990) advocated a multidisciplinary team approach to evaluating and remediating LD in deaf children, involving experts in pediatrics, physical therapy, occupational therapy, psychology, special education, and speech and language. They argued that different professionals' perspectives on the same symptoms yield a crucial measure of interevaluation reliability. They listed 29 published evaluation tools and indicated the 15 they consider most important to use with deaf children. Their approach synthesizes formal testing and curriculum-based evaluation. However, the validities of their evaluation tools require further study.

Sikora and Plapinger (1994) evaluated a series of standardized diagnostic measures for identifying LD in deaf students, including audiological, speech and language, psychological, psychoeducational, and occupational therapy measures. Their results show that standardized measures used to evaluate LD in hearing children give specific information about deaf children necessary for educational programming beyond the information given by teachers' impressions.

According to Rush and Baechle (1992), evaluators responsible for psycho-educational assessment at Gallaudet University observed that deaf and hearing students with LD share many characteristics. These include difficulties in (a) one academic area despite superior performance in other classes, (b) expressive or receptive language including reading, writing, or signing, (c) social perception and competence, (d) problem solving, (e) gross and fine motor coordination, (f) test taking, (g) remembering specific tasks and rules, (h) organization and time management, (i) following directions or instructions, (j) spelling or handwriting, (k) memory, (l) perceptual discrimination, (m) attention and concentration, and (n) distinguishing essential from nonessential information.

Some items on this list segregate naturally into crude taxonomic categories of executive function (ADD) and specific processing disorders (LD). However, lists of largely undifferentiated characteristics are only starting places for future research to develop a useful nosology of LD and ADD in the deaf population. Once such a nosology is available, the impression that affected deaf and hearing individuals have similar characteristics may turn out to be valid only at specific levels of taxonomic description. The interactive developmental effects of LD, ADD, and deafness may induce some syndromes and comorbidity patterns that are unique to the deaf population.

Current ADD Evaluation Practices

ADD evaluation for hearing and deaf populations typically involves subjectively classifying an individual student or client based on several lines of converging evidence. These include (a) teacher or physician referral, (b) teacher, parent, or self-rating scales for ADD (Brown, 1996; Conners, 1990), (c) intake interviews to obtain developmental and academic background information, (d) clinical evaluation most likely using the DSM-IV (1994) criteria, (e) continuous performance tests (Conners, 1992; Leark, Dupuy, Greenberg, Corman, & Kindschi, 1996), and (f) neuropsychological–psychoeducational tests to assess executive functions, to rule out other causes, and to detect comorbidities.

Protocols for attention and activity evaluation should be carefully examined for potential cultural and language biases before use with a deaf population. A few studies offer useful guidelines. Morgan and Vernon (1994) evaluated four scales for identifying ADD in the deaf population, including the Conners Rating Scales (Conners, 1990), the School Behavior Checklist (Miller, 1974), the Behavior Problem Checklist (Quay & Peterson, 1967), and the Child Behavior Profile (Achenbach, 1978). Kelly et al. (1993b) listed several rating scales and other instruments that may be useful for deaf populations. They also described a school-wide system for addressing the needs of deaf children with ADD through interviews and observations, psychoeducational evaluation, medical evaluation, specific rating-scale and psychometric measures of attention, and a comprehensive management program encompassing academic, counseling, and medical interventions in home, residential, and classroom settings.

Problems for Progress in Evaluating LD and ADD in the Deaf Population

The development of better procedures to identify LD deaf individuals, including a standardized test battery and collaboration with LD specialists, has often been identified as an essential priority (Bunch & Melnyk, 1989; Mauk & Mauk, 1992; Roth, 1991; Rush & Baechle, 1992). Clearly, developing procedures to identify ADD in deaf individuals is also essential, given its impact on learning and social communication (Kelly et al., 1993b). Several factors complicate this effort.

Evaluation Philosophy.   The literature on LD and ADD evaluation has undergone repeated pendular shifts since the 1960s between emphasis on discrete point assessment procedures on the one hand and dynamic assessment on the other. Discrete point assessment, in which diagnostic labels and processing deficit descriptions (e.g., ADHD, LD, visual learner, sequential processing deficit) are applied to children based on one-time clinical observation and testing, were popular in the 1960s but waned in the 1970s and 1980s following growing concerns over the validity of endless batteries of standardized tests. In its place, there arose a trend toward context-based and curriculum-based classroom assessment (Wallach & Butler, 1994).

Discrete point testing experienced a resurgence in the 1990s powered in part by new neuropsychological testing technology (Conners, 1992; Korkman & Pesonen, 1994). In counterpoint to this resurgence, several authors eschewed the "one size fits all system" (Wallis, 1994) of LD and ADD evaluation and reasserted the need to develop "authentic assessment" approaches "situated in the classroom, designed by the teacher, and used to evaluate student performance within the classroom curriculum context" (Garcia & Pearson, 1994, p. 357). Thus, several authentic assessment methods have been pursued, including ethnographic interviews, observational inventories, and portfolio assessment (Paratore, 1995; Wallach & Butler, 1994).

Generally, this ongoing philosophical debate has not been explicitly played out in the literature on LD and ADD evaluation in the deaf population, although several authors have advocated comprehensive teacher-assisted and team-based evaluation. It is clear, however, that the debate has produced a conceptual foundation and technically advanced assessment methodologies on both sides that should be eclectically sampled in future work to develop appropriate evaluation protocols for the deaf population. Striking a balance between these two assessment traditions is complicated. Discrete point testing is subject to violations of construct validity due to variability among deaf individuals in language and cultural factors. Authentic assessment is subject to violations of observational validity due to potential cultural biases, imperfect communication skills, and varying educational attitudes on the part of teachers and other observers.

Cultural and racial bias in educational assessment is a reality that has a deleterious impact on educational achievement (Cummins, 1984; Delgado, 1984; Parasnis, 1997; Skutnabb-Kangas & Cummins, 1988). These biases apparently extend to LD assessment of deaf individuals. Delgado (1981) found a 23% incidence of LD classification in deaf children from non-English speaking homes compared to 5% for all deaf children, and Lerman (1976) found that a disproportionate number of Hispanic deaf students were placed in the low achieving or LD groups in educational programs for the deaf. The proportion of deaf children who are from minority groups increased from 24% to 40% between 1974 and 1994 (Schildroth & Hotto, 1996) and is now 43.5% (Gallaudet Research Institute, 1997). These findings reveal the urgent need to develop culturally fair LD evaluation protocols and educational programs that respect the cultural and linguistic diversity of minority students.

Sufficiently Restrictive Definitions. Definitions are needed that restrict the classification of individuals to neurobehaviorally and psychoeducationally homogeneous groups—that is, to groups with similar etiologies, learning difficulties, or neural bases of LD or ADD (Shaywitz et al., 1994). Achieving such restrictive definitions is particularly difficult with respect to deaf individuals.

Achievement/potential discrepancies are frequently used indicators of LD. However, difficulty in obtaining an accurate assessment of intelligence for deaf individuals makes the quantitative assessment of achievement/potential discrepancy a "nebulous criterion" for identifying LD deaf children (Powers et al., 1988). Typically, LD evaluation of deaf children relies on nonverbal measures of IQ under the assumptions that they are likely to avoid language achievement confounds and to be culturally unbiased. For example, the Performance Scale of the WISC-R (Wechsler, 1974) is the traditional nonverbal intelligence test used with deaf children (Levine, 1974) and several psychometric studies have supported its predictive validity for their academic achievement (Hirshoren, Hurley, & Hunt, 1997; Hirshoren, Hurley, & Kavale, 1979; Hirshoren, Kavale, Hurley, & Hunt, 1977; Paal, Skinner, & Reddig, 1988). However, cross-cultural factor analytic work (Parmar, 1989) showed that, even when a nonverbal test meets standard specified conditions for "cultural fairness," it may contain intrinsic biases that prevent accurate estimation of a child's intellectual abilities. Parmar advised using multiple measures, including indigenously developed tests, teacher evaluation, and informal assessment procedures rather than abstract figural tests and tests not standardized on relevant populations.

A deep problem is separating canonical forms of LD from potentially novel forms specific to a deaf population or from non-LD conditions that mimic LD. For example, different factors can produce atypical English language development in deaf individuals that may precipitate sustained learning difficulties. This complicates the definition of language learning disabilities (LLD). Such factors include (a) *sociolinguistic factors*, including restrictions on or alterations of normal social language interaction with parents, relatives, teachers, and peers (Cummins, 1984; Lederberg, 1993), (b) *experiential factors*, including variable access to language data in the environment due to restricted hearing and possibly additional sensory or motor problems (Marschark, 1993a, 1993b), (c) *neurological factors*, including prenatal and perinatal neurological damage or cellular and system development errors due to genetics, toxicity, and infectious disease, and other factors (Chase, 1996).

It is important to recognize the etiological distinctions among these factors when constructing LD definitions for deaf people. The LD literature in the general population typically emphasizes neurological factors in definitions of LD, excluding sociolinguistic and experiential factors. However, sociolinguistic and experiential factors peculiar to the deaf population can exert a sustained and atypical influence on neural development and on the perception of language forms during early critical periods. These factors may alter the normal developmental process of pruning neural connections and of fixing the parameters of the adult language in a way that may depend on their severity and interaction with neurological factors (Berent & Samar, 1990; Laughton, 1989; Parasnis & Samar, 1982). Some deaf children may therefore develop atypical language processing and usage patterns that resist remediation, constituting essentially novel LD syndromes.

Because the factors listed here tend to interact in perplexing ways during language acquisition (Laughton, 1989), it is tempting to lump learning difficulties in the deaf population due to atypical language development from all sources into a general category of language learning disabilities. Yet, the question is empirical whether this would be taxonomically sensible. Until further data on syndrome validity are available, sociolinguistic, experiential, and standard neurobiological factors should be thought of as dimensionally distinct but interactive factors when developing definitions of LD for the deaf population. Such distinctions at this early stage of study will promote the eventual development of a meaningful LD nosology and of effective methods of diagnostic evaluation and intervention.

Finally, LD definitions need to exclude explicitly as primary causes the myriad psychological, cognitive, and situational factors that can adversely affect learning behavior without an organic foundation of neural misorganization. This will help protect deaf children from being automatically labeled as LD without careful consideration of the role of other factors (Clark & Kendall, 1980).

Similar cautions can be made regarding the definition of ADD. ADD appears to be a heterogeneous disorder, with both behavioral and cognitive components that need not all occur together and that may break out into distinct neurobehavioral subtypes (Shaywitz et al., 1994). However, many medical, emotional, or psychological conditions produce educational or behavioral problems that can mimic the symptoms of ADD without possessing a genuine neurobiological substrate for ADD. Kelly et al. (1993a) specifically cautioned that language and communication disorders can be misdiagnosed as ADD in deaf children who have difficulty following directions or completing tasks and that the relatively higher prevalence of communication disorders in children who are deaf increases the likelihood of such misdiagnosis.

Kelly et al. (1993a) listed a number of conditions that purportedly produce ADD as a secondary condition, although their specific list should be regarded cautiously because strong evidence for such secondary ADD is lacking (Pennington, 1991). However, recent evidence does suggest that ADD can be produced as a symptomatic reaction to the experience of failure at reading without involving a neurobiological disorder of executive functions (Pennington, 1991). Given the difficulties that deaf children typically experience learning to read (Vernon & Andrews, 1990), it is an open but important question whether secondary ADD occurs within the deaf population, how it might be expressed in specific mechanisms at the neural level, how it might affect language development and academic achievement, and so on.

LD and ADD definitions for both hearing and deaf populations are currently not established facts. Rather they are hypotheses that should guide research heuristically toward their own refinement and taxonomic differentiation.

Communication, Cultural, and Developmental Factors.
Well-managed communication is central to achieving reliable and valid LD and ADD evaluation. Certain barriers to communication in common evaluation procedures—for example, the language of instructions—are tractable, if somewhat problematic. However, valid assessment is not merely a straightforward issue of translating scales and instructions into an accessible language format (Roth, 1991). Deaf individuals have an ethical right to be tested in their own language (Individuals with Disabilities Education Act of 1990), and ensuring a deaf individual's comprehension of the purposes and requirements of any evaluation requires that evaluation personnel be able to communicate proficiently with that person. Yet, both cultural factors and the variety of languages and language modalities used by the deaf population can complicate the communication process. Evaluation personnel should minimally have certification training in LD and ADD evaluation (Elliot et al., 1988), have expertise in deafness that includes cultural awareness, have flexible communication competencies consistent with the multilingual competencies of the deaf population, and take explicit measures to ensure a deaf individual's understanding and cooperation (Morgan & Vernon, 1994).

Any attempt to develop a valid LD and ADD evaluation regimen for the deaf population must confront intricately related cognitive, cultural, and developmental factors that determine behavior and test performance, influence the emergence of cognitive styles and competencies, and regulate both the cognitive and the behavioral domains of attention. Besides guarding against culturally and ethnically biased evaluation decisions, testing protocols must be sensitive to confounds that lurk beneath the surface of cognitive performance measures. For example, Marschark

(1996) demonstrated that the highly replicable depression of working memory measures, such as digit span, that deaf children and adults tend to show is largely an artifact of the articulatory loop duration for linguistic rehearsal in sign and does not reflect a genuine cognitive capacity deficit. Accordingly, LD memory evaluation protocols should correct for this effect by using validated norms, and evaluation protocol developers should remain vigilant of similar confounds.

Evaluating ADD in the deaf population in particular requires close attention to a few specific cultural and communication issues. The DSM-IV (1994) criteria implicitly presume culturally valid reference behaviors. However, the criteria entail both superficial and deep discrepancies in the cultural appropriateness of some of the items. Items like "Often does not seem to listen when spoken to directly" can be modified to avoid reference to speech and hearing while retaining the intent of communicative receptivity and attentional focus. However, items like "Is easily distracted by extraneous stimuli (other things going on)," if accepted uncritically, may belie basic differences of type and degree in normal social and communicative behavior for deaf and hearing individuals.

For example, deafness may lead to highly adaptive strategic behaviors and neural system reorganizations that may present as a disability when none exists. Deaf children adopt compensatory attentional strategies such as looking around the room to manage attention for communication purposes (Morgan & Vernon, 1994; Swisher, 1993). The requirement to use their peripheral vision to alert them to novel events in the environment also suggests that deaf individuals may distribute their visual attention more broadly over the visual field (Parasnis & Samar, 1982). The attentional system of some deaf individuals has been shown to undergo an adaptive behavioral and neural reorganization due either to auditory deprivation per se or to the acquisition of ASL (Neville, 1988; Parasnis & Samar, 1985; Parasnis, Samar, Bettger, & Sathe, 1996). Collectively, these considerations suggest that the normative behavior of deaf individuals on tests designed to measure attention, impulsivity, and frontal lobe function may be both quantitatively and qualitatively different from that of hearing people, raising the possibility of misdiagnosis. Therefore, LD and ADD evaluators must be aware of behaviors that are the norm for deaf individuals but appear atypical for hearing individuals (Morgan & Vernon, 1994; Roth, 1991). Potential validity violations should be considered automatically when conceptual definitions and evaluation procedures from the mainstream are adopted.

The Lack of Normative Data.   Most standardized instruments are normed on hearing populations; using them with deaf individuals is typically inappropriate (Roth, 1991). The few intelligence and achievement tests[5] available for the deaf population are sometimes useful for assessing LD and ADD but are generally inadequate due to the use of typically small samples of deaf participants within limited age ranges for their normative samples. Some universities, schools, and private practitioners have developed idiosyncratic protocols and limited normative data bases for their own use to evaluate LD in deaf individuals (Rush & Baechle, 1992). However, adequate validation studies are not available for most instruments in use.

Without appropriate norms for the deaf population, standard LD assessment procedures would classify approximately 75% of deaf children as LD (LaSasso, 1992). In addition, the possibility exists that elevated scores on continuous performance tests of executive functions for ADD evaluation might reflect normal cultural or developmental influences on some deaf individuals rather than the presence of ADD (Brice & Kerman, 1995). In practice, many deaf individuals are misdiagnosed by psychologists and neuropsychologists as having LD (Morgan & Vernon, 1994). This misdiagnosis results from inappropriate use of normative data from the general population and from the indiscriminate use of inappropriate test instruments such as the Wechsler verbal scales (but see Rush, Blennerhassett, Epstein, & Alexander, 1991, for evidence supporting the use of the WAIS-R verbal scales with deaf students). To prevent misdiagnosis, large-scale, age-referenced norms for deaf children and adults must be developed on any diagnostic LD and ADD measures, including language, IQ, and academic achievement measures (Morgan & Vernon, 1994).

CURRENT AND FUTURE RESEARCH DIRECTIONS

Phonological Coding/Awareness Deficits in Dyslexia in the Deaf Population

Some deaf children and adults, even those with profound deafness, are capable of coding written words phonologically to various degrees, and this ability seems to be correlated positively with their development of reading skills (Leybaert, 1993; Parasnis, 1996b). A complex set of factors associated with deafness may influence the level of development of a phonological code in the deaf population (Leybaert, 1993). However, we

[5]These tests include the Kaufman Assessment Battery for Children (Kaufman & Kaufman, 1983), the Stanford Achievement Test™, Special Edition for Hearing-Impaired Students (Madden, Gardner, Rudman, Karlsen, & Merwin, 1972), the Test of Early Reading Ability—Deaf or Hard of Hearing (Reid, Hresko, Hammill, & Wiltshire, 1991), and an adaptation of the WISC-R (Ray, 1979). Some norms for deaf children are also available for the Behavior Problem Checklist, useful for ADD screening (Goulder & Trybus, 1971).

propose that the ordinary limitations of speech-based language experience stemming from deafness per se are not sufficient to explain all of the cases of deaf individuals who have poor phonological coding skills and may therefore have relatively poor reading skills. The deaf population must be at least as vulnerable as the hearing population to inheriting a dyslexia genotype and perhaps more vulnerable to environmentally induced dyslexia. Extrapolating from standard incidence figures (Benton & Pearl, 1978), a minimum of 5 to 10% of the deaf population should be dyslexic due to either genetic or environmental causes unrelated to deafness and should therefore be predisposed to having poor phonological awareness and phonological coding skills underlying their reading difficulties.

Developmental dyslexia in the hearing population is primarily a deficit in phonological coding with genetic and environmental etiologies (Galaburda et al., 1989; Pennington, 1991; Semrud-Clikeman & Hynd, 1994; Shaywitz et al., 1995). Furthermore, a deficit in phonological awareness is a heritable precursor to heritable deficits in phonological coding (Olsen et al., 1989). Phonological awareness has been shown repeatedly to be a necessary condition for the development of good reading skills in hearing children (Birnbaum & Samar, 1997; Stanovitch, 1986). Similarly, phonological awareness may be a necessary condition for the development of good reading skills in deaf children, and the heritability of phonological awareness deficits might account for some of the significant individual differences that deaf children display in developing such skills despite equivalent hearing losses, language exposure, and school experiences. These findings suggest that future work should focus on establishing the behavioral genetics of dyslexia and phonological coding/awareness deficits in the deaf population. The substantial heritability of these conditions in the hearing population (approximately 50%) suggests that family history will help to predict which deaf children are at risk for reading problems.

A related issue is whether phonological awareness can be trained in deaf children as it can be in hearing children and whether such training will ameliorate reading problems. For example, early intervention to train phonological awareness and other precursors of reading in preliterate hearing children produces lasting improvements in reading decoding and comprehension skills (Birnbaum & Samar, 1997; Torgesen, Morgan, & Davis, 1992). Furthermore, Matthew effects govern the benefits of such early intervention. Matthew effects refer to a positive feedback cycle that operates during literacy acquisition. Positive experiences and new knowledge about the reading process gained during reading lead in turn to further success in reading. Like the so-called "miracle of compound interest," Matthew effects compound modest early gains in reading ability into disproportionately larger gains over time during early childhood in a rich-get-richer fashion (Birnbaum & Samar, 1997; Stanovich, 1986). If deaf children at risk for reading disabilities can be identified early, it will be possible to engage them in early intervention programs designed to capitalize on phonological awareness training and Matthew effects in their acquisition of literacy. Therefore, future research should focus directly on methods of identifying preliterate deaf children at risk for phonological coding/awareness deficits. This may include the use of familial history information as well as direct measures of phonological awareness. Gerber (1993) noted that current practices for evaluating reading disability in the general population are deficient because the psychometric tests used fail to assess phonological awareness, including the ubiquitous Verbal Scale of the WISC-R (Wechsler, 1974). Future work on evaluating reading disabilities in the deaf population should focus on finding an objective psychometric measure of this cognitive variable and developing an appropriate set of norms.

ADD as a Secondary Syndrome to Reading Difficulties

Behavioral genetic studies indicate that ADD and dyslexia are genetically independent syndromes. Pennington (1991) proposed that their substantial comorbidity might be due to a form of ADD that arises as a secondary syndrome to the school failure that some dyslexic children experience, possibly interacting with factors such as family environment. Such children become inattentive, impulsive, and distractible as a symptomatic reaction without an underlying executive system dysfunction. Behavioral genetic studies (Gilger, Pennington, & DeFries, 1991) and neuropsychological studies (Javorsky, 1996; Pennington, Groisser, & Welsh, 1993) support the claim that ADD can be produced as a secondary syndrome (i.e., an ADD phenocopy) in some children with reading problems.

The average reading achievement of the adult deaf population is approximately at the fourth-grade level (Center for Assessment and Demographic Studies, 1992). The finding that ADD might be induced by the experience of failure at reading suggests, therefore, that some deaf individuals may be at high risk for developing secondary ADD. Because executive functions seem to be unaffected in secondary ADD despite the presence of typical ADD symptoms (Pennington et al., 1993), secondary ADD would add significantly to the heterogeneity of ADD subtypes in the deaf population.

This has implications for evaluation and remediation. Evaluation protocols for a deaf population must distinguish primary from secondary

ADD in order to achieve neurobehaviorally homogeneous ADD subclassifications and to design appropriate remediation efforts. In this respect, executive function tests can help to motivate the correct subclassification of individuals with ADD.

One clear prediction of the occurrence of secondary ADD within the deaf population is that the incidence of ADD should increase with age, unlike genetically caused ADD. Future research using appropriate behavioral genetic techniques (Gilger, 1995) coupled with standard neuropsychological evaluation should directly address the prevalence and identification of secondary ADD in the deaf population and its implications for evaluation and remediation.

Specific Markers for English Language Learning Disabilities

A desideratum of LLD research is the discovery of a pathognomic marker—that is, "a linguistic form or principle that can be shown to be characteristic of children with Specific Language Impairment" (Rice & Wexler, 1996, p. 1239) but not of unaffected children. A pathognomic marker would facilitate the investigation, identification, and remediation of LLD. Although such markers have been hard to come by due to the large variation that children normally display in their progress toward the acquisition of the adult grammar (Leonard, 1987), recent work suggests that such a marker might exist for hearing children (Rice & Wexler, 1996; Rice, Wexler, & Cleave, 1995).

The same motivation exists to seek a marker for LLD in the deaf population. This task is problematic because the reduced and atypical English language input due to many factors associated with deafness itself results in enormous variation in English language development, including individual variation in the rates of acquisition of grammatical forms (Bochner, 1982) and in the setting of the grammatical parameters that determine the distribution of lexical and grammatical forms in English (Berent & Samar, 1990). Over time, the cumulative effect of variable rates of acquisition reveals tremendous variation among deaf students of comparable age in very specific aspects of English language knowledge (Berent, 1996b).

To worsen matters, deafness and LLD individually produce very similar difficulties for learning the grammatical structures and other domains of English language knowledge. Virtually the same lists of English forms, structures, and usage patterns summarized as areas of language difficulty in the literature on LD (e.g., Gerber, 1993; Wiig & Semel, 1984) appear in the literature on the English language characteristics of deaf individuals (e.g., Berent, 1988, 1996a; Mogford, 1993; Paul & Quigley, 1994; Quigley & King, 1980). In both cases, these difficulties span the full spectrum of English language knowledge, including difficulties at the phonological, lexical, morphological, syntactic, semantic, and pragmatic levels.

Considering the complicated contribution of deafness itself to variation in English language knowledge, it is unlikely that a simple pathognomic marker can be found that only arises in deaf children who have LLD. It is more likely that deaf children who are affected by LLD will possess differential degrees of difficulty on individual grammatical forms or domains of language knowledge compared with unaffected deaf children. This suggests that a useful generalization of the construct of a pathognomic marker for use with the deaf population would be the notion of a pathognomic *profile*—a differential *pattern* of difficulty over a series of grammatical forms and domains of language knowledge that uniquely identifies a deaf individual as belonging to a specific LLD category. Recent research has bearing on this possibility.

Teacher Intuitions. The intuitions of experienced teachers can provide clues to a possible pathognomic profile for LLD in the deaf population. Berent et al. (1997) had 28 teachers of English to deaf college students rate the comparative difficulty of 30 English grammatical structures, usage patterns, and language knowledge domains for imagined typical deaf students versus LLD deaf students separately. For each item, teachers rated the frequency with which students would have usage or comprehension difficulty on a 5-point scale ranging from *always* to *never*. The results showed that teachers perceived typical and LD deaf students to have similar, but not identical, orders of difficulty for the 30 items.

Certain items stood out as potentially discriminating markers for LLD. These fell into four categories: (a) spelling, (b) lexical knowledge and usage, (c) discourse processes, and (d) syntactic processes involving movement. English teachers perceived spelling as distinguishing typical from LLD deaf students the most. Items pertaining to lexical knowledge and usage referred to word meaning, associations, concepts, storage, and retrieval; figurative language; and temporal, spatial, and causal relationships. Items pertaining to discourse processes alluded to semantic, syntactic, and pragmatic knowledge required for following directions and organizing sentences logically; distinguishing important from unimportant ideas; recognizing structures used as indirect requests and other illocutionary and perlocutionary speech acts; and establishing coreference among elements (e.g., pronouns) within and across sentences. Items pertaining to syntactic processes involving movement included structures in which moved constituents bind the deep structure positions that they vacate and establish scope relations required for interpretation. Such processes occur in questions, relative clauses, quantifier phrases, passives, and negative sentences.

These results suggest that LLD in deaf individuals might alter the typical pattern of competency orders, with many grammatical structures and domains of language knowledge remaining in place in the difficulty hierarchy created by deafness alone, whereas certain others are promoted to positions of greater difficulty. If future research confirms that deaf students with LLD show a distinct order of difficulty (or acquisition) for grammatical structures and domains of language knowledge, then that order would constitute a pathognomic profile. Such a profile would directly motivate the development of a psychometrically valid battery designed to identify deaf individuals with LLD.

Extended Language Development Stages. Wexler (1994) reported that very young children exhibit an "optional infinitive" stage during which they use nonfinite (infinitival) forms of verbs as well as finite forms in clauses where the adult grammar requires the use of the finite form. Apparently, children are capable of projecting the structural representation of grammatical tense in their underlying syntactic representation of a finite clause but may choose not to do so. Rice, Wexler, and Cleave (1995) and Rice and Wexler (1996) showed that preschool children with specific language impairment (SLI) display an extended optional infinitive stage, whereas optional infinitive usage in age-matched, non-SLI children hardly occurs. Their results indicate strong discrimination of SLI from non-SLI children based on the frequency with which children employ nonfinite verb forms in obligatorily finite contexts. The set of morphemes that mark tense in English (e.g., *-s*, *-ed*, *BE*, and *DO*) might therefore be a clinical marker for SLI.

This work on an extended optional infinitive stage provides the most convincing evidence to date for a pathognomic marker for LLD. For deaf children and adults, tense marking is a persistent area of difficulty and individual variation (Paul & Quigley, 1994). Dinner (1981) reported that tense errors were the best discriminator of LLD deaf children, and Berent et al. (1997) reported that sentences involving *DO* were rated as among the grammatical items expected to show the largest difference between deaf students with and without LLD. Given the findings of Rice et al. (1995, 1996), quantitative studies of the use of infinitival forms in the spontaneous and elicited productions of deaf children and adults with and without suspected LLD should be undertaken to determine if optional tense marking is a pathognomic marker for LLD in the deaf population.

Text Analysis. LLD children have difficulty with discourse structure including the production and comprehension of narrative forms and figurative language such as metaphor (Abrahamsen & Sprouse, 1995). Discourse structure studies of the language of LLD children might show patterns of "derailed discourse" that provide a marker for LLD (Wallach & Butler, 1995).

Such text analysis holds promise for evaluating LLD in the deaf population. Plapinger and Sikora (1990) described an 11-year-old deaf girl with LLD whose narrative stories lacked cohesion thematically and syntactically, being below expected levels for non-LLD deaf peers. Berent et al. (1997) confirmed that discourse-level language skills are rated among the most distinguishing characteristics of LLD deaf students. Text analysis studies are needed to verify these impressions.

Cross-Language Evaluation

Just as LD affects the acquisition and use of speech-based languages in hearing and deaf populations, LD might affect the acquisition and use of sign language. Hence, markers might exist for specific sign-language learning disabilities. Language processing difficulties might also exist that are common across a deaf individual's different languages (e.g., English and ASL). If so, cross-language evaluation procedures might help identify LLD individuals in the deaf population.

For example, in English certain noun and verb forms of words are distinguished by derivational morphological endings. In ASL, derivational–morphology movement mechanisms such as reduplication distinguish many noun and verb forms. LLD children and deaf children tend to have difficulty acquiring derivational morphological endings in English (Gerber, 1993). A deaf individual who simultaneously has difficulty with derivational endings in English and derivational movement in ASL would be a candidate for an LLD, whereas difficulty with derivational endings in English only might simply reflect the impact of deafness per se on English language skills.

Only one study has explicitly examined the possible use of sign language performance to differentially diagnose LLD. Dinner (1981) had teachers rate 64 deaf children for LD behavior patterns in their motor coordination, personal social skills, and English-based sign language performance (Signing Exact English II [SEE-II]). Children rated as having LD showed worse receptive SEE-II language performance than children rated as non-LD. The worse the LD behavioral rating, the worse were children's receptive SEE-II skills. The best discriminator of LD from non-LD children was a test of morphology related to the comprehension of verb tense markers.

Although intriguing, Dinner's (1981) results confound knowledge of English language structure with the use of sign language and therefore do not provide evidence that LLD occurs for natural sign languages such as ASL. The future demonstration of a genuine relationship between LLD and cross-language indices of a common underlying linguistic phenomenon could provide a method of differentially diagnosing some LLD individuals in the deaf population.

Disorders of Spatial Cognition

The prevalence of spatial cognition disorders in the deaf population is unknown but could be relatively high due to the broad neurological impact of environmental etiologies. Ratner (1985) speculated extensively on the pervasive damage to a deaf child's language and cognitive development, social acceptance, academic achievement, and self-image that can result from spatial cognition disorders. These disorders underlie disorders of mathematical reasoning (Strang & Rourke, 1985), suggesting serious consequences for the life success of affected deaf children in an increasingly technological world. Furthermore, visual perceptual deficits in deaf children are associated with impaired ability to comprehend the spatial components of sign language (Ratner, 1988), suggesting that spatial cognition disorders might result in specific sign-language learning disabilities. With the increasing use of ASL in educational settings, discovering ways to evaluate both English and ASL LLD is crucial to refining the classification of children into groups having learning strengths and weaknesses in distinct language domains.

The use of spatial cognition by a deaf child differs in important and adaptive ways from that of a hearing child (Parasnis, 1983b; Parasnis & Samar, 1982). Many deaf children may possess enhanced spatial cognition skills (Bellugi, O'Grady, Lillo-Martin, O'Grady, van Hoek, & Corina, 1990; Emmorey, Kosslyn, & Bellugi, 1993; Parasnis & Samar, 1982; Parasnis et al., 1996) and they are known to rely on their spatial skills to a greater extent than hearing children for some purposes. For example, deaf children are less efficient than same-age hearing children at using spontaneous rehearsal strategies in problem-solving tasks biased toward verbal or sequential processing (Bebko, 1984). However, they excel on tasks with significant spatial requirements, and they use their spatial processing skills to compensate for their spontaneous rehearsal inefficiency (Bebko, Lacasse, Turk, & Oyen, 1992).

These findings have important implications for academic performance and for LD evaluation in the deaf population. Deaf children with spatial cognition deficits can be expected to be at serious risk for more generalized learning problems than their hearing peers due to the potential unavailability of compensatory spatial cognition mechanisms. Furthermore, spatial cognition deficits in deaf children may project a different profile on neuropsychological tests than in hearing children, who presumably do not require spatial cognition skills in tasks where they can efficiently use spontaneous rehearsal strategies, suggesting that the use of hearing norms can result in serious misdiagnosis.

Spatial cognition disorders can be more devastating to the social, language, and cognitive development of deaf children than that of hearing children (Ratner, 1985) because the visual modality is the primary modality for learning and communication (Parasnis & Samar, 1982; Parasnis et al., 1996). Therefore, spatial cognition disorders deserve special attention in future research on the deaf population.

Objective Psychometric and Neuropsychological Measures of LD and ADD

There is little work on objective psychometric and neuropsychological tests of LD in the deaf population. A few studies have suggested that deaf and hearing children with LD may behave similarly on standard psychometric tests. Sikora and Plapinger (1994) gave deaf children standard psychometric tests designed for hearing children and reported effective LD detection based on achievement/potential discrepancy measures. Their instruments measured expressive vocabulary, IQ, verbal and visual memory, reading, math, general knowledge, visual–motor integration, and visual–perception skills. They reported that deaf LD and deaf non-LD students did not substantially differ in more concrete academic areas like math computation or in experiential areas like science. However, the deaf LD group had substantially greater difficulty than the deaf non-LD group in language-based areas such as reading, applied math, social studies, and humanities. Sikora and Plapinger (1994) noted that this pattern is typical of a student with normal hearing and a language-based LD. Marlowe (1991) compared the performance of LD and non-LD secondary school children who were either deaf or hearing on a temporal and on a spatial sequential memory task, statistically controlling for IQ. The LD groups were defined by large achievement/potential discrepancy scores and prior teacher referral for LD evaluation. LD children showed short-term sequential memory deficits regardless of whether or not they were deaf. Kelly, Aylward, Jones, Parker-Fisher, Bell, and Verhulst (1993) reported that ADD slows visual reaction time of both deaf and hearing children to comparable degrees.

These initial results provide direct experimental evidence for the existence of ADD and LD in the deaf population and suggest that at least some forms of LD may be manifested in similar psychometric deficits in deaf and hearing children. However, given the extensive evidence for strategy and processing differences between deaf and hearing populations, fundamental differences in the psychometric behavior of deaf and hearing LD children are likely to emerge in future studies.

A promising area for immediate future research is the use of continuous performance tests (CPT) to screen for ADD in the deaf population. CPTs require a child to repeatedly detect a simple visual target like a little black square or a letter in a sequence of other similar objects. These tests examine the child's response times for norm-referenced patterns that suggest inattentive or impulsive responding. CPTs have become part of ADD diagnostic programs because of their objective scoring, their ability to contribute to differential diagnosis of ADD subtypes, and their utility in objectively tracking medication dosage. CPTs are among the most reliable measures of frontal lobe function to discriminate children with ADD from children without ADD (Barkley et al., 1992). They may therefore be useful for ADD evaluation and monitoring in deaf children.

However, limited evidence from a small sample of children at the Kendall School suggests that the mean CPT performance of deaf children is shifted toward scores denoting ADD (Brice & Kerman, 1995). It is unclear whether this shift reflects a higher incidence of ADD in deaf children or is an artifact of normal cultural or developmental differences in target detection performance. Nevertheless, CPTs are beginning to be used with deaf children in school and clinical settings. Therefore, the possibility that CPTs might overdiagnose ADD in deaf children if hearing norms are used suggests that large-scale, age-referenced normative and cross-validation studies should be conducted immediately to motivate the use of CPTs with deaf individuals.

Diagnostic Neural Imaging

Functional magnetic resonance imaging (fMRI) technology is a harmless method of directly visualizing the brain structures responsible for specific types of cognitive and language processing. It has been used to study the neuroanatomy of language processing in both hearing and deaf individuals (Corina et al., 1996) and has revealed important neuroanatomical differences between normal and disabled readers in the hearing population (Shaywitz, 1996; Shaywitz et al., 1995). Eden et al. (1997) showed that fMRI can detect and localize abnormal visual system processing in hearing dyslexics, providing a potential biological marker for dyslexia. Certainly, fMRI will play a major immediate role in diagnosing LD and ADD because it can directly reveal the underlying neural misorganization responsible for these conditions.

Neuroelectric imaging (EEG) is another imaging technology that can identify neural misorganization associated with LD and ADD. EEG patterns have been shown to discriminate both hearing individuals (Ackerman, Dykman, Oglesby, & Newton, 1994; Klorman, 1995) and deaf individuals (Wolff, 1986) who were either known to have or were at risk for LD or ADD from unaffected or low risk individuals. Advances in dense-array EEG electrode technology (Tucker, 1993), neuroelectric source localization theory (Achim, 1995), and neuroelectric signal processing methods (Samar & Molfese, 1995; Samar, Swartz, & Raghuveer, 1995) will soon make inexpensive neuroelectric imaging technology commonplace. Neuroelectric imaging will complement fMRI by providing superior time resolution of the disordered processing underlying LD and ADD.

Together, fMRI and neuroelectric imaging will soon provide neurobehaviorally precise evaluation and monitoring of LD and ADD by allowing the specific neural misorganization responsible for LD and ADD to be directly visualized in individuals. Therefore, the extension of fMRI and neuroelectric imaging technology to LD and ADD evaluation in the deaf population will help to solve the problem of separating the role of deafness versus LD and ADD in producing learning difficulties. This will substantially improve the accuracy of LD and ADD evaluation and subclassification of deaf children and will lead to more correctly focused intervention. Given the dramatic recent advances in the development of these technologies, research on diagnostic neural imaging for LD and ADD in the deaf population should be an immediate priority.

Interactive Multimedia Remediation

Interactive computer technology improves problem-solving accuracy and impulsivity control in impulsive deaf adolescents and impulsive LD hearing adolescents, suggesting that computer-aided intervention can remediate the impulsivity symptoms of ADD (Campbell et al., 1986). More recently, Merzenich et al. (1996) and Tallal et al. (1996) showed that highly entertaining video computer games can be used to train fundamental perceptual language processing skills in children with LLD, producing a 2-year gain in language skills after just a month of intensive training. Tallal, Merzenich, and their colleagues are beginning generalization trials in 25 or more special education schools and clinics in the United

States and Canada to determining whether their remedial techniques work with children with dyslexia, other forms of LD, and ADD (Horgan, 1996).

These results raise the intriguing possibility that interactive multimedia applications could be developed to ameliorate at least some of the underlying processing disabilities of LD and ADD deaf individuals. By identifying specific psychophysical processing difficulties in deaf children and then embedding appropriate auditory and visual discrimination exercises into video game platforms, it may be possible to take advantage of the developing deaf child's neural plasticity to alter the course of LD or ADD at an early stage. The multimedia technology now exists to implement such games easily and to evaluate their effectiveness in modern educational environments.

CONCLUSION

A decade and a half ago, Sabatino (1983) pointed out that it was only in the deaf population, not the hearing population, that there was any empirical evidence for a neural foundation for learning disabilities. LD in the hearing population was merely *presumed* to be caused by neural dysfunction, whereas the exogenous causes of deafness were *known* sometimes to produce neural damage in cognitive systems beyond the sensorineural damage responsible for deafness per se. Today the neural dysfunction that produces some forms of LD in the hearing population can be directly visualized by brain scanning techniques whereas, ironically, even the existence of LD in the deaf population remains largely unproven for the lack of focused research.

Almost nothing is known directly about the cognitive and learning characteristics of deaf individuals with LD and ADD. Anecdotal evidence, survey opinions, and limited empirical studies suggest that deaf LD and ADD individuals may display many of the same characteristics as hearing LD and ADD individuals including difficulties with spelling, discourse organization, grammatical knowledge, visual perception, memory, attention, planning, organization, problem solving, and social behavior. Generally, it seems sensible to pursue models of ADD and LD in the deaf population that maintain the hierarchical distinction between ADD as a set of metacognitive disorders of overarching executive functions and LD as a set of cognitive disorders of specific domains of information processing such as reading, spatial cognition, social reasoning, and memory processes.

However, adequate comprehensive, norm-referenced evaluation instruments are not available to operationalize the measurement of these functions in an individual referred for LD or ADD evaluation. Nor is there any empirical data on the types and variety of LD and ADD syndromes that arise within the deaf population. That is, we do not have a classification scheme that ensures, through validated testing methodology, that a deaf individual will be identified correctly as belonging to a group of individuals who all have the same basic cognitive, neural, and learning characteristics. Without such a scheme we cannot know what specifically causes an individual's learning disability and therefore we cannot know how specifically to intervene. This vacuous state of knowledge can only be overcome by an energetic and comprehensive research initiative like that which has occurred in the mainstream of LD and ADD research.

The educational relevance of evaluating deaf individuals for LD and ADD is broadly recognized as an urgent priority. With the upcoming reauthorization of the IDEA, a new federal definition of disabilities will shortly rise from the ashes of the current definitional crisis. The exclusionary language of the current federal definition is likely to be eliminated, and operational criteria will be called for that directly tie LD and ADD evaluation to the curricular needs and educational goals of all affected children. To meet the challenge of operationalizing the definition for the deaf population, research on LD and ADD must expand its scope and vision to heed developments in the mainstream literature on LD and ADD, on educational and cognitive psychology broadly defined, and on the educational and cognitive psychology of deaf people in particular.

The evaluation of LD and ADD in the deaf population is inherently less tractable than in the hearing population. The potential for cultural bias in LD and ADD evaluation is particularly acute due to the lack of adequate norms on the deaf population, inconsistent control over communication and language factors during evaluation, and the potentially pervasive reliance of deaf individuals on adaptive attentional and cognitive coping strategies in testing and learning situations. However, recent developments in behavioral genetics, neuropsychology, neuroimaging, applied linguistics, reading research, interactive multimedia technology, and the philosophy of assessment provide rich opportunities for research toward a meaningful nosology of LD and ADD in the deaf population and toward the consequent development of effective and culturally fair evaluation and remedial programs and services for deaf individuals.

ACKNOWLEDGMENT

We greatly appreciate the thorough and enthusiastic assistance of our research assistant Poorna Kushalnagar in conducting the literature search for this chapter.

REFERENCES

Abrahamsen, E. P., & Sprouse, P. T. (1995). Fable comprehension by children with learning disabilities. *Journal of Learning Disabilities, 28,* 302–308.
Achenbach, T. M. (1978). *Child Behavior Profile,* Bethesda, MD: National Institute of Mental Health, Laboratory of Developmental Psychology.
Achenbach, T. M., & Edelbrock, C. S. (1981). Behavioral problems and competencies reported by parents of normal and disturbed children aged 4 through 16. *Monographs of the Society for Research in Child Development, 46* (Serial No. 188).
Achim, A. (1995). Cerebral source localization paradigms: Spatiotemporal source modeling, *Brain and Cognition, 27,* 256–287.
Ackerman, P. T., Dykman, R. A., Oglesby, D. M., & Newton, J. O. E. (1994). EEG power spectra of children with dyslexia, slow learners, and normal reading children with ADD during verbal processing. *Journal of Learning Disabilities, 27,* 619–630.
Algozzine, B., & Ysseldyke, J. E. (1986). The future of the LD field: Screening and diagnosis. *Journal of Learning Disabilities, 19,* 394–398.
Altshuler, K. Z., Deming, W. E., Vollenweider, J., Rainer, J. D., & Tendler, R. (1976). Impulsivity and profound early deafness: A cross cultural inquiry. *American Annals of the Deaf, 121,* 331–345.
American Psychiatric Association. (1980). *Diagnostic and statistical manual of mental disorders* (3rd ed.). Washington, DC: Author.
American Psychiatric Association. (1987). *Diagnostic and statistical manual of mental disorders* (3rd ed., revised). Washington, DC: Author.
American Psychiatric Association. (1994). *Diagnostic and statistical manual of mental disorders* (4th ed.). Washington, DC: Author.
August, G. J., & Garfinkel, B. D. (1990). Co-morbidity of ADHD and reading disability among clinic-referred children. *Journal of Abnormal Child Psychology, 18,* 29–45.
Auxter, D. (1971). Learning disabilities among the deaf population. *Exceptional Children, 4,* 573–577.
Barkley, R. A. (1990). *Attention deficit hyperactivity disorder: A handbook for diagnosis and treatment.* New York: Guilford.
Barkley, R. A., Grodzinsky, G., & DuPaul, G. J. (1992). Frontal lobe functions in attention deficit disorder with and without hyperactivity: A review and research report. *Journal of Abnormal Child Psychology, 20,* 163–188.
Bebko, J. M. (1984). Memory and rehearsal characteristics of profoundly deaf children. *Journal of Experimental Child Psychology, 38,* 415–428.
Bebko, J. M., Lacasse, M. A., Turk, H., & Oyen, A-S. (1992). Recall performance on a central–incidental memory task by profoundly deaf children. *American Annals of the Deaf, 137,* 271–277.
Bellugi, U., O'Grady, L., Lillo-Martin, D., O'Grady, M., van Hoek, K., & Corina, D. (1990). Enhancement of spatial cognition in deaf children. In V. Volterra & C. Erting (Eds.), *From gesture to language in hearing and deaf children* (pp. 278–298). New York: Springer-Verlag.
Benton, A. L., & Pearl, D. (1978). *Dyslexia.* New York: Oxford University Press.

Berent, G. P. (1988). An assessment of syntactic capabilities. In M. Strong (Ed.), *Language learning and deafness* (pp. 133–161). Cambridge, UK: Cambridge University Press.

Berent, G. P. (1996a). The acquisition of English syntax by deaf learners. In W. Ritchie & T. Bhatia (Eds.), *Handbook of second language acquisition* (pp. 469–506). San Diego, CA: Academic Press.

Berent, G. P. (1996b). Learnability constraints on deaf learners' acquisition of English *wh*-questions. *Journal of Speech and Hearing Research, 39,* 625–642.

Berent, G. P., & Samar, V. J. (1990). The psychological reality of the subset principle: Evidence from the governing categories of prelingually deaf adults. *Language, 66,* 714–741.

Berent, G. P., Samar, V. J., & Parasnis, I. (1997, March). *English-based learning disabilities in the deaf student population.* Paper presented at the annual convention of Teachers of English to Speakers of Other Languages, Orlando, FL.

Birnbaum, R. K., & Samar, V. J. (1997). *The role of method of instruction, phonological awareness, and letter knowledge in literacy acquisition of kindergarten children.* Manuscript submitted for publication.

Bochner, J. H. (1982). English in the deaf population. In D. G. Sims, G. G. Walter, & R. L. Whitehead (Eds.), *Deafness and communication: Assessment and training* (pp. 107–123). Baltimore: Williams and Wilkins.

Brice, P., & Kerman, M. (1995, April). *Use of the Test of Variables of Attention with deaf students.* Paper presented at the meeting of the American Orthopsychiatric Society, Chicago, IL.

Brown, T. E. (1996). *Brown Attention-Deficit Disorder Scales manual.* San Antonio, TX: The Psychological Corporation.

Bunch, G. O., & Melnyk, T.-L. (1989). A review of the evidence for a learning-disabled, hearing-impaired sub-group. *American Annals of the Deaf, 134,* 297–300.

Campbell, D. S., Neill, J., & Dudley, P. (1986). *Computer aided self-instruction training with impulsive deaf students and learning disabled students: A study on teaching reflective thought.* Toronto: Ontario Institute for Studies in Education.

Center for Assessment and Demographic Studies, Gallaudet Research Institute (1992). Score summary for Stanford Achievement Test, Hearing Impaired Version, 8th ed. Washington, DC: Author.

Chase, C. H. (1996). Neurobiology of learning disabilities. *Seminars in Speech and Language, 17,* 173–182.

Chess, S., & Fernandez, P. (1980). Impulsivity in rubella deaf children: A longitudinal study. *American Annals of the Deaf, 125,* 505–509.

Clark, B. R., & Kendall, D. C. (1980). Learning disabled or hearing impaired: A folly of forced categories. *British Columbia Journal of Special Education, 4,* 13–27.

Conners, C. K. (1990). *Conners rating scales manual.* North Tonawanda, NY: Multi-Health Systems.

Conners, C. K. (1992). *Users guide: Continuous performance test computer program.* North Tonawanda, NY: MultiHealth Systems.

Corina, D., Bavelier, D., Jezzard, P., Clark, V., Padmanhaban, S., Rauschecker, J., Braun, A., Turner, R., & Neville, H. (1996). Processing of American Sign Language and English in native deaf signers: An fMRI study at 4T [Abstract]. *Brain and Cognition, 32,* 100–101.

Coutinho, M. J. (1995). Who will be learning disabled after the reauthorization of IDEA? Two very distinct perspectives. *Journal of Learning Disabilities, 28,* 664–668.

Craig, W. N., & Craig, H. B. (1987). Tabular summary of schools and classes in the United States. *American Annals of the Deaf, 132,* 124.

Cummins, J. (1984). *Bilingualism and special education: Issues in assessment and pedagogy.* San Diego, CA: College Hill Press.

236 SAMAR, PARASNIS, BERENT

Davila, R. R., Williams, M. L., & MacDonald, J. T. (1991). *Clarification of policy to address the needs of children with attention deficit disorder within general and/or special education.* Washington, DC: U.S. Department of Education, Office of Special Education and Rehabilitation Services.

Delgado, G. (1981). Hearing-impaired children from non-native language homes. *American Annals of the Deaf, 126,* 118–121.

Delgado, G. (Ed.). (1984). *The Hispanic deaf: The issues and challenges for bilingual special education.* Washington, DC: Gallaudet University Press.

Delong, G. R. (1992). Autism, amnesia, hippocampus, and learning. *Neuroscience and Biobehavioral Reviews, 16,* 63–72.

Dinner, M. B. (1981). *A proposed sign language test battery for use in the differential diagnosis of language/learning disability in deaf children* (Doctoral dissertation, University of Colorado at Boulder, 1981). University Microfilms International, 8209815.

Eden, G. F., VanMeter, J. W., Rumsey, J. M., Maisog, J. M., Woods, R. P., & Zeffiro, T. A. (1996). Abnormal processing of visual motion in dyslexia revealed by functional brain imaging. *Nature, 382,* 66–69.

Elliot, R., & Powers, A. (1988). Preparing teachers to serve the learning disabled hearing impaired. *The Volta Review, 90,* 13–18.

Elliot, R., Powers, A., & Funderburg, R. (1988). Learning disabled hearing impaired students: Teacher survey. *The Volta Review, 90,* 277–285.

Emmorey, K., Kosslyn, S. M., & Bellugi, U. (1993). Visual imagery and visual spatial language: Enhanced imagery abilities in deaf and hearing ASL signers. *Cognition, 46,* 139–181.

Epstein, M. A., Shaywitz, S. E., Shaywitz, B. A., & Woolstein, J. L. (1991). The boundaries of attention deficit disorder. *Journal of Learning Disabilities, 24,* 78–86.

Faraone, S. V., Biederman, J., Lehman, B. K., Keenan, K., Norman, D., Seidman, L. J., Kolodny, R., Kraus, I., Perrin, J., & Chen, W. J. (1993). Evidence for the independent familial transmission of attention deficit hyperactivity disorder and learning disabilities: Results from a family genetic study. *American Journal of Psychiatry, 150,* 891–895.

Freeman, R. (1979). Psychosocial problems associated with childhood hearing impairment. In L. Bradford & W. Harding (Eds.), *Hearing and hearing impairment* (pp. 405–415). New York: Grune & Stratton.

Friedlander, M. J., Martin, K. A. C., & Wassenhove-McCarthy, D. (1991). Effects of monocular visual deprivation on geniculocortical inervation of area 18 in cat. *Journal of Neuroscience, 11* 3268–3288.

Galaburda, A. M., Rosen, G. D., & Sherman, G. F. (1989). The neural origin of developmental dyslexia: Implications for medicine, neurology, and cognition. In A. M. Galaburda (Ed.), *From reading to neurons* (pp. 377–388). Cambridge, MA: MIT Press.

Gallaudet Research Institute. (1997). [Annual survey of deaf and hard-of-hearing children and youth, 1995–96 school year.] Unpublished tabulations.

Garcia, G. E., & Pearson, P. D. (1994). Assessment and diversity. In L. Darling-Hammond (Ed.), *Review of research in education* (Vol. 20, pp. 337–391). Washington, DC: American Educational Research Association.

Gerber, A. (1993). *Language-related learning disabilities: Their nature and treatment.* Baltimore: Brookes.

Gilger, J. W. (1995). Behavioral genetics: Concepts for research and practice in language development and disorders. *Journal of Speech and Hearing Research, 38,* 1126–1142.

Gilger, J. W., Pennington, B. F., & DeFries, J. C. (1991). Risk for reading disabilities as a function of parental history in three samples of families. *Reading and Writing, 3,* 205–217.

Gillis, J. J., Gilger, J. W., Pennington, B. F., & DeFries, J. C. (1992). Attention deficit disorder in reading-disabled twins: Evidence for a genetic etiology. *Journal of Abnormal Child Psychology, 20,* 303–315.

Goulder, T. J., & Trybus, R. J. (1971). *The classroom behavior of emotionally disturbed, hearing impaired children.* Washington DC: Gallaudet University.

Griffith, A., & Scott, D. (1985). *Looking back.* Toronto: The Canadian Hearing Society.

Hammill, D. D., Leigh, J. E., McNutt, G., & Larsen, S. C. (1981). A new definition of learning disabilities. *Learning Disabilities Quarterly, 4,* 336–342.

Harris, R. (1978). The relationship of impulse control to parent hearing status, manual communication, and academic achievement in deaf children. *American Annals of the Deaf, 123,* 52–67.

Hechtman, L. (1994). Genetic and neurobiological aspects of attention deficit hyperactivity disorder: A review. *Journal of Psychiatry and Neuroscience, 19,* 193–201.

Hersh, C. A., Stone, B. J., & Ford, L. (1996). Learning disabilities and learned helplessness: A heuristic approach. *International Journal of Neuroscience, 84,* 103–113.

Hill, J. W., Luetke-Stahlman, B., & Kapel, D. E. (1985). *Validating teacher-suspected dual diagnosis among select deaf students also thought to be learning disabled.* (Eric Document Reproduction Service No. ED 276 231).

Hirshoren, A., Hurley, O. L., & Hunt, J. T. (1977). The WISC-R and the Hiskey–Nebraska Test with deaf children. *American Annals of the Deaf, 122,* 392–394.

Hirshoren, A., Hurley, O. L., & Kavale, K. (1979). Psychometric characteristics of the WISC-R performance scale with deaf children. *Journal of Speech and Hearing Disorders, 44,* 73–79.

Hirshoren, A., Kavale, K., Hurley, O. L., & Hunt, J. T. (1977). The reliability of the WISC-R performance scale with deaf children. *Psychology in the Schools, 14,* 412–415.

Horgan, J. (1996, November). Playing past learning disabilities. *Scientific American 275*(5), 102.

Hynd, G. W., Hern, K. L., Novey, E. S., Eliopulos, D., Marshal, R., Gonzalez, J. J., & Voeller, K. K. (1993). Attention deficit–hyperactivity disorder and asymmetry of the caudate nucleus. *Journal of Child Neurology, 8,* 339–347.

Individuals with Disabilities Education Act, 20th Cong., PL 101-476, §1400–1495 (1990).

Israelite, N. K., & Hammermeister, F. K. (1986). A survey of teacher preparation programs in education of the hearing impaired. *American Annals of the Deaf, 131,* 232–237.

Javorsky, J. (1996). An examination of youth with attention-deficit/hyperactivity disorder and language learning disabilities: A clinical study. *Journal of Learning Disabilities, 29,* 247–258.

Kandel, E. R. (1985). Early experience, critical periods, and developmental fine tuning of brain architecture. In E. R. Kandel & J. H. Schwartz (Eds.), *Principles of neuroscience* (2nd ed., pp. 757–770). New York: Elsevier.

Karchmer, M. A. (1985). A demographic perspective. In E. Cherow, N. D. Matkin, & R. J. Trybus (Eds.), *Hearing impaired children and youth with developmental disabilities: An interdisciplinary foundation for service* (pp. 36–56). Washington, DC: Gallaudet University Press.

Kaufman, A., & Kaufman, N. (1983). *Kaufman Assessment Battery for Children.* Circle Pines, MN: American Guidance Service.

Keim, J., McWhirter, J. J., & Bernstein, B. L. (1996). Academic success and university accommodation for learning disabilities: Is there a relationship? *Journal of College Student Development, 37,* 502–509.

Kelly, D. P., Aylward, G. P., Jones, M. L., Parker-Fisher, S. J., Bell, S. A., & Verhulst, S. J. (1992). Visual reaction time in deaf and hearing children with attention deficit disorders. *American Journal of Diseases of Children, 146,* 466–467.

Kelly, D. P., Forney, G. P., Parker-Fisher, S. J., & Jones, M. L. (1993a). The challenge of attention deficit disorder in children who are deaf or hard of hearing. *American Annals of the Deaf, 138,* 343–348.

Kelly, D. P., Forney, G. P., Parker-Fisher, S. J., & Jones, M. L. (1993b). Evaluating and managing attention deficit disorder in children who are deaf or hard of hearing. *American Annals of the Deaf, 138*, 349–357.

Kelly, D. P., Kelly, B. J., Jones, M. L., Moulton, N. J., Verhulst, S. J., & Bell, S. A. (1993). Attention deficits in children and adolescents with hearing loss: A survey. *American Journal of Diseases of Children, 147*, 737–741.

Klorman, R. (1991). Cognitive event-related potentials in attention deficit disorder. *Journal of Learning Disabilities, 24*, 130–140.

Klorman, R. (1995). Psychophysiological determinants. In M. Hersen & R. T. Ammerman (Eds.), *Advanced abnormal child psychology* (pp. 59–85). Hillsdale, NJ: Lawrence Erlbaum Associates.

Klorman, R., Brumaghin, J. T., Salzman, L. F., Straus, J., Borgstedt, A. D., McBride, M., & Loeb, S. (1990). Effects of methylphenidate on processing negativities in patients with attention-deficit hyperactivity disorder. *Psychophysiology, 27*, 328–337.

Korkman, M., & Pesonen, A. (1994). A comparison of neuropsychological test profiles of children with attention deficit–hyperactivity disorder and/or learning disorder. *Journal of Learning Disabilities, 27*, 383–392.

Lahey, B. B., Pelham, W. E., Schaughency, E. A., Atkins, M. S., Murphy, H. A., Hynd, G., Russo, M., Hartdagen, S., & Lorys-Vernon, A. (1988). Dimensions and types of attention deficit disorder. *Journal of the Academy of Child and Adolescent Psychiatry, 27*, 330–335.

Larsen, J. P., Hoien, T., Lundberg, I., & Odegaard, H. (1990). MRI evaluation of the size and symmetry of the planum temporale in adolescents with developmental dyslexia. *Brain and Language, 39*, 289–301.

LaSasso, C. J. (1992). Speaking of learning disabilities, "Whatever happened to Erin?" *Perspectives, 11* (2), 2–6.

Laughton, J. (1989). The learning disabled, hearing impaired student: Reality, myth, or overextension? *Topics in Language Disorders, 9*(4), 70–79.

Leark, R. A., Dupuy, T. R., Greenberg, L. M., Corman, C. L., & Kindschi, C. L. (1996). *T.O.V.A., Test of variables of attention: Professional manual, version 7.0.* Los Alamitos, CA: Universal Attention Disorders, Inc.

Lederberg, A. (1993). The impact of deafness on mother–child and peer relationships. In M. Marschark & M. D. Clark (Eds.), *Psychological perspectives on deafness* (pp. 93–119). Hillsdale, NJ: Lawrence Erlbaum Associates.

Leonard, L. B. (1987). Is specific language impairment a useful construct? In S. Rosenberg (Ed.), *Advances in applied psycholinguistics: Vol. 1. Disorders of first language development* (pp. 1–39). Cambridge: Cambridge University Press.

Lerman, A. (1976). *Discovering and meeting the needs of Hispanic hearing impaired children.* (Final report, CREED VII project). New York, NY: Lexington School for the Deaf.

Levine, E. S. (1974). Psychological tests and practices with the deaf: A survey of the state of the art. *The Volta Review, 76*, 298–319.

Leybaert, J. (1993). Reading in the deaf: The roles of phonological codes. In M. Marschark & M. D. Clark (Eds.), *Psychological perspectives on deafness* (pp. 269–309). Hillsdale, NJ: Lawrence Erlbaum Associates.

Livingstone, M. S., Rosen, G. D., Drislane, F. W., & Galaburda, A. M. (1991). Physiological and anatomical evidence for a magnocellular defect in developmental dyslexia. *Proceedings of the National Academy of Science, 88*, 7943–7947.

Madden, R., Gardner, E. F., Rudman, H. L., Karlsen, B., & Merwin, J. L. (1972). *Stanford Achievement Tests: Special Edition for Hearing Impaired Students*, Washington, DC: Gallaudet University.

Marazita, M., Ploughman, L., Rawlings, B., Remington, E., Arnos, K., & Nance, W. (1993). Genetic epidemiological studies of early-onset deafness in the U.S. school-age population. *American Journal of Medical Genetics, 46*, 486–491.

Marlowe, B. A. (1991). Identifying learning disabilities in the deaf population (Doctoral dissertation, The Catholic University of America, 1991). *University Microfilms International*, 9117152.

Marschark, M. (1993a). Origins and interactions in the social, cognitive, and language development of deaf children. In M. Marschark & M. D. Clark (Eds.), *Psychological perspectives on deafness* (pp. 7–26). Hillsdale, NJ: Lawrence Erlbaum Associates.

Marschark, M. (1993b). *Psychological development of deaf children.* New York: Oxford University Press.

Marschark, M. (1996, April). *Mental representation and memory: Cognitive implications for deaf learners.* Paper presented at the Learning Disability, Neuropsychology and Deaf Youth: Theory, Research & Practice meeting, Seattle, WA.

Mauk, G. W., & Mauk, P. P. (1992). Somewhere, out there: Preschool children with hearing impairment and learning disabilities. *Topics in early childhood special education: Hearing impaired preschoolers, 12,* 174–195.

Meadow, K., & Trybus, R. (1979). Behavioral and emotional problems of deaf children: An overview. In L. Bradford & W. Harding (Eds.), *Hearing and hearing impairment* (pp. 395–403). New York: Grune & Stratton.

Merzenich, M. M., Jenkins, W. M., Johnston, P., Schreiner, C., Miller, S. L., & Tallal, P. (1996). Temporal processing deficits of language-learning impaired children ameliorated by training, *Science, 271,* 77–81.

Miller, L. C. (1974). *School behavior checklist.* Louisville, KY: University of Louisville Press.

Mogford, K. (1993). Oral language acquisition in the prelingually deaf. In D. Bishop & K. Mogford (Eds.), *Language development in exceptional circumstances* (pp. 110–131). Hove, UK: Lawrence Erlbaum.

Moores, D. F. (1996). *Educating the deaf: Psychology, principles, and practices* (4th ed.). Boston: Houghton Mifflin.

Morgan, A., & Vernon, M. (1994). A guide to the diagnosis of learning disabilities in deaf and hard-of-hearing children and adults. *American Annals of the Deaf, 139,* 358–370.

National Joint Committee on Learning Disabilities. (1994). *Collective perspectives on issues affecting learning disabilities.* Austin, TX: PRO-ED.

Neville, H. J. (1988). Cerebral organization for spatial attention. In J. Stiles-Daves, M. Kritchevsky, & U. Bellugi (Eds.), *Spatial cognition: Brain bases and development* (pp. 327–341). Hillsdale, NJ: Lawrence Erlbaum Associates.

O'Brien, D.H. (1987). Reflexivity-impulsivity in total communication and oral deaf and hearing children: A developmental study. *American Annals of the Deaf, 132,* 213–217.

Olsen, R. K. (1985). Disabled reading processes and cognitive profiles. In D. B. Gray & J. K. Kavanaugh (Eds.), *Behavioral measures of dyslexia* (pp. 215–243). Parkton, MD: York Press.

Olsen, R. K., Wise, B., Conners, F., Rack, J., & Fulker, D. (1989). Specific deficits in component reading and language skills: Genetic and environmental influences. *Journal of Learning Disabilities, 22,* 339–348.

Paal, N., Skinner, S., & Reddig, C. (1988). The relationship of non-verbal intelligence measures to academic achievement among deaf adolescents. *Journal of Rehabilitation of the Deaf, 21,* 8–11.

Paul, P. V., & Quigley, S. P. (1994). *Language and deafness* (2nd ed.). San Diego, CA: Singular Publishing Group.

Parasnis, I. (1983a). Vision and deafness: A review of ophthalmological studies. *Journal of the Academy of Rehabilitative Audiology, 16,* 148–160.

Parasnis, I. (1983b). Visual perceptual skills and deafness: A research review. *Journal of the Academy of Rehabilitative Audiology, 16,* 161–181.

Parasnis, I. (Ed.). (1996a). *Cultural and language diversity and the deaf experience.* New York: Cambridge University Press.

Parasnis, I. (1996b, April). *Relationship between rhyme generation and English skills in profoundly deaf skilled signers.* Paper presented at the annual meeting of the American Educational Research Association, New York, NY.

Parasnis, I. (1997). Cultural identity and diversity in deaf education. *American Annals of the Deaf, 142,* 72–79.

Parasnis, I., & Samar, V. J. (1982). Visual perception of verbal information by deaf people. In D. G. Sims, G. G. Walter, & R. L. Whitehead (Eds), *Deafness and communication: Assessment and training* (pp. 53–71). Baltimore: Williams & Wilkins.

Parasnis, I., & Samar, V. J. (1985). Parafoveal attention in congenitally deaf and hearing young adults. *Brain and Cognition, 4,* 313–327.

Parasnis, I., Samar, V., Bettger, J., & Sathe, K. (1996). Does deafness lead to enhancement of visual spatial cognition in children? Negative evidence from deaf non-signers. *Journal of Deaf Studies and Deaf Education, 1,* 145–152.

Paratore, J. R. (1995). Assessing literacy: Establishing common standards in portfolio assessment. *Topics in Language Disorders, 16,* 67–82.

Parmar, R. E. (1989). Cross-cultural transfer of non-verbal intelligence tests: An (in)validation study. *British Journal of Educational Psychology, 59,* 379–388.

Pennington, B. (1991). *Diagnosing learning disorders: A neuropsychological framework.* New York: Guilford.

Pennington, B. F., Groisser, D., & Welsh, M. C. (1993). Contrasting cognitive deficits in attention deficit hyperactivity disorder versus reading disability. *Developmental Psychology, 29,* 511–523.

Plapinger, D., & Sikora, D. (1990). Diagnosing a learning disability in a hearing-impaired child. *American Annals of the Deaf, 135,* 285–292.

Powers, A., Elliot, R., Fairbank, D., & Monaghan C. (1988). The dilemma of identifying learning disabled hearing-impaired students. *The Volta Review, 90,* 209–218.

Powers, A., Elliot, R., & Funderburg, R. (1987). Learning disabled hearing-impaired students: Are they being identified? *The Volta Review, 89,* 99–105.

Quay, H. C., & Peterson, D. R. (1967). *Behavior problem checklist.* Champaign, IL: University of Illinois Press.

Quigley, S. P., & King, C. M. (1980). Syntactic performance of hearing impaired and normal hearing individuals. *Applied Psycholinguistics, 1,* 329–356.

Ratner, V. L. (1985). Spatial-relationship deficits in deaf children: The effect on communication and classroom performance. *American Annals of the Deaf, 130,* 250–254.

Ratner, V. L. (1988). New tests for identifying hearing-impaired students with visual perceptual deficits: Relationship between deficits and ability to comprehend sign language. *American Annals of the Deaf, 133,* 336–343.

Ray, S. (1979). *An adaptation of the Wechsler Intelligence Scale for Children–Revised for the deaf.* Natchitoches, LA: Northwestern State University of Louisiana.

Reid, D. K., Hresko, W. P., Hammil, D. D., & Wiltshire, S. (1991). *Test of Early Reading Ability: Deaf or Hard of Hearing.* Austin, TX: PRO-ED.

Rice, M. L., & Wexler, K. (1996). Toward tense as a clinical marker of specific language impairment in English-speaking children. *Journal of Speech and Hearing Research, 39,* 1239–1257.

Rice, M. L., Wexler, K., & Cleave, P. (1995). Specific language impairment as a period of extended optional infinitive. *Journal of Speech and Hearing Research, 38,* 850–863.

Ross, R. G., Hommer, D., Breiger, D., Varley, C., & Radant, A. (1994). Eye movement task related to frontal lobe functioning in children with attention deficit disorder. *Journal of the American Academy of Child and Adolescent Psychiatry, 33,* 869–874.

Roth, V. (1991). Students with learning disabilities and hearing impairment: Issues for the secondary and postsecondary teacher. *Journal of Learning Disabilities, 24,* 391–397.

Rourke, B. P. (1989). *Nonverbal learning disabilities: The syndrome and the model.* New York: Guilford.

Rourke, B. P., & Conway, J. A. (1997). Disabilities of arithmetic and mathematical reasoning: Perspectives from neurology and neuropsychology. *Journal of Learning Disabilities, 30,* 34–46.

Rush, P., & Baechle, C. (1992, Spring). Learning disabilities and deafness: An emerging field. *Gallaudet Today,* 20–26.

Rush, P., Blennerhassett, L., Epstein, D., & Alexander, D. (1991). WAIS-R verbal and performance profiles of deaf adolescents referred for atypical learning styles. In D. Martin (Ed.), *Advances in cognition, education, and deafness* (pp. 82–88). Washington, DC: Gallaudet University Press.

Sabatino, D. (1983). The house that Jack built. *Journal of Learning Disabilities, 16,* 26–27.

Samar, V. J., & Molfese, D. (Eds.). (1995). Contemporary trends in neurometric waveform analysis [Special issue]. *Brain and Cognition, 27*(3).

Samar, V. J., Swartz, K. P., & Raghuveer, M. R. (1995). Multiresolution analysis of event-related potentials by wavelet decomposition. *Brain and Cognition, 27,* 398–438.

Satterfield, J. H., Schell, A. M., Nicholas, T. W., Satterfield, B. T., & Freese, T. E. (1990). Ontogeny of selective attention effects on event-related potentials in attention-deficit hyperactivity disorder and normal boys. *Biological Psychiatry, 28,* 879–903.

Schildroth, A. N., & Hotto, S. A. (1996). Annual survey of deaf and hard-of-hearing children and youth: Changes in student characteristics, 1984–85 and 1994–95. *American Annals of the Deaf, 141,* 68–71.

Semrud-Clikeman, M., & Hynd, G. W. (1990). Right hemisphere dysfunction in non-verbal learning disabilities: Social, academic, and adaptive functioning in adults and children. *Psychological Bulletin, 107,* 196–209.

Semrud-Clikeman, M., & Hynd, G. W. (1994). Brain-behavior relationships in behavior. In N. C. Jordan & J. Goldsmith-Phillips, *Learning disabilities: New directions for assessment and intervention* (pp. 43–65). Boston, MA: Allyn & Bacon.

Shaw, S. F., Cullen, J. P., McGuire, J. M., & Brinkerhoff, L. C. (1995). Operationalizing a definition of learning disabilities. *Journal of Learning Disabilities, 28,* 586–597.

Shaywitz, S. E. (1996, November). Dyslexia. *Scientific American,* 98–104.

Shaywitz, S. E., Fletcher, J. M., & Shaywitz, B. A. (1994). Issues in the definition and classification of attention deficit disorder. *Topics in Language Disorders: ADD and Its Relationships to Spoken and Written Language, 14* (4), 1–25.

Shaywitz, B. A., Shaywitz, S. E., Pugh, K. R., Constable, R. T., Skudlarski, P., Fulbright, R. K., Bronen, R. A., Fletcher, J. M., Shankweiler, D. P., Katz, L., & Gore, J. C. (1995). Sex differences in the functional organization of the brain for language. *Nature, 373,* 607–609.

Shelton, T. L., & Barkley, R. A. (1994). Central issues in the assessment of attention deficit disorders in children. *Topics in Language Disorders: ADD and Its Relationships to Spoken and Written Language, 14* (4), 26–41.

Shroyer, V. (1982). Assessing and remedying perceptual problems in hearing impaired children. In D. Tweedie & E. H. Shroyer (Eds.), *The multihandicapped hearing impaired: Identification and instruction* (pp. 135–147). Washington, DC: Gallaudet University Press.

Shue, K. L., & Douglas, V. I. (1992). Attention deficit hyperactivity disorder and the frontal lobe syndrome. *Brain and Cognition, 20,* 104–124.

Sikora, D., & Plapinger, D. (1994). Using standard psychometric tests to identify learning disabilities in students with sensorineural hearing impairments. *Journal of Learning Disabilities, 27,* 352–359.

Skutnabb-Kangas, T., & Cummins, J. (Eds.). (1988). *Minority education: From shame to struggle.* Phillidelphia, PA: Multilingual Matters, Ltd.

Stanovich, K. E. (1986). Matthew effects in reading: Some consequences of individual differences in the acquisition of literacy. *Reading Research Quarterly, 21,* 360–407.

Strang, J. D., & Rourke, B. P. (1985). Arithmetic disability subtypes: The neuropsychological significance of specific arithmetic impairment in childhood. In B. P. Rourke (Ed.), *Neuropsychology of learning disabilities: Essentials of subtype analysis* (pp. 167–183). New York: Guilford.

Swanson, J. M., Potkin, S., Bonforte, S., Fiore, C., Cantwell, D., & Crinella, F. (1991). Activating tasks for the study of visual–spatial attention in ADHD children: A cognitive anatomic approach. *Journal of Child Neurology, 6* (Suppl. S), 119–127.

Swisher, M. V. (1993). Perceptual and cognitive aspects of recognition of signs in peripheral vision. In M. Marschark & M. D. Clark (Eds.), *Psychological perspectives on deafness* (pp. 209–227). Hillsdale, NJ: Lawrence Erlbaum Associates.

Tallal, P., Miller, S. L., Byma, G., Wang, X., Nagarajan, S., Schreiner, C., Jenkins, W. M., & Merzenich, M. M. (1996). Language comprehension in language-learning impaired children improved with acoustically modified speech. *Science, 271,* 81–84.

Torgesen, J. K., Morgan, S. T., & Davis, C. (1992). Effects of two types of phonological awareness training on word learning in kindergarten children. *Journal of Educational Psychology, 84,* 364–370.

Tucker, D. M. (1993). Spatial sampling of head electrical fields: The geodesic head sensor net. *Electroencephalography and Clinical Neurophysiology, 87,* 154–163.

Ullman, R. K., Sleator, E. K., & Sprague, R. L. (1984). A new rating scale for diagnosis and monitoring of ADD children. *Psychopharmacological Bulletin, 20,* 160–164.

U.S. Office of Special Education Programs. (1995). *Improving the Individuals with Disabilities Education Act: IDEA reauthorization.* Washington, DC: Author.

Vernon, M., & Andrews, J. F. (1990). *Psychology of deafness: Understanding deaf and hard of hearing people.* New York: Longman.

Wallach, G. P., & Butler, K. G. (1995). Language learning disabilities: Moving in from the edge. *Topics in Language Disorders, 16,* 1–26.

Wallis, C. (1994, July 18). Life in overdrive. *Time,* 42–50.

Wechsler, D. (1974). *Wechsler intelligence scale for children–revised.* New York: The Psychological Corporation.

Welsh, M. C. (1994). Executive function and the assessment of attention deficit hyperactivity disorder. In N. C. Jordan & J. Goldsmith-Phillips, *Learning disabilities: New directions for assessment and intervention* (pp. 43–65). Boston, MA: Allyn & Bacon.

Westby, C. E., & Cutler, S. K. (1994). Language and ADHD: Understanding the bases and treatment of self-regulatory deficits. *Topics in Language Disorders: ADD and Its Relationships to Spoken and Written Language, 14* (4), 58–76.

Wexler, K. (1994). Optional infinitives. In D. Lightfoot & N. Hornstein (Eds.), *Verb movement* (pp. 305–350). New York: Cambridge University Press.

Wiig, E. H., & Semel, E. (1984). *Language assessment and intervention for the learning disabled* (2nd ed.). Columbus, OH: Merrill.

Wolff, A. (1986, August). *Neurophysiological differences among deaf children.* Paper presented at the meeting of the American Psychological Association, Washington, DC.

Zametkin, A. J., & Rapoport, J. L. (1987). Neurobiology of attention deficit disorder with hyperactivity: Where have we come in 50 years? *Journal of the American Academy of Child Adolescent Psychiatry, 26,* 676–686.

10

Assessing Pragmatic Language Skills in Deaf Children: The Language Proficiency Profile

James M. Bebko
Elaine E. McKinnon
York University

The assessment of the full range of language skills of deaf children is a complex task due to the varied forms and modalities of language used by many deaf children. In this chapter, we discuss the development of a measure to assess the language proficiency of deaf children. The basic premise for the development of the measure was that any scale that is identified with a single means of expression, such as spoken English or signed skills, necessarily underestimates the deaf child's full range of language skills. Therefore, as becomes apparent in subsequent sections of the chapter, the focus for our scale was less on the form of the child's language and more on the content and use components of language skills (Bloom & Lahey, 1978).

LANGUAGE DEVELOPMENT IN THE DEAF CHILD: A BRIEF OVERVIEW

Research over the past few decades has left no room for doubt that language can and does develop in the absence of hearing. As Bellugi and

her associates concluded, "the human capacity for language is not linked
to some privileged cognitive/auditory connection" (Bellugi, Poizner, &
Klima, 1989, p. 380). Children who are deaf can acquire and utilize a
manual language that exhibits all of the complexities of linguistic organization found in spoken languages.

The form of language acquired by deaf children necessarily varies
depending on the forms of language presented by parents or other
caregivers and available within their environment. In particular, in North
America, deaf children born of deaf parents will likely be exposed to
American Sign Language (ASL), an autonomous language used by the
deaf with its own mechanisms for relating visual form with meaning. Deaf
children born to hearing parents may be exposed to a variety of forms of
language input, including ASL, forms of Signed English, fingerspelling,
speech, and forms that incorporate many of these methods simultaneously (e.g., Simultaneous Communication, Pidgin Signed English). In
addition to parental hearing status and type of language input received,
other factors that influence the actual language performance of deaf
children include the age at onset of deafness; type, degree, and etiology
of the hearing impairment; age of identification of the child's hearing loss;
education; parental acceptance of deafness; and hearing-aid use
(Thompson, Biro, Vethivelu, Pious, & Hatfield, 1987).

The basic course of language acquisition in deaf children immersed in
a signing environment from birth is fairly well understood. Studies of deaf
children of deaf parents who use ASL have confirmed that, despite the
differences in modality of language (that is, manual vs spoken), deaf
children acquire ASL as a first language in ways that are remarkably similar
to those of hearing children acquiring spoken language (Newport & Meier,
1986). ASL exhibits formal structuring at the same levels as spoken
languages, namely phonemic, morphological, and syntactic levels. However, the form that this grammatical structuring assumes is influenced by
the visual–manual modality in which the language is expressed and
understood (Bellugi, Klima, and Poizner, 1988). ASL makes linguistic use
of visual–spatial information, insofar as it presents a layered organization
of linguistic information in space (Petitto & Bellugi, 1988). It can be
assumed that other signed language systems also make use of these spatial
devices to convey a range of features of the language structure and
meaning. However, we must acknowledge that our understanding of the
developmental sequence of language acquisition in deaf children of
hearing parents is less well understood.

This cursory review highlights several issues of importance when
considering language development in the deaf child and, particularly, our
ability to adequately assess this language. First, there is no one uniform

language system acquired by all deaf children; ASL is only one form of manual language learned (c.f., signed English).Variations within the population of deaf children are often found to be greater than variations between deaf and hearing children (Meadow, 1978). Second, there are many forms of manual language acquired by deaf children that are unstandardized, with the result that young deaf children may communicate in somewhat idiosyncratic ways. Taken together, these two issues highlight both the complexity and the diversity of language that can be observed in the deaf child. Understanding this makes the job of assessing the deaf child's language all the more challenging.

ASSESSMENT MEASURES

Assessing the language and communication skills of deaf children is an essential step to furthering our understanding of language development in deaf children. More generally, this assessment can help inform general theories of language development to enable these theories to encompass a wider range of language acquisition experiences. In addition, the information gained can help further our understanding of the development of other language skills, as well as cognitive skills that are language-based, such as literacy, metalinguistic development, and a range of memory and problem-solving skills. Nonetheless, assessing the language of the deaf child has been found to be a particularly challenging and elusive exercise.

Language assessment measures can broadly be classified as those that assess receptive language abilities—children's understanding of what is communicated to them—and those measures that are concerned with evaluating expressive language abilities—what children are able to produce and how effectively they use the language being produced. Because the focus of this chapter is on the development of a particular expressive language measure, we restrict our review to a sample of tests that evaluate expressive language abilities. The following review is by no means exhaustive, and the interested reader is referred to others who discuss at greater length the issues of language asssessment in the deaf child and the various measures available (e.g., Thompson et al., 1987).

ASSESSMENT OF EXPRESSIVE LANGUAGE SKILLS

Bates (1976) pointed out that "language is acquired and used in a social context" (p. 412). More directly, Thompson et al. (1987) contended that, for hearing-impaired children, the major focus for assessment of language skills should be the social use of language. They further asserted that informal assessment or informal use of formal assessment tools may be the most informative and useful approach. This perspective is clearly evident in the development and utilization of many of the measures reviewed here.

Measures that have been used with deaf populations in the past can be generally clustered into two forms of assessment. One is based on language samples of the child, and these have varied according to whether they use elicited, spontaneous, or interview-generated samples. The second form can be grouped into rating methods, using developmental checklists with an informed rater.

A number of tests use as their basis the analysis of a language sample. This allows the examiner to study the child's use of language within various contexts. This is particularly important given the observation of Thompson et al. (1987) that some hearing-impaired children use language inappropriately, even though syntactically correct sentences may be produced. Language samples may be spontaneous, allowing a child to talk about presented materials or proposed situations or activities. Alternatively, the child may be asked to repeat or imitate what the examiner has communicated, providing an elicited language sample.

The elicited language sample approach is popular because it is more proscribed and allows for scores to be derived in a shorter period of time. It is, however, inherently more limited in the range of language structures being examined. A less-structured approach often results in more, and more complex, language than a structured, prescribed approach (Longhurst & Grubb, 1974). Moreover, within elicited samples of language, there is not necessarily communicative intent on the part of the speaker (Thompson et al., 1987). Furthermore, the language produced may simply be a product of good rote memory (Miller, 1973), clearly a confound in this form of evaluation.

An example of the elicited language approach to evaluating language in the deaf population is the Grammatical Analysis of Elicited Language (GAEL; Moog & Geers, 1979). This measure evaluates important elements of spoken language in young hearing-impaired children and provides norms for oral hearing-impaired children aged 5 to 9 years. Target sentences are constructed within the context of various activities using a set of toys and are scored on the basis of the presence of 16 grammatical categories. This approach has application to orally trained deaf children and may, with modification, be used with children who use a simultaneous communication approach. The language system being evaluated is, however, clearly English, so this measure could not be utilized with groups of children who use sign systems with nonstandardized English or ASL. Further, the GAEL does not evaluate the child's use of language, and the role of memory in the child's performance is certainly a confound.

Hoemann and Gonter-Gaustad (1990) developed an imitation test to assess both ASL and Manually Coded English (MCE) based on the Imitation, Comprehension, and Production (IPC) measure described by Fraser, Bellugi, and Brown (1963). They examined the productions of deaf children who used both of these systems of signing with the aim of comparing their developing proficiency within these two systems. The children were presented sets of contrasting sentences via videotape, these sentences differing only in the grammatical feature being examined. The children were then required to imitate the model's execution. The authors found this approach to measuring developing knowledge and acquisition of ASL and MCE very useful, although some refinement in the assessment of certain features was warranted. It is noteworthy that this approach does not evelute use of language, but is rather overly focused on development of syntactic skill. Moreover, memory may play an important role in the child's productions.

In the case of evaluating a spontaneous language sample, one measure that has been widely used with the deaf population is the Developmental Sentence Analysis approach developed by Lee (1974). The examiner selects and scores a series of consecutive sentences within a spontaneous language sample, analyzing each sentence on the basis of the presence of eight categories of grammatical forms. There are, however, no norms available for deaf children. Further, only standard English language can be evaluated using this approach, whether it is spoken or signed, limiting the use of this measure to a select group of deaf children.

Printz and Strong (1994) developed a set of production and comprehension measures to assess ASL skills within the context of a spontaneous language sample. With regard to ASL production, the authors devised two measures. In the "Classifier Production Test," children were required to sign in ASL the actions from segments of a cartoon movie just viewed. Responses were videotaped and scored for the presence of different size, shape, and movement markers known as classifiers (Strong & Prinz, 1997). The second production measure required children to look at pictures from a children's storybook that had no text, and to sign the story in ASL. Again, videotaped productions were scored using a checklist for the presence of ASL grammatical and narrative structures.

It is noteworthy that none of the measures evaluated thus far make provision for evaluating a child's skill in the areas of semantics and pragmatics. Caccamise, Newell, and their associates have promoted the development and use of the Sign Communication Proficiency Interview (SCPI), an interview method of evaluating language competency based on the Language Proficiency Interview (Newell, Caccamise, Boardman, & Holcomb, 1983; Caccamise, Newell, & Mitchell-Caccamise, 1983). This approach captures natural language as it occurs within the context of a social exchange. Adult interviewees are engaged in a conversational format by proficient signers and the topics or content of the interview vary according to the communicative needs and interests of the participant. Given that the purpose of the measure is to evaluate signed communicative competence, raters evaluate sign skills along a continuum from ASL to Pidgin Signed English/natural signed English. Interviews are videotaped and scored by skilled raters. A rating is provided that captures a general overview of the interviewee's skills in using signing for communication, ranging from "no functional skills in signing" to "superior plus." This methodology taps both expressive and receptive skills in signing. Further, there is consideration of use of vocabulary and ability and ease of conversing, including how well the interviewee is able to ask clarifying questions and use other conversational strategies, both aspects of pragmatic functioning. This measure has been used primarily with adults. The authors acknowledge that adaptation of the interview technique for assessment of younger children's communication skills still needs to be investigated (Caccamise & Newell, 1986).

The measures reviewed thus far examine language within the context of a language sample that is either spontaneous or elicited in a structured manner. In addition, the SCPI makes use of a flexible interview format for generating a language sample that is evaluated by trained raters.

Individuals interested in evaluating the language of deaf children also have available to them language rating scales. These are generally comprised of a checklist of language skills or behaviors arranged in a developmental progression. The Kendall Communicative Proficiency Scale (KCPS) Worksheet (Francis, Garner, & Harvey, 1980) is an example and is examined in greater detail in the next section.

The SKI-HI scale was developed for use with hearing-impaired infants and children. The scale is developmentally ordered and lists expressive and receptive language skills that children from 0 to 5 years of age would normally demonstrate. Each age interval is represented by enough observable language skills to obtain a good profile of a child's language ability (Thompson et al., 1987). Parents are the raters of the child's language capabilities, and the focus is on English language skills.

RATIONALE AND DEVELOPMENT
OF A PRAGMATIC LANGUAGE ASSESSMENT
TOOL: THE LANGUAGE PROFICIENCY PROFILE

As is apparent from the preceding review, a choice of measures for evaluating the language skills of deaf adults is available, depending on the purposes for the evaluation. However, a more limited selection is available to assess deaf children's developing skills. More importantly, there is no one measure available that can be broadly utilized for making comparisons among deaf children who use various language forms and modalities. For example, assessment of ASL and English language skills alone, although useful for evaluating the proficiency of a person within each single modality, may not capture the full range of the child's linguistic or communicative abilities. Combined forms of expression may be used as well as nonstandardized language forms, yieding a situation in which the sum of the child's language skills may be greater than the individual parts. Therefore, when the goal is to evaluate skills across populations of deaf children, as well as between hearing and deaf children, whether for research or for educational purposes, a measure is needed that is relatively modality-free and non-language specific.

As an example, in our own research work, we were exploring a hypothesis that children's (deaf or hearing) language proficiency was a predictor of their use of certain memory strategies (e.g., Bebko, 1979, 1984; Bebko, Bell, Metcalfe-Haggert, & McKinnon, in press; Bebko & McKinnon, 1990; Bebko & Metcalfe-Haggert, 1997). However, it quickly became apparent that the measures available were not comprehensive enough to enable us to evaluate the full range of the deaf children's expressive language skills. Therefore, Bebko and McKinnon (1987) developed a measure whose emphasis was on more pragmatic/semantic aspects of language that would be common to both the spoken and signed languages of the hearing and deaf child. Our goal was a measure that was less single-language bound than other measures available. We were interested in one that would be useful and valid to examine the overall developing expressive language skills of young children, encompassing as much of the variety of their expressive skills as possible. In addition, we hoped to eliminate barriers to its use by minimizing the amount of training required to use the instrument. Our efforts lead us to develop the Language Proficiency Profile (LPP).

The LPP was adapted from the Kendall Communicative Proficiency Scale (Francis et al., 1980), a 15-point scale designed for rating the communicative proficiency of deaf children within educational settings. The KCPS used trained raters who, on the basis of a cluster of judgments in five critical categories—namely Reference, Content, Cohesion, Use, and Form—would assign a level of proficiency to the child. Each of the categories was assumed to tap somewhat different roots of communicative competence. The level of proficiency ascribed to each child ranged from 0 to 7 (including half-level scores), tapping the range of language abilities from prelinguistic communicative abilities to fully proficient and sophisticated expressive language functioning. The raters made these judgments on the basis of their natural interactions with the children, primarily in the school environment.

The KCPS was designed as a measure of developmental growth in language and, as such, raters were to maintain a perspective that was sensitive to "the developmental continuum along which the child evolves within each category as his communicative proficiency grows" (Francis et al., 1980, p. 262). The same five categories of Reference, Content, Cohesion, Use, and Form make up the basic framework of the LPP, insofar as the LPP has used the critical features or "markers" in each of the categories, at each of the levels, and placed these in the context of a question that could be answered by an individual familiar with the child's language.

The Structure of the LPP: Categories and Levels

The structure of the LPP (and the KCPS) was derived from Bloom and Lahey's (1978) model, which emphasized that there are three basic dimensions to language: content, form, and use. Language competence is assumed to be comprised of the integration of these three dimensions. Therefore, they are represented directly in the scale.

During prelinguistic development, form, content, and use seem to represent separate strands of development (Bloom & Lahey, 1978). Because the LPP was not intended to evaluate prelinguistic levels of development, we did not incorporate the earliest levels of the KCPS in the scale; therefore, the LPP begins at the equivalent of level two in the KCPS. In addition to content, form, and use, as early communicators come to learn the needs of listeners and the requirements of specific communication situations, cohesion and reference become equally important dimensions of language proficiency. There is no reason to doubt that these same dimensions are present in the development of any language, including signed languages—or, indeed, any combined communication system that may incorporate more than a single modality of expression. Therefore, each of these five dimensions is represented in the LPP and are described individually.

The Form criterion refers to the structure of language. At earlier levels, the child is capable of producing single word/sign units from the adult speech/sign inventory, followed by producing two syntactically related elements, and so on. Eventually the child is able to code all required elements of his or her message and is able to communicate easily with peers and adults within the content framework appropriate for the child's developmental level. Later developments in form include the ability to communicate in short narratives and in a manner that is idiomatic and free of circumlocution.

The Use category refers to the various functions of language. As was noted with the KCPS, almost all language functions found at higher levels of proficiency can be observed in more rudimentary forms at earlier levels (Francis et al., 1980). Judgments within this category require addressing of such increasingly complex functions as: Does the child use language to interact with or gain the attention of others, to describe objects, events, and actions, to create worlds of make believe, to solve problems, or to influence the opinions of others?

The Content category refers to the topics of the child's communication; what sorts of objects, actions, and relationships are reflected in communication. At the lower proficiency levels, Bloom and Lahey's (1978) semantic categories are represented in communications that include information about existence or disappearance, rejection, denial, causality, and so on. Early on, the content of the child's communication will concern the things and actions that originate from or have some direct bearing on him or her. Content will later extend to the ability to specify relations between events and conditions, eventually leading to the ability to report on essentially all his or her experience and any ideas within intellectual reach.

The Reference component refers to the child's capacity to refer to information beyond the immediate context. It relates to the degree to which the child's use of language is freed from the present. The Reference criteria overlap with the Content criteria in some respects. This is not unexpected given the obvious relationship between what a child refers to and how far removed it is in terms of time or degree of abstraction from the here and now. In the Reference scale, raters evaluate, for example, if the child restricts his or her communication to the things around him or her, or whether things are discussed from the past or future. As the child's language proficiency increases, language comes to be used to present imaginary or hypothetical ideas. Eventually, the child will demonstrate the capacity to refer to things that have no concrete form, such as rules, principles, or abstract relationships (Francis et al., 1980).

Finally, Cohesion is considered an aspect of communicative function and deals with how, and how effectively the child links his or her communication to the listener and the messages that preceded and followed his or her utterances (Bloom & Lahey, 1978). Thus, assessment within this category is associated with control of syntax and the ability to take into account the perspective, knowledge, and opinions of the conversational partner. In the early stages of proficiency, the child repeats segments of preceding utterances of others or may share a common focus of attention within the immediate environment. Progressively, the child is able to initiate new topics by providing new information or asking questions about events or intentions. At the final stages of proficiency within this category, the child is able to engage in sustained dialogue and narrative and demonstrates the ability to repair conversations should there be misunderstandings or confusion.

Four of the five components of the LPP (excluding Form) evaluate the child's language primarily from the perspective of semantics, function, and use. Thus, for these parts of the measure, our intent not to link assessment directly to the actual form in which the language is expressed is satisfied. As for the Form category, questions are not directly linked to any modality of expression, because, as noted earlier, the LPP is not concerned with what we might refer to as a microanalysis of language; that is, it does not query the appearance of language-specific features (for example, the emergence of irregular verb forms or spatial referencing that conveys past tense). Rather, the LPP is focused on whether children are able to express accurately various aspects of language in a form that would be acceptable in their particular language modality (for example, is the child able to convey past tense within his or her utterance?). As a result of these considerations, it would seem reasonable to presume that any manner or modality of language can be evaluated equally with the LPP. It follows, then, that the LPP may be a valuable tool to enable comparisons to be made across languages and modalities, for example within deaf populations or across hearing groups who use multiple languages.

Finally, a central difference between the LPP and the KCPS is that the LPP uses an informed rater methodology, with the rater evaluating the child's language using a developmental scale. This mitigates the need for extensive training of the rater for interviews and, thus, enables a wider range of people to rate the child's skills. As is shown next, it has been used successfully with teachers and with parents as raters, with no additional training on the scale.

From its earliest conception in 1987 to the present, the LPP has been through several revisions. These revisions have included rewording of questions to improve understanding, and revisions in how questions may be answered. These modifications incorporated feedback provided to the authors from parents, teachers, and language experts who completed the measure. Finally, recent versions have reduced the amount of redundancy in questions across categories, thus providing an approximately equal number of questions across categories in determining overall levels of proficiency. These changes occured in the context of a series of validation studies for the LPP that are summarized in the next sections.

Evaluations of Construct and Concurrent Validity of the LPP

The First Version: LPP-1.　In the first study utilizing the LPP (version LPP-1; Bebko & McKinnon, 1987), McKinnon (1987) evaluated whether language experience and proficiency might be related to the emergence of a rehearsal stategy on a memory task for both hearing children and a sample of deaf children who used signed and spoken language. In this and in all the studies we discuss relating to the LPP, the deaf samples were children with profound deafness (i.e., hearing loss > 85 db in the better ear), and whose deafness was endogenous or of unknown etiology. Children with identified emotional, behavioral, medical, or learning difficulties were excluded from participating.

The sample evaluated using the LPP in McKinnon (1987) consisted of 41 deaf children who were in a Total Communication program (that is, utilizing sign, speech, gesture, and other forms) aged 5 to 15 years, and 45 hearing children aged 5 to 8 years. The teachers most familiar with the child's language skills served as the raters. An initial finding was that the LPP-1 was significantly correlated with the age of the deaf children (r = .631), indicating that, in general, increasing age was associated with higher scores on the LPP. However, of greater interest from the validity standpoint was that the LPP was correlated with estimates of the years of language experience in the deaf children, that is, the number of years of continuous language training for deaf children of hearing parents, or the number of years since birth for deaf children of deaf parents. The corresponding r values were r = .706 for the total years of language experience since identification of deafness and r = .604 for the years of experience in the child's currently most-used language system (i.e., if there had been a change in approach, for example, from auditory only to manual only or simultaneous communication approach, it was the number of years of experience with the child's current system). All three of these correlations provided initial confirmation of the construct validity of the LPP as a developmental measure of language proficiency with deaf children. That is, increased scores were positively associated with age, and more importantly, with years of language training. The correlation of the LPP with age in the hearing sample was not significant, however, due to a ceiling effect; many of the hearing children's skills were rated near the maximum of the scale.

Refinements in the measure were undertaken to improve the wording of specific questions, in particular when earlier skills had disappeared with the appearance of more sophisticated skills, which led to the LPP-Revised (LPP-R). In addition, we began to explore two additional issues: the applicability of the measure with other groups of children, namely younger hearing children and orally trained deaf children, as well as different ways to score the LPP.

Evaluation of the LPP-R.   The LPP-R was scored in a variety of ways for statistical analyses. The levels method used in the KCPS was the original method adapted for use with the LPP. In scoring, the LPP questions were grouped according to the levels of the KCPS to which they corresponded. The result was a score for each of the five subscale components (Reference, Content, Cohesion, etc.), which indicated the highest level of proficiency for that subscale (Subscale Level). An overall level was determined by recording the maximum level achieved across all five categories/subscales (LPP Total Level). A new sum method was also developed, which corresponds to the sum of the "yes" responses for the questions in each subscale (Subscale Sum Score) and the total "yes" responses across all 5 subscales (LPP Total Sum Score). The sum methods were developed because the levels methods were seen as potentially too insensitive to developmental change, as the level can range from only level 2 to level 7. In contrast, using the sums, the scores for each subscale can range from 0 to the maximum for each subscale, and the LPP total sum score can range from 0 to 112. As a result, this method is potentially more sensitive to small differences in proficiency.

In the first follow-up study[1] in 1992, the LPP-R was given to the teachers of 18 orally trained deaf students ranging in age from 6 to 14 years. Concurrent validity was explored using the Bankson Language Screening Test (Bankson, 1977) in addition to the LPP. The Bankson is a test of English language skills that assesses children in up to five areas. Two of the subscales evaluate perceptual skills (visual perception and auditory perception) and were not included in the study as they were not deemed germane to the goals of the study. Therefore, the students' language skills were evaluated using the remaining three psycholinguistic subscales of the Bankson, tapping semantic knowledge and understanding of morphological and syntactic rules.

---

[1]We wish to acknowledge the contributions of Diana Frawley and Beth Posen to the completion of these studies of the LPP-R.

Language proficiency as measured by the LPP was found to be significantly correlated with age (r = .649), again pointing to its utility as a measure of developmental language proficiency. Concurrent validity was evaluated by comparing the Bankson scores with the various LPP-R scores. The correlations between the Bankson total score and both the LPP total level score (r = .775) and the LPP total sum score (r = .796) were highly significant, providing good evidence for concurrent validity. The high degree of concurrence indicates that the LPP-R and the Bankson share a degree of commonality in the language skills they measure. Nonetheless, the lack of a perfect correlation indicates that they also differ somewhat, as expected, likely due to the semantic, morphological, and syntactic focus of the Bankson, whereas the LPP intentionally minimized the latter two aspects of language proficiency.

Strong correlations were found with each of the subscale level scores of the LPP-R and the Bankson total: correlations ranged from .539 to .829. When the Bankson subscale scores were compared to the LPP subscale level scores, correlations were significant at the .05 level or higher for all but one comparison; these significant correlations ranged from .512 to .885. The one nonsignificant comparison was found between Bankson Morphological and LPP Cohesion (r = .366); these variables would not necessarily be expected to be highly correlated, as they are at best only indirectly related to one another.

The relationship between the LPP total sum and subscale sum scores and the Bankson total and subscale scores was also examined. These correlations were all at least as high or higher than was the case for the levels analyses (see Table 10.1). All correlations except LPP Cohesion and Bankson morphology were again significant at least at the .05 level. These findings pointed to the utility of the sum scoring approach over and above the method that established levels of language proficiency, at least for the purposes of research. Interestingly, the subscales on the LPP that tapped more semantic and pragmatic aspects of language, Content and Cohesion,

TABLE 10.1
Correlations Between LPP-R Sum Scores and Bankson Scores

LPP-R	Total	Semantic	Bankson Morphological	Syntactic
Subscale Sum Scores				
Reference	.87	.82	.74	.84
Content	.67	.57	.60	.77
Cohesion	.55	.56	.39	.54
Use	.85	.89	.59	.79
Form	.73	.69	.61	.72
Total Sum Score	.80	.79	.60	.49

proved to be less well correlated with the Bankson language scores, compared to the correlations derived with Reference, Form, and Use. This finding is not suprising, because, as discussed earlier, the Bankson taps more structural aspects of language, including morphological and syntactic rule generation and usage.

The LPP was also compared to another measure of language development, the Communication subscale from the Vineland Adaptive Behaviour Scales (Sparrow, Balla, & Cicchetti, 1984), in a sample of 39 hearing children ages 2 years to 6 years. In this case, a parent of the child served as the rater on the LPP, and also participated in an interview using the survey form of the Vineland. The Vineland was used as a comparison measure because both it and the LPP utilize a questionnaire format rather than relying on direct observation of language skills. Further, both measures were designed to tap language skills across a similar age range: the LPP from single-word utterances onwards and the Vineland from birth to 9 years of age or higher. The Vineland's strong emphasis on the social use of language skills also makes it a particularly viable measure for comparison with the LPP.

Both the Vineland and the LPP were highly correlated with age. Moreover, the Vineland correlated highly with the LPP overall level score ($r = .765$) and the LPP total sum score ($r = .754$). When examined more closely, the Vineland written and receptive subscale scores showed only weak correlation with the LPP scales, as expected: correlations between the written score and the individual LPP scales ranged from .520 to .558 and correlations between the receptive score and the LPP scores ranged from .488 to .530. In contrast, correlations between the Vineland expressive score and the LPP scores were significantly stronger; ranging from .76 to .813. This pattern of findings is important in that they corroborate the intended use of the LPP, to measure expressive language skills, and reinforce the concurrent validity of the LPP with single-language measures.

The LPP-2.   As a result of feedback from raters using the LPP-R in these two studies, several questions were reworded to facilitate interpretation and reduce ambiguity. In addition, the scale used to rate each question was revised to reflect a more graduated emergence of skills. Response choices were expanded from "yes," "no," and "unsure" on the earlier versions of the LPP to "past this level," "yes," "emerging," "not yet," and "unsure" on the newest version (LPP-2). Further, some questions were deleted if they were present across more than one subscale; as a result, the number of questions in each subscale became more equal.

An evaluation of concurrent and construct validity with the LPP-2 was conducted in 1993.[2] First, we studied a group of 104 hearing children,

[2]We wish to acknowledge the contributions of Susan Koehler and Catherine Beach to the completion of the studies with the LPP-2.

aged 2 to 7 years, with equivalent representation of males and females. Parents were given the LPP-2 to complete and were interviewed using the survey format of the Vineland Adaptive Behavior Scale—Communication subscale. Correlations were highly significant between LPP and Vineland scores in this sample. Table 10.2 summarizes the correlations found among the LPP-2 scores and the Vineland subscale scores. The strongest correlations were again noted when the Vineland Expressive domain subscore was compared to scores within the LPP-2. Correlations ranged from .66 to .76 when the sum score within each subscale was used in the analysis. Correlations were weaker although still significant when the Receptive domain subscore on the Vineland was compared to the the sum scores within each subscale; correlations ranged from .51 to .59. Correlations were found to be weaker still when the Written domain subscore was included in the analyses, although all correlations continued to be significant; correlations ranged from .36 to .51 for these analyses.

Construct validity was next examined in the LPP-2 by examing the structure of LPP subscale sum scores across ages in this larger sample of hearing children (Table 10.3). The results confirmed that there was a developmental trend to increasing levels being attained by progressively higher age groups for each of the subscales. Language proficiency increased at each age level, approaching the ceiling of each scale at the 6 year level. The Form subscale was found to have a lower ceiling than the other scales.

Finally, construct validity was examined from a different persective, using the expert opinions of three psycholinguistics/speech and language specialists.[3] Individual questions from the LPP-2 were printed on separate filing cards and given to these experts, randomly arranged within each subscale. The experts were asked to sort the questions into a developmental order within each subscale, starting with the lowest-level skill and

TABLE 10.2
Correlations of LPP-2 Scores with Vineland Adaptive Behavior Scores

LPP-2	Vineland Expressive	Vineland Receptive	Vineland Written
Subscale Scores			
Reference	.74	.59	.51
Content	.75	.57	.43
Cohesion	.66	.51	.42
Use	.76	.56	.48
Form	.71	.52	.36
Total Score	.79	.60	.49

---

[3]We are indebted to Dr. Joanna Blake, Dr. Philip Dale, and Dr. Donna Thal for donating their time to complete these rankings.

TABLE 10.3
Mean LPP-2 Scores Obtained Across Subscales and Age Groups

LPP-2 Subscales	Age in Years (N)				
(Maximum #)	2 (20)	3 (29)	4 (24)	5 (19)	6 (11)
Reference (22)	15.20	18.00	19.25	19.37	21.27
Content (24)	18.00	20.57	21.88	22.42	23.73
Use (26)	17.25	21.37	23.54	23.32	25.18
Cohesion (22)	12.70	17.63	18.13	18.79	20.82
Form (18)	14.60	17.13	17.13	17.47	17.91

progressing to higher-level skills. Questions that were thought to reflect a similar level of functioning were to be grouped together.

Discrepancy scores were computed for each question; that is, a score was computed for each rater that represented the degree to which the new question placement was discrepant from its original LPP placement level. Across the raters, there was 74% agreement with the original scale for developmental resortings for Form, 97% agreement for Content, 94% agreement for Reference, 88% agreement for Cohesion, and 69% agreement for Use. Kendall's Coefficient of Concordance (W), a nonparametric measure of relative agreement across the raters, was significant for all subscales; .87 for Form, .89 for Content, .92 for Reference, .68 for Cohesion, and .54 for Use. The experts had somewhat greater difficulty sorting items from the Use, Cohesion, and Form subscales, as revealed by a greater number of tied ranks within these subscales.

The results of these various investigations indicate good validity for the LPP-2 and its predecessors, both in terms of its ability to measure language proficiency as an emerging developmental skill and in terms of its comparability to other related criterion measures (Bankson and Vineland measures), both for hearing and deaf children.

Use in Research

The LPP was demonstrated in the aforementioned studies to be an effective and valid measure of language proficiency whose particular strength lies in the fact that it is not language-specific and hence has application with a variety of populations of children. This cross-language group applicability makes this measure especially useful within the context of research, particularly with children who use more than one language to communicate.

McKinnon (1987) examined the degree to which language proficiency may account for the emergence of memory-strategy use in a group of deaf children who were educated in a simultaneous-communication approach to language instruction. The LPP-1 was determined to be a useful predictor of strategy emergence within the deaf sample. Level of language proficiency was found to discriminate deaf children who produced a rehearsal strategy from those deaf children who did not do so, classifying correctly 81.25% of the children.

The LPP-R was used in a further project examining language proficiency, automatization (overlearning) of language skills, and use of spontaneous rehearsal strategies by children who were deaf (Bebko, et al., in press). The assumption in this study was that a degree of language proficiency was required before children would be able to use language-based strategies, such as rehearsal, effectively. Prior to achieving this level of proficiency, rehearsal would be too effortful to be used effectively. As predicted, the children's language proficiency, as measured by their scores on the LPP-R proved to be the strongest predictor of rehearsal use. Closer examination revealed that it was the children's performance on more advanced questions, in particular, that was the strongest determinant of whether a child was likely to be a rehearser. The authors concluded "it was the proficiency with which children used these particularly abstract ... language skills that was more discriminating in predicting their use of spontaneous rehearsal strategies" (Bebko et al., in press, p. xx). A parallel study using a different language measure with hearing children corroborated the predicitive importance of language skills for rehearsal use (Bebko, Kennedy, Metcalfe-Haggert, & Ricciuti, in preparation)

Clinical and Educational Applications

I. Communicative Competence and Academic Performance.
The role of language proficiency in the establishment of language-based academic skills is fundamental. It can be argued whether it is language proficiency in general, or English language proficiency in particular, that is related to emerging literacy skills in deaf children (e.g., Mayer & Wells, 1996). Therefore, it becomes ever more important to be able to evaluate deaf children's language abilities. The LPP-2, as has been well-established here, is a reliable and valid tool to evaluate the deaf child's overall language skills, and its particular strength lies in its ability to assess communicative competence irrespective of the modality or form this communication takes.

One particular advantage of the LPP-2 and its earlier forms is that it measures language across a range of pragmatic, semantic, and syntactic abilities. In other words, it taps the cross-sectional nature of the child's capabilities within the various subscales, as well as maintaining a perspective on the developmental nature of this language competence. There is a degree of overlap among some of the criteria across subscales due to the fact that the various components of the child's language skills are related to some of the same underlying cognitive–interpersonal skills. Therefore, if a child satisfies the criteria of one subscale at a particular level of development, it is highly likely he or she will also satisfy the criteria of the other subscales at that level. This was acknowledged by the authors of the KCPS as well (Francis et al., 1980). For this reason, the levels method for scoring the LPP may be more appropriate than the sum method when the measure is being used for certain clinical or educational purposes.

From a clinical perspective, if a lack of consistency across the various subscales is observed for a particular child, this finding may point to some relative weaknesses within that child's emerging language abilities. Because each subscale taps different but related roots of communicative competence, an asymmetry in development across the subscales may point to areas requiring some form of intervention by educators and language specialists. To illustrate, a child may achieve consistent levels of ability within all subscales on the LPP-2 except the Cohesion subscale, where his or her skills may be markedly lower. Educators may be able to pinpoint this deficiency and devise ways of teaching the child improved strategies for using language, from a pragmatic point of view, within social settings. For example, the child may be taught ways to connect utterances to those of their conversational partner, to be sensitive to the subtle signs that there is some confusion about what has been communicated, and to utilize techniques to repair miscommunications or request clarifications when needed.

Further applications of the LPP-2 may involve profiling the language abilities of a large and diverse sample of deaf children. This would allow for some examination of the prevalence of concordance or asymmetry in achievement across the various subscales. This profiling may then be examined in relation to the child's predominant language system and manner of coding communication, as well as in relation to other language-based abilities like literacy, problem-solving, or strategy usage.

II. *Communicative Competence and Mental Health.* Social and behavioral problems have been identified at rates of up to 5 times greater among deaf compared to hearing children (Schlesinger & Meadow, 1972). Language/communication difficulties, among other potential difficulties, including child-rearing environment, cognitive, personality, and immaturity difficulties, have been linked to adjustment problems in deaf children (Greenberg & Kusche, 1988; Reivich & Rothrock, 1972).

White (1981) found that personal adjustment in deaf children is positively associated with their understanding of affective vocabulary.

Harris (1978) and Levine and Wagner (1974) reported that the communication ability of deaf children was related to the degree of impulsivity versus self-control observed. Further, Greenberg and Kusche (1988) summarized three additional areas in which poor language skills impact on the deaf child: difficulty in establishing secure, trusting relationships, which may lead to feelings of powerlessness and decreased self-efficacy; difficulty learning role-appropriate behaviours and values; and difficulty learning the dynamics of their social world (e.g., cultural and subcultural differences). Greenberg and Kusche (1988) noted, "these [findings] should alert us to the crucial importance of communicative competence for developing self-control, self-esteem, identification, and an understanding of one's environment" (p. 3).

Given the important role played by language in both school-related skills and more general psychosocial adjustment, and the impact of difficulties in school achievement on adjustment (e.g., self-worth), the LPP-2 may prove of benefit in identifying deaf children with language difficulties, and, thus, increased risk for difficulties in school and/or longer-term mental-health problems.

SUMMARY

In this chapter, we review the development, validation, and application of the LPP, a measure of language proficiency that has been developed for use with deaf children. The advantages of the LPP over other standardly available measures of language proficiency are multifold: The measure is capable of evaluating language competency that is non-language specific; the measure taps into diverse aspects of language competency, including pragmatic and semantic skills; the measure is easily administered and scored by parents and teachers; and it does not require prior training on the part of the rater.

REFERENCES

Bankson, N. (1977). *Bankson language screening test.* Austin, TX: Pro-Ed.
Bates, E. (1976). *Language in context: The acquisition of pragmatics.* New York: Academic Press.
Bebko, J. (1979). Can recall differences among children be attributed to rehearsal effects? *Canadian Journal of Psychology, 33,* 96–105.
Bebko, J. (1984). Memory and rehearsal characteristics of profoundly deaf children. *Journal of Experimental Child Psychology, 38,* 415–428.
Bebko, J., Bell, M., Metcalfe-Haggert, A., & McKinnon, E. (in press). Language proficiency and the prediction of spontaneous rehearsal in children who are deaf. *Journal of Experimental Child Psychology.*

Bebko, J., Kennedy, C., Metcalfe-Haggert, A., & Ricciuti, C. (in preparation). *Language proficiency and metacognition as predictors of spontaneous rehearsal in children.*

Bebko, J., & McKinnon, E. (1987). *The language proficiency profile.* Unpublished document. York University, Department of Psychology, North York, Ontario, Canada.

Bebko, J., & McKinnon, E. (1990). The language experience of deaf children: Its relation to spontaneous rehearsal in a memory task. *Child Development, 61,* 1744–1752.

Bebko, J., & Metcalfe-Haggert, A. (1997). Deafness, language skills and rehearsal: A model for the development of a memory strategy. *Journal of Deaf Studies and Deaf Education, 2,* 131–139.

Bellugi, U., Klima, E., & Poizner, H. (1988). Sign language and the brain. In F. Plum (Ed.), *Language, communication and the brain.* (pp.). New York: Raven Press.

Bellugi, U., Poizner, H., & Klima, E. (1989). Language, modality and the brain. *Trends in Neurosciences, 12,* 380–388.

Bloom, L., & Lahey, M. (1978) *Language development and language disorders.* New York: Wiley. Caccamise, F., & Newell, W., January (1986). *Assessing sign communication skills via interview techniques.* Paper presented at the fourth National Symposium on Sign Language Research and Teaching. Silver Spring, MO.

Caccamise, F., Newell, W., & Mitchell-Caccamise, M. (1983). Use of the Sign Language Proficiency Interview for assessing the sign communicative competence of Louisiana School for the Deaf dormitory counselor applicants. *Journal of the Academy of Rehabilitative Audiology, 16,* 283–304.

Francis, J., Garner, D., & Harvey, J. (1980). *KCPS: A pragmatic approach to language for teachers of deaf children.* Washington: KDES, Gallaudet University.

Fraser, C., Bellugi, U., & Brown, R. (1963). Control of grammar in imitation, comprehension and production. *Journal of Verbal Learning and Verbal Behavior, 2,* 121–135.

Greenberg, M., & Kusche, C. (1988). *Promoting social competence in deaf children: The PATHS project.* Final report to the William T. Grant Foundation. Department of Psychology, University of Washington, Seattle, Washington.

Harris, R. (1978). The relationship of impulse control to parent hearing status, manual communication, and academic achievement in deaf children. *American Annals of the Deaf, 123,* 52–67.

Hoemann, H., & Gonter-Gaustad, M. (1990, July/August). *Assessing deaf children's bilingual competence.* Paper presented at the International Congress on Education of the Deaf, Rochester, NY.

Lee, L. (1974). *Developmental sentence analysis: A grammatical assessment procedure for speech and language clinicians.* Evanston, IL: Northwestern University Press.

Levine, E., & Wagner, G. (1974). Personality patterns of deaf persons. *Perceptual and Motor Skills,* (Monograph Supplement 4–V39).

Longhurst, T., & Grubb, J. (1974). A comparison of language samples collected in four situations. *Language, Speech and Hearing Services in the Schools, 5(2),* 71–78.

Mayer, C., & Wells, G. (1996). Can the linguistic interdependence theory support a bilingual–bicultural model of literacy education for deaf students? *Journal of Deaf Studies and Deaf Education, 1,* 93–107.

Meadow, K. (1978). The "natural history" of a research project. In L. Liben (Ed.), *Deaf children: Developmental perspectives* (pp. 21–40). New York: Academic Press.

McKinnon, E. (1987). *An investigation of language experience and proficiency in deaf children: Its relationship to language mediation in a memory task.* Unpublished master's thesis, York University, North York, Ontario, Canada.

Miller, J. (1973). Sentence imitation in preschool children. *Language, Speech and Hearing Services in the Schools, 16,* 1–14.

Moog, J., & Geers, A. (1979). *Grammatical analysis of elicited language.* St. Louis, MO: Central Institute for the Deaf.
Newell, W., Caccamise, F., Boardman, K., & Holcomb, B. (1983). Adaptation of the Language Proficiency Interview (LPI) for assessing sign language competence. *Sign Language Studies, 41,* 311–352.
Newport, E., & Meier, R. (1986). The acquisition of American Sign Language. In D.I. Slobin (Ed.), *The crosslinguistic study of language acquisition, volume 1: The data* (pp. 881–938). Hillsdale, NJ: Lawrence Erlbaum Associates.
Petitto, L., & Bellugi, U. (1988). Spatial cognition and brain organization: Clues from the acquisition of a language in space. In J. Stiles-Davis, M. Kritchevsky and U. Bellugi (Eds.), *Spatial cognition: Brain bases and development* (pp. 299–326). Hillsdale, NJ: Lawrence Erlbaum Associates.
Printz, P., & Strong, M. (1994). *A test of ASL.* Unpublished manuscript. San Francisco State University, California Research Institute.
Reivich, R., & Rothrock, I. (1972). Behavior problems of deaf children and adolescents: A factor-analytic study. *Journal of Speech and Hearing Research, 15,* 93–104.
Schlesinger, H., & Meadow, K. (1972). *Sound and sign.* Berkeley: University of California Press.
Sparrow, S., Balla, D., & Cicchetti, D. (1984). *Vineland Adaptive Behaviour Scales.* Circle Pines, MN: American Guidance Services.
Strong, M., & Prinz, P. (1997). A study of the relationship between American Sign Language and English literacy. *Journal of Deaf Studies and Deaf Education, 2,* 37–46.
Thompson, M., Biro, P., Vethivelu, S., Pious, C., & Hatfield, N. (1987). *Language assessment of hearing-impaired school age children.* Seattle: University of Washington Press.
White, F. (1981). *Affective vocabulary and personal adjustment of deaf and hearing adolescent populations.* Unpublished doctoral dissertation, East Texas State University.

11

Development and Use of a Conversational Proficiency Interview With Deaf Adolescents

C. Tane Akamatsu
Toronto Board of Education

Carol Musselman
Ontario Institute for Studies in Education

Explorations of deaf students' language and communication development have either focused on very early language and communication development (Moores, 1996), or English grammatical development during school-age years (McAnally, Rose, & Quigley, 1987; Moores, 1996). Very few studies have looked at the quality of the face-to-face communication that deaf students possess or have access to in spoken English (Wood, Wood, Griffiths, & Howarth, 1986), simultaneous communication (SC; Akamatsu & Stewart, 1992), and American Sign Language (ASL). In this chapter, we describe the development and use of a Conversational Proficiency Interview that we used for research purposes, and suggest clinical and educational uses for this interview.

The Role of Language in an Overall Conception of Intelligence: Conceptual Framework

Within a social constructivist framework, an examination of the quality of face-to-face communication is very important because it is in interaction between and among people that cognitive processes are born, whether the child is deaf or hearing (Trevarthen, 1979; Vygotsky, 1978, 1987; Wertsch, 1979, 1985, 1991; Wood, Wood, Griffiths, & Howarth, 1986). According to Vygotsky, higher-order cognitive functions appear at two levels: first on the intermental plane, or between individuals, and later in the intramental plane, or within an individual. This means that the necessary skills for thinking using language, and indeed any culture's ways of mediating experience, can be found in the kinds of dialogue in which students are engaged, both inside and outside the classroom (Halliday, 1975, 1993; Wells, 1986). Face-to-face communication allows for the establishment of intersubjectivity (Rommetveit, 1985, Trevarthen, 1979), contextualization of language, and for the use of paralinguistic features such as pointing, facial expression, use of real world objects, vocal modulation, and such. It is in this arena that language development (and by extension cognitive development) begins (Nelson, 1996; Wertsch, 1985). These ideas are elaborated next.

Igniting the Linguistic and Cognitive Cycle

In the usual case, in which a child's language and communication needs can be met by people in the environment, language and cognition eventually intertwine to the extent that language becomes thoughtful and cognition verbal. This is not to say that all forms of cognition are verbal, but that verbal forms of cognition are enabled. The interrelation of language and cognition allows for language to be used not just communicatively, or referentially, but also reflectively, and for cognition to be used not just for nonverbal problem solving but for verbal problem solving as well.

In a social constructivist framework, learning is viewed as a *transactional* process, with the child and a more knowledgeable *other* coconstructing knowledge in an interactive partnership. The mastery of semiotic systems, including language, is believed to transform an individual's existing (i.e., natural) forms of mental functioning (e.g., arousal, attention) into higher psychological processes (e.g., controlled attention, intentional memory, logical thinking). Dialogue, a unique form of linguistic collaboration, provides children with an initial point of entry into many of the concepts and strategies found in a culture.

The psychological *space* in which language and cognition develop was characterized by Harre (1986) along two orthogonal but related dimensions: The public-to-private and the individual-to-social, which exist over time. Expanding on the notion that cognition has its origins in interpersonal interaction, Vygotsky suggested that the publicly observable social dialogue that occurs in day-to-day life contains the necessary raw material from which a child begins to build a conceptual representation, not only of the world but of the meaning systems that become the tools for higher-level thinking. Bakhtin (1986) discussed the *multivoicedness* that characterizes the the dialogic nature of interactions by insisting that "meaning can come into existence only when two or more voices come into contact: when the voice of a listener responds to the voice of a speaker" (Wertsch, 1991, p. 52). An important factor in individuals' appropriation of social speech into the private world is *intersubjectivity*. Rommetveit (1985) characterized intersubjectivity as the agreement of two individuals on a given task, and the awareness that such an agreement has been reached. Each individual's subjectivity or subjective participation in activity is therefore influenced by the others.

Individuals eventually appropriate, in like form, the observable, public, social speech[1] for their own use. Vygotsky (1987) termed the kind of speech used for this appropriation *egocentric speech* to reflect the beginnings of intramental functioning. The distinction between social and egocentric speech typically begins around 3 or 4 years of age (Vygotksy, 1987). At this point, language begins to be used as a cognitive as well as an interactive tool. Initially this egocentric speech resembles the public language because it is still not clearly dissociated from its earlier social function. Indeed, egocentric speech was viewed by Wertsch & Stone (1985) as the "bridge between external interpsychological functioning and internal intrapsychological functioning" (p. 172). Unlike Piaget, who believed that children are socialized out of using egocentric speech, Vygotsky believed that egocentric speech goes underground and transforms into an intramental psychological tool for verbal thought.

Assuming adequate intersubjective interaction has taken place, the language and associated ways of thinking are assimilated and transformed into the individual, idiosyncratic, unobservable representation that Vygotsky termed *inner speech*. It is this inner speech that forms the basis for the cognitive tools necessary for self-regulated thinking, and the eventual making public of what was formerly private.

---

[1]Vygotsky referred to this as social speech. Following Vygotsky's convention, "speech" refers to language *in action*, rather than the oral form of language. Thus, "speech" can refer to signed language as well as spoken language. Throughtout this chapter, references to "social speech," "egocentric speech," and "inner speech" have this connotation in mind.

Individuals who have developed enough inner speech[2] (how much is enough is open to debate) to ignite the cognitive cycle and use it for regulated thought become able to make public the kinds of linguistic and/or cognitive behaviors that they as individuals are able to generate on their own. Thus, the transformation from social to individual and back to social language is possible through inner speech. Social language generated by an individual may then be taken up in interactive dialogue. From such a perspective, higher-level cognitive and metacognitive strategies are seen to be born of an individual's interactions with other members of one's culture, within the contexts of symbolically mediated, goal-oriented activity.

Vygotsky (1978) termed the "distance between the actual developmental level as determined by independent problem solving and the level of potential development as determined through problem solving under adult guidance or in collaboration with more capable peers" the "zone of proximal development." (p. 86) The study of the difference between assisted and unassisted performance on a given task is important because it is through assisted performance, especially linguistically mediated performance, that learning occurs.

In studying the development of an individual within a sociocultural context, Vygotsky described four types of development: phylogenesis (development of the species), cultural history (development as a result of cultural or historic changes in a society), ontogenesis (development of an individual over a lifespan), microgenesis (development over a very short time span). For the purposes of this chapter, ontogenesis and microgenesis are important. Ontogenesis results in a qualitative transformation caused by an individual's use of cultural–historical tools, of which language is an example. Ways of thinking are culturally bound, as well. Therefore, the kinds of language and social instantiations of language are particularly important to study. Microgenesis refers to learning that happens within a very short time frame, for example, within a lesson, a conversation, or even in a single interchange. A fine-grained analysis of such interactions can reveal zones of proximal development and instances of microgenetic development.

The Special Case of Deaf Children

Most deaf children live in hearing families. From the time of birth (and possibly before), members of the family, especially the primary caregiver,

---

[2]The term *inner speech* in the context of deaf individuals, particularly signing deaf individuals, refers to the idiosyncratic, verbal thought that individuals use for themselves. The nature of the inner speech is still an open question (e.g., Conrad, 1979; Cook & Harrison, 1995; Mayer & Wells, 1996).

were likely unaware of the child's deafness. Assuming they were interacting with a hearing child, interaction behaviors were geared to a child who could hear, including using voice and spoken language. The kinds and amount of tactile and visual stimulation that would be appropriate for a deaf child would not have been used. Thus, the deaf child would have found itself in a situation in which important knowledgeable others could not respond initially in communicatively appropriate ways (reviewed in Marschark, 1993a).

The establishment of intersubjectivity between a hearing caregiver and deaf child, *especially when the caregiver is unaware that the child is deaf*, is likely to be difficult. Yet, without intersubjectivity, the participants in any goal-oriented, mediated activity may be working at cross-purposes without being aware. The normal interaction patterns that would lead to intersubjectivity would not be present to the extent that they might be with deaf parents, who would presumably interact with a deaf child in ways appropriate to *them*, and by extension to the deaf child. Therefore, the mechanisms by which cognition becomes verbal are thwarted at the very beginning by the deaf child not having accessible, comprehensible interaction, communication, and eventually language. Similarly, the interactions through which language is even acquired are not suited to the communicative needs of the child. Bonkowski, Gavelek, and Akamatsu (1991) pointed out that a failure to understand the communicative contexts in which deaf children find themselves, and the resulting misfit between deaf children and hearing (especially nonsigning) adults, can result in the prevention of the development of intersubjectivity necessary for engaging successfully in public, social language.

The extent to which spoken language is accessible to deaf children is questionable. Furthermore, although signed language may indeed be visually accessible, the quality and quantity of signed language that deaf children receive is far less than the spoken language in which normally hearing children are bathed. The opportunities to engage in true dialogue are restricted severely in most deaf children. Even deaf children who are fortunate enough to be born into signing families may receive less linguistic exposure relative to hearing children *simply because language must occur in the child's visual field*. Audition, being omnidirectional, combined with vision, provides hearing children with a different multisensory experience with which to collect data about the world.

"Dialogue provides a rich opportunity for participants to reflect upon and revise thoughts within temporarily shared realities" (Bonkowski, Gavelek, & Akamatsu, 1991, p. 189). However, the problem of mediating meaning and learning is especially acute in deaf children because of the difficulties of establishing the necessary inner speech that forms the basis

270 AKAMATSU AND MUSSELMAN

for higher-level cognition and verbal thought (Bernstein & Finnegan, 1983; Conrad, 1979; Jamieson, 1995; Kaiser-Grodecka & Cieszynska, 1991; Webster, 1986; Wood, Wood, Griffiths, & Howarth, 1986). This state of affairs can result in potentially serious cognitive repercussions affecting both language and school-based learning (cf. Curtiss, 1977; Fischer, in press) unless specific interventions are undertaken.

The introduction of *Total Communication* programs, and especially the enactment of total communication as simultaneous speech and sign (SC) was an attempt to bridge the gap between the spoken language and the visual language needs of severe to profoundly deaf children. Research has shown, however, that there has been limited success of such programs in upgrading the academic achievement of the very children the programs were designed to serve (Moores, 1996). A social constructivist perspective suggests that visible language is not enough to overcome the communicative and cognitive needs of these children. Rather, engagement in certain kinds of dialogue would seem to be necessary to enable the children to acquire higher-level cognitive functioning. We also need assessment instruments that tap that dialogic capability.

Since the acceptance of signing into many programs for deaf students, it is now high time to look at the attendant verbal thought development and processes in deaf students. Marschark (1993b) pointed out that "it does not seem to be of any service to the deaf population to ignore the possible role of language skills, manual or oral, in the ability to deal effectively with problem-solving in the real world" (p. 136). We are only now beginning to develop a body of research that goes explicitly beyond the nonverbal thought processes of deaf individuals, and taps the verbal processes. Bonkowski, Gavelek, and Akamatsu (1991) reiterated Vygotsky's call for both an ontogenetic and microgenetic analysis of language and cognitive development in deaf children. The interaction between language and cognition is very obvious, particularly when observing the linguistic and cognitive abilities of deaf teenagers. Therefore, for a deaf child, an ontogenetic approach to development must take into account factors such as the age at which the deafness occurred and was discovered, modes of communication used by the caregivers before and after diagnosis, types of educational programs a child attended, the number of people with whom the child has regular contact, the language(s) to which the child has been exposed, the skills of the adults at providing the various languages, and their match with the child's communicative needs.

Static forms of assessment, which sample behavior and knowledge at a particular point in time, have been used to assess ontogenetic development by sampling behaviors and abilities at various points in time, for example, at different ages of an individual's life. However, static forms of assessment do not take into account opportunity for the individual to stretch, or to demonstrate proximal development. Dynamic assessments, in which more capable others lead the child to maximal performance, allow for comparisons of assisted and unassisted performance, as well as for analyses of what facilitates performance, under what conditions. Microgenetic development may be observed under dynamic assessment conditions. The conversational proficiency interview format allows us to explore the development of language and communication in a dynamic format, allowing for students' maximum potential while maintaining the integrity of the language and communication mode being tested.

Modality Issues in Conversation With Deaf Partners

Because we are interested in how deaf adolescents communicate, and particularly how they use language, we believe that it is important to assess how well they function in both American Sign Language (ASL) and English. Yet, ASL and English are different languages, which evolved in different sensory modalities. Furthermore, most deaf students are instructed via the simultaneous use of speech and sign, with varying degrees of correspondence to both ASL and English. Therefore, it was important to address conversational proficiency in two languages (ASL and English) and three modalities (sign only, speech only, simultaneous sign and speech).

Naturally, the more hearing one has, the easier it is to learn spoken language. Hearing is the primary modality through which spoken language is learned, but for deaf students, vision takes over as the primary modality for language learning. The most immediate implication of this sensory fact is that reception of *spoken* language must be supplemented visually, through speechreading, cued speech, or sign support. Therefore, hard-of-hearing students can be expected to acquire spoken language through hearing (and good supplemental training), and signed language through vision. On the other hand, deaf students cannot be expected to acquire spoken language through hearing alone, but may learn some aspects of speech through the visual modality. They can, of course, be expected to learn signed language through the visual modality.

Both English and ASL in their primary forms are face-to-face languages, or languages used in interaction. As such, each has as much potential to ignite cognitive and linguistic development as does any other language. However, there are some important differences between ASL and English.

Skillful signers of ASL can be expected to be familiar with the various genres of ASL literature (e.g., ABC and number stories, "origin" stories, poetry; reviewed in Christie & Wilkins, 1997). This literature is akin to an *oral* tradition, in that it uses and elaborates on mechanisms found within the language to create specialized uses such as ASL poetry, story-telling, and sign-mime for dramatic effect. ASL literature is primarily designed for an audience immediate in both time and space, to be delivered "live." Videotechnology has allowed some decontextualization of the literature in much the same way that audiotaping allowed oral, nonwritten, languages to be decontextualized. However, the face-to-face nature of such literatures are constrained by the same cognitive factors (attention, memory, learning) that constrain face-to-face communication. There is no external memory in the form of a written text *in that language*. As in many languages with rich oral traditions, ASL has a well-developed storytelling style, and its community of users considers skilled storytelling a hallmark of linguistic ability. Skill in storytelling, and a dramatic genre known as *sign-mime*, add a dramatic dimension to the usual face-to-face interaction.

English in its primary form is an auditory–oral language. It is also important to investigate the extent to which deaf students are capable of functioning in face-to-face English, whether this English is spoken or signed. There is still much controversy about the status of signing in English as a language. However, if, as is the case for hearing students, interaction in English forms the basis for internalizing English for use as a means of verbal thought in English, then whether this face-to-face English occurs in speech alone or through some form of English-based signing is less important than if it occurs at all. Another factor in becoming proficient in English is the development of literacy skills in English, because mastery of literate genres can influence some kinds of face-to-face interaction in its users (Olson, 1977; Olson & Torrance, 1991).

This is not to imply that ASL is an inferior language, nor that ASL users cannot think in complex or abstract ways. Rather, within a social–constructivist framework, it is important to remember that culturally afforded thinking tools also happen with the acquisition of various forms of language within and across languages. Therefore, it became important in developing this measure that hallmarks of strong skill in ASL be afforded the same status that hallmarks of strong skill in English provide.

The Social Context of Simultaneous Communication: Languages in Contact

Simultaneous communication is fundamentally an educational phenomenon, the goal of which is to enhance the ability of deaf students to understand and produce English. Although it is generally agreed that ASL, as a visual–gestural language, cannot be conveyed simultaneously with spoken English, there are aspects of ASL that are a part of SC (Akamatsu & Stewart, in press; Stewart, Akamatsu, & Bonkowski, 1990). In particular, ASL lexicon figures heavily in the use of SC. ASL grammatical markers such as facial expressions, eye-gazing, and body movements are also found in the SC of people who are proficient in ASL (Newell, Stinson, Castle, Mallery-Ruganis, & Holcomb, 1990). Moreover, Maxwell and Doyle (1996) found that the mixing of ASL and English served to meet the *communication* goals of the deaf and hearing interlocutors of a school for the deaf. What is unique about SC is the variability in the extent to which the auditory and visual modalities are used (Akamatsu & Stewart, in press; Maxwell, 1990; Maxwell, Bernstein, & Maer, 1991; Maxwell & Doyle, 1996; Stewart, Akamatsu, & Bonkowski, 1990).

Because we were studying the communication practices of students in the context of their schools, it was important to examine their use of SC. As we stated earlier, the linguistic status of SC is ambiguous. On one hand, the presence of running speech and resulting English word order combined with various levels of incorporation of English grammatical morphemes, ASL spatial grammar, and largely ASL lexicon suggest that SC may, for its users, be a form of relexicalized English. On the other hand, in their comparison of ASL and contact signing, Lucas and Valli (1990, 1992) suggested that contact signing (without audible speech but with *English-like mouthing in basic English word order*) may be a specialized register of ASL.

In any event, we would expect that students who are strong users of either ASL or spoken English (or both) should also be strong users of SC. There is no research evidence that the proficient use of SC is not suitable for the communicative needs of deaf students, although early SC research tended to focus on the difficulty of manually encoding many of the invented English grammatical morphemes (e.g., Marmor & Petitto, 1979). Indeed, because of its affinity to both English and ASL, as well as its historical[3] use in the schools, we would expect SC to be the students' strongest modality, linguistic status notwithstanding.

DEVELOPING THE CONVERSATIONAL PROFICIENCY INTERVIEW

The basis of our conversational proficiency is the foreign language interview used by the U.S. Foreign Service (Jones, 1979). This foreign language

---

[3]Historical in the sense that students in total communication classrooms were exposed to SC throughout their educational careers.

interview was adapted for use with ASL by Caccamise and Newell at the National Technical Institute for the Deaf (Newell, Caccamise, Boardman, & Holcomb, 1983) and is currently the most widely used form of ASL assessment in the form of the Sign Communication Proficiency Interview (SCPI). Other studies of deaf adolescents showed that with adaptation, the SCPI is a viable tool for assessing language and communication proficiency in this population (Johnson, nd). We further adapted the SCPI by emphasizing *conversational appropriateness* over specific linguistic purity. This interview builds on similar work by Lou, Fischer, and Woodward (1987), who developed a measure of communicative competence that could be used with any deaf person, regardless of the individual's preferred mode of communication or preferred language. Lou, Fischer, and Woodward attempted to use a single conversational interview with a scoring system that rated communicative competence, linguistic competence, and organizational ability. They claimed that their interview was language independent because they found no significant differences among the abilities in participants with differing language and communication mode preferences.

Guiding Principles for Development
of the Interview

We wanted this interview to tap a variety of linguistic and pragmatic functions. Therefore, we attempted to sample vocabulary breadth and depth, simple and complex syntactic structures, specific linguistic functions present in the languages being tested (e.g., word order, subject–verb agreement, tense marking in English; classifier use, three-dimensional grammar, appropriate use of nonmanual markers in ASL; a rule-governed combination of the two in SC). We also sampled a variety of pragmatic functions, including naming and referring, establishing and maintaining stable relationships for logical thought, planning, describing, explaining, offering opinion, justifying opinion, creating hypotheses, and situating oneself in a sociocultural context. These functions were suggested as functions that language serves in the development of cognition (e.g., Nelson, 1996).

The interview itself uses a highly structured, yet flexible protocol. Because an interview format is used, the assessment can be characterized as *dynamic* in the sense that it provides opportunities for examinees to enhance their performance by building on the linguistic and cognitive opportunities provided by the examiner. The open-ended nature of the questions allows the examinee freedom of expression, ranging from gestures and one-word utterances through extended, lengthy, and detailed explanations. Thus, responses to a seemingly simple question such as "How do you feel about having deaf teachers?" could range from simple, unelaborated answers such as "It's okay," to highly detailed comparisons and contrasts between deaf and hearing teachers, to a lengthy discussion about what a school with exclusively deaf teachers might be like. Therefore, the students are given the opportunity to demonstrate maximal competence in language and cognition simultaneously.

In cases where an individual is very competent in Language A and only minimally competent in Language B, we would expect that some aspect of that person's cognitive competence would be reflected through Language A but not Language B. Of concern would be students who demonstrate marginal competence in both Languages A and B. It would be these students who lack the tools and the interaction with which to develop and manipulate their thinking.

USING THE CONVERSATIONAL PROFICIENCY INTERVIEW

Participants

As part of a larger study on psychosocial development of deaf adolescents, 69 students, ages 14 to 19 ($\bar{x}$ = 6.8 years) were interviewed in three modalities (speech only, simultaneous speech and sign, and sign only) and two languages (English and ASL). These students were recruited from across the province of Ontario, and attended school in a variety of settings, ranging from fully mainstreamed in local schools, to self-contained classrooms in residential schools for the deaf. The average unaided hearing thresholds of the students was 98.0 dB. Of this group, 16 had primarily attended oral–hearing programs since childhood. An additional 7 were deaf children of deaf parents. The students were enrolled in a variety of programs, including self-contained oral classes, self-contained total communication classes, both with partial or full integration, with and without sign language interpreters. The self-contained classes were located in schools for deaf students as well as in local public high schools. Thus, the full range of educational options was represented. Because males were more reluctant to participate, two thirds of the sample was female. As a group, the students achieved an average performance IQ (PIQ) of 98.3 (SD = 13.7), as measured on the Wechsler Intelligence Scales for Children–Third Edition (WISC-III, Wechsler, 1991) for students under 16, and the Wechsler Adult Intelligence Scales–Revised (WAIS-R, Wechsler, 1981) for students 16 and older. This demonstrated that the students had nonverbal abilities within the *average* range, compared to hearing students. These data are not surprising, and replicated previous findings (Blennerhassett, 1987; Blennerhassett, Moores, Hannah, & Woolard, 1988; Braden, 1984, 1985), and suggest that these students are not unusual in this respect.

Procedures

Using the adapted conversational proficiency interview, each student was assessed in three communication conditions: spoken English (Oral condition), simultaneous communication (SC condition), and ASL (ASL condition). All of the interviews were videotaped for later analysis using two cameras, one trained on the interviewer and the other trained on the interviewee. The resulting images were recorded using split-screen technology so that both interlocutors could be seen simultaneously.

Each interview consisted of an introduction phase, during which the interviewer introduced herself, got the student to introduce him or herself, and explained the purpose of the interview. Because the interviews were conducted in the student's preferred mode of communication, we were assured first that they understood the task by the third (least-favored mode) interview, and were able at least to introduce themselves to the interviewer.

Interviewers

The spoken English assessments were conducted by a hearing anthropologist with a teaching background, yet who knew no sign language. She was not familiar with deaf speech at the outset of the project, although she did become somewhat familiar with it by the end of the project. Her increasing familiarity with deaf speech did not seem to affect the administration of the interviews over time. The SC assessments were conducted by a certified interpreter who was a child of deaf parents. This interviewer was capable of code-switching between SC, contact sign, and ASL. However, she maintained running speech most of the time, and only occasionally signed an ASL idiomatic expression without voice. She always backed up such an expression with an English translation, signed in SC. The ASL assessments were conducted by a culturally Deaf research assistant who had signed since childhood, and who was a graduate of Gallaudet University. This interviewer was also an excellent speechreader. In spite of the fact that the ASL interviewer could probably have interacted with most of the oral students in speech, she maintained a deaf, nonspeaking persona throughout the ASL interviews. Thus, the SC and

ASL interviews were conducted by individuals bilingual in both ASL and English, but who maintained different communication styles for the purpose of administering the interview.

Conditions of the Interviews

Spoken English was assessed through speech only (Oral condition), and American Sign Language (ASL condition) through sign only. The simultaneous communication condition was assessed through a combination of simultaneous speech and sign. The signing used was a natural blend of ASL and a few English sign system signs, in English word order, much like the kind of signing found in contact sign (Lucas & Valli, 1992). The interviewer occasionally used mouthings and other oral gestures found in ASL (e.g., bilabial raspberry, "PAH"), but generally used spoken English in the oral channel. We allowed the signing interviewers some flexibility in using both ASL and signed English signs, depending on the skills of the students and the topics discussed, thereby creating a more ecologically valid communicative situation. All participants, including the interviewers, were allowed to use paper and pencil if they so requested when communication broke down.

Each student participated in three interviews, one for each communication condition. The purpose of this was to engage the students in communication conditions in which they might actually find themselves. Most of the students came from hearing families and had to communicate with members of the hearing world who do not sign (Oral condition). Most of the students were educated in Total Communication classrooms where simultaneous speech and sign were used (SC condition). Most of the students sign among themselves, purportedly in ASL (ASL condition).

Prior to the interview, each student had been engaged in conversation about his or her preferred mode of communication. They were told that we were interested in their development, and especially in their communication development. They were told they would be communicating with different types of people. The first interview was conducted in the student's preferred mode of communciation. The second interview was conducted in the students' next favored mode of communication, followed by the least preferred mode. Each student was assessed in order from most-preferred to least-preferred mode over a period of several weeks. This allowed the students to become familiar with the task, so that by the time they entered the condition in which they would experience the greatest difficulty, they would not be hindered by a lack of understanding of the expectations of the interview. The tone of the interview was conversational throughout, with the interviewer following the students' topics of interest. By doing this, we anticipated obtaining the best sample of the student's language and communicative abilities in each of the three conditions.

During each interview, students were told that the purpose of the interview was to get to know the students and to find out how they communicated best across a variety of communication modalities. They were encouraged to use their "best speech/ASL/communication," depending on the interview condition. In the first interview, they received the most explicit explanation, and were told that in subsequent interviews, they would have a similar conversation in their next preferred modality. For example, an orally skilled student would be told in the Oral condition that the next interview would be in both speech and sign, and the third interview would be only in sign. In subsequent interviews, the students were reminded of the requirements of the interview and in spite of knowing that it was a difficult situation, they were cooperative.

Scoring

Holistic Rating of the Interviews. The protocols were rated initially by using holistic rating scales, which simultaneously take into consideration both linguistic and cognitive sophistication. In addition to the categories suggested by Newell et al. (1983), we added two new categories, "Adaptive" and "Adaptive+" to the rating scale. These categories reflected the abilities of students who managed to keep a rudimentary conversation going without using the target language of the interview, but by using other strategies such as gesture, vocalizations, and pantomime. The final rating scale had 11 points, ranging from "no functional communication" to "Advanced+". For ease of statistical analysis, each rating level was assigned a numerical value from 0 (no functional communication) to 5.5 (Advanced+; definitions of these skills for each language are presented in Appendix A).

Each interviewer rated each interview in which she participated. In addition, 20% of the interviews in each modality were rated by a second person. The second rater for the Oral interviewers was a hearing researcher who had basic signing skills and was familiar with deaf speech. The second rater for the SC condition was a hearing researcher who had fluent ASL skills and worked with school-age deaf children. The second rater for the ASL condition was the interviewer for the SC condition. All raters participated in the development of the CPI, and were very familiar with the rating system. Given the nature of the data, the ratings were subjective. Nevertheless, the interrater reliability was .91 for the oral condition, .72 for SC, and .98 for ASL. Although the interrater reliability is rather high for all conditions, the lower rate for the SC condition is probably due to the more varied form of communication that existed in this condition. The students were classified as strong, developing, and weak in each modality condition. It is important to understand that the terms *strong* and *weak* refer to the students' performances under enabling vs. disabling conditions. That is, the ASL condition would be an enabling condition for a strong ASL user, but a disabling condition for a novice signer. Using the definitions of the rating scale, the *strong* groups were comprised of students who were rated from "Advanced" to "Advanced+." The *developing* groups were made up of those students who were rated from "Survival" to "Intermediate+." Students in the *weak* groups were rated from "No functional skills" to "Novice+." Thus, each student had a language–communication profile (e.g., weak oral, strong SC, developing ASL).

Detailed Examination of the Interviews

Because we were interested in the relationship between language proficiency and cognitive functioning within that language, we examined the performances of the students who were rated as Strong Oral, Strong ASL, Weak Oral, and Weak ASL. The performances of 41 individuals were studied (most of the strong oral students were also in the weak ASL category; a few of the strong ASL students were in the weak oral category). We did not do a detailed examination of the SC protocols, because in that condition, students could potentially use elements of both English and ASL, making it difficult to ascertain which language contributed when to communicative and/or cognitive functioning. Future examination of the relationship between performance on the SC condition and the stronger language of individual students might shed light on how specific language knowledge contributes to performance in SC.

We developed a detailed matrix comprising various linguistic and cognitive skills (see Appendix B). Using this detailed matrix, we looked for the component skills that allowed strong performance, or conversely, that limited performance on the CPI conditions. Because we were dealing not only in two languages and cultures but also in two modalities, there were certain skills that were important in some modalities that were unimportant in others. For example, eye contact has different functions and conveys different meanings in ASL and English. Storytelling is more central to illustrate points in ASL than in English. Vocabulary size (i.e., different words) is a mark of English proficiency; classifier usage is a mark of ASL proficiency. Yet, both languages share the potential for one to hypothesize, support opinion, negotiate, and tailor one's language to the audience. Therefore, the detailed rating matrix contains certain elements that are common to both languages, and other elements that apply to only one or the other language.

RESULTS

Quantitative Findings: Overall Sample

Figure 11.1 depicts the distribution of the 69 students by holistic rating in all three conditions. In all conditions, the distribution is skewed toward the high end, although the spread at the high end is slightly greater for the spoken English than for the ASL condition. The SC distribution is highly skewed toward the high end. In fact, with the exception of one student, all the SC scores were above 3.

Overall, the differences among the three conditions are negligible: The students' mean score for spoken English was (x = 3.5 (Survival+), SD = 1.5), followed by ASL (x = 3.6 (Survival+), SD = 1.3), and SC (x = 4.1 (Intermediate), SD = 0.6) . This suggests that as a group, students were performing at the Survival+ level in spoken English and in ASL, and at the Intermediate level in SC.

Students for whom ASL is their stronger language (x = 8.1, SD = .91) scored slightly higher in their weaker language (i.e., spoken English, x = 3.8, SD = 2.14) than students whose stronger language is spoken English (x = 8.9, SD = 1.00) did in their weaker language (i.e., ASL, x = 2.9, SD = 2.79). These differences are not significant, and in both cases, the weaker language skills fall in the Novice to Novice+ range category.

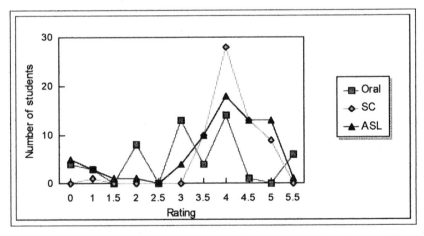

FIG. 11.1. Frequency of ratings by condition (0 = no functional proficiency, 5.5 = Advanced+).

Performance on the SC condition was slightly positively correlated with performance in the Oral condition ($r = .33$), and in the ASL condition ($r = .20$). Performance on the SC condition was also moderately positively correlated with performance on the stronger of the other two conditions ($r = .64$). In addition, performance on the Oral condition correlated negatively with performance on the ASL condition ($r = -.26$). Not surprisingly, hearing threshold (in dB) correlated very negatively with performance on the Oral condition ($r = -.63$), and correlated slightly positive with performance on the ASL condition ($r = .15$). This is because performance on the ASL condition has more to do with how much exposure to ASL one has, regardless of hearing ability.

Profiles

Four general profiles emerged from the data. The most common profile was that of students whose language skills were more or less evenly matched across the three conditions ($n = 22$). About one third of these students scored *at most* at the Intermediate level. This group might be termed *balanced bilinguals*.

Another common profile was that of the *developing bilingual*. Of this group, 12 were ASL-dominant, scoring in the Strong range in the SC and ASL conditions, and in the Developing-to-Weak range in the Oral condition. Another 15 were English-dominant, scoring in the Strong range in the SC and Oral conditions, and in the Developing-to-Weak range in the ASL condition.

A very small number of students ($n = 5$) actually scored better in the SC condition than in either of the two unimodal language conditions. The maximum scores of three of these students was Intermediate, and their scores in the two unimodal language conditions were Survival to Survival+, also suggesting that these students were not strong users of either English or ASL. Perhaps for these students, combining information from the two language conditions (perhaps speech reading English in combination with the signs) provided the most enabling communicative situation.

A sample profile from each type is presented in Fig. 11.2.

Qualitative Findings

The interviews selected for more detailed examination were analyzed for communicative and linguistic competence. Communicative competence included the domains of topic choice, discourse levels and register, and repair strategies. Linguistic competence included vocabulary and lexical choice, and morphological and syntactic sophistication (see Appendix B).

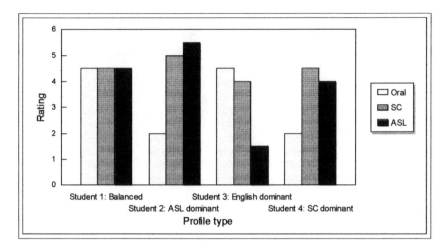

FIG. 11.2. Profiles from four different students, illustrating the four general profiles, based on ratings received in each condition (0 = no functional proficiency, 5.5 = Advanced+).

Performance in an Enabling Condition

Students who were strong in either spoken English or ASL could deal typically with complex topics within their experience. However, they often had difficulty dealing with hypothetical situations, even when they were talking about something with which they had a good deal of experience. Their vocabularies were typically broad, colloquial, and idiomatic, and precise reference could be made to the topics at hand. Expressive fluency for nonexperiential or hypothetical topics often could not be rated because they simply could not deal cognitively with these topics. Their grammar was good, and if mistakes were made, they did not interfere with communication.

Skilled English speakers included complex components of English grammar such as subordinate clauses and cleft constructions. By and large, the students who were strong users of English had a slight deaf accent, which is characterized by minor errors in articulation that do not interfere with communication. These errors occur because they cannot hear well enough to monitor their speech, particularly for high-frequency sounds such as voiceless fricatives (e.g., /s/ /sh/, etc). Students who performed well in spoken English often continued either to use speech exclusively (typically *without* gestures) or to resort to paper and pencil when communicating with a signing deaf person.

Strong ASL users included extensive use of the verb classifier system, well-sculpted space, and nonmanual grammatical signals for subordinate clauses, topic–comment constructions, and verb inflections. The students who were strong ASL users had *native-like* ASL accents in their signing. That is, they looked like they had been signing from early childhood. Some of the strong ASL users code-switched to English when discussing technical aspects of their topics. This was done through fingerspelling the English word, and then explaining what it meant in ASL, or sometimes signing in contact signing (English word order with mouthing). We found that the students who could perform well in ASL often could *communicate* well with nonsigning hearing people, using a variety of strategies. For the strong ASL students, particularly those with no speech, their gestural and mouthing patterns were precise and modified to that of the hearing world.

Strong ASL users typically included several lengthy narratives in their interviews. The interviewers and raters often commented that with the skilled ASL users, "you ask a question and get a story." These narratives tended to be more descriptive of action than of actors, which is not surprising given the highly verb-centered structure of the language. One student in particular presented a series of narratives all related to the topic of an international dance competition, in which she discussed the importance of deaf culture in the style of dance she does and in her choreography.

In sum, the skilled teens in either the Oral or ASL condition were able to ask and answer questions, clarify and demand clarification of communication, give information and instruction, compare and contrast topics, and give definitions and supported opinions. As stated earlier, the nature of the interview format allows an interviewee maximum freedom to demonstrate linguistic and cognitive sophistication by requiring the interviewer to stretch the interviewee's language by challenging the student to state an opinion and support it, or by demanding clarification of details. We found that the students more skilled in their enabling condition regularly offered supported opinion in the way of comparisons and contrasts without the need for the interviewer to challenge them. The students less skilled in their enabling condition typically did not operate at their highest levels until they were challenged by the interviewer.

This excerpt from an interview illustrates the concept of dynamic assessment that provided opportunities for examinees to enhance their performance by building on the linguistic and cognitive opportunities provided by the examiner. This student, age 16, scored at the Advanced+ level in the Oral condition, and at the Survival+ level in the ASL condition. Here, in the Oral interview, she is talking about her impression of a videotape that was taken when she was 6 years old:

> Adult(A): When you look at the little girl that you were and you think
>   about yourself now, has your personality changed?
> Teen(T):   [nods yes] Yes.

The question posed by the examiner is a yes–no question, which the teen could have elaborated on spontaneously. At this point, the teen has merely offered a one-word answer. When she was challenged to expand on her answer, it became clear that she was not quite sure what the question was:

> A: And how has that changed?
> T: [puzzled look] Could you be more specific re: In what way are you asking me?

Here, the teen has asked for clarification, and the adult begins to scaffold the teen's thinking:

> A: You know what I mean by personality?
> T: My stubbornness or...[indicates a question by gesture].
> A: Yes, your characteristics.

Here, the teen begins to struggle with the conceptual information:

> T: I'm very ... to my personality. It goes wherever I want. I mean, I get really stubborn sometimes. Nothing much has changed. I mean I'm learning a lot. I have increased knowledge through the past 10 years.

The answer here contradicts her earlier claim that her personality has changed:

> A: So you know more?
> T: Yeah.

Now the adult goes back to the question of any change in personality, using a concept the teen raised (stubbornness):

> A: Now, you said that you are very self-determined.
> T: [nods yes].
> A: And you like to get a goal and go for it.
> T: [nods yes].
> A: Is that the way you were when you were 6 or 7?
> T: No.

At this point, the teen is consistent with her first answer. The interviewer then begins to provide the student with ways of thinking about her answer:

A: Were you self-determined when you were 6 or 7?

T: No, my mom would just, my mom was the one. She put a lot of force on me to learn, learning how to talk and stuff. And that way, I just became that kind of ... It's basically my mom's.

A: Your mom's influence?

T: [nods yes] Yes.

A: So your mom was very influential in making you self-determined? Was there anyone else who helped you to become more self-determined in your childhood?

T: My mom, my speech therapist Miss C____. Have you heard of her?

A: I've heard of the name, yes.

T: Yeah. She was giving me that kind of thing. And it's my mom mostly. It's really my mom.

A: Mostly your mom.

T: Yeah.

The interview continues with the interviewer asking the student to provide more detailed information about how she came to be more self-determined:

A: Can you tell me what your mother did that helped you to be more self-determined?

T: Well, almost everyday during my childhood, we were having lessons together and sometimes I don't want to do it. I don't want to do it because I really don't have any time to play and enjoy myself. And what she does is she puts all these cards, these little papers and stuff like pictures and she'd ask me what are these pictures? And she says we will time it. And sometimes I say no more. I just don't want to do it. And she said, no, we have to do it. It's really important. And we would probably sit together for 15 minutes or ½ hour and do that kind of work. Classes and stuff and we would talk and that's part of it.

A: And so you think that was a large part of how your mother influenced you to be self-determined?

T: Yeah.

The description of how this teen's mother worked with her, and her conjecture that that is how she became self-determined illustrates more

clearly than her earlier claim that she was stubborn and nothing much
had changed. Had the interviewer dropped the subject at that point, this
student might only have been rated at an intermediate, rather than at the
Advanced level. The dynamic give-and-take of this format allowed the
interviewer to take the student to her maximum level.

Performance in a Disabling Condition

For the purposes of this interview technique, and within the context of
socially constructed and constituted communication situations, we refer
to the condition in which the students performed their worst as the
disabling condition. We might expect, and indeed found, that regardless of
their maximal performance in another condition, some of the students
were truly stymied when asked either to speak only or sign only.

Those students who were not skilled in spoken English, regardless of
their skill in SC or ASL, could deal with social formulas such as greeting
and leave-taking, but not substantively with any topics, simple or complex. Here, there are clear differences between how the teens dealt with
spoken English and ASL. Because all the students had experience dealing
with people who do not sign, they used a variety of strategies for
communicating with the interviewer in the spoken English condition.
Many of the signing students resorted to paper and pencil. In addition,
they would repeat themselves, mime, gesture, trace letters in the air and
on the palm of their hands.

In contrast, about half of the "oral" students who did not know ASL
had also never met a profoundly deaf adult before, and continued to
communicate in the ASL condition as *if they were talking to a hearing person*.
These students made no attempt whatsoever to modify communication,
even to the point of gesturing or writing in the air. This was true in spite
of the fact that the interviewer was signing and using a variety of strategies
(the same strategies mentioned above) to communicate with the student,
making it abundantly clear that exclusively oral communication was not
appropriate. One student adopted a strategy of mouthing words without
voice, acknowledging that the interviewer was deaf. However, she ultimately resorted to paper and pencil, as well. Another student knew the
manual alphabet and made his way through the interview by *fingerspelling*
with the interviewer. However this fingerspelling was not done in the way
that fluent fingerspelling is used in ASL. Rather he spelled out each word
letter-by-letter. Even then, he made errors in production and was imper-
vious to correction. By and large, students who knew no ASL were less
able to *sculpt* space than those who also knew some sign. In all cases, this
communication was rudimentary linguistically.

When an individual is placed in a disabling situation, however, even valiant attempts at communication leave little opportunity to display maximum levels of cognitive manipulation. For example, one student had no functional skills in ASL, and indeed, made no attempt to sign or gesture. He did, however, score at the Advanced level in the spoken English condition and continued to use his speech skills in the ASL interview. Considering the difficulty this dyad had in establishing the topic—it took 20 turns to establish mutual understanding of the first topic (what is your name?)—one can see that this student simply would not be able to demonstrate his maximum cognitive abilities if he had continued to rely on speech alone in the ASL condition.

Another example comes from a student who was rated with "No Functional Skills" in spoken English, and Intermediate+ in ASL. This student could only manage a few very common, everyday words in speech. Communication was marked by the need for frequent repetition and punctuated by long pauses. As in the previous interview, this dyad took 13 turns to establish understanding of the simple question "Are you busy here?" They finally had to resort to paper and pencil to be successful at communication. This interview also included communication strategies such as rudimentary mime, as well as tracing letters on the hand. At one point, the teen attempted to "mime" what she intended, but the adult did not pick up on the message. In fact, it appeared as if the adult ignored some important cues, for example, suggesting the word *teacher* after the student had said *busy* (pronounced as "bih") several times, while miming writing. At that point, the adult caught onto the meaning of *write*, but misunderstood its intent. The student was trying to portray what it means to be busy (i.e., writing a lot), but the adult thought she was asking to use paper and pencil. Both the teen and the adult were able to communicate adequately through writing, but the teen's functional ability in *spoken* English was severely hampered by the quality of her speech, rather than by her knowledge of English *per se*, as she was able to make herself understood in writing.

DISCUSSION

The conversational proficiency interview allowed us to explore issues such as; (a) how the students and interviewers were able to establish and extend their communication, (b) what communication strategies the students used in the three interviews, including insuring that the other person could understand them and could detect and repair breakdowns), and (c) how these kinds of skills might inform the study of language, communication, and cognitive development in deaf students.

Overall, we found few differences between students who have a strong spoken-language base and students who have a strong signed-language base in terms of their performance on the CPI. This suggested that through the CPI, students were permitted to demonstrate maximum performance in a dynamic mode. This replicated the findings of Lou, Fischer, and Woodward (1987). However, whereas Lou et al. determined initially the relative contribution of ASL and English to candidate's language *prior* to rating, the CPI process attempted to determine, through three separate interviews, the conditions that enabled or disabled maximal performance. In other words, our goal to seek conditions and strategies for enabling maximal performance was outside the set of goals for the Lou et al. measure.

When placed in *enabling* conditions, some students were able to demonstrate strong language skills regardless of the specific language (in this case, English vs. ASL) or of the modality of that language (spoken vs. signed), but other students were not able to demonstrate strong language skills regardless of condition. In an enabling condition, we are able to collect data that lend themselves to microgenetic analysis. The contributions of specific strategies that the interlocutors used, and even the specific words that were used, can be studied. When placed in *disabling* conditions, the students drew on a variety of communication strategies but were linguistically unable to perform to their maximum ability.

Revisiting the Linguistic and Cognitive Cycle

In studying the development of an individual within a sociocultural context, Vygotsky described four types of development: phylogenesis (development of the species), cultural history (development as a result of cultural or historic changes in a society), ontogenesis (development of an individual over a lifespan), and microgenesis (development over a very short timespan). For the purposes of this chapter, ontogenesis and microgenesis are important. Ontogenesis results in a qualitative transformation caused by an individual's use of cultural–historical tools, of which language is an example. Ways of thinking are bound culturally, as well. Therefore, the kinds of language and social instantiations of language are particularly important to study. Microgenesis refers to learning that happens within a very short time frame, for example, within a lesson, a conversation, or even in a single interchange. A fine-grained analysis of such interactions can reveal instances of microgenetic development. It is clear from the performance of these students that the linguistic and cognitive cycle has been in operation for a number of years.

The students in our study were enrolled in school systems where the choice between oral and total communication programs was available and has always been available. Therefore, we know that those students who remained in oral programs were a select group of students who continued to be educable in that modality. It is not surprising that the students who managed well in spoken English actually had more hearing than the others, and in their special programs, had learned to maximize the use of that hearing for the acquisition of spoken language.

In contrast, many of the students who are currently in signing programs have been there since switching from oral preschool and kindergarten programs. The age at which the switch was made is of some concern. There are studies that suggested that the critical period for signed language acquisition may be more flexible than for spoken-language acquisition (e.g., Fischer, 1985, 1994), and other studies suggest that certain disparities between native or near-native signers (those who learned between birth and 5 years of age) and nonnative signers appear *and persist for as much as 40 years*, in both production and grammatical analysis (Mayberry & Eichen, 1991; Mayberry & Fischer, 1989; Newport, 1990). We are left to wonder about any concomitant, cognitive repercussions of delayed language acquisition. Social constructivist theory suggests that, to the extent that language is involved in verbal thought, limitations in language ability have a negative impact on verbal thinking and problem solving. We also suggest that in spite of the fact that for these students, the signing modality is more successful for education than the oral modality, we must consider the quantity and nature of the interactions they have had in the oral and signed (either alone or in combination) modalities to explain the differences in performance that we observe.

We know that in oral programs, all of the teachers received their formal education in spoken English, and are required to be able to handle English in both the printed and oral–aural modalities. In total communication programs, all of the teachers, even the deaf teachers, also received their formal educations in English, in a combined form of signs and speech. However, because most of these children had hearing parents with varying degrees of communicative skills in signing, these students did not receive the same quantity or quality of dialogic interaction in either ASL or SC that oral students did in spoken English.

Research and Clinical Uses for the CPI

In the past decade, changes in language and communication policies in a few schools for deaf children have recognized ASL as a language of instruction. Subsequent changes in practices call for a careful examination and documentation of how these changes affect the cognitive and linguistic abilities of both teachers and children and how these abilities are measured. Multiple means of measuring cognitive and verbal abilities must be included in a comprehensive evaluation of deaf students' abilities (Braden, 1991; Rush, Blennerhassett, Epstein, & Alexander, 1991), not only in the cognitive arena, but also in the specific English and ASL language abilities of the students (see, e.g., Mayer & Wells, 1996; Paul, 1992).

Whereas researchers have found a positive correlation between language ability and intellectual functioning (Arnold & Walter, 1979; Zweibel, 1987), any direct relationship between language abilitiy and either verbal or nonverbal cognitive abilities is difficult to ascertain (see Marschark, 1993b, for a review of the issues). Most of the research either suffers from methodological flaws (e.g., lack of control groups) or from a theoretical perspective that equates language ability with literacy. Very few studies have attempted to examine verbal intellectual ability in ASL (e.g., Maller, 1994; Nizzero, Musselman, & MacKay-Soroka, 1993). Because ASL has not been used as a primary language of education, the necessary criteria for judging the quality of an argument, the succinctness of prose, or the beauty of metaphor in the context of educational achievement are absent in a standardized fashion.

Within a social constructivist perspective, the CPI allows us to begin to explore verbal abilities in deaf students in both ASL and English (signed and spoken) through dialogic interaction in both enabling and disabling conditions. Detailed analyses of the conversations revealed instances of microgenetic development, and operation in the zone of proximal development. As the adults raised issues with the teens and asked for increasingly sophisticated kinds of thinking through their dialogues, the language skills of the teens were stretched to their limits.

Hickmann (1985) suggested that inner speech is fully developed when "language becomes its own context" (p. 264). When this happens, decontextualization from the real world of temporally and spatially shared interlocution is possible, and independent control over higher psychological processes begins. If independent learning in school requires the use of decontextualized language, then the intermediate level ability demonstrated by the averages of the current sample (which still uses contextualized language) may not be enough for independent school-based learning and achievement. Students whose highest CPI score is in the *developing* range may not yet have the necessary control over inner speech and may be at academic risk, even when their PIQ is within average limits. Nizzero, Musselman, and MacKay-Soroka (1993) showed that it is the verbal, not the nonverbal, IQ scores that are correlated with other measures of academic achievement.

The CPI scores of the majority of the teens suggested that they lack sufficient skill at using either ASL or spoken English as effective tools for higher-level cognition and verbal thought. Intermediate-level skills do not allow for precision and sophistication in language use for complex ideas. For the signing teens, ASL and SC, as they are currently provided in the school systems, are functioning as an effective means of *communication*, but not as an academic register for the students. This would also suggest that those students whose strongest condition was SC and who scored in the developing range are at greatest risk for academic achievement. These would be students who have difficulty in class simply with class discussions, conversations, and day-to-day routine verbal interactions (skills tested in the CPI).

We can speculate, given the large number of students who switched from Oral to SC programs, that verbal ability in general developed later in these students. In spite of the fact that sign language is often used successfully to ameliorate the effects of early language deprivation caused by deafness, we suggest that sign language, by itself, is not an academic panacea for late-language learning individuals. Having missed the most crucial early language learning years, as well as possibly endured other psychosocial and/or neurological stressors, may have caused a permanent language delay that cannot be entirely made up through the use of sign language alone (Mayberry & Eichen, 1991; Mayberry & Fischer, 1989; Newport, 1990). The number of fluent signers (in either ASL or "good" SC), compared with the number of fluent speakers, in a deaf child's environment is relatively small. Therefore, signing deaf students have fewer good language models, and spend far less time in linguistic interactions than do normal hearing, or even hard-of-hearing children. These social–environmental conditions, a by-product of deafness, would predict lower verbal cognitive ability.

The CPI may also become a useful tool in determining whether clients have enough verbal ability to benefit from certain types of counselling. Any counselling that requires the client to imagine new and different situations, or the "what if" type scenario may prove difficult for clients whose strongest communication or language is at an intermediate level. These clients may have a difficult time decontextualizing their thinking. This would require the therapist to change the approach of the therapy to rely solely on the client's personal experiences.

The application of interview format assessment such as the CPI to younger populations has been attempted, but further refinements rest on collecting normative data on large numbers of deaf children. However, its use as an additional tool for sampling information about a person's language and cognitive development appears promising. The emphasis in deaf education has been on developing language, but we must also ask "language for what?" Providing accessible language is not enough; we must ensure that students have the opportunity to use their language in ways that make it functional. This means attending to the social implications of various language skills. For example, speech is important for interacting with hearing peers and ASL for interaction with deaf peers. Educators must also attend to the cognitive functions of language in addition to literacy, and provide the type of interactions that allow complex cognitive skills to develop. Instruments such as the CPI can help to evaluate the extent to which students are developing these important social and cognitive skills.

ACKNOWLEDGMENTS

The authors gratefully acknowledge the contributions of Adele Churchill, Sherri MacKay, Anne Miller, Irene Nizzero, and Phyllis Vazquez, who assisted in the development, data collection, and analysis of the interview and intelligence data. All errors of interpretation are, of course, our own.

REFERENCES

Akamatsu, C. T., & Stewart, D. (1992). Socially constructing language use for cognitive empowerment in deaf children. *Curriculum and Teaching: International Review of Curriculum and Instruction 7*, 1–12.

Akamatsu, C. T., & Stewart, D. (in press). Constructing simultaneous communication: The contributions of natural sign language. *International Review of Sign Linguistics, Vol. 2.*

Arnold, P., & Walter, G. (1979). Communication and reasoning skills in deaf and hearing signers. *Perceptual and Motor Skills, 49*, 192–194.

Bakhtin, M. (1986). *Speech genres and other late essays.* (C. Emerson & M. Holquist, Eds., V. W. McGee, trans.). Austin, TX: University of Texas Press.

Bernstein, M., & Finnegan, M. (1983). Internal speech and the deaf child. *American Annals of the Deaf, 128*, 483–489.

Blennerhassett, L. (1987). Experimental use of the WISC-R and WAIS-R verbal scales with hearing impaired adolescents. Paper presented at the National Association of School Psychologists, March, New Orleans, LA.

Blennerhassett, L., Moores, D., Hannah, J., & Woolard, L. (1988). The impact of parental deafness on WISC-R and WAIS-R verbal and performance scores of deaf adolescents. Paper presented at the National Association of School Psychologists, April, Chicago, IL.

Bonkowski, N., Gavelek, J., & Akamatsu, C. T. (1991). Education and the social construction of mind: Vygotskian perspectives on the cognitive development of deaf children. In D. Martin (Ed.), *Advances in cognition, education, and deafness* (pp. 185–194). Washington, DC: Gallaudet University Press.

Braden, J. (1984). The factorial similarity of the WISC-R Performance Scale in deaf and hearing samples. *Journal of Personality and Individual Differences, 5,* 403–410.

Braden, J. (1985). The structure of nonverbal intelligence in deaf and hearing subjects. *American Annals of the Deaf, 131,* 496–501.

Braden, J. (1991). A meta-analytic review of IQ research with deaf persons. In D. Martin (Ed.), *Advances in cognition, education, and deafness* (pp. 56–62). Washington, DC: Gallaudet University Press.

Christie, K., & Wilkins, D. (1997). A feast for the eyes: ASL literacy and ASL literature. *Journal of Deaf Studies and Deaf Education, 2,* 57–59.

Conrad, R. (1979). *The deaf school child.* London: Harper & Row.

Cook, J., & Harrison, M. (1995). Private sign and literacy development in preschoolers with hearing loss. *Sign Language Studies, 88,* 201–226.

Curtiss, S. (1977). *Genie: A case study of a modern wild child.* New York: Academic Press.

Fischer, S. (1985). The effects of age on acquisition: A critical period? (pp. 66–71). In K. Kanda (Ed.), *Proceedings of the 10th annual meeting of the Japanese Sign Language Association,* Tokyo, Japan.

Fischer, S. (1994). Critical periods: Critical issues. In B. Schick & M. P. Moeller (Eds.), Proceedings of the 7th annual conference on Issues in Language and Deafness: The use of sign language in educational settings: Currents concepts and controversies (pp. 1–11). Omaha, NE: Boys Town National Research Hospital.

Fischer, S. (in press). Critical periods for language acquisition: consequences for deaf education. In A. Weisel (Ed.), *Deaf education in the 1990s: An international perspective.* Washington, DC: Gallaudet University Press.

Halliday, M. A. K. (1975). *Learning how to mean.* London: Arnold.

Halliday, M. A. K. (1993). Towards a language-based theory of learning. *Linguistics and Education, 5,* 93–116.

Harre, R. (1986). *The social construction of emotions.* Oxford, England: Blackwell.

Hickmann, M. (1985). The implications of discourse skills in Vygotsky's developmental theory. In J. Wertsch (Ed.), *Culture, communication and cognition: Vygotskian perspectives* (pp. 236–257). London: Cambridge University Press.

Jamieson, J. (1995). Visible thought: Deaf children's use of signed and spoken private speech. *Sign Language Studies, 86,* 63–80.

Johnson, R. E. (undated). Language proficiency interview. Part of final report for NIH grant. ms.

Jones, R. L. (1979). The oral interview of the Foreign Service Institute. In B. Spolsky (Ed.), *Advances in language testing series: 1, Some major tests* (104–115). Washington, DC: Center for Applied Linguistics.

Kaiser-Grodecka, I., & Cieszynska, J. (1991). The understanding of time by deaf pupils. In D. Martin (Ed.), *Advances in cognition, education, and deafness* (pp. 201–204). Washington, DC: Gallaudet University Press.

Lou, M., Fischer, S., & Woodward J. (1987). A language independent measure of communicative competence. *Sign Language Studies, 57,* 353–370.

Lucas, C., & Valli, C. (1990). ASL, English, and contact signing. In C. Lucas (Ed.), *Sign language research: Theoretical issues* (pp. 288–307). Washington, DC: Gallaudet University Press.

Lucas, C., & Valli, C. (1992). *Language contact in the American deaf community.* Washington, DC: Gallaudet University Press.

Maller, S. (1994). Item bias in the WISC-III with deaf children. Paper presented at the American Educational Research Association, New Orleans, LA, April 4–8.

Marmor, G., & Petitto, L. (1979). Simultaneous communication in the classroom: How well is English grammar represented? *Sign Language Studies, 23,* 99–136.

Marschark, M. (1993a). Origins and interactions in social, cognitive, and language development of deaf children. In M. Marschark & M. D. Clark (Eds.), *Psychological perspectives on deafness* (pp. 7–26). Hillsdale, NJ: Lawrence Erlbaum Associates.

Marschark, M. (1993b). *Psychological development of deaf children.* New York: Oxford University Press.

Maxwell, M. (1990). Simultaneous communication: The state of the art and proposals for change. *Sign Language Studies, 69,* 333–390.

Maxwell, M., Bernstein, M., & Maer, K. (1991). Bimodal language production. In P. Siple & S. Fischer, (Eds.), *Theoretical issues in sign language research, volume 2: Psychology* (pp. 171–190). Chicago: University of Chicago Press.

Maxwell, M., & Doyle, J. (1996). Language codes and sense-making among deaf schoolchildren. *Journal of Deaf Studies and Deaf Education, 1,* 122–137.

Mayberry, R., & Eichen, E. (1991). The long-lasting advantage of learning sign language in childhood: Another look at the critical period for language acquisition. *Journal of Memory and Language, 30,* 486–512.

Mayberry, R., & Fischer, S. (1989). Looking through phonological shape to lexical meaning: The bottleneck of non-native sign language processing. *Memory and Cognition, 17,* 740–754.

Mayer, C., & Wells, G. (1996). Does the linguistic interdependence theory support a bilingual–bicultural model of literacy education for deaf students? *Journal of Deaf Studies and Deaf Education, 1,* 93–107.

McAnally, P., Rose, S., & Quigley, S. (1987). *Language learning practices with deaf children.* Boston: College Hill.

Moores, D. (1996). *Educating the deaf: Psychological principles and practices.* (4th ed.). Boston: Houghton Mifflin.

Nelson, K. (1996). *Language in cognitive development: The emergence of the mediated mind.* London: Cambridge University Press.

Newell, W., Caccamise, F., Boardman, K., & Holcomb, B. R. (1983). Adaptation of the Language Proficiency Interview (LPI) for assessing sign communicative competence. *Sign Language Studies, 41,* 311–351.

Newell, W., Stinson, M., Castle, D., Mallery-Ruganis, D., & Holcomb, B. R. (1990). Simultaneous communication: A description by deaf professionals working in an educational setting. *Sign Language Studies 69,* 391–414.

Newport, E. (1990). Maturational constraints on language learning. *Cognitive Science, 14,* 11–28.

Nizzero, I., Musselman, C., & MacKay-Soroka, S. (1993). Verbal and nonverbal intelligence as predictors of academic achievement in deaf teenagers. Paper presented at the meeting of Convention of American Instructors of the Deaf, June, Baltimore, MD.

Olson, D. (1977). From utterance to text: The bias of language in speech and writing. *Harvard Educational Review, 47,* 257–281.

Olson, D., & Torrance, C. (Eds.). (1991). *Literacy and orality.* London: Cambridge University Press.

Paul, P. (1992). The use of ASL in teaching reading and writing to deaf students: An interactive theoretical perspective. In *Bilingual considerations in the education of deaf students: ASL and English* (Conference proceedings). Washington, DC: Gallaudet University Press.

Rommetveit, R. (1985). Language acquisition as increasing linguistic structuring of experience and symbolic behavior control. In J. Wertsch (Ed.), Culture, communication, and cognition, Vygotskian perspectives (pp. 183–204). London: Cambridge University Press.

Rush, P., Blennerhassett, L., Epstein, K., & Alexander, D. (1991). WAIS-R Verbal and Performance profiles of adolescents referred for atypical learning styles. In D.

Martin (Ed.), *Advances in cognition, education, and deafness* (pp. 82–88). Washington, DC: Gallaudet University Press.

Stewart, D., Akamatsu, C. T., & Bonkowski, N. (1990). Synergy effects: Sign driven and speech driven simultaneous communication. In W. Edmondson & F. Karlsson (Eds.), *SLR '87: Papers from the fourth international symposium on sign language research* (pp. 235–242). Hamburg: Signum-Press.

Trevarthen, C. (1979). Communication and co-operation in early infancy: A description of primary intersubjectivity. In M. Bullowa, (Ed.), *Before speech* (pp. 321–347). London: Cambridge University Press.

Vygotsky, L. S. (1978). *Mind in society: the development of higher psychological processes* (M. Cole, V. John-Steiner, S. Scribner, & E. Souberman, Eds.). Cambridge, MA: Harvard University Press.

Vygotsky, L. S. (1987). *Thinking and speech.* (N. Minick, Trans.). New York: Plenum.

Webster, A. (1986). *Deafness, development and literacy.* London: Methueun.

Wechsler, D. (1981). *Manual for the Wechsler Adult Intelligence Scales, Revised.* San Antonio, TX: The Psychological Corporation.

Wechsler, D. (1991). *Wechsler Intelligence Scales for Children, Third Ed.* San Antonio, TX: The Psychological Corporation.

Wells, G. (1986). *The meaning makers: Children learning to talk and talking to learn.* Portsmouth, NH: Heinemann.

Wertsch, J. (1979). From social interaction to higher psychological processes: A clarification and application of Vygotsky's theory. *Human Development, 22,* 1–22.

Wertsch, J. (1985). *Vygotsky and the social formation of mind.* Cambridge, MA: Harvard University Press.

Wertsch, J. (1991). *Voices of the mind: A sociocultural approach to mediated action.* Cambridge, MA: Harvard University Press.

Wertsch, J., & Stone, C. A. (1985). The concept of internalization in Vygotsky's account of the genesis of higher mental functions. In J. Wertsch (Ed.), *Culture, communication, and cognition: Vygotskian perspectives* (pp. 162–182). London: Cambridge University Press.

Wood, D., Wood, H., Griffiths, A., & Howarth, I. (1986). *Teaching and talking with deaf children.* New York: Wiley.

Zweibel, A. (1987). More on the effects of early manual communication on the cognitive development of deaf children. *American Annals of the Deaf, 132,* 16–20.

Appendix A
Holistic Rating Categories for Each Condition

Rating	Description
No functional proficiency	Does not possess skills prerequisite to language interview
	ASL: little or no attempt to communicate in sign SC: little or no attempt to communicate in sign or speech Oral: little or no attempt to communicate in speech
	Oral: little or no attempt to communicate in speech
Adaptive	Can accomplish social formulas with difficulty, can answer yes/no questions. May have one or two intelligible words–signs, has some success communicating using isolated gestures, sound patterns, and mime adapted to needs of interviewer
	ASL: 1–2 intelligible signs, some success communicating using isolated gestures, pantomime, signs adapted to needs of interviewer SC: 1–2 intelligible signsor words, some success communicating using isolated gestures, pantomime, signs and sound patterns adapted to needs of interviewer Oral: 1–2 intelligible signs or words; some success communicating using isolated gestures, pantomime, and sound patterns to needs of interviewer
Novice	Can accomplish social formulas without difficulty. Can converse on simple, familiar topics, but only with difficulty and not with precision or sophistication
	Vocabulary is sufficient for only the most elementary needs. Fluency is limited by frequent repetition, long pauses, shortness of constructions, and frequent paraphrasing of interviewer. Basically limited to single word utterances, simple phrases. Grammar and articulation are characterized by frequent errors that interfere with communication. Comprehension is limited to simple questions and statements at a slowed rate and requires frequent and often multiple repetitions
	ASL: single signs SC: single signs or spoken words or simultaneously produced sign–word Oral: single spoken words
Novice +	Exhibits some survival level skills, but not all and not consistently
Survival	Can accomplish all of novice requirements with ease. Can ask/answer basic questions, has some skill in creating novel utterances. Can converse on complex, unfamiliar topics, but only with difficulty and not with precision or sophistication
	Vocabulary is sufficient for simple expression, but groping for words and lengthy, imprecise circumlocutions characterize attempts at more complex topics. Expressive and receptive fluency is usually close to normal rate. Inappropriate pausing and paraphrasing of interviewer are infrequent when talking about familiar topics. Pronunciation, although occasionally inexact, does not interfere with communication. Grammatical errors only interfere occasionally with communication. Miscues may require multiple repetitions

296

Appendix A (cont'd.)

Rating	Description
	ASL: uses fingerspelling productively, but cannot read it unless slow and clear
	TC: uses fingerspelling productively, but cannot read it unless slow and clear
	Oral: Comprehension requires *work*; repetition frequently required
Survival +	Exhibits some intermediate-level skills, but not all and not consistently.
Intermediate	Can accomplish survival requirements with ease. Can converse on complex, unfamiliar topics, but only with difficulty and not with precision or sophistication
	Vocabulary is broad, but complex topics may require circumlocution. Receptive and expressive fluency generally good, may deteriorate with complex topics. Pronunciation and grammatical errors are infrequent, do not interfere with communication. Single, normally produced repetitions will usually repair miscues
	ASL: Classifier system is rudimentary; natural miscues with fingerspelling are reasonable and easily repaired
	SC: Conveys notions of plurality and time; inflection in either speech or sign, although inconsistently and with errors
	Oral: inflectional morphology may contain errors; speech may contribute to these errors
Intermediate +	Exhibits some advanced-level skills, but not all and not consistently
Advanced	Can accomplish all intermediate requirements, and can converse with sophistication and precision on complex, unfamiliar, and technical topics at age-appropriate level
	Vocabulary is broad, colloquial, idiomatic, and sufficient for precise reference to any topic. Receptive and expressive fluency is always smooth. Grammar is characterized by full range of constructions. Mispronunciation is rare, never interferes with communication
	ASL: rich description, well-developed stories; classifier system is complete; signing is clear
	SC: English and/or ASL features may be present in any of the above; *deaf* accent does not impede comprehension of speech; generally coordinates speech and sign if bimodal
	Oral: any *deaf* accent does not impede comprehension
Advanced +	Exhibits some Superior skills, but not all and not consistently

Appendix B
Conversational Proficiency Interview (CPI) Rating Matrix (ASL)

Name _____	Test Date _____	1	Always/consistently
		2	Frequently
OID# _____	Test Age _____	3	Sometimes/rarely
		4	Never
CPI# _____	Gender M F	NA	Not applicable/No opportunity

	Topics		*Rating*				*Comments*
1a.	Social formulas (e.g., hello, thank you); yes/no questions	1	2	3	4		
1b.	Some everyday topics and questions	1	2	3	4		
1c.	Most familiar topics, but with difficulty and without precision; barely manages common survival situations	1	2	3	4		
1d.	Familiar topics with precision and ease	1	2	3	4		
1e.	Unfamiliar and/or complex concrete topics without precision	1	2	3	4	NA	
1f.	Unfamiliar and/or complex concrete topics with precision	1	2	3	4	NA	
1g.	Hypothetical topics without precision	1	2	3	4	NA	
1h.	Hypothetical topics with precision	1	2	3	4	NA	

	Vocabulary		*Rating*				*Comments*
2a.	A few signs, primarily limited to everyday social situations, familiar names, common objects, colors, numbers, days of the week, and time	1	2	3	4		
2b.	Sufficient for simple expression, but gropes for words and uses lengthy circumlocutions, mime, and pantomime to attempt more complex topics	1	2	3	4		
2c.	Good control of everyday vocabulary; complex topics require circumlocution	1	2	3	4		
2d.	Vocabulary is broad and precise	1	2	3	4		

Appendix B (cont'd.)

	Vocabulary	Rating					Comments
2e.	Uses colloquialisms, idioms, slang appropriately	1	2	3	4		

	Fingerspelling	Rating					Comments
3a.	Can form letters of the manual alphabet, but does not use in conversation	1	2	3	4	NA	
3b.	Uses productively, but is labored and difficult to read	1	2	3	4	NA	
3c.	Fluent production	1	2	3	4	NA	
4a.	Reads with difficulty, requiring a slow rate and/or frequent repetition	1	2	3	4	NA	
4b.	Reads with fluency	1	2	3	4	NA	

	Grammar	Rating				Comments
5a.	Uses single word utterances	1	2	3	4	
5b.	Constructs short novel utterances; emergence of basic grammatical features	1	2	3	4	
5c.	Constructs simple and some complex sentences	1	2	3	4	
5d.	Uses a variety of simple and complex sentences to produce clearly connected text; emergence of classifier system	1	2	3	4	
5e.	Native-like mastery of grammar; "plays" with language including hand-switching, classifiers	1	2	3	4	

	Articulation	Rating					Comments
6.	Is there discernible sign?	2 Yes		1 No			
7a.	Signs are difficult to understand	1	2	3	4	NA	
7b.	Signs can be understood, but comprehension requires work; frequent repetition required	1	2	3	4	NA	
7c.	Easy to understand; few errors, but signs may be "mushy" or "sloppy"	1	2	3	4	NA	
7d.	Clear articulation; errors, if any, are consistent, characterizable, as accent, and do not interfere with communication (sophisticated speaker)	1	2	3	4	NA	

Articulation		Rating					Comments
7e.	Production is smooth and clear; variation enhances meaning and interest	1	2	3	4	NA	
8.	Mouths English equivalent of signs	1	2	3	4		

Fluency ("The Look")		Rating					Comments
9a.	Production labored	1	2	3	4		
9b.	Production very slow and choppy	1	2	3	4		
9c.	Production reasonably paced and fluid, although a bit slow	1	2	3	4		
9d.	Production at normal rate for experiential topics, with appropriate rhythm and stress	1	2	3	4		
9e.	Production at normal rate for hypothetical topics, with normal rhythm and stress	1	2	3	4		
9f.	Varies rhythm and stress to enhance meaning	1	2	3	4		
10a.	Receptive fluency very slow	1	2	3	4		
10b.	Receptive fluency at normal rate for experiential topics	1	2	3	4		
10c.	Receptive fluency at normal rate for hypothetical topics	1	2	3	4		

Narrative (Story) Structure		Rating					Comments
11.	Evidence of narration?	2 Yes		1 No			
12a.	Some narrative elements present with simple plot and sequence	1	2	3	4	NA	
12b.	Simple, concise narrative with discernible plot and sequence, and some descriptive elaboration	1	2	3	4	NA	
12c.	Complex, elaborated narrative	1	2	3	4	NA	
12d.	Series of interrelated narratives	1	2	3	4	NA	
13a.	Elaborative detail related to actors (e.g., how actors are related to each other)	1	2	3	4	NA	
13b.	Elaborative detail related to action	1	2	3	4	NA	

Narrative (Story) Structure		Rating					Comments
14a.	Stories are detached from speaker	1	2	3	4	NA	
14b.	Stories use shifting perspective	1	2	3	4	NA	
Narrative (Story) Function		**Rating**					**Comments**
14c.	Narrative elicited by interviewer	1	2	3	4	NA	
14d.	Constructs narrative to illustrate a point	1	2	3	4	NA	
14e.	Constructs narrative to argue a point	1	2	3	4	NA	
15a.	Meaning in narrative specifically related to deaf culture	1	2	3	4	NA	
15b.	Teen makes meaning of narrative explicit	1	2	3	4	NA	
15c.	Teen conveys feeling through narrative	1	2	3	4	NA	
15d.	Narrative elicits emotional response from interviewer	1	2	3	4	NA	
Communication Repair Strategies		**Rating**					**Comments**
16.	Communication miscues occur	2 Yes		1 No			
17a.	Requests clarification	1	2	3	4	NA	
17b.	Spontaneous repetition	1	2	3	4	NA	
17c.	Rephrasing	1	2	3	4	NA	
17d.	Resorts to mime	1	2	3	4	NA	
17e.	Resorts to writing	1	2	3	4	NA	
17f.	Resorts to writing on hand	1	2	3	4	NA	
17g.	Resorts to writing in aid	1	2	3	4	NA	
17h.	Resorts to fingerspelling	1	2	3	4	NA	
Discourse		**Rating**					**Comments**
18a.	Social formulas; yes/no questions	1	2	3	4		
18b.	Describes, asks/answers basic questions	1	2	3	4		
18c.	Narrates, describes, compares, and contrasts; uses rudimentary stories which are detached from speaker	1	2	3	4		
18d.	Hypothesizes, provides supported opinion	1	2	3	4		
18e.	Negotiates, persuades, counsels; tailors language to audience	1	2	3	4		

12

A Hitchhiker's Guide to Holes and Dark Spots: Some Missing Perspectives in the Psychology of Deafness

M. Diane Clark
Shippensburg University

A Deaf man is driving along and stops to pick up a hitchhiker, who cannot understand his signs but welcomes the ride. The Deaf man, anxious to reach his destination, is speeding and eventually is pulled over by a cop. Of course, the policeman begins talking with pursed lips to the driver. When it is clear that the driver is deaf, the officer, who cannot sign, decides to gesture a simple warning to slow down. The hitchhiker observes this with interest. Later on that night, the weary Deaf man pulls over and trades places with his passenger. The hitchhiker, also in a hurry, does exactly what the Deaf man did—he speeds. He too sees the flashing police lights behind him and pulls over. Again, an officer starts speaking to the driver. The hitchhiker, expecting to take advantage of his new-found trick, shakes his head and points to his ears. However, this time, the police officer begins to sign, "My parents were deaf. I know sign language. You were speeding ..." (Bienvenu, 1994, p. 21).

The term *hitchhiker* is used to represent the types of errors that can be made when hearing people attempt to understand deaf individuals solely from a hearing viewpoint. For many of these hitchhikers, their view of deafness focuses on a lack of hearing or a sensory deficit. This "broken ear" view was clearly captured on the March 11, 1990 *60 Minutes* (Hewitt, 1990) segment with I. King Jordan, the first deaf president of Gallaudet University. The interviewer asked Jordan if he would take a pill to regain his hearing. This comment caused a strong response from Jordan, who told the interviewer, "I don't live in silence. I live in a beautiful, visual world, and so many things catch my attention visually that you may miss." In an attempt to show the interviewer how ridiculous her question was, Jordan asked: "Would you be offended if I asked you, 'Suppose I could give you a pill and it would make you a man?' Would you be interested in becoming a man?" This comment clearly caught the interviewer off guard, but demonstrated how insulting it is when hearing individuals assume that deaf individuals feel broken. Jordan's comment, "But still you see something missing," again highlights how the hitchhiker often views a deaf person. Jordan's response to a question about deafness causing a significant absence was that deafness is not a significant absence but is a significant difference.

Jordan's words reflect how members of the Deaf community view their world from a different center (Padden & Humphries, 1988). For members of this culture, "the condition of not hearing, or of being hard of hearing, cannot be described apart from its placement in the context of categories of cultural meaning" (Padden & Humphries, 1988, pp. 54–55). This definition focuses on the context in which deaf individuals develop and is vital if a psychology of deafness is to discuss issues related to deaf and hard-of-hearing individuals accurately from an insider's point of view (referred to in anthropology as an *emic* view.) The hitchhiker's or outsider's view can lead to a bias referred to as *audism* (Lane, 1992), being hearing-centered.

Because most research within the field of the psychology of deafness has been created by hitchhikers who wanted to capitalize on the "natural experiment" of deafness, research often highlighted deficits in deaf individuals' performances. Books titled *Psychology of Deafness*, utilizing a medical or clinical model, led to an ongoing debate that questions whether or not there is a psychology of deafness. Lane (1988, 1996) stated that what has been labeled as a psychology of the Deaf is, in effect, hearing researchers and educators trying to fix deaf and hard-of-hearing individuals (representing an audistic framework). Lane stated that there is no psychology of the Deaf and that "it is, in fact, not clear that there can be one" (p. 16). From his perspective, only if psychology of deafness could "capture ways in which deaf people as a group differ from hearing people more than the individuals in either group differ among themselves" (p. 8) could a valid claim be made to a field titled *psychology of deafness*.

After reviewing the literature, Lane concluded that what has passed as a psychology of deafness is in reality a paternalistic view of colonizers (hearing people) about those colonized (deaf people). The accusation about hearing researchers and educators who are "commonly ignorant of the language, institutions, culture, history, mores, and experiences of deaf peoples" (p. 16) described some research within the field. Lane's (1988) conclusion that the "most effective remedy ... would be to involve deaf people themselves ... in research design and implementation" (p. 17) suggested a challenge to the audistic views of the hitchhiker and a refocusing on the experiences of the deaf driver.

In contrast to Lane's views, Paul (1996a, 1996b; Paul & Jackson, 1993) compared a clinical view of deafness to a cultural view of deafness. The clinical view (Paul & Jackson, 1993) was defined as a disease or disability focus that "assumes that the improvement of the performance of deaf individuals in certain psychoeducation areas is facilitated by theories and research on hearing individuals" (p. XIV). In contrast, the cultural view "has called into question the indiscriminate application of mainstream developmental theories to deaf individuals ... [and] argued that there is a need for Deaf theorists and researchers" (p. XIV). Paul then argued that both frameworks fit within a developmental–interactive conceptual framework that "explore[s] the interactions of hearing children of hearing parents as well as those of deaf children of both hearing and deaf parents" (p. XIV).

So where is our hitchhiker? From our opening analogy, he is sitting there with a ticket in his hand that he received from a police officer who had a special status; that of a hearing child of deaf signing parents. One might imagine him wondering how his perspective could be so mistaken or simplistic. Let us propose that this hitchhiker reaches his destination and sets out to understand what it might be like to be deaf. If he only plugs up his ears and then believes that he understands what it must be like to be deaf, his world view would be much like that of the earlier mentioned clinical view. He might then go out and attempt to create programs and develop schools that help deaf individuals to understand what the hearing world takes for granted. The focus would be on programs *for* deaf persons.

On the other hand, what if our hitchhiker had a background in probabilistic epigenesis and the contextual–interactionist world view? The explicit, as well as implicit, assumptions that he would bring to bear in understanding deaf individuals would include bidirectional interactions occurring between the deaf individual and the environment in which the person was embedded. Here the deaf person would be seen as being actively involved with his or her context as a third source of development. Interactions would involve the deaf person, the environment, and the person's genetic makeup. All new experiences would be filtered through the historical context in which this deaf person had been placed.

For example, the following questions would be vital to understand the current development state of the deaf individual: When did the hearing loss occur, prelingually or postlingually? What type of educational program was the individual enrolled in during the elementary years and beyond? How supportive or nonsupportive was the environment of an individual who was deaf or hard-of-hearing? Was the individual exposed to a sign language, an oral regime, or a manual sign system? With how many family members was the individual able to communicate naturally and fluently?

These questions and many more need to be investigated to understand the psychological development of deaf individuals. Research and any resulting programs developed based on this research would be developed not *for* or *about* deaf individuals but in relation to the context in which specific deaf groups find themselves. This world view would result in a psychology *of* deafness that uses methodologies like the ecological systems approach (Bronfenbrenner, 1977) to understand developmental and educational outcomes experienced by deaf persons.

This ecological systems theory investigates reciprocal or bidirectional relations between an active organism and an active context (Lerner, 1986) where it is assumed that individuals are creating their own context as well as being influenced by this context. One must pay attention to many systems within the context, such as the *microsystem, mesosystem, exosystem,* and *macrosystem* (Bronfenbrenner, 1977). Microsystems consist of the immediate settings in which the deaf individual interacts. Each individual is embedded within many different microsystems. Two examples are school and home. Is the school a residential school or a mainstream public school system; is the individual a member of a deaf family or a hearing family? The mesosystem focuses on the interactions of these different microsystems.

One can examine how the school, the peer, and the family microsystems interact. Exosystems are those systems that do not directly contain an individual but impact her or him. Given that many deaf adults are underemployed, the family SES would impact this family's deaf or hearing child (note that the child is not involved in the work system). Finally, the macrosystem includes historic events and cultural beliefs. A common cultural belief concerning deafness is that deaf individuals must learn an oral language to fit into society and become productive members of that society. Armed with an ecological systems theory (based on the contextual–interactionism model), our hitchhiker evaluates carefully the questions included within a psychology of deafness. This hitchhiker knows that question selection is based on one's values and that the frame of the question is related to these underlying values, some explicit and others implicit, and would notice that questions framed by Deaf individuals tend to be framed in a positive way, as are those in the volume, *The Deaf Way* (Erting, Johnson, Smith & Snider, 1994). This individual notices that *Psychology of Deafness* texts are often written by other hitchhikers and questions the writer's world views regarding topics selected for inclusion within the text, evaluating whether or not hearing status was used in a normative manner. This hearing norm tends to conceptualize deaf individuals as the deviation, possibly leading to negative inferences. The normative bias influenced many early studies that found deaf individuals had significantly higher scores on some tasks than did hearing controls, but the researchers' conclusions stated that the deaf individual showed skill deficits (Blair, 1957; Myklebust & Brutten, 1953; Olson, 1967).

Because of an understanding of his or her outsider perspective, our hitchhiker is careful about designing research that investigates deaf participants and evaluates published research carefully to see if it reflects an audistic bias. One such discussion can be found in Clark and Hoemann (1991) who described methodological issues causing concern to researchers (mostly hitchhikers) in deafness. One concern was that many older published studies did not clearly describe their deaf participants. The use of phrases such as "fluent in ASL" have often been used without clear-cut definitions regarding what it means to be fluent in ASL. They also pointed to the "clear advantages to having deaf researchers as [an] investigator" (p. 424).

Another issue for the hitchhiker may be in establishing rapport with deaf participants. Many older published studies presented experimental instructions in oral English (Allen, 1971; Blanton & Nunnally, 1967; Frumkin & Anisfeld, 1977; Hartung, 1970) or through pantomime and mouthing (Mandes, Allen, & Swisher, 1971). Given these types of instructions, how can the hitchhiker be sure that the deaf participants clearly understand what they are being asked to do? Additionally, how can one be sure that the deaf individual is motivated to perform at his or her best for a hitchhiker?

So how will a hitchhiker—coming from a contextual–interactionist perspective evaluate literature that is typically referred to as "psychology of deafness"? This individual selects paradigms like that of Bronfenbrenner's ecological systems to investigate the effects of context on the development of deaf individuals. The researcher's contextual–interactionist world view leads to the understanding that there are different outcomes for deaf individuals in comparison to hearing individuals. Consequently, a textbook written from this viewpoint would look quite different from one written from a clinical hitchhiker's point of view. The following ideal table of contents was developed by our enlightened hitchhiker.

Chapter 1—Is There a Psychology of Deafness?
    Contexts in which deafness occurs
        Onset and severity of hearing loss
        Family context
        School context
        Sociocultural context
        Linguistic context
    History of psychology of deafness
        Deficit or difference?
        Brief overview of the Mykelbust (1960) and Paul and Jackson (1993) *psychology of deafness* books
    Metatheoretical issues
        The cultural versus clinical views
    Contextual–interactionism world view
        Ecological systems theory
    Thinking critically—The hitchhiker's dilemma
        Emic versus etic views

Chapter 2—Biology Within Psychology of Deafness
    Audiological issues
    Heritability of deafness
    Effects of deafness on prenatal sensory integration
    Prenatal effects related to congenital deafness or parental deafness
    "What the hands reveal about the brain"
        Lateralization
        Recruitment and reorganization of brain function
        Signers with strokes

Chapter 3—Perception
    Spatial cognition
        Mental rotation
    Figure–ground disambiguation
    Kinesthetic effects on perceptual motor skills
    Effects on peripheral vision

Chapter 4—Intelligence
Theoretical issues—Is it g or EKS?
Development of Elaborate Knowledge Domains and Elaborate
Knowledge Structures (EKS)
Impact of Schooling on EKSs
   Effects of educational policies
   Time on academics for the deaf child
   Concept formation
   Microlevel cognitive processes
      Central processing capacity
      Speed of encoding
   Effects of task complexity
   Effects of practice
Assessment issues
   Validity and reliability issues
   Standardization issues

Chapter 5—Language and Language Development
Sign languages
   Grammar
   Acquisition
   Code switching and registers
Issues in language development
   Language input to Deaf Children
   Deaf families and hearing families
   Oral, manual, or American Sign Language (ASL)?
   Deaf children and the development of an L1
   Bilingual issues
      Acquisition
      Schooling
Linguistic creativity of deaf individuals
   In English
   In Sign Language
The relationship between language and thought

Chapter 6—Memory and Memory Development
Attention and pattern recognition
   Visual sensory registers—Same or different?
Visual short-term memory
   English stimuli
   ASL stimuli
   Codes: Acoustic–articulatory, visual and/or kinesthetic?

Articulatory loop issues
Priming
Episodic memory
Semantic memory
Concept formation
Expert performance
Implicit versus explicit paradigms
Problem solving
Cognition and emotion
Retrieval cues and successes
Memory development
Piaget's theory related to deaf children
Vygosty's theory related to deaf children

Chapter 7—Social–Emotional Development
Infancy
Attachment
Infant-caregiver synchronicity
Play
Early childhood
Perspective taking
Gender development
Theories of mind
Middle childhood
Family issues
Literacy and schooling
Residential schools versus mainstreaming
Reading
Arithmetic
Understanding games and group regulation
Emotional development
Prosocial development
Peer relations
Adolescence
Sexuality
Identity formation
Peer group interactions
Deaf peers
Hearing peers
Adulthood
Careers
Family

Partner choices and lifestyle preferences
Friendships

Chapter 8—Mental Health Issues
Diagnostic and assessment issues
Treatment issues
  Uses of interpreters
  Therapist training in issues related to deaf clients
Cultural issues related to possible misdiagnosis
Primary prevention

Chapter 9—The Deaf Individual as a Member of the Group
Social cognition
  Scripts
Attitudes
  Conformity and obedience
  Political ideologies
Attribution theory
  Fundamental attribution error
  Just world hypothesis

Chapter 10—Deaf Culture
Deaf history
International views of deaf culture
Deaf clubs and sports
Diversity issues
Deaf cultures views regarding education
Political activism
Deaf people and their art
  Deaf humor
  Deaf theater

The previous potential table of contents is surely not complete. Many additional areas could be and should be included. Using this table as a starting point might help to highlight the areas that were adequately researched and those that need more work to clarify remaining issues.

Chapter 1, on the psychology of deafness, includes several different areas, some of which can be written now. Marschark (1993) and Rodda and Grove (1987) have introductory chapters that discuss issues related to the onset of hearing loss and the effects of this loss on an individual's ongoing contexts. A review of books such as Myklebust (1960) and Paul and Jackson (1993) provides an historical overview of the field of psychology of deafness. The author can then evaluate whether or not a hearing-centered approach was adopted and, if so, how this approach impacted the results of the studies reported.

Moving into metatheoretical issues enters the field of philosophy of science. Paradigms and world views within psychology of deafness would benefit from a discussion of their explicit and implicit assumptions and how these assumptions influence or guide research and theory related to each. This type of dialogue has begun (see Clark, 1993; Lane, 1988, 1996; Paul, 1996a, 1996b), but additional clarification would be beneficial and shed additional light on a somewhat murky area. This type of discussion should aid in the ongoing dialogue about whether or not there is a psychology of deafness.

The focus of this book is on embedding deaf children and deaf adults within their many contexts. The working assumption of the book is that in "the domains of linguistic, cognitive, and social functioning, it is assumed that (deaf) children (and adults) both shape their worlds and are shaped by them" (Marschark, 1993, p. 6). Given this assumption, Brofenbrenner's (1977) ecological system approach was suggested as a tool to aid in uncovering similarities and differences among individuals who find themselves in different contexts (i.e., deaf children in signing deaf families, deaf children in oral deaf families, deaf children in signing hearing families, deaf children in families with no or limited signing, as well as, in some cases, hearing children in hearing families). Many studies compare some of these groups but few studies have been able to collect data from all these contexts and make fine-grained comparisons among them. Design and implementation of these types of questions, which could be analyzed using structured equation models, will go a long way toward disambiguating many confounds within the field.

Another aspect of the ecological systems approach is Brofenbrenner's focus on ecological validity or a "focus on how (individuals) develop in settings representative of their actual world" (Lerner, 1986, p. 26). Studies that employ ecologically valid situations have often shown that deaf individuals have abilities that are not demonstrated in less familiar contexts (Christie & Wilkins, 1997; Rutherford, 1993; Valli, 1993). As noted in Clark and Hoemann (1991) and again in Marschark (1993), selecting methodologies and control groups to determine the impact of deafness is vital to obtaining valid and reliable results. If we add the notion of ecologically valid contexts in which deaf individuals interact on a continuous basis to our concerns about methodologies and control groups, our research will provide more accurate detail about the skills, abilities, and/or deficits of deaf individuals.

The final section of chapter 1 would discuss suggestions to enable us to critically evaluate research. One such topic for evaluation is the differences between an *emic* view—individuals within a culture—versus an *etic* view of detached observers (see Pollio & Pollio, 1991, for a brief discussion of these notions as related to deafness). Newport (1996) called attention to this emic–etic distinction with her statement that native speakers of a language keep nonnative speakers honest. Therefore, a blending of emic and etic views strengthens our understanding of the deaf individual. Finally, to insure our critical thinking, eight rules of logic (Wade & Tavris, 1996) are proposed:

1. Ask questions and be willing to wonder;
2. define the problem;
3. examine the evidence;
4. analyze assumptions and biases;
5. avoid emotional reasoning;
6. do not oversimplify;
7. consider other interpretations; and
8. tolerate uncertainty.

Chapter 2, biology within psychology of deafness, is typically the next section in a general psychology text. The biology of deaf individuals should not be assumed to be the same as that of a hearing individual, and similarities and differences need to be addressed carefully. The table of contents here starts with issues typically included in a book on deafness (e.g., Paul & Jackson, 1993; Rodda & Grove, 1987), such as audiological issues and the heritability of deafness. These issues are fairly well-understood and can be easily included within the text.

As one moves on to the prenatal effects, one finds limited sources of information. For example, what is the impact of deaf parents on the prenatal development of hearing infants, and how does congenital deafness impact the development of the cortex? This area is a hole in our research and is in dire need of being addressed. Suggestions such as, "under atypical conditions of development, reducing input from an earlier developing system may result in precocial utilization of a later developing system" (Turkewitz & Kenny, 1985, p. 303), pointed out interesting areas of potential research. Given that the auditory system develops prenatally before the visual system, what are the effects of this early deprivation on the intramodal development integration of the remaining senses? Neville and colleagues (Neville & Lawson, 1987a; Neville, Schmidt, & Kutas, 1983) found that visually evoked brain potentials (VEP) differ in deaf and hearing adults. The effects of auditory deprivation and the acquisition of a visual language were also found to impact adult VEPs differentially (Neville & Lawson, 1987b.) These findings are important in and of themselves in a chapter such as this, but they also lead to additional questions relating to the origins of these effects. Additional work utilizing infant paradigms needs to be conducted in this area.

What the Hands Reveal about the Brain is the title of Poizner, Klima, and Bellugi's (1987) book about the linguistic and visuospatial brain organization of deaf stroke victims. It provided a strong basis on which to build this section. Additional works by Corina et al. (Corina, Poizner, Bellugi, & Feinberg, 1992; Corina, Vaid, & Bellugi, 1992; Emmorey & Corina, 1993) and Wolff et al. (Cantor, Wolff, Thatcher, Kammerer, & Gardner, 1986; Wolff, Cantor, Thatcher, Kammerer, & Gardner, 1986; Wolff & Thatcher, 1990) showed that deaf individuals develop different cortical organizations. Again the works of Neville et al. provided many insights into the reorganization of cortical functions within deaf adults. The question of the relationship between lateralization and deafness has resulted in many conflicting findings (see Kelly, 1978; Kelly & Tomlinson-Keasey, 1977, 1981; Lubert, 1975; Muendel-Atherstone & Rodda, 1982; McKeever, Hoemann, Flovian, & Van Deventer, 1977; Phippard, 1977; Poizner, Battison, & Lane, 1979.) Rodda and Grove (1987) suggested that each study has had "serious defects, such as: (a) failure to control incidental variables; (b) insensitive response measures; (c) inadequate stimulus ensembles; (d) small subject groups; (e) failure to introduce subject variables into the design; (f) use of statistically unreliable indices of laterality; (g) inappropriate methods of statistical analysis; (h) insufficiently thought-out hypotheses" (p. 286). Given these concerns and inconsistencies, additional work on lateralization with more controlled methodologies and statistical analyses is needed. All of these areas will benefit from continued research, as they have the potential to inform us about other related aspects of deafness.

Issues that are related to chapter 3 have seen an explosion of research within the past 10 years. Parasnis et al. (Parasnis, 1983; Parasnis & Samar, 1982; Parasnis, Samar, Bettger, & Sathe, 1996) investigated the effects of deafness as well as ASL knowledge on spatial cognition. Emmorey et al. investigated the effects of deafness and ASL knowledge on mental rotation, face recognition, and motion detection. Additionally, how deaf individuals process information in their peripheral visual field was investigated (Neville & Lawson, 1987a; Parasnis & Samar, 1985; Swisher, 1993).

Additional work would shed light on the areas of perceptual skills that underlie successful performance on IQ tests (perception of visual–spatial organizations as in the Wechsler Block Design subtest and figure–ground disambiguation as in the Children's Embedded Figures Test) and the effects of deafness on kinesthetics. Some studies (Butterfield, 1985; Butterfield & Ersing, 1987) investigated the effects of deafness on balance and found delays in deaf children's gross motor skills. The area of kinesthetics within deafness needs clarification and integration into other perceptual areas to finish illuminating this dim spot.

Chapter 4, on intelligence, includes two issues: an exploration of intelligence and related assessment issues. The exploration component has been constructed in such a way as to question the traditional view of a g factor that underlies IQ by comparing g to elaborate knowledge domains (EKD) and structures (EKS). Braden (1994) provided an excellent picture of IQ in deaf individuals given a g perspective. An interesting comparison would be to evaluate deaf individuals' EKSs and the impact that different schooling contexts had on these EKSs. These types of questions and their corresponding answers could then be evaluated as to whether they provided more insight into an ecologically valid view of deaf persons' intelligence-related behaviors. Issues related to intelligence in deaf children and adults have been problematic, given that nonverbal IQ tests may be tapping into different skills and abilities than do the traditional types of verbal tests. This comparison could provide insight into new ways of conceptualizing intelligence and of more directly comparing the impacts of different schooling contexts on deaf children. Moreover, this type of comparison may provide insight into the debate about superior IQs in deaf children of deaf parents (e.g., Braden, 1987 vs. Brill, 1970).

Assessment issues were clearly problematic for Lane (1988) in his discussion of whether or not there is a psychology of deafness. Flaws noted by Lane included test administration, test scoring, test language, poor test reliability and validity, inappropriate test norms, and a cultural bias. Recent work has started to develop deaf norms for the Wechsler tests but not all tests have been restandardized on deaf populations. Validity and reliability issues could benefit from additional work and may be related to many of the just-cited flaws (i.e., administration, language, and cultural bias).

Research on many of the contents of chapter 5 seems to be scarce to nonexistent. The types of questions posed here could benefit from collaborative work with educators and psychologists as well as an emic and etic collaboration to bring light to a dark spot that directly impacts the development of deaf children.

Since Stokoe's (1960) *Sign Language Structure* was published, the study of ASL has blossomed, establishing the first part of chapter 5 in a well-developed manner. Over the years, several books have been published that lay out general characteristics of ASL such as Klima and Bellugi's (1979) *The Signs of Language* and Schein's (1984) *Speaking the Language of Signs.* Markowicz's (1980) introduction to Lane and Grosjean's *Recent Perspectives on American Sign Language*, titled "Myths about American Sign Language," pointed out the ways in which our hitchhiker might have viewed deafness prior to his speeding ticket. Cutting edge linguistic and psycholinguistic research in this area has been presented at many conferences including Theoretical Issues in Sign Language Research (TISLR), the most recent one in Montreal, September, 1996. Therefore, topics suggested in the first sections of chapter 5 are easily accessible, and most are available in published forms.

Research on ASL acquisition has come of age in the past ten years. Many studies suggest that ASL acquisition parallels oral language acquisition (Meier, 1991; Meier & Newport, 1990; Petitto, 1987) in important ways. An ongoing debate within the field has developed in regard to whether or not language acquisition occurs earlier in sign languages (see Bonvillian & Folven, 1993) than it does in oral languages (see Petitto & Marentette, 1991). One outcome created by these different points of view has been excellent research on manual babbling (Meier, 1992; Pettito, 1996) as well as the relationship between gesture and language in deaf and hearing children (e.g., Volterra & Erting, 1990). Just to suggest a few of the most recent topics within the field, the following is a sample from research presented at the 1996 TISLR conference:

Acquisition of first signs: Place, handshape, and movement (Conlin, Mirus, & Meier, 1996);
The development of syntax in deaf toddlers learning ASL (Schick & Gale, 1996);
"Parentese" in American Sign Language (Holzrichter, 1996);
Grammaticization in a newly emerging sign language in Nicaragua (Morford & Kegl, 1996).

This area has many exciting ongoing projects that provide important insights and information about the acquisition of signed languages.

Another exciting area of research is code switching and registers in sign languages. Native speakers of a language understand different contexts that allow for more formal or informal language usage. This area of research has begun with sign languages (Mackay, Reed, & Taylor, 1996; D. Wilkins, personal communication, November, 1995) and adds to our understanding of how to teach hitchhikers to lecture in the classroom as well as to teach reverse interpretation so as to reduce confusions between deaf individuals and hearing individuals while presenting the ideas of the deaf individuals in a professional manner.

"Unlocking the Curriculum" (Johnson, Liddell, & Erting, 1989) opened the door to a heated dialogue about many language and educational issues. This particular working paper left no one without an opinion; either strongly for the proposed changes or strongly against the suggestions. Given a "cycle of low expectations" where it is expected "that deaf children cannot perform as well as hearing children" (Johnson et al., 1989, p. 12), one sees students who have fallen through the cracks and lack many basic skills as demonstrated by the letter in Fig. 12.1. These issues continue to be debated and need to be carefully investigated to provide unemotional answers to highly emotional issues and questions. New research suggests a positive relationship between literacy and ASL (Hoffmeister, 1996; Padden, 1996; Prinz & Strong, 1996). Additionally, new research suggests that ASL fluency leads to higher levels of literacy than does knowledge of manual codes for English (MCE; Singleton & Supalla, 1996). Moreover, research on bilingual issues needs to be continued in order to fully understand how a bilingual–bicultural approach to language acquisition and education will benefit or hinder the cognitive, social–emotional, and affective development of deaf children.

Linguistic creativity has been reviewed in both Marschark and Clark (1987) and Marschark (1993). These reviews start the work of looking at creativity in English versus creativity in a signed language (ASL in this case). For example, Everhart and Marschark (1988) found different results when evaluating creativity in written productions versus creativity in signed productions. Marschark (1993) concluded that additional evidence is needed in regard to linguistic creativity in deaf children but "what evidence is available ... strongly suggests that they are not as literal in their language and cognition as early observations suggested" (p. 201).

Exciting new work has been emerging in regard to creativity in ASL. Christie and Wilkins (1997) noted that ASL literacy has developed in informal settings, such as Deaf families, residential schools for the deaf, and other DEAF-WORLD contexts. Because ASL literacy was so deeply embedded with Deaf culture, it has not been researched in a formal way until recently. Conferences such as the 1991 and 1996 National American Sign Language Literature conferences have provided an impetus to this research and one can now start to find discussions about ASL linguistic creativity. Rutherford (1993) investigated American Deaf folklore, exploring ABC stories, group narratives of deaf children, plays on signs, and many more forms of linguistic creativity. The work is an excellent example of an emic–etic collaboration and brings aspects of the context found within Deaf culture to light. Valli (1993) collected videotaped ASL poems and investigated aspects of their poetics, rhyme, and meter. He compared the rhyme of visual poetry and the rhyme found in written poetry.

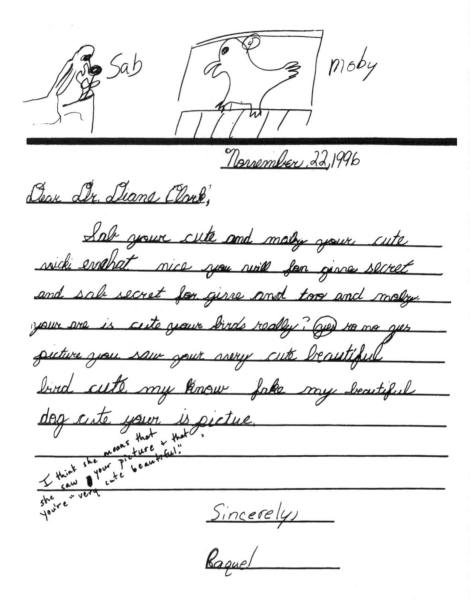

FIG. 12.1. Letter from a fourth grader at a residential school for the deaf. (Letter sent to the author of this chapter in response to pen-pal letters about the author's birds.)

Research in this vein needs to continue and to expand into a comparison between signed productions of ASL poetry and examples of written poetry by deaf individuals. Deaf poets often use visual forms within their written poems (e.g., NO!, Madsen, 1977; see Fig 12.2). The use of typeface and forms within the written works need to be investigated in terms of the linguistic creativity that is borrowed from the individuals' preferred use of space, such as, visual space. Given our preferred methodologies, all contexts for creative expression (English vs. ASL, written vs. signed) must be included to provide a well-balanced view of deaf individuals' creative abilities.

Chapter 5 concludes with a theoretical discussion regarding the relationship between language and thought. Paul and Jackson (1993) had a brief section on this topic, but much more needs to be included. The impact of delayed language acquisition and the effect of language input systems needs to be addressed. Issues around a bilingual–bicultural philosophy need to be discussed to understand how they impact language and thought. Mayer and Wells (1996) related a linguistic interdependence model to question whether or not a bilingual–bicultural theory can develop literacy for deaf students, yet others suggest that ASL fluency aids in the development of literacy (Singleton & Supalla, 1996; Strong & Prinz, 1997). A focus on issues revolving around this philosophical question will lead to productive research in the future.

"The deafness literature is rife with examples of explicit and implicit rejections of apparent performance differences that go against deaf children while accepting those in their favor. With the possible exception of literature concerning IQ … the memory literature is clearly the worst offender in this regard" (Marschark, 1993, p. 151). Given this warning, it is clear that additional work is needed in the area of memory and memory development (chapter 6) to resolve the conflicting findings available in the published literature. The table of contents for this chapter was developed by looking at a cognitive psychology text rather than looking at the published research within the field of deafness. This organization should prove useful when evaluating what is known about deaf individuals' memory and what areas are still "holes and dark spots." The first rule of logic suggested earlier was to "ask questions and be willing to wonder." Starting here and continuing to use the remaining seven rules of logic, our hitchhiker will start to fill in the holes and resolve the contradictions.

Marschark and Mayer's view (this volume) about the nature of mental representations and their impact on cognitive processes provides a way to untangle the existing labyrinth. The preferred linguistic modality for each individual must be entered in the equation before one can understand how this preference has interacted with memory development, memory performance, and the strategies used for problem solving. Careful design and implementation of future research will allow us to fill in gaps in our

NO!

I'm tired of hearing
That old refrain:
"*Teach the deaf to speak–to talk,
And they'll be whole again!*"

How well I know
That's just not so!
I live; I grow,
And everyday
Quite simply tells me:
"NO!"

I'm deaf–
I cannot hear,
And I know–
No magic will
Ever transform me
Into being otherwise!

I talk.
You smile;
You understand
My simple message spoken.
"*Bravo!*"
"*What marvellous speech!*"

You pat me on the back and say:
"*It's a hearing world you must live in
Or be, quite simply,
Relegated to
A stigmatized*

DEAF GHETTO Ghetto Ghetto Ghetto

*A world of silence:
A world of signs;
A limited world
Apart from the rest!*"

No!
That's not the world at all!
Not the world I know;
My world is
BEAUTIFUL
N
L
I
M
T
E
D

Not perfect,
but
Neither void!

How can it be
When all around me
Are
Hands,
Faces,
Whole beings
Communicating?
No guessing,
Doubting,
Struggling,
And I understand all that's said;
To fill in the gaps–
Words unrecognised or missed!

You praise my speech;
My comprehension.
That's fine, but....
You soon forget
Frustrations endured...
The difficulties faced!
I cannot be like you.
No!
We're set apart....
But only by one small difference–
A difference at times
That overwhelms:
I do not hear;

Yes! Teach the deaf
To speak–to talk,
But teach them first
How to walk
With confidence,
With heads held high,
And full knowledge
To converse by
With "words" FLOWING from the hand

Let them carry
Throughout this land
A simple banner
Called "Self-Esteem",
And teach the world at large
to sign–
To make us all
One world at heart
And not a world
That's set apart!
No!

Willard J. Madsen
1977

FIG. 12.2. Example of use of visual space in a deaf poet's written poetry. (Permission received from the author for inclusion of the poem "NO!")

knowledge base and clear up the current conflicting results. Utilization of statistical tools such as path analysis, factor analysis, and structured equation modeling will provide ways to understand how linguistic contexts interact with cognitive outputs.

Development within the social–emotional realm lays the foundation for all later cognitive and linguistic development. For these reasons, chapter 7 becomes vital to our understanding of development within a psychology of deafness. Attachment has been studied in hearing mother–deaf child dyads (Greenberg & Marvin, 1979; Lederberg & Mobley, 1990) with results showing interactions between mothers' communication effectiveness and attachment. Several methodological limitations have been noted for these studies (see Marschark, 1993) that limit their generalizability. Therefore, it is suggested that attachment in deaf children is an area where work remains to be completed to have a picture of rates of secure versus insecure attachment as well as to understand the effects of these types of attachments for later social–emotional development.

Symbolic play serves as an indicator of the cognitive development of young children and is therefore important to understand in deaf children. Play and mother responsiveness have been investigated by Spencer and her colleagues (Spencer, 1996; Spencer & Deyo, 1993; Spencer & Meadow-Orlans, 1996) who found that many factors can help to develop symbolic play across deaf and hearing mother–child dyads. A closer look at infant caregiver synchronicity (cf., Meadow-Orlans, 1997) will help to fill remaining gaps in our understanding of the social–emotional development of deaf children and its relationship to all later aspects of development—social–emotional, cognitive, and linguistic.

In regard to the remaining topics in chapter 7, the research is limited or even hit-and-miss. Gregory's (1976) longitudinal studies (Gregory, Bishop, & Sheldon, 1995) provide information that allows one to start to understand the long-range impact of parenting and schooling decisions on the adult years of a deaf individual. One can note that a significant proportion of her participants had no language skills and therefore had become totally isolated as adults. Gregory's chapter in this volume shows the impact of early experience in later adolescence and the transition into early adulthood. Findings such as this should cause us to look for predictors of success given early social–emotional factors.

The field is currently seeing findings coming from areas that prior to this time had either been black holes or dark spots. These areas include research on theories of mind (Clark, Schwanenflugel, Everhart, & Bartini, 1996; Gray & Hosie, 1996; Courtin, chap. 4, this volume), literacy (Schirmer & Woolsey, 1997; Strong & Prinz, 1997), and the social adjustment of deaf adolescents in various educational settings (Musselman, Mootilal, & MacKay, 1996). Still, additional research needs to focus on middle childhood and adolescence to fill the gaps in our knowledge base.

In terms of adult development, little is known about deaf adults. Higgins (1980) provided insights into aspects of what it means to be "outsiders in a hearing world," touching on identity, deviance, the stigma often associated with being deaf, as well as the types of encounters deaf people often have with "the hearing world." In terms of identity formation, Gutman and Hecht (1997) found that identification with both the Deaf culture and the lesbian culture was beneficial in creating positive self-esteem in deaf lesbians. More research focusing on lifestyle choices, career paths, family, and friendships will add to our understanding of deaf adults.

All general psychology texts cover mental health and treatment issues, and so would this psychology of deafness text. Issues within this area are complicated by the fact that most therapists who see deaf clients are hitchhikers who often have no background in deafness, sign language, or Deaf culture. Pollard (chap. 8, this volume) provides clear insight into the problems that can occur when an interpreter and a hearing therapist attempt to provide services to a deaf client. What has been a deep, dark, black hole has now received the type of attention that has been needed for many years. Pollard's chapter clearly outlines areas for future research and gives cautions that will benefit service delivery for deaf persons.

An additional positive note is that Gallaudet University will graduate its first doctoral class from an APA-approved clinical psychology program this spring (V. Gutman, personal communication, March, 1997). Clinicians from this program are fluent in sign, understand Deaf culture, and have been trained for service delivery to a deaf population. Additionally, this program has deaf as well as hearing students enrolled. One final note, the issue of primary prevention deserves special attention. With a clearer understanding of the impact of a hearing loss on all aspects of the developing child's contexts, it will be possible to arrange these contexts to maximize the development of deaf children, allowing them to reach their fullest potential. These advances will allow the lights within all deaf individuals to shine through any dark spot.

Social psychology looks at how individuals are impacted by the group, and the table of contents for this chapter was developed based on what typically appears in a section of this sort. Because of the types of individuals who historically have engaged in research within this interdisciplinary field (teacher education programs, communication disorders programs, linguistic departments, psychology departments, and human development programs), topics of interest to a social psychologist have rarely been the focus of research projects using deaf participants.

A few books touch on related ideas. Lane (1992) looked at members of the Deaf community as an oppressed linguistic minority who have started to join together, forming political identities to obtain their civil rights. His presentation in chapter 3 on representation, power, and oppression could serve as the foundation for additional studies on conformity and obedience issues. Higgins (1980) approached the issue from the point of view of a sociologist, thereby giving some background on which to build. Attitudes-toward-deaf-individuals scales need to be developed as a way to cross the bridge from being hearing centered into understanding Deaf culture (Padden & Humphries, 1988). This area is a rich one for many new and exciting research collaborations utilizing insiders and hitchhikers.

The final chapter in the "hitchhikers" table of contents discusses Deaf culture. *Deaf in America: Voices from a Culture* (Padden & Humphries, 1988) and *The Deaf Way* (Erting, Johnson, Smith, & Snider, 1994) are cornerstones of a chapter such as this one. Highlighting issues like deaf humor (Bienvenu, 1994; Bouchauveau, 1994; Rutherford, 1983) works toward an emic–etic understanding of how deaf individuals see themselves and the place they hold in society. Bienvenu (1994) analyzed deaf humor, pointing out its visual nature and how it is used to pass on Deaf culture. For example, the hitchhiker joke at the beginning of this chapter is based on the oppression felt within Deaf culture. She continued by showing how deaf humor situates the deaf person as victorious in a confrontation with a hearing person, like the hitchhiker. Deaf theater has developed into an art form that integrates a visual language with aspects of Deaf life (Rutherford, 1993), again serving as a mechanism to continue Deaf culture.

A rich tradition of deaf history can be found in the *Gallaudet Encyclopedia of Deaf People and Deafness* (Van Cleve, 1987) as well as *A Place of Their Own: Creating the Deaf Community in America* (Van Cleve & Crouch, 1989). Recent historic victories can also be understood through books like *Deaf President Now!: The 1988 Revolution at Gallaudet University* (Christiansen & Barnartt, 1995). Deaf Studies programs have been developed and act as a mechanism to study "deaf history, culture, language, and literature" (Lane, 1988, p. 16). Concluding with a chapter of this nature brings us back to the starting point—why a psychology of deafness?

Psychology has studied deaf individuals often only as a deviation from what were considered *normal* participants (i.e., hearing people; Lane, 1988). Research of this nature reflects an audistic bias, where what hearing people do is considered normative but what deaf people do is regarded as a deficient deviation from that standard. For a psychology of deafness to pass Lane's (1988) criteria of showing more differences between deaf and hearing groups than are found within either group, the field would have to avoid positioning itself within a hearing-centered stance. Research would need to clarify similarities and differences between deaf and hearing participants, working to resolve any derogatory views. Moreover, this psychology of deafness would have to include all deaf individuals, recognizing special needs and talents within the differing contexts where deaf individuals are found. This psychology would have to avoid focusing on research areas that only attempted to see how deaf individuals were lacking skills (such as English literacy, math abilities, and traditional IQ scores), and sample from the broad range of activities and events occurring within deaf individuals' lives.

The use of a word that labels a bias, *audism*, communicates that the members of the group (deaf individuals) have been denied full access to resources. The issues reflected within the -isms—racism, sexism, heterosexism, as well as audism—call attention to biases that empower one group while subjugating others. One way to redress these power inequities has been to name the problem and develop courses (Deaf Studies), print media and journals (*Deaf American, American Annals of the Deaf, Sign Language Studies*), and recognized organizations (World Federation of the Deaf) that strive to refocus energy on an emic viewpoint rather than one that is only etic. Groups representing the other -isms—African Americans, women, lesbians, gays, bisexuals—present their voices within contexts and courses titled, "Psychology of" formats. Until deaf researchers are equally represented within all aspects of psychology (cognitive, developmental, clinical, counseling, social, history, testing, and health psychologies), thereby including deaf voices within the field of psychology, this hitchhiker believes that there is a need for a psychology of deafness. The field should work toward correcting an audistic bias by carefully employing the suggested eight rules of logic:

1. Ask questions and be willing to wonder,
2. define the problem,
3. examine the evidence,
4. analyze assumptions and biases,
5. avoid emotional reasoning,
6. do not oversimplify,
7. consider other interpretations, and
8. tolerate uncertainty.

In this manner, a psychology of deafness will enlighten those frozen with a hearing framework and reallocate resources in a more equitable way.

Finally, it is this hitchhiker's belief that the field of psychology of deafness will increase knowledge in all of the subfields included under the umbrella of psychology.

ACKNOWLEDGMENTS

I acknowledge Angela Bartoli and Kim Weikel who read earlier drafts of this chapter and worked with me on clarifying "holes and dark spots" in my logic. Nina Weaver proofed the manuscript, and any remaining errors are solely my own. Ellen Faynberg took many hours to sort through my piles of references and type them into the manuscript; thank you for your patience and energy. Finally, I am grateful to David Martin of Gallaudet University who took the role of another hitchhiker to make sure that my map would take me to my stated destination.

REFERENCES

Allen, D. V. (1971). Color–word interference in deaf and hearing children. *Psychonomic Science, 24,* 295–296.
Bienvenu, M. J. (1994). Reflections of deaf culture in deaf humor. In C. J. Erting, R. C. Johnson, D. L. Smith, & B. D. Snider, (Eds.), *The deaf way: Perspectives from the international conference on deaf culture* (pp. 16–23). Washington, DC: Gallaudet University Press.
Blair, F. X. (1957). A study of the visual memory of deaf and hearing children. *American Annals of the Deaf, 102,* 254–263.
Blanton, R. L., & Nunnally, J. C. (1967). Retention of trigrams by deaf and hearing subjects as a function of pronunciability. *Journal of Verbal Learning and Verbal Behavior, 6,* 428–431.
Bonvillian, J.D., & Folven, R.J. (1993). Sign language acquisition: Developmental aspects. In M. Marschark & M. D. Clark (Eds.), *Psychological Perspectives on Deafness* (pp. 229–265). Hillsdale, NJ: Lawrence Erlbaum Associates.
Bouchauveau, G. (1994). Deaf humor and culture. In C. J. Erting, R. C. Johnson, D. L. Smith, & B. D. Snider (Eds.), *The deaf way: Perspectives from the international conference on deaf culture* (pp. 24–30). Washington, DC: Gallaudet University Press.
Braden, J. P. (1987). An explanation of the superior performance IQs of deaf children of deaf parents. *American Annals of the Deaf, 132,* 263–266.
Braden, J. P. (1994). *Deafness, deprivation, and IQ.* New York: Plenum.
Brill, R. G. (1970). The superior I.Q.'s of deaf children of deaf parents. *Maryland Bulletin, 90* 97–111.
Bronfenbrenner, U. (1977). Toward an experimental ecology of human development. *American Psychologist, 32,* 513–531.
Butterfield, S. A. (1985). Gross motor profiles of deaf children. *Perceptual and Motor Skills, 62,* 68–70.
Butterfield, S. A., & Ersing, W. F. (1987). Age, sex, hearing loss, and balance in development of jumping by deaf children. *Perceptual and Motor Skills, 64,* 942.

Cantor, D. S., Wolff, A. B., Thatcher, R. W., Kammerer, B. L., & Gardner, J. K. (1986). *Neurophysiological differences between deaf and hearing children.* Paper presented at the International Neuropsychological Society Meeting, Veldhoven, The Netherlands.

Christiansen, J. B., & Barnartt, S. N. (1995). *Deaf president NOW!: The 1988 revolution at Gallaudet University.* Washington, DC: Gallaudet University Press.

Christie, K., & Wilkins, D. M. (1997). A feast for the eyes: ASL literacy and ASL literature. *Journal of Deaf Studies and Deaf Education, 2,* 57–59.

Clark, M. D. (1993). A contextual/interactionist model and its relationship to deafness research. In M. Marschark & M. D. Clark, (Eds.), *Psychological Perspectives on Deafness.* Hillsdale, NJ: Lawrence Erlbaum Associates.

Clark, M. D., & Hoemann, H. W. (1991). Methodological issues in deafness research. In D. S. Martin, (Ed.), *Advances in Cognition, Education, and Deafness* (pp. 423–426). Washington, DC: Gallaudet University Press.

Clark, M. D., Schwanenfluegel, P. J., Everhart, V. S., & Bartini, M. (1996). Theory of mind in deaf adults and the organization of verbs of knowing. *Journal of Deaf Studies and Deaf Education, 1,* 179–189.

Conlin, K. E., Mirus, G. R., & Meier, R. P. (1996). *Acquisition of first signs: Place, handshape, and movement.* Presented at the Fifth International Conference on Theoretical Issues in Sign Language Research, Montreal, Quebec, Canada.

Corina, D., Poizner, H., Bellugi, U., & Feinberg, T. (1992). Dissociation between linguistic and nonlinguistic gestural systems: A case for compositionality. *Brain and Language, 43,* 414–447.

Corina, D., Vaid, J., & Bellugi, U. (1992). The linguistic basis of left hemisphere specialization. *Science, 255,* 1258–1260.

Emmorey, K., & Corina, D. (1993). Hemispheric specialization for ASL signs and English words: Differences between imageable and abstract forms. *Neuropsychologia, 31,* 645–653.

Erting, C. J., Johnson, R. C., Smith, D. L., & Snider, B. D. (1994). *The deaf way: Perspectives from the international conference on deaf culture.* Washington, DC: Gallaudet University Press.

Everhart, V. S., & Marschark, M. (1988). Linguistic flexibility in the written and signed/oral language productions of deaf and hearing children. *Journal of Experimental Child Psychology, 46,* 174–193.

Frumkin, B., & Anisfeld, M. (1977). Semantic and surface codes in the memory of deaf children. *Cognitive Psychology, 9,* 475–493.

Gray, C. D., & Hosie, J. A. (1996). Deafness, story understanding, and theory of mind. *Journal of Deaf Studies and Deaf Education, 1,* 217–233.

Greenberg, M. T., & Marvin, R. S. (1979). Attachment patterns in profoundly deaf preschool children. *Merrill–Palmer Quarterly, 25,* 265–279.

Gregory, S. (1976). *The deaf child and his family.* New York: Halsted.

Gregory, S., Bishop, J., & Sheldon, L. (1995). *Deaf young people and their families.* London: Cambridge University Press.

Gutman, V., & Hecht, A. A. (1997). *Identity formation and self-esteem in deaf lesbians.* Poster presented at the annual meeting of the Association for Women in Psychology, Pittsburgh, PA.

Hartung, J. E. (1970). Visual perceptual skill, reading ability, and the young deaf child. *Exceptional Children, 36,* 603–608.

Hewitt, D. (Executive Producer.) (1990, March 11). *60 Minutes.* New York: CBS.

Higgins, P. C. (1980). *Outsiders in a hearing world: A sociology of deafness.* Beverly Hills, CA: Sage Publications.

Hoffmeister, R. J. (1996). *A piece of the puzzle: ASL and reading comprehension in deaf children.* Presented at the Fifth International Conference on Theoretical Issues in Sign Language Research, Montreal, Quebec, Canada.

Holzrichter, A. S. (1996). *"Parentese" in American Sign Language.* Presented at the Fifth International Conference on Theoretical Issues in Sign Language Research, Montreal, Quebec, Canada.

Johnson, R. E., Liddell, S. K., & Erting, C. J. (1989). *Unlocking the curriculum: Principles for achieving success in deaf education.* Gallaudet Research Institute Working Paper, 89-3.Washington, DC: Gallaudet University Press.

Kelly, R. R. (1978). Hemispheric specialization of deaf children: Are there any implications for instruction? *American Annals of the Deaf, 123,* 637–645.

Kelly, R. R., & Tomlinson-Keasey, C. (1977). Hemispheric laterality of deaf children for processing words and pictures visually presented to the hemifields. *American Annals of the Deaf, 122,* 525–533.

Kelly, R. R., & Tomilinson-Keasey, C. (1981). The effect of auditory input on cerebral laterality. *Brain and Language, 13,* 67–77.

Klima, E., & Bellugi, U. (1979). *The signs of language.* Cambridge, MA: Harvard University Press.

Lane, H. (1988). Is there a "Psychology of the Deaf"? *Exceptional Children, 55,* 7–19.

Lane, H. (1992). *The mask of benevolence: Disabling the Deaf community.* New York: Vintage Books.

Lane, H. (1996, June). Is there a psychology of deafness?: A response. *BRIDGE: Bridging Research in Deafness and General Education, 15(1),* 4–8.

Lederberg, A. R., & Mobley, C. E. (1990). The effect of hearing impairment on the quality of attachment and mother–toddler interaction. *Child Development, 61,* 1596–1604.

Lerner, R. M. (1986). *Concepts and theories of human development, (2nd edition).* New York: Random House.

Lubert, B. J. (1975). The relation of brain asymmetry to visual processing of sign language, alphabetic and visuo-spatial material in deaf and hearing subjects. Unpublished masters thesis, University of Western Ontario, Ontario, Canada.

Mackay, B., Reed, M., & Taylor, C. (1996). *The evolution of a BSL formal register within legal settings.* Presented at the Fifth International Conference on Theoretical Issues in Sign Language Research, Montreal, Quebec, Canada.

Madsen, W. J. (1977). *No!,* Presentation of Gallaudet Universities New Faculty Orientation. Washington, D.C.

Mandes, E. A., Allen, P. R., & Swisher, C. W. (1971). Comparative study of tachistoscopic perception of binary figures in deaf children and normally hearing children. *Perceptual and Motor Skills, 33,* 195–200.

Markowicz, H. (1980). Myths about American Sign Language. In H. Lane & F. Grosjean, *Recent perspectives on American Sign Language* (pp. 1–6). Hillsdale, NJ: Lawrence Erlbaum Associates.

Marschark, M. (1993). *Psychological Development of Deaf Children.* New York: Oxford University Press.

Marschark, M., & Clark, D. (1987). Linguistic and nonlinguistic creativity of deaf children, *Developmental Review, 7,* 22–38.

Mayer, C., & Wells, G. (1996). Can the linguistic interdependence theory support a bilingual–bicultural model of literacy education or deaf students? *Journal of Deaf Studies and Deaf Education, 1,* 93–107.

McKeever, W. F., Hoemann, H. W., Florian, V. A., & VanDenventer, A. D. (1976). Evidence of minimal cerebral asymmetries for the processing of English words and American Sign Language stimuli in the congenitally deaf. *Neuropsychologia, 14,* 413–423.

Meadow-Orlans, K. P. (1997). Effects of mother and infant hearing status on interactions at twelve and eighteen months. *Journal of Deaf Studies and Deaf Education, 2,* 26–36.

Meier, R. P. (1991). Language acquisition by deaf children. *American Scientist, 79,* 60–70.

Meier, R. P. (1992). *Language acquisition in sign and speech.* Paper presented at the XXV International Congress of Psychology, Brussels, Belgium.

Meier, R. P., & Newport, E. (1990). Out of the hands of babes: On a possible sign advantage in language acquisition. *Language, 66,* 1–23.

Morford, J. P., & Kegl, J. (1996). *Grammaticization in a newly emerging signed language in Nicaragua.* Presented at the Fifth International Conference on Theoretical Issues in Sign Language Research, Montreal, Quebec, Canada.

Muendel-Atherstone, B., & Rodda, M. (1982). *Differences in hemispheric processing of linguistic material presented visually to deaf and hearing adults.* Unpublished mansucript, University of Alberta.

Musselman, C., Mootilal, A., & MacKay, S. (1996). The social adjustment of deaf adolescents in segregated, partially integrated, and mainstreamed settings. *Journal of Deaf Studies and Deaf Education, 1,* 52–63.

Myklebust, H. (1960). *The psychology of deafness*; Sensory deprivation, learning & adjustment. New York: Grune & Stratton.

Myklebust, H., & Brutten, M. (1953). A study of the visual perception of deaf children. *Acta Otolaryng, (Suppl. 105).*

Neville, H. J., & Lawson, D. (1987a). Attention to central and peripheral visual space in a movement detection task: An event-related potential and behavioral study: II. Congenitally deaf adults. *Brain Research, 405,* 268–283.

Neville, H. J., & Lawson, D. (1987b). Attention to central and peripheral visual space in a movement detection task: An event-related potential and behavioral study: III. Separate effects of auditory deprivation and acquisition of a visual language. *Brain Research, 405,* 284–294.

Neville, H. J., Schmidt, A., & Kutas, M. (1983). Altered visual evoked potentials in congenitally deaf adults. *Brain Research, 266,* 127–132.

Newport, E. (1996, September). *Sign Language Research in the Third Millennium.* Closing Plenary, presented at the Fifth International Conference on Theoretical Issues in Sign Language Research, Montreal, Quebec, Canada.

Olson, J. R. (1967). A factor analytic study of the relation between the speed of visual perception and the language abilities of deaf adolescents. *Journal of Speech and Hearing Research, 26,* 354–360.

Padden, C. (1996). *ASL and reading ability in deaf children.* Presented at the Fifth International Conference on Theoretical Issues in Sign Language Research, Montreal, Quebec, Canada.

Padden, C., & Humphries, T. (1988). *Deaf in America: Voices from a culture.* Cambridge, MA: Harvard University Press.

Parasnis, I. (1983). Visual perceptual skills and deafness: A research review. *Journal of the Academy of Rehabilitation Audiology, 16,* 161–181.

Parasnis, I., & Samar, V. J. (1982). Visual perception of verbal information by deaf people. In D. G. Sims, G. G. Walter, & R. L. Whitehead (Eds.), *Deafness and communication: Assessment and training* (pp. 53–71). Baltimore, MD: Williams & Wilkins.

Parasnis, I., & Samar, V. J. (1985). Parafoveal attention in congenitally deaf and hearing young adults. *Brain and Cognition, 4,* 313–327.

Parasnis, I., Samar, V. J., Bettger, J., & Sathe, K. (1996). Does deafness lead to enhancement of visual spatial cognition in children: Negative evidence from deaf non-signers. *Journal of Deaf Studies and Deaf Education, 1,* 145–152.

Paul, P. V., (1996a, March). Is there a psychology of deafness?: The influence of clinical and cultural perspectives. *BRIDGE: Bridging Research in Deafness and General Education, 15(3),* 8–11.

Paul, P. V., (1996b, November). Is there a psychology of deafness?: A reply to Harlan Lane. *BRIDGE: Bridging Research in Deafness and General Education, 15(4), 5–7.*
Paul, P. V., & Jackson, D. W. (1993). *Toward a psychology of deafness.* Boston: Allyn & Bacon.
Petitto, L. A. (1987). On the autonomy of language and gesture: Evidence from the acquisition of personal pronouns in American Sign Language. *Cognition, 27,* 1–52.
Petitto, L. A. (1996). In the beginning: On the genetic and environmental factors that make early language acquisition possible. In M. Gopnik & S. Davis (Eds.), *The Genetic Basis of Language* (pp. 46–71). Hillsdale, NJ: Lawrence Erlbaum Associates.
Petitto, L. A., & Marentette, P. F. (1991). Babbling in the manual mode: Evidence for the ontogeny of language. *Science, 251,* 1493–1496.
Phippard, D. (1977). Hemifield differences in visual perception in deaf and hearing subjects. *Neuropsychologia, 15,* 555–561.
Poizner, H., Klima, E. S., & Bellugi, U. (1987). *What the hands reveal about the brain.* Cambridge, MA: MIT Press.
Poizner, H., Battison, R., & Lane, H. L. (1979). Cerebral asymmetry for perception of American Sign Language. *Brain and Language, 7,* 351–362.
Pollio, H. R., & Pollio, M. R. (1991). Some observations from a different point of view. In D. S. Martin (Ed.), *Advances in Cognition, Education, and Deafness* (pp. 429–442). Washington, DC: Gallaudet University Press.
Prinz, P. M., & Strong, M. (1996). *Proficiency in American Sign Language (ASL): Leading the way to the acquisition of English literacy.* Presented at the Fifth International Conference on Theoretical Issues in Sign Language Research, Montreal, Quebec, Canada.
Rodda, M., & Grove, C. (1987). *Language, Cognition and Deafness.* Hillsdale, NJ: Lawrence Erlbaum Associates.
Rutherford, S. (1993). *A study of American Deaf folklore.* Burtonsville, MD: Linstok Press, Inc.
Schein, J. D. (1984). *Speaking the language of signs.* Garden City, NY: Doubleday.
Schick, B., & Gale, E. (1996). *The development of syntax in deaf toddlers learning ASL.* Presented at the Fifth International Conference on Theoretical Issues in Sign Language Research, Montreal, Quebec, Canada.
Schirmer, B. R., & Woolsey, M. L. (1997). Effect of teacher questions on the reading comprehension of deaf children. *Journal of Deaf Studies and Deaf Education, 2,* 47–56.
Singleton, J., & Supalla, S. (1996). *The effects of sign language fluency upon literacy development.* Presented at the Fifth International Conference on Theoretical Issues in Sign Language Research, Montreal, Quebec, Canada.
Spencer, P. E. (1996). The association between language and symbolic play at 2 years: Evidence from deaf toddlers. *Child Development, 67,* 867–876.
Spencer, P. E., & Deyo, D. A. (1993). Cognitive and social aspects of deaf children's play. In M. Marschark and D. Clark (Eds), *Psychological perspectives on deafness (pp.65–91).* Hillsdale, NJ: Lawrence Erlbaum Associates.
Spencer, P. E., & Meadow-Orlans, K. P. (1996). Play, language, and maternal responsiveness: A longitudinal study of deaf and hearing infants. *Child Development, 67,* 3176–3191.
Stokoe, W. (1960). Sign language structure: An outline of the visual communication systems of the American deaf. *Studies in Linguistics Occasional Papers, No. 8.* Washington, DC: Gallaudet University Press.
Strong, M., & Prinz, P. M. (1997). A study of the relationship between American Sign Language and English literacy. *Journal of Deaf Studies and Deaf Education, 2,* 37–46.
Swisher, M. V. (1993). Perceptual and cognitive aspects of recognition of signs in peripheral vision. In M. Marschark & M. D. Clark (Eds.), *Psychological Perspectives on Deafness* (pp. 209–227). Hillsdale, NJ: Lawrence Erlbaum Associates.

Turkewitz, G., & Kenny, P. A. (1985). The role of developmental limitations of sensory input on sensory/perceptual organization. *Journal of Developmental and Behavioral Pediatrics, 6,* 302–306.

Valli, C. (1993). *Poetics of American Sign Language poetry.* Unpublished doctoral dissertation, The Union Institute Graduate School.

Van Cleve, J. (1987). *Gallaudet encyclopedia of deaf people and deafness.* New York: McGraw-Hill.

Van Cleve, J., & Crouch, B. (1989). *A place of their own.* Washington, DC: Gallaudet University Press.

Volterra, V., & Erting, C. J. (1990). *From gesture to language in hearing and deaf children.* Berlin: Springer-Verlag.

Wade, C., & Tavris, C. (1996). *Psychology, (4th ed.).* New York: HarperCollins.

Wolff, A. B., Cantor, D. S., Thatcher, R. W., Kammerer, B. L., & Gardner, J. K. (1986). *Neurophysiological differences among deaf children with different eitiologies of deafness.* Paper presented at the American Psychological Assoication annual meeting, Washington, DC.

Wolff, A. B., & Thatcher, R. W. (1990). Cortical reorganization in deaf children. *Journal of Clinical and Experimental Neuropsychology, 12(2),* 209–211.

Author Index

Johnson, R. E., 274, *293*, 307, 317, 323, *325*, *326*, *327*
Johnson-Morris, J. E., 87, *99*
Johnston, P., 200, *239*
Jones, C. J., 104, *130*
Jones, D. A., 186, *194*
Jones, E. M., 186, *194*
Jones, M. L., 202, 211, 229, *237*, *238*
Jones, R. E. 273, *293*
Jordan, I. K., 7, *18*, 63, *76*

K

Kagan, J., 94, *100*
Kaiser-Grodecka, I., 270, *293*
Kammerer, B. L., 314, *326*, *330*
Kandel, S., 104, *127*
Kapel, D. E., 213, *237*
Karchmer, M. A., 158, *170*, 201, *237*
Karlsen, B., 221, *238*
Karzon, R. K., *193*
Katon, W., 186, *196*
Katz, D., 191, *194*
Katz, L., *241*
Kaufman, A., 221, *237*
Kaufman, N., 221, *237*
Kavale, K., 217, *237*
Kedward, H. B., *328*
Kelly, C., 133, *150*
Kelly, D. P., 202, 203, 210, 211, 212, 213, 214, 218, 229, *237*, *238*
Kelly, R. R., 314, *327*
Kendall, D. C., 218, *235*
Kendel, E. F., 207, *238*
Kendon, A., 9, *18*
Kennedy, C., 259, *262*
Kenny, P. A., 313, *330*
Kerman, M., 221, 230, *235*
Kimura, D., 3, 4, *18*
Kindschi, C. L., 215, *238*
King, B., 5, 7, *18*
King, C. M., 225, *240*
King, S. J., 190, *197*
Kingdon, J., 15, *18*
Klima, E. S., 7, *18*, 20, 23, 24, 35, 42, 43, 49, *50*, *51*, *52*, 60, 62, 66, *74*, 77, 85, *100*, 103, *127*, *129*, 244, *262*, 314, 316, *327*, *329*
Koester, J. S., 142, 146, *150*
Klorman, R., 202, 210, 231, *238*
Klutas, M., 313, *328*
Kluwin, T. N., 153, 158, 159, *170*
Kolodny, R., *236*,
Korkman, M., 216, *238*
Kosslyn, S. M., 35, 38, 39, 40, 41, 42, 44, 49, *50*, *52*, 228, *236*

Kozlowski, K., 191, *197*
Krakow, R. A., 60, 62, 72, *75*
Kramer, S. J., 26, *49*
Kraus, I., *236*
Krauss, R. M., 54, *74*
Kretschmer, R. E., 104, *129*
Kuhl, P., 22, *50*, 106, *128*
Kusché, C. A., 89, *99*
Kuse, A. R., 37, *52*
Kyle, J. G., 61, 62, 63, *75*

L

Lacasse, M. A., 61, *73*, 228, *234*
Ladd, G. W., 165, *170*
Lahey, B. B., 206, *238*
Lahey, M., 243, 250, 251, 252, *262*
Lane, H., 39, *50*, 171, *175*, 185, 187, 189, *194*, 304, 305, 312, 314, 315, 316, 323, *327*, *329*
Lane, K. E., 187, *194*
Larew, S. J., 186, 187, 188, *194*
Larsen, J. P., 208, *238*
Larsen, S. C., 203, *237*
LaSasso, C. J., 221, *238*
Laughton, J., 205, 218, *238*
Lawler, D. M., 191, *194*
Lawson, D., 20, 21, *51*, 104, *129*, 313, 314, *328*
Layton, T. L., 87, *100*
Leark, R. A., 215, *238*
Lederberg, A., 87, *100*, 142, 143, 144, 146, *150*, *152*, 154, *170*, 217, *238*, 321, *327*
Lee, L. ,247, *262*
Leekam, S. R., 83, 84, 88, *101*
Lehman, B. K., *236*
Leigh, I. W., 157, 167, *170*, 188, *194*
Leigh, J. E., 203, *237*
Lenel, J. C., 115, *128*
Lentz, E. M., 186, *193*
Leonard L. B., 224, *238*
LePoutre, D., 64, *76*
Lerman, A., 158, 159, *170*, 216, *238*
Lerner, R. M., 306, 312, *327*
Levine, D., 43, *50*
Levine, E., 172, *195*, 209, 217, *238*, *261*, *262*
Levinson, S., 47, *50*
Levitan, L., 171, 184, *195*
Lewis, C., 80, *100*
Leybaert, J., 107, 115, 116, 120, 121, 123, *126*, *127*, *128*, 221, 222, *238*
Liben, L. S., 56, 71, *75*
Lichtenstein, E. H., 61, *75*
Liddell, S., 39, *51*

Subject Index

Simultaneous communication, 246, 258,
   272, 273
Social skills, 164, 260
Socio-economic status, 158
Speech, 1, 3
   intelligibility, 124
   module, 107
   reception, 110, 111
   surrogates, 16
Spelling, 107, 111, 117, 120, 121, 123
Strategies
   memory, 56–58, 65, 71, 73, 249, 253,
      258, 259
   reading, 68
   social interaction, 260

V

Visuospatial processing, 59, 68

W

Word-length effect, 66
Working memory, 55, 59ff., 249, 258–259,
   309, 310, 319
Writing, 114, 118

Z

Zone of proximal development, 268